SO-ATM-913

Blueprints for exchange-rate management

Centre for Economic Policy Research

The Centre for Economic Policy Research is a registered charity with educational purposes. It was established in 1983 to promote independent analysis and public discussion of open economies and the relations among them. Institutional (core) finance for the Centre has been provided through major grants from the Leverhulme Trust, the Esmée Fairbairn Trust, the Baring Foundation and the Bank of England. None of these organizations gives prior review to the Centre's publications nor do they necessarily endorse the views expressed therein.

The Centre is pluralist and non-partisan, bringing economic research to bear on the analysis of medium- and long-run policy questions. The research work that it disseminates may include views on policy, but the Board of Governors of the Centre does not give prior review to such publications, and the Centre itself takes no institutional policy positions. The opinions expressed in this volume are those of the authors and not those of the Centre for Economic Policy Research.

Board of Governors

Chairman	Mr Jeremy Hardie
Vice-Chairman	Sir Adam Ridley

Professor Giorgio Basevi	Professor Richard Layard
Dr Christopher Bliss	Ms Kate Mortimer
Dr Paul Champsaur	Mr Michael Posner
Ms Honor Chapman	Ms Sheila Drew Smith
Admiral Sir James Eberle	Professor David Stout
Mr Michael Emerson	Mr Angus Walker
Ms Sarah Hogg	Sir Douglas Wass

Officers

Director	Professor Richard Portes
Assistant Director	Mr Stephen Yeo
Director of Finance and Research Administration	Mrs Wendy Thompson

3 January 1989

Blueprints for exchange-rate management

edited by

MARCUS MILLER

BARRY EICHENGREEN

and

RICHARD PORTES

ACADEMIC PRESS
Harcourt Brace Jovanovich, Publishers
London   San Diego   New York   Berkeley
Boston   Sydney   Tokyo   Toronto

ACADEMIC PRESS LIMITED
24/28 Oval Road
London NW1 7DX

United States Edition published by
ACADEMIC PRESS INC.
San Diego, CA 92101

Copyright © 1989 by
ACADEMIC PRESS LIMITED

All Rights Reserved
No part of this book may be reproduced in any form by photostat,
microfilm, or by any other means, without written permission
from the publishers

Typeset by Lasertext Ltd., Stretford, Manchester
Printed in Great Britain by St. Edmundsbury Press Ltd., Bury St Edmunds,
Suffolk

Contents

Part II   Theoretical issues

List of figures

List of tables

Preface

This volume contains the proceedings of the conference on *International Regimes and Macroeconomic Policy* organized by the Centre for Economic Policy Research and held in London on 8–9 September 1988.

This is the latest in a sequence of conferences and resulting volumes arising from CEPR's research programme on *Macroeconomic Interactions and Policy Design in Interdependent Economies*, operating during 1985–88 in collaboration with the Brookings Institution. Financial support for the programme, including the conference as well as some of the research reported here, was provided by the Ford Foundation and the Alfred P. Sloan Foundation. The research underlying some of the papers also benefited from funding by the Economic and Social Research Council. We are happy to express our gratitude for this support.

We also wish to thank Jacqui Eggo and Eve Jagusiewicz at CEPR for ensuring that the conference ran smoothly. Paul Compton, the Centre's Publications Officer, guided this volume to press rapidly and efficiently; he and we were pleased to work again with John Black of the University of Exeter, who served as Production Editor. They have kept editors, authors and discussants to CEPR's very tight production schedule, so that these timely, policy-relevant analyses by leading researchers would quickly reach a wide audience.

All this has been a cooperative effort. We hope that our colleagues, sponsors and readers will find it as worthwhile as we have and that the research reported here will inform the current debate on exchange-rate management and macroeconomic policy coordination.

Marcus Miller
Barry Eichengreen
Richard Portes

2 January 1989

List of conference participants

George Alogoskoufis *Birkbeck College, London, and CEPR.*
David Begg *Birkbeck College, London, and CEPR.*
John Black *University of Exeter.*
James Boughton *IMF.*
Stephen Broadberry *University of Warwick.*
Andrew Brociner *Birkbeck College, London.*
David Currie *London Business School and CEPR.*
John Driffill *University of Southampton and CEPR.*
Hali Edison *Federal Reserve Board.*
Barry Eichengreen *University of California at Berkeley and CEPR.*
Peter Ellehøj *LSE.*
Alberto Giovannini *Columbia University and CEPR.*
Thorvaldur Gylfason *University of Iceland and CEPR.*
Gerald Holtham *Shearson Lehman Hutton.*
Warwick Hood *HM Treasury.*
Alison Hook *Foreign and Commonwealth Office.*
Andrew Hughes Hallett *University of Newcastle-upon-Tyne and CEPR.*
Pierre Jacquet *Institut Français des Relations Internationales, Paris.*
Nigel Jenkinson *Bank of England*
Peter Kenen *Princeton University.*
Paul Levine *London Business School and CEPR.*
Marcus Miller *University of Warwick and CEPR.*
Patrick Minford *University of Liverpool and CEPR.*
Anton Muscatelli *University of Glasgow.*
Richard Portes *CEPR and Birkbeck College, London.*
Neil Rankin *Queen Mary College, London, and CEPR.*
Mark Salmon *University of Warwick and CEPR.*
Guido Tabellini *University of California at Los Angeles and CEPR.*
Niels Thygesen *University of Copenhagen.*
Paul Turner *University of Southampton.*
Frederick van der Ploeg *Tilburg University and CEPR.*

David Vines   *University of Glasgow and CEPR.*
David Walton   *Goldman Sachs International.*
John Williamson   *Institute for International Economics, Washington, D.C.*
Simon Wren-Lewis   *National Institute of Economic and Social Research and CEPR.*

Chapter 1

Editors' introduction

Marcus Miller, Barry Eichengreen and Richard Portes

In the 1980s, both academics and policy-makers have rediscovered the economics of interdependence. Dramatic swings in the value of exchange rates, large-scale movements of financial capital across national borders, and persistent imbalances in trade accounts have highlighted international policy and performance linkages. These international imbalances are attributed, alternatively, to conflict in the stance of macroeconomic policies in Europe, the United States and Japan and to disarray in the international monetary system. This has given rise to two separate literatures, one concerned with international policy coordination, the other with the stabilization of exchange rates through reform of the international monetary system. This volume is designed to bring these two currents together.

The case for international policy coordination and the case for exchange-rate management clearly may be linked. In the extreme view, stating that national economic policies should be coordinated and that exchange rates should be stabilized are two ways of making the same point. Insofar as imbalances in national economic policies are the source of exchange-rate volatility, by coordinating their policies nations can eliminate exchange rate swings. From this standpoint, policy coordination is the key; exchange-rate stabilization is a byproduct, though a desirable one. The premise that policy coordination can all but eliminate exchange-rate movements assumes, however, that changes in macroeconomic policies are the main source of exchange-rate variability. If other factors such as inefficiencies in financial markets are an important source of macroeconomic disturbances, then the optimal, internationally coordinated policy response still may not eliminate undesirable exchange-rate movements. Clearly, the cases for international

BLUEPRINTS FOR EXCHANGE RATE MANAGEMENT
0-12-497060-5

Copyright © 1989 Academic Press, Ltd
All rights of reproduction reserved

economic policy coordination and for stable exchange rates, while related, are distinct.

The question is whether an alternative exchange-rate arrangement, such as Williamson's target zones or the European Monetary System's adjustable parities, is consistent with the exchange rates which would emerge from optimally coordinated macroeconomic policies. This question is critical for those who argue that exchange-rate rules can facilitate coordination. The optimal, internationally coordinated response to a macroeconomic disturbance can be very difficult to compute in a complex, interdependent world, and very difficult to implement when responsibility for policy-making is decentralized internationally. A common set of exchange-rate targets, either target rates or target zones, may provide a useful surrogate for national policy-makers seeking to coordinate their initiatives. This argument is particularly attractive to those who view greater exchange-rate stability as a desirable goal in its own right.

A related argument is that international monetary reform can help to solve the credibility and enforcement problems that plague efforts to coordinate policies internationally. Even if all nations are better off when they coordinate their policies than when they behave non-cooperatively, it still may be in the interest of each participant to 'cheat' by altering its policies and defecting from the agreement so long as it has no reason to anticipate foreign retaliation. An agreement to cooperate will not be credible in the absence of an enforcement mechanism. Negotiating exchange-rate rules or a formal exchange-rate arrangement can be understood as an investment in credibility. Nations invest political and economic capital when they join an exchange-rate arrangement like the European Monetary System (EMS). If they fail to coordinate their policies so as to maintain their membership, that investment is lost, generally at the expense of the politicians responsible. Hence establishing an exchange-rate arrangement can be understood as a precommitment to policy coordination.

The papers in this volume consider these issues in turn. Part I contains two papers exploring historical experiences with alternative exchange rate systems and their implications for international policy coordination. Alberto Giovannini analyses the common features of the nineteenth century gold standard, the Bretton Woods system, and the EMS, asking how the convergence of national economic policies was achieved under each of these systems. Steve Broadberry examines the experience of interdependence and deflation in the UK and US in the 1920s and 1930s, challenging the notion that common participation in a fixed-rate system helped these countries to coordinate their economic policies.

Part II consists of four theoretical contributions to the current debate on world monetary reform. In the first, George Alogoskoufis uses a stochastic model to evaluate the welfare costs and benefits of Williamson's extended target zone proposal (extended, that is, to include a role for fiscal policy). The analysis allows for either symmetric or asymmetric equilibria, and examines the second-best outcomes that emerge if fiscal policy is denied a stabilization role in support of the exchange-rate regime. Alison Hook and David Walton simulate a stochastic rational expectations model to assess whether commodity prices might be a useful leading indicator of aggregate OECD inflation, robust enough to guide monetary policy for the developed countries as a whole.

Whatever indicators may be used to guide the overall stance of monetary policy, it is the exchange rate that has pride of place for setting international interest differentials in a target zone system (at least at the edges of the zone). James Boughton challenges this assignment, arguing instead that national monetary policy should be assigned to stabilizing domestic nominal income, and fiscal policy assigned to external balance, specified as a current-account target. On these grounds, he advocates floating exchange rates. Both the target zones proposed by Williamson and the Exchange Rate Mechanism of the EMS involve a band which in principle allows the rate to float inside the band and only requires monetary policy to stabilize the rate when it is at or near the edges. Marcus Miller and Paul Weller study the hybrid nature of such regimes in a stochastic model where, in addition, the market allows for some possibility of realignment at the edge of the band.

In Part III, empirically estimated global models are used to give practical content to such speculations and to examine other issues central to the current debate. Using a global model and historical data from 1975 to 1986, David Currie and Simon Wren-Lewis run a competition between extended target zone rules (as specified in the Williamson-Miller blueprint) and the alternative assignment analyzed by Genberg and Swoboda (1987) and advocated here by James Boughton. Patrick Minford similarly assesses the hybrid Exchange Rate Mechanism of the EMS, modifying his empirically estimated rational-expectations model for the purpose. Two themes central to the debate on monetary reform are highlighted in the last two papers. First, Andrew Hughes Hallett and his colleagues use the Federal Reserve Board's model to see whether exchange rates are, after all, useful surrogates for international cooperation: they emerge sceptical. Second, Paul Levine and his colleagues see how well simple rules do as surrogates for more complicated forms of cooperation and how sustainable such rules may prove: they are more optimistic.

As each of the papers published in the volume is critically discussed by an expert in the relevant field, we do not duplicate their efforts here. Instead we set the scene by reviewing earlier contributions to these fields and indicating themes which are the focus of attention in this volume. First we take up issues highlighted by the study of earlier exchange-rate regimes. Then we turn to the current debate on blueprints for reform of the international monetary system.

I Historical experience

Alberto Giovannini's wide-ranging paper stresses that fixed exchange-rate systems have always operated asymmetrically and have been maintained with restrictions on convertibility and capital mobility. Earlier analyses by Robert Triffin, Alec Ford and Marcello De Cecco also emphasized asymmetries in the operation of the classical gold standard. Ford (1962) contrasted the experiences of Britain and Argentina in the three decades preceding World War I; and he argued that creditor countries had a much happier experience with the gold standard than net foreign debtors. Whenever the world economy moved into recession and the volume of international trade contracted, this created more serious difficulties for borrowers than for lenders, since the former still had to service the foreign debts they had contracted in the course of previous years. Moreover, creditor countries could respond to the recession by calling a halt to foreign lending, redirecting those funds toward domestic investment and thereby moderating the downturn. Debtors, in contrast, were battered by mutually reinforcing current- and capital-account shocks.

De Cecco (1974) also contrasted the operation of the gold standard in different countries. One contrast was between countries with advanced and underdeveloped financial markets. The standard response under the gold standard to an external deficit was a tighter monetary policy, implemented by a rise in the central bank discount rate. This policy had very different effects when adopted by countries with different kinds of financial markets. One asymmetry lay in the power of central bank discount rates. The Bank of England, cooperating closely with the City of London, could succeed in altering the direction of international capital movements regardless of what other central banks did with their own discount rates. Therefore, other central banks had to follow the Bank of England, which led to the parallel movement of interest rates and national price levels noted by Triffin (1964), rather than the inverse movements predicted by Hume's specie-flow mechanism.

In addition, Triffin suggested that Britain could shift the burden of adjustment onto primary producers through commodity markets. The price-specie flow mechanism predicted that a monetary contraction induced by an external deficit should have restored external balance by worsening Britain's terms of trade (enhancing her competitiveness). In practice, the opposite response of the terms of trade was frequently observed. Triffin suggested that the mechanism was the liquidation of stocks of commodities induced by higher interest rates in London. A rise in the Bank of England's discount rate induced holders of inventories to dump stocks on the market, which restored balance to Britain's external accounts by reducing the cost of her imports and shifted the burden of adjustment onto primary-producing countries.

It is claimed that there were similar asymmetries in the Bretton Woods system between the experience of the reserve-currency country, the United States, and that of other participants. The same comparisons can be made for the EMS, although here Germany plays the role of the centre country (see Giavazzi, Micossi and Miller, 1988).

Giovannini, Giavazzi and others have argued that fixed exchange rates have so far been reconciled with the sovereignty of national economic policy-making in the EMS only through the maintenance of exchange controls. Historical experience suggests that this should not be attributed to unusually high capital mobility within present-day Europe or to the peculiar inability of European governments to harmonize their national economic policies; similar restrictions prevailed during the gold standard years and under Bretton Woods.

Both of these points have implications for international monetary reform. If any global system of limited exchange-rate flexiblity is likely to perform asymmetrically, the architects of a new system would be advised to take the existence of those asymmetries into account. If exchange-rate stability and perfect international capital mobility are incompatible, the only feasible alternatives may be a regime which retains a role for exchange-rate flexibility or else a common central bank (like that currently under discussion in Europe – see De Cecco and Giovannini, 1989).

The one notable 20th century experience with fixed exchange rates not considered by Giovannini, the interwar gold standard, is the subject of the paper by Stephen Broadberry. International economists are drawn to this experience by the fact that the short existence of the interwar gold standard coincided with the onset of the Great Depression. The coincidence has led some observers to blame the operation of the system for the macroeconomic crisis of the 1930s. Others, notably Clarke (1967), indict not the structure of the fixed exchange-rate system but the failure of governments to coordinate their macroeconomic policies during the period when it prevailed. Broadberry uses a formal model to show that, even in the absence of country-specific supply shocks or other international asymmetries, adherence to a fixed exchange-rate system will not permit central banks formulating policies independently to approach the cooperative solution to their policy game if they possess incompatible price-level or reserve targets. He demonstrates that under such circumstances adherence to a fixed-rate system may be counterproductive. Broadberry shows that, following the collapse of the gold standard in the 1930s, countries were better able to approach the policy optimum. This work serves as an important caution to the view that exchange-rate rules necessarily provide a good approximation to the cooperative solution to international policy games.

II   The current debate on international monetary reform

Experience with floating rates since 1973 has proved disappointing in a number of respects. In the first place, exchange rates have moved far more in response to fundamentals than seems rational: the US dollar appreciated by roughly 50% in real effective terms over 1980–85, only to fall by an even larger amount subsequently. Second, these 'misalignments' have been associated with unsustainably large payments imbalances. Finally, the credibility of national monetary targets (designed to supply a nominal achor under floating) has been substantially undermined by the speed of financial innovation and deregulation.

Recent developments, notably the Plaza Agreement (to drive the dollar down) and the Louvre Accord (to stabilize the dollar and to shift domestic demand in ways that would accommodate an improvement in the US deficit) have demonstrated a marked shift in attitudes towards exchange rates and put the subject of international monetary reform firmly on the agenda. In Table 1.1 we have classified international monetary systems (both past and proposed) by two criteria, flexibility of exchange rates and symmetry of operation. The hegemony exercised by the US from 1968 was suspended between 1973 and 1985 as countries floated and pursued domestic money supply targets. Here we focus on the alternative proposals for international

Table 1.1   International monetary systems

	Hegemony	Symmetric decision-making
Fixed exchange rates	Dollar standard (1968–73)	McKinnon's 'Paper Gold Standard'
Managed exchange rates	Plaza-Louvre (1985–88)	Williamson's Target Zones and the Blueprint Boughton's 'Alternative Assignment'
Floating rates	—	National monetary targets (1973–85)

monetary reform put forward by Ronald McKinnon, John Williamson and James Boughton, shown in the right-hand column.

McKinnon's (1984) plan for a symmetric Paper Gold Standard envisaged fixed exchange rates between the United States, Japan and Germany and a target for the growth rate of the aggregate price level. The G3 economies would set interest differentials so as to stabilize exchange rates and adjust the average level of interest rates to preserve price stability. Fiscal policy would be directed to achieving current-account balance. McKinnon was probably right to argue that some type of symmetric system is more likely to be acceptable (especially to Germany) than a return to US hegemony, and that monetary policy is easier to coordinate than fiscal policy. But his plan, which rests upon explicit cooperation among G3 central banks, assumes more consensus among national policy-makers than is the case now or in the foreseeable future; at the Toronto summit, for example, monetary coordination was hardly discussed.

The prolonged deviations from equilibrium ('misalignments') during the 1980s arose because nominal rates did not adjust simply to keep real rates stable, but moved independently of relative prices, driven largely by financial asset price considerations. It is this difficulty that Williamson's target zone proposal (1983, 1985) was designed to remedy: the G7 countries should adopt targets for central exchange rates that are designed to deliver sustainable current account balances at the highest level of output at which inflation is stable, while monetary policy should be used when rates deviate by more than 10% from such targets. Target values for nominal exchange rates would in effect be adjusted to offset inflation, thus becoming effectively target real exchange rates. To counter the objection that there would be insufficient check on inflation, the proposal was extended to include use of average G7 interest rates to stabilize aggregate nominal growth, while individual countries' fiscal policies could be adjusted to influence domestic nominal growth. This 'extended target zone' proposal (co-authored with one of the present editors) was offered as a blueprint for the international coordination of economic policy. For convenience, we reprint a summary in the Box below.

This extended target zone system resembles the McKinnon plan in emphasizing multilateral cooperation on stabilizing exchange rates (but involving G7 rather than G3). Despite their different exchange-rate targets, both proposals employ similar mechanisms for controlling global inflation, each assigning the average level of interest rates to stabilize a nominal target. The alternative use of commodity price indicators, suggested in 1987 by both James Baker and Nigel Lawson, is discussed by Hook and Walton here. The extended target zone system was evaluated by David Currie and Simon Wren-Lewis (1988), using the National Institute Global Econometric Model

---

The Blueprint Williamson and Miller (1987)

The participating countries (the Group of Seven) agree that they will conduct their macroeconomic policies with a view to pursuing the following two intermediate targets:
(1) A rate of growth of domestic demand in each country calculated according to a formula designed to promote the fastest growth of output consistent with gradual reduction of inflation to an acceptable level and agreed adjustment of the current account of the balance of payments.
(2) A real effective exchange rate that will not deviate by more than (10) percent from an internationally agreed estimate of the 'fundamental equilibrium exchange rate,' the rate estimated to be consistent with simultaneous internal and external balance in the medium term.

To that end, the participants agree that they will modify their monetary and fiscal policies according to the following principles:

(A) The *average level* of world (real) short-term interest rates should be revised up (down) if aggregate growth of nominal income is threatening to exceed (fall short of) the sum of the target growth of nominal demand for the participating countries.

(B) *Differences* in short-term interest rates among countries should be revised when necessary to supplement intervention in the exchange markets to prevent the deviation of currencies from their target ranges.

(C) National *fiscal policies* should be revised with a view to achieving national target rates of growth of domestic demand.

The rules (A) to (C) should be constrained by the medium-term objectives of maintaining the real interest rate in its historically normal range and of avoiding an increasing or excessive ratio of public debt to GNP.

(GEM). Their results suggested that applying such rules in practice would have led to a significant improvement in economic performance during 1975–85.

Subsequently, however, the policy assignment embodied in the extended target zone system has been challenged by James Boughton, who argues here against using monetary policy for exchange-rate targets. Instead, he recommends a return to floating rates, but with two major provisions: that monetary policy be guided by targets for nominal income rather than for money supply, and that fiscal policy be assigned to balance-of-payments targets. We are pleased to include in this volume the second study by Currie and Wren-Lewis in which they compare the Blueprint and this alternative assignment. What they find is that the 'J-curve' response of current accounts and the weak link between money and nominal income prevent Boughton's policy assignment from working effectively.

In addition to the topics mentioned above – the appropriate choice of indicator for global monetary policy and the question of how best to 'assign' national monetary and fiscal policy – there has been a lively debate on the merits of adopting currency bands. The EMS has ECU bands – although the operation of capital controls mitigates somewhat the loss of monetary autonomy this implies. It was reported that the Louvre Accord involved bands of plus or minus five per cent *vis-à-vis* the dollar. As these were not publicly acknowledged, however, they involved no explicit monetary policy commitment. The issue of how currency bands might work if they are publicly acknowledged and capital movements are not inhibited is an important one at this time – both for the EMS and for the G3 – and is another of the themes discussed in theory and tested using econometric models in the papers included here.

References

Clarke, S.V.O. (1967) *Central Bank Cooperation, 1924–31*, New York: Federal Reserve Bank of New York.

Currie, David, and Simon Wren-Lewis (1988) 'Evaluating the extended target zone proposal for the G3', CEPR Discussion Paper No. 221, London: Centre for Economic Policy Research.

De Cecco, Marcello (1974) *Money and Empire*, Oxford: Blackwell.

De Cecco, Marcello, and Alberto Giovannini, eds. (1989) *A European Central Bank? Perspectives on Monetary Unification after ten years of the EMS*, Cambridge: Cambridge University Press for CEPR.

Ford, A.G. (1962) *The Classical Gold Standard, 1880–1913: Britain and Argentina*, Oxford: Clarendon Press.

Genberg, Hans, and Alexander K. Swoboda (1987) 'The current account and the policy mix under flexible exchange rates', IMF Working Paper No. 87/70, Washington, D.C.: International Monetary Fund.

Giavazzi, Francesco, Stefano Micossi and Marcus Miller, eds. (1988) *The European Monetary System*, Cambridge: Cambridge University Press for CEPR.

McKinnon, Ronald I. (1984) *An International Standard for Monetary Stabilization*, Washington, D.C.: Institute for International Economics.

Triffin, Robert (1964) 'The myth and realities of the so-called gold standard', in *The Evolution of the International Monetary System: Historical Reappraisal and Future Perspectives*, Princeton: Princeton University Press.

Williamson, John (1983, revised 1985) *The Exchange Rate System*, Washington, D.C.: Institute for International Economics.

Miller, Eichengreen and Portes

Williamson, John, and Marcus Miller (1987), *Targets and Indicators: A Blueprint for the International Coordination of Economic Policy*, Washington, D.C.: Institute for International Economics.

Part I

Historical perspectives

Chapter 2

How do fixed-exchange-rate regimes work? Evidence from the gold standard, Bretton Woods and the EMS

Alberto Giovannini

I Introduction

Few countries freely float their currencies: the *International Financial Statistics Supplement on Exchange Rates* (1985) lists only 12 out of 147 members of the IMF as 'independently floating'. While this list includes large countries like the United States, Japan and the United Kingdom, as many as 34 countries, for example, peg their currencies to the US dollar. Even so, in the current open-economy macroeconomics literature most theoretical and empirical papers deal with aspects of flexible-exchange-rate regimes.

There exist two competing hypotheses on the working of fixed exchange rates. The 'symmetry' hypothesis states that every country is concerned with the good functioning of the system, and cannot afford to deviate from world averages. Every country is just left to follow the 'rules of the game', that is to avoid sterilizing balance of payments flows. This hypothesis is masterfully described by McCloskey and Zecher (1976).

If every country is just concerned with accommodating reserve flows in order to maintain its exchange-rate parities, however, the international monetary system as a whole suffers from an indeterminacy: there is no system-wide nominal anchor. According to the proponents of the symmetry hypothesis, this nominal anchor is provided by an external numeraire like

BLUEPRINTS FOR EXCHANGE RATE MANAGEMENT
0-12-497060-5

Copyright © 1989 Academic Press, Ltd
All rights of reproduction reserved

gold, or is agreed upon by member countries through a process of inter-national cooperation. Hence Helpman's (1981) labeling of this regime as a 'cooperative peg'.

The competing hypothesis states that fixed-exchange-rate regimes are inherently asymmetric: they are characterized by a 'centre country' which provides the nominal anchor for the others, either by managing the gold parity in a centralized fashion, or by arbitrarily setting some other nominal anchor. This hypothesis has been proposed by Keynes (1930), and has been labeled by Helpman (1981) a 'one-sided peg'.[1]* This paper organizes and discusses the empirical evidence on the two hypotheses, by studying the institutional features and the data on three experiences with fixed rates: the international gold standard (from 1870 to 1913), the Bretton Woods regime (which lasted from 1958 to 1971) and the European Monetary System (EMS, started in March 1979, still in place).

Section II describes the institutional features of the three systems, with the objective of determining whether the institutions, *per se*, induce asymmetry. Section III describes another significant institutional aspect: the use of capital controls to limit the effectiveness of external constraints on monetary policy. Section IV illustrates the two competing hypotheses with a simple theoretical model. Section V discusses the empirical evidence. Section VI offers a few concluding observations.

II. Common features of fixed exchange rates: Institutional setup

All the international monetary systems I study in this paper are characterized by codified sets of rules, which bind countries adhering to them. These rules have increased in coverage and complexity in the more recent years, but conserve a number of common features that it is useful to highlight. I divide the institutional arrangements of the three exchange regimes into three categories: a numeraire to set target exchange rates; 'bands' for exchange rates, setting limits within which exchange rates could fluctuate without implying any actions by central banks to maintain the central parities; and provisions for central bank financing of balance-of-payments discrepancies and for correcting external imbalances.

II.1   Numeraire

Both the gold standard and the Bretton Woods regime were characterized by the use of gold as external numeraire. Under the gold standard, each

---

* Superscript numerals refer to numbered notes at the end of each chapter.

currency had a specified official value in terms of gold – the mint par. At this value the central bank was ready to exchange domestic banknotes for gold coins.[2]

Under the Bretton Woods system, the IMF Articles of Agreement[3] stipulated that each member country declare its par value in terms of gold.[4] The dollar price of gold was $35 an ounce, and it was never changed, until the Smithsonian conference of December 1971. The main difference between the gold standard and the Bretton Woods system is that in the former regime monetary authorities – at least in those countries on a full gold standard (Britain, Germany and the US)[5] – were required by law to exchange domestic banknotes with gold coins at the par value (plus or minus transactions costs), whereas after World War II central banks used gold in transactions among themselves, and intervened in the private bullion market at their own discretion. Since the private sector had no rights of official conversion of national currencies into gold[6], gold was much less of a direct constraint on national monetary policies than in the gold standard era.[7]

With gold as an external numeraire, the gold standard and the Bretton Woods system provide, in different degrees, an official nominal anchor for all member countries. In the EMS, by contrast, this official nominal anchor is altogether absent. Each EMS currency, and each currency in the European Community, has a central rate determined in terms of the European Currency Unit (ECU), a basket unit of account that comprises a specified quantity of every currency in the European Community. The ratio of any two ECU central rates is used to obtain bilateral central rates, which are the target rates for monetary authorities. Given that the ECU is just a weighted average of the member countries' currencies, if n is the number of currencies in the ECU, there are only $n-1$ bilateral exchange rates to be pegged: for this reason a nominal anchor is absent from the rules governing the EMS.[8]

II.2 Bands

In the gold standard regime, individual currencies' gold parities, and the costs of shipping gold internationally, jointly implied bilateral bands within which exchange rates could fluctuate without requiring any action by monetary authorities. Whenever bilateral exchange rates reached the limits of the bands, arbitrage opportunities would be available, involving trades of gold with the central banks, and of foreign exchange in the market. Examples of these bilateral fluctuation bands are reported in Table 2.1. As the table shows, when the price of dollars in terms of francs in the foreign exchange market rose above 5.215, it was profitable to obtain gold at the mint par from the Bank of France, ship it to the US, sell it to US banks at the mint

Table 2.1   Bilateral fluctuation bands

Currency (x-rate)	Parity	Lower Limit	Upper Limit
Gold Standard			
Sterling ($/pound)	4.866	4.827	4.890
Franc (FF/$)	5.183	5.148	5.215
Mark (DM/$)	4.198	4.168	4.218
Bretton Woods			
Sterling ($/pound)	2.8	2.772	2.828
Franc (FF/$)	4.937	4.887	4.986
Mark (DM/$)	4.2	4.158	4.242
European Monetary System			
Franc (FF/DM)	2.310	2.258	2.362

Sources: *Gold Standard*: Morgenstern (1959). Sterling points are computed
for gold trade from Britain to the US (in 1879). Franc and mark points
are computed for trade from Paris and Berlin (respectively) to New York
(in 1901). *Bretton Woods*: *International Financial Statistics*. Data refer to
the year 1960. *EMS*: *European Economy*. Data refer to March 1979.

par, and simultaneously sell dollars for francs in the foreign exchange
markets, thus profiting from the arbitrage. The width of the gold standard
band was determined by the cost of transporting gold to different national
markets: thus it varied over time and across different markets. The estimates
by Morgenstern reported in Table 2.1 have been recently reassessed by Clark
(1984), Officer (1986) and Spiller and Wood (1988). The authors' results
suggest that the volatility of the gold points was considerable, making it
difficult to determine whether international gold arbitrage was indeed an
effective constraint on domestic monetary policies.

In the Bretton Woods regime, in the absence of an obligation for central
banks to trade in the gold market with the public – which implies fluctuation
bands whose size is determined by the available arbitrage technology –
bilateral fluctuation bands were set by fiat: central banks were required to
keep their respective currencies within ±1 percent of their stated parities.
Although par rates were set in terms of gold, bilateral fluctuation bands were
around dollar parities. As a result, all cross rates (not involving the dollar)
had 2 percent fluctuation margins on each side.[9]

The bilateral fluctuation bands involving the EMS currencies are, for all
currencies except the lira, 2.25 percent on each side of bilateral central rates.
The lira can fluctuate up to 6 percent on each side of bilateral central rates.
Thus, the fluctuation bands for all European bilateral rates excluding the
lira rates are only slightly larger than those prevailing during the Bretton
Woods years: 4.5 percent in the EMS, 4 percent during Bretton Woods. The

EMS regime is further complicated by an 'indicator of divergence', measuring the weighted average deviation of each currency from the other currencies in the ECU. When the indicator of divergence reaches a certain threshold, a country is supposed to take corrective actions.[10] These corrective actions, however, are not compulsory.[11]

II.3 Adjustment and financing

During the gold standard central banks were compelled to take corrective actions by a combination of two mechanisms: the convertibility of banknotes into gold coin, which encouraged arbitrage by the private sector whenever exchange rates exceeded bilateral fluctuation limits, and the coverage of banknotes by gold, which forced central banks to maintain a certain ratio of gold reserves to circulating banknotes, thus reacting to fluctuations of their gold reserve.[12] Changes in the discount rate and open market operations (Bloomfield, 1959) were the standard corrective actions. Various central banks also resorted to the so called 'manipulation of gold points' which I discuss below in Section III.

No central-bank financing arrangment was part of the institutional setup of the gold standard. However, a number of instances are recorded when central banks granted bilateral credit to each other. Ford (1962) notes that the Bank of France discounted Sterling bills to ease the strain on London in the Autumn of 1906, 1907, 1909 and 1910. Kindleberger (1984) describes the cooperation between European central banks in the crisis of 1890, when the Bank of England asked the Russian State Bank not to draw on its deposits in London and obtained from the State Bank an 800,000 sterling gold loan, and from the Bank of France a loan of 3,000,000 sterling in gold.[13].

The Bretton Woods system and the EMS, by contrast, are characterized by a complex structure of loans available to finance balance-of-payments needs. These financial resources support the foreign exchange market intervention required to keep currencies within their fluctuation bands. Neither the IMF Articles of Agreement, nor the rules governing the EMS, spell out the actions that central banks have to take when exchange rates reach bilateral fluctuation margins. In both systems the modality of adjustment to external disequilibria is only specified through the rules governing the financing of central banks' external imbalances, though there are some concessions to the principle of symmetry (in the Bretton Woods regime through the clauses on 'scarce' currencies, see Argy 1981, in the EMS with the divergence indicator, and the Very Short Term Financing Facility, described below).

Under the BrettonWoods regime member countries could draw on various tranches of their IMF 'quota'. These tranches are characterized by different degrees of 'conditionality', that impose progressively tighter constraints on monetary and fiscal policies: resources are made available to the borrowers subject to their meeting certain prespecified performance criteria.[14]

The EMS rules for balance-of-payments financing appear to be designed to avoid crises: the central banks of the currencies reaching bilateral intervention margins are supposed to grant each other automatic credit (not subject to authorization) in unlimited amounts under the Very Short Term Financing Facility.[15] The Very Short Term Financing Facility can also be used to support foreign exchange market intervention within the marginal fluctuation bands, subject to the authorization of the central bank whose currency is being drawn. The Short Term Monetary Support, another form of financial assistance available to EMS central banks experiencing temporary balance-of-payments difficulties, is instead governed by a 'quota' system similar to that used by the IMF.

II.4   Is asymmetry induced by the institutions?

The very brief survey of institutional features of the three fixed-exchange-rates regimes suggests two observations. First, the basic structure of international monetary systems has not changed dramatically in the last century. In particular, despite the efforts of policymakers to improve upon the IMF Articles of Agreement, the features of the Bretton Woods system and the EMS are noticeably similar. Both systems are characterized essentially by a lack of an external nominal anchor (given the minor role played by gold during the Bretton Woods regime), and by elaborate structures of balance-of-payments financing arrangements, which stand in contrast to the absence of any explicit rules for central banks to follow when bilateral fluctuation margins are reached. The added complications of the EMS, regarding the divergence indicator, have proved impractical.[16] In the gold standard, instead, adjustment rules were provided by the market mechanism, and by each country's coverage system.

The second observation suggested by my survey is that the rules of the gold standard, Bretton Woods and the EMS do not seem *per se* to induce an asymmetric working of international adjustment. Except in the case of Bretton Woods – where the bilateral fluctuation bands of the dollar are narrower than those of the other currencies – none of the basic institutional features of the three fixed-exchange-rate regimes seems asymmetric. At the same time, all the provisions of the EMS explicitly designed to avoid asymmetries, like the indicator of divergence and the Very Short Term

Financing Facility, were never seriously binding. The indicator of divergence does not force any country to take specific actions, while the automatic and symmetric foreign exchange intervention that takes place under the VSTFF appears to be a small fraction of the total volume of foreign exchange market intervention by member countries.[17]

III Capital controls

It is often argued by international economists that 'capital controls' are more frequently resorted to by countries belonging to fixed-exchange-rates arrangements (see, for example, Stockman, 1987). In this paper I use the term 'capital controls' to denote various regulatory manipulations of the market mechanism which underlies the adjustment to external imbalances. These regulations were directed at different markets in different periods. Hence, for example, international bond and money markets were relatively free from regulation during the gold standard (a time where the gold market was subjected to various controls), but not in the more recent fixed-rate regimes, Bretton Woods and the EMS. In all three cases central banks resorted to capital controls as an additional instrument of monetary management. Controlling international financial transactions allows a country to gain limited freedom from the 'rules of the game' imposed by the domestic and international monetary system, by preventing or slowing down the adjustment that would occur if financial transactions were free.

Controls were frequently imposed in emergencies. The Bank of England suspended the convertibility of notes into gold, thereby freeing itself to issue fiat money, in 1847, 1857 and 1866 (Kindleberger, 1984). While some of these crises were domestic in origin, the suspension of convertibility was also a response to external gold drains: see, for example the discussion in Dornbusch and Frenkel (1984). Following Keynes (1930), they argue that the suspension of gold standard rules during crises suggests they were effective only in periods of quiet.[18] Another popular regulatory measure affecting financial and gold flows was the so-called manipulation of gold points, that is the change in the bid-ask spread on bullion charged by the central bank. The Bank of England increased its buying price for bar gold in the crisis year of 1890, and according to Scammell (1965) followed the same practice on several other occasions in the following years. Similar devices were used by the Bank of France and the Reichsbank (Bloomfield, 1959).

The use of regulatory controls as emergency measures is common also in the Bretton Woods and EMS years. Article VI of the IMF Articles of Agreement even allows the Fund to request countries with balance-of-payments problems to impose capital controls for a limited time, in order to prevent the use of Fund resources. In response to capital account deficits, the Kennedy Administration proposed an investment tax credit in 1961, and passed the Interest Equalization Tax in 1963 – a tax on US residents' purchases of foreign securities – followed by the Foreign Credit Restraint Program and the Foreign Direct Investment Program – aimed at limiting foreign investments by commercial banks, other financial institutions, and industrial companies. French and Italian authorities tightened various measures to prevent capital outflows after the Summer of 1968 and the Fall of 1969.

The practice of using capital controls as a fine-tuning device to stem speculative flows has survived in the EMS. Countries like France and Italy, which until recently have prohibited the non-firm private sector from trading in financial assets with the rest of the world, have used restrictions on international trade credits to slow down or speed up the response of short-term capital flows.[19]

Giavazzi and Giovannini (1986) argue that in the EMS France and Italy rely crucially on capital controls, witness the large divergences between domestic offshore interest rates on franc and lira assets. They see asymmetries of capital controls as a reflection of the central role played by the Bundesbank, and capital controls as instrumental for countries other than Germany to maintain their exchange rate targets in the EMS, without having to surrender completely their monetary sovereignty. This observation raises two related questions. Are all fixed-exchange-rate regimes characterized by asymmetries in the degree to which capital controls are used? Is the presence of these asymmetries an indication of the existence of a central country?

A broad overview of the use of capital controls suggests a positive answer to the first question. There is ample qualitative evidence and opinion (see, for example, Bloomfield, 1959; Ford, 1962; Scammell, 1965) that the Bank of England tended to use administrative devices less frequently than its counterparts on the Continent. It is well known that the convertibility of banknotes into gold was not guaranteed by law in France, but was left to the central bank's discretion. The much less frequent changes of the discount rate by the Bank of France, relative to the Bank of England and the Reichsbank, tends to imply the effectiveness of the threat of inconvertibility, which was accompanied by numerous changes of the gold points. In Germany international shipments of gold were apparently discouraged by moral suasion. As Bloomfield (1959) reported, Reichsbank officials questioned by the United States National Monetary Commission denied that the central bank discouraged commercial banks from obtaining gold for export when the gold export point was reached, but admitted that at certain times German banks refrained from shipping gold when it was profitable to do so. This phenomenon is independently confirmed by Birch (1887), in his presidential address to the London Institute of Bankers:

I was raising the question, only a few days since, with some of the leading bankers in Berlin, whether the Bank of Germany would give large amounts of gold in exchange for its notes, and they explained to me that, if gold was required to use as currency, they had no difficulty in getting what they wanted, but that they were too Patriotic to think of going to the bank for gold with a view to making a profit on the export (Birch, 1887, p. 510).

The evidence on asymmetric use of capital controls during the Bretton Woods years is, to some extent, less clearcut. While in the second postwar period as a whole the United States has regulated international capital flows less than its European conterparts, episodes like the Interest Equalization Tax were clearly motivated by concern for the external influence on domestic monetary management.

The imposition of capital controls was resorted to not only by deficit countries. In the months preceding the revaluation of the Deutsche mark in March 1961, the Bundesbank struggled with capital inflows by imposing a series of discriminatory measures meant to discourage foreign residents' purchases of German assets.[20] These measures included higher reserve requirements on foreign-owned deposits at German commercial banks, prohibition of the payment of interest on foreign-owned sight and time deposits, and prohibition of the sale of money-market paper to nonresidents.

In summary, the evidence on both the gold standard and the EMS suggest that countries other than Britain (during the gold standard) and Germany (in the EMS) imposed regulations in order to avoid compliance with the 'rules of the game': in an asymmetric system the rules of the game consist of accommodating fully the centre country's monetary policies.[21] Hence these regulations might have been suggested by a desire to maintain some degree of monetary sovereignty. The evidence on Bretton Woods seems to indicate that capital controls were resorted to more often outside of the US, although even the US experimented with them in a number of cases.

IV   Symmetric and asymmetric fixed-exchange-rate regimes: A definition

The alternative hypotheses about the working of fixed exchange rates can be illustrated using the canonical model of the gold standard.[22] This model concentrates on the external influences on domestic monetary policy and on domestic aggregate variables. It relies on the assumption that monetary policy is powerless in affecting real variables, so that real and nominal variables are determined independently. This assumption, which is probably not accurate in practice, is not essential for the conclusions I will draw here, but is quite helpful to sharpen the distinction between the alternative hypotheses on the working of the international monetary system.

There are two countries, a domestic and a foreign country – whose variables are identified by an asterisk. The rate of inflation in each country is determined by the rate of money growth and a velocity shock, that is independent of monetary factors:

$$p = m + v \qquad p^* = m^* + v^* \tag{1}$$

where m is the rate of growth of money, and p the rate of inflation. v represents the rate of growth of velocity. The law of one price holds in the goods market.[23] Hence the rates of inflation at home and abroad are the same in equilibrium. Real rates of return on domestic and foreign securities are equalized except for a variable, x representing international portfolio shifts. x is independent of monetary policies:[24]

$$p = p^* \tag{2}$$

$$r^* = r + x \tag{3}$$

The balance sheets of the two central banks imply:

$$m = d - f \qquad m^* = d^* - f^* \tag{4}$$

In a fiat currency system, d could be interpreted as the change in domestic credit relative to the initial stock of nominal money. f is the outflow of foreign exchange reserves, also measured in terms of the initial stock of money. Under the gold standard, d and f are the rate of growth of the fiduciary issue and the outflow of gold, respectively. Since there are only two countries in the model, one country's gold or reserve outflows are the other country's inflows. Assuming that the two countries are of equal size, we have:

$$f = -f^* \tag{5}$$

Equations (1) to (5) imply the following expression for the world rate of inflation, and the flow of international reserves:

$$p = 0.5[(d + d^*) + (v + v^*)] \tag{6}$$

$$f = 0.5[(d - d^*) + (v - v^*)] \tag{7}$$

As equations (6) and (7) show, the world rate of inflation is a weighted average of the domestic and foreign rates of growth of domestic credit (adjusted for velocity shocks), while reserve flows are determined by the deviations of the domestic and foreign monetary policies and money demand shocks. Nominal interest rates are determined by the Fisher equation:

$$i = r + p \qquad i^* = r^* + p^* \tag{8}$$

I define the symmetric fixed-exchange-rate regime as follows. Under a symmetric fixed-exchange-rate regime each central bank attempts to control a domestic target and a foreign target, represented by the nominal interest rate, and the rate of change of foreign exchange reserves: the two target variables have the same weights and desired values in central banks' objectives. I borrow the assumption that central bankers' objectives can be determined by a domestic target and a foreign target from Giovannini (1986), Eichengreen (1987), Giavazzi and Giovannini (1989) and Barsky *et al.* (1988). The specification of the domestic target in terms of the nominal rate of interest is due to Barro (1988) and Barsky *et al.* (1988). In a symmetric system, the objective (loss) functions are:

$$W = (i - \bar{i})^2 + bf^2 \tag{9}$$
$$W^* = (i^* - \bar{i})^2 + bf^{*2} \tag{10}$$

In a commodity-based system like the gold standard, the similarity of the two objective functions would arise from the common rules governing the convertibility of banknotes into gold coins, and from the similarity of the rules about specie coverage of banknote circulation. In a fiat system like the EMS, the similarity of the two objective functions would arise as a result of systematic international consultations among member countries, whose objective is to define common guidelines for monetary policy.

When central banks maximize (9) and (10) world interest rates and reserve flow are as follows:

$$i = \bar{i} - 0.5x \qquad i^* = \bar{i} + 0.5x \tag{11}$$
$$f = (0.5/b)x \tag{12}$$

International disturbances are equally shared by the two countries, and international reserve flows are inversely proportional to the importance of the external target in the two countries' objectives.

By contrast, I define the asymmetric system as follows: the centre country targets the domestic interest rate, while the other country minimizes fluctuation of international reserves. Hence countries' objective functions differ:

$$W = (i - \bar{i})^2 \tag{9'}$$
$$W^* = f^{*2} \tag{10'}$$

The reaction functions implied by (9′) and (10′) are:

$$d = 2(\bar{i} - r) - d^* - (v + v^*) \tag{13}$$

$$d^* = d + (v - v^*) \tag{14}$$

Equations (13) and (14) show that the centre country accommodates world money demand shocks, but – given the real rate of interest and money demand – it offsets any changes of domestic credit policy in the periphery. The country at the periphery accommodates the centre country's policy, and offsets differences in money demand shocks, which tend to give rise to international reserve flows. The equilibrium interest rates and reserve flows are:

$$i = \bar{i} \qquad i^* = \bar{i} + x \tag{15}$$

$$f = 0 \tag{16}$$

Equations (15) and (16) reveal most clearly the fundamental difference between symmetric and asymmetric fixed-exchange-rate systems: in an asymmetric system countries at the periphery give up control of their domestic target to achieve stability of foreign reserve flows. In equilibrium all international portfolio shifts are fully reflected in changes in the interest rates at the periphery, but do not change the interest rate of the centre country.

The illustration of the symmetric and asymmetric regimes adopted in this section – based on postulated asymmetries in the objectives of central bankers – was preferred to an alternative specification, based on the hypothesis that the centre country is a 'Stackelberg leader'. That model relies on the assumption that changes in monetary policies by countries other than the leader cannot elicit the leader's reaction. By contrast, the model I use has in my opinion the virtue of being based on a symmetric game structure, but is silent on what gives rise to the asymmetries in the objective functions. The asymmetries could be generated by four different phenomena, which I briefly review below. They include Mundell's (1968) 'proper division of the burden of international adjustment', the presence of a 'reserve currency' country, liquidity constraints affecting differently surplus and deficit countries, and the issue of 'imported reputation'.

Robert Mundell (1968) demonstrates that the adjustment to country-specific disturbances should be divided in inverse proportion to the sizes of the countries involved. In our problem, the adjustment to relative interest-rate shocks is carried out by the small country: the interest rate in the large country is unaffected. This result can be illustrated considering a world made up by two equally-sized regions: one occupied by a single large country (the 'domestic country'), and the other by a large number of small countries (denoted by an asterisk, *), indexed by $j = 1, \ldots, N$.[25] In this world, the rate of inflation is:[26]

$$p^*_j = p = 0.5[(d_j + (1/N)\Sigma d^*_j) + (v + (1/N)\Sigma v^*_j)].$$ (17)

Each small country's domestic credit policy has a negligible effect on its own rate of inflation. By contrast, the small countries' reserve flows are:

$$f^*_j = d^*_j + v^*_j - 0.5[(d + (1/N)\Sigma d^*_j) + (v + (1/N)\Sigma v^*_j)]$$ (18)

In equilibrium, deviations of the two target variables from their desired values are inversely related to the relative effectiveness of the instrument: hence the small countries end up nearly pegging their foreign exchange reserves, while the task of pegging the world interest rate is left to the centre country. This corresponds to the asymmetric regime postulated above.

A similar result would obtain if one of the two countries issues a 'reserve' currency: this case is discussed by Swoboda (1978) and Genberg, Saidi and Swoboda (1982). An increase in high-powered money by the reserve-currency country has a larger effect on world inflation than the same increase from a non-reserve-currency country. The foreign exchange reserves of the other country increase by a multiple of the original monetary expansion, equal to the money multiplier of the reserve currency. Hence the non-reserve-currency central bank would be relatively ineffective at targeting the rate of interest, and, as above, would end up targeting foreign exchange reserves.

A third reason for the endogenous establishment of an asymmetric regime is the presence of constraints on the size of balance-of-payments deficits, justified, for example, by liquidity constraints. With identical objective functions, the equilibrium reserve outflow from the domestic country is given by equation (12). If the domestic country faces systematically positive realizations of x, i.e. it is a 'deficit country', and if the costs of financing reserve outflows are large, the domestic country would find it advantageous to forego interest rate stability by accommodating fully the monetary policy of the centre country.

Finally, asymmetric exchange rate regimes could arise in the 'imported credibility' models of Giavazzi and Giovannini (1987) and Giavazzi and Pagano (1988). These authors show that, when exchange-rate targets are fully credible, inflation-prone central banks might find it advantageous to accommodate fully to a central bank which has an 'inflation fighter' reputation.[27]

V Empirical evidence

In this section I discuss the empirical evidence on the hypothesis that the three fixed-exchange-rates regimes worked asymmetrically. I first review the evidence on the timing of discount rate changes during the gold standard. Then I study the behaviour of interest rates around parity realignments, both during the Bretton Woods and the EMS. And finally I derive and test some stochastic implications of the model of Section IV.

V.1   The timing of discount-rate changes during the gold standard

During the gold standard, changes in Bank rate were considered the main policy instruments used by central banks to affect their gold reserves and international capital flows. Bloomfield (1959) and Eichengreen (1987) argue that British rate changes followed immediately by changes on the Continent are evidence suggestive of the central role of the Bank of England in the gold standard. To verify this hypothesis, I have looked at the data published by the US National Monetary Commission (1910), reporting dates and amounts of discount rate changes for Britain, France and Germany in the period from January 1889 to December 1907.

First, I have computed the number of occurrences when a change in the British discount rate was followed (within 1 week) by a change in the discount rate in France or Germany. During the period, the Bank of England changed the discount rate 104 times, increasing it 59 times, and decreasing it 45 times. The Reichsbank followed increases in the British discount rate 11 times, and followed rate decreases 14 times. There are also 14 cases when the Reichsbank discount rate changes preceded those of the Bank of England.[28] France, by contrast, followed changes of Bank rate much less frequently (a reflection of less intensive use of discount rate policy by the Bank of France). Only three British rate changes were followed by France within a week (2 negative and 1 positive), while France's discount rate adjustments were also followed by the Bank of England on three occasions (2 negative changes, 1 positive). In the case of France, there are also three instances of discount rate changes occuring the same day.[29]

Table 2.2 contains statistical tests of the timing of discount rate changes, using 992 weekly observations for the period mentioned above. I estimate a vector autoregression including 8 lags of the British, French and German rates, and test the joint significance of the coefficients of each set of lagged rates in each regression. The table shows no evidence of temporal precedence in the changes in the British rate. Instead, lagged values of the German discount rate are significantly correlated with Bank rate and the French discount rate.[30] In summary, there is very little evidence in support of the hypothesis that Bank rate changes preceded changes in discount rates on the continent. As I argue in Giovannini (1986), at least in the monthly data, there is a strong contemporaneous correlation between the British and the

Table 2.2   The timing of discount rate changes under the gold standard

	Dependent Variables		
	GB	GER	FRA
R^2	0.434	0.956	0.982
DW	2.000	2.000	2.001
F-tests			
GB	0.000	0.432	0.780
GER	0.000	0.000	0.038
FRA	0.117	0.574	0.000

Sample: Weekly from January 1890 to December 1907. The entries denoted by F-test are the marginal significance levels of the null hypothesis that the coefficients of the lagged discount rates of the country of the corresponding row are not significant in the regressions whose dependent variable is the country of the corresponding column.

German rates.[31] This correlation, however, is almost entirely due to the common seasonal component in discount rate policies, and therefore cannot be interpreted as supporting the hypothesis of the leadership of the Bank of England.[32]

How should we interpret these results? The temporal pattern of discount-rate changes being tested in this section is consistent with a leader-follower structure, where the centre country's central bank always moves first, independently of the other central banks' actions, and taking their reactions into account. The empirical evidence presented here rejects this hypothesis.[33] This evidence, however, has no conclusive implications for the asymmetric model of the gold standard in Section IV.[34]

V.2   The asymmetric behaviour of interest rates

A rather general implication of the model in Section IV regards the behaviour of interest rates. While in a symmetric regime international portfolio shifts are reflected in both countries' interest rates, in an asymmetric regime the centre country's rate is unaffected, and international portfolio disturbances perturb only the other countries' rates.[35]

This result suggests a simple test of the asymmetry hypothesis, based on the observation of countries' interest rates in response to observable international portfolio shifts. The most natural choice of episodes of shifts between countries' assets is the periods preceding devaluations. Both under the Bretton Woods regime and in the EMS there have been several realignments of central parities, which have been prompted by countries' inability to withstand balance-of-payments difficulties, and have been anticipated – though to different degrees – by financial markets. In this section I analyze the behaviour of interest rates around the Bretton Woods realignments of March 1961 (Deutsche mark revalued), November 1967 (devaluation of sterling), August 1969 (French franc devalued), and October 1969 (Deutsche mark revalued).

Figures 2.1, 2.2 and 2.3 report monthly observations of 1-month Eurodollar deposit rates, and of the differential between the Eurodollar rate and a domestic money market in the US, during an interval of two years around the realignments of 1961, 1967 and 1969.[36] Figures 2.4, 2.5, 2.6 and 2.7 report weekly data (taken on Fridays) on the US Treasury Bills rate and the forward premium. The sources are the *Wall Street Journal* for the US interest rate, and the *Economist* for the forward premium. The forward premium is

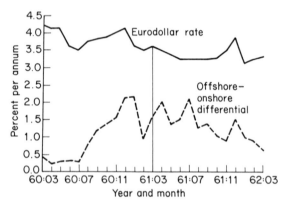

Figure 2.1 Dollar interest rates around the 1961 realignment

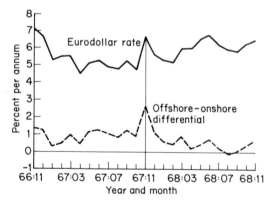

Figure 2.2 Dollar interest rates around the 1967 realignment

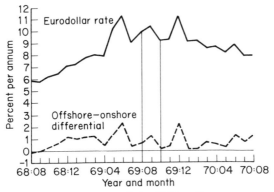

Figure 2.3   Dollar interest rates around the 1969 realignments

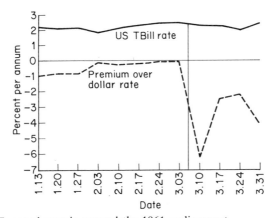

Figure 2.4   Forward premia around the 1961 realignment

calculated using bilateral rates against sterling: it is the ratio of the 1-month forward rate (expressed in units of the currency per dollar) and the spot exchange rate, less 1 (the result is multiplied by 1200 to express the implied interest rate differential in percent per annum).

Figures 2.1 and 2.4 illustrate the behaviour of dollar interest rates and the DM/dollar forward premium corresponding to the revaluation of the mark on March 6, 1961. Figure 2.4 shows that the volatility of the interest rate differential implied by the forward market much exceeds the volatility of the US Treasury bill rate. On January 13 the foreign exchange market implies a negative DM-dollar differential of about 1 percent. That differential decreases to −6 percent and −2.5 percent the weeks following the realignment. These large fluctuations of the interest-rate differential implied by the forward rate are accompanied by a much smaller increase of the Eurodollar

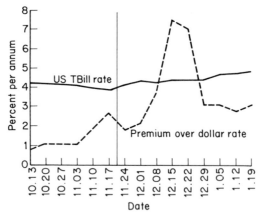

Figure 2.5   Forward premia around the 1967 realignment

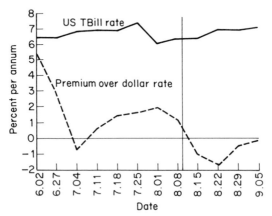

Figure 2.6   Forward premia around the August 1969 realignment

rate (shown in Figure 2.1), which reached 4.14 percent in December 1960, but fell to about 3.5 percent the February before the revaluation of the DM.

Figures 2.2 and 2.5 report US rates and forward premia around the devaluation of sterling on November 20, 1967. Figure 2.2 shows a large peak in the Eurodollar interest rate and the offshore-domestic differential for the dollar in the month of November – suggesting that the sterling crisis had some repercussion on the dollar (evidence against the asymmetry hypothesis). Figure 2.5 shows wide swings in the forward discount on sterling, especially after the date of the devaluation, and a slight increase in the US TBill rate in the weeks preceding the devaluation.

Finally, Figures 2.3, 2.6 and 2.7 illustrate the data for the August 11, 1969

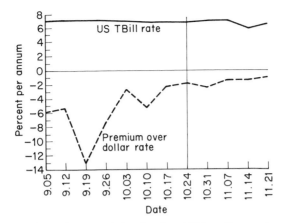

Figure 2.7 Forward premia around the October 1969 realignment

devaluation of the franc, and the October 24 revaluation of the DM. As Figure 2.3 shows, 1969 was a year of high and volatile Eurodollar interest rates. Figure 2.6 presents the data for the French devaluation. It shows that the forward market implied a very high differential between French and US interest rates at the end of June, without any large swings in the US TBill rate. The TBill rate, however, fell from 7.4 to 6.05 percent in the week preceding the devaluation. Figure 2.7 contrasts the relative stability of the US TBill rate with a sharp increase of the dollar-DM interest rate differential implied by the forward premium, which reached 13 percent on September 19.

Figures 2.8 and 2.9 report domestic and offshore interest rates for the lira,

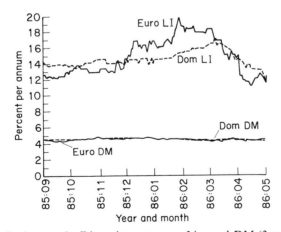

Figure 2.8 Onshore and offshore interest rates: Lira and DM (3-month deposits)

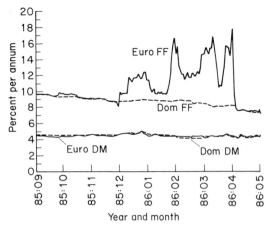

Figure 2.9 Onshore and offshore interest rates: French franc and DM (1-month deposits)

the French franc and the Deutsche mark, in the weeks preceding and immediately following the EMS realignment of April 7, 1986, when both the lira and the French franc were devalued relative to the Deutsche mark. This episode was first studied by Giavazzi and Giovannini (1987). The large swings of the offshore interest rates on the franc and the lira occur despite a strikingly stable pattern of domestic and offshore DM rates.

In summary, the behaviour of interest rates around devaluations strongly suggests the presence of asymmetry in the two EMS episodes. The sharp movements of dollar rates around the sterling devaluation in 1967 are in contrast to the hypothesis that the US was the centre country during the Bretton Woods years. The Bretton Woods data, however, should be interpreted with caution, since this analysis cannot identify and control for portfolio shifts that did not involve dollar assets: the maintained assumption is that the observed international interest rate differentials reflect incipient portfolio reallocations between dollar assets and the assets denominated in the depreciating or appreciating currency.

V.3 Exploring the stochastic implications of the asymmetric model of fixed exchange rates

Following the analysis of Section IV, I assume that central banks minimize the following objective functions:

$$W_t = - E_t[(y_{1t+j} - \bar{y}_{1t+j})^2 + b(y_{2t+j} - \bar{y}_{2t+j})^2] \tag{19}$$

$$W_t^* = - E_t[(y_{1t+j}^* - \bar{y}_{1t+j}^*)^2 + b(y_{2t+j}^* - \bar{y}_{2t+j}^*)^2] \tag{19'}$$

where y_1 and y_2 are the home and external target variables in both countries (foreign-country variables denoted by a *). This maximization is performed subject to equations describing the dynamics of the target variables:

$$Y_t = A(L)Y_{t-1} + B(L)Y^*_{t-1} + C(L)Z_t \tag{20}$$

$$Y^*_t = A^*(L)Y_{t-1} + B^*(L)Y^*_{t-1} + C^*(L)Z_t \tag{21}$$

where $A(L)$, $B(L)$ and $C(L)$, and the corresponding starred variables are polynomials in the lag operator. Y and Y^* are the vectors of targets for the domestic and the foreign country, and Z is a vector which includes exogenous variables, stochastic disturbances, and the instruments available to the two central bankers.

The first-order condition for the domestic central bank is

$$E_t(y_{1t} - \bar{y}_{1t}) = -bE_t(y_{2t} - \bar{y}_{2t}) \tag{22}$$

A similar condition holds for the foreign central bank.

Equation (22) implies that, if b equals zero, deviations of the domestic target variable from its desired value should be uncorrelated with information at time t, and in particular with past realizations of the external target variable. Under the alternative hypothesis, lagged realizations of the external target variable – presumably correlated with the right-hand side of equation (22) – are correlated with the term on the left-hand side. Intuitively, in the centre country the deviations of the domestic target from its desired value are white-noise errors.[37]

In order to derive testable implications, I need identifying assumptions about the unobservable term $\bar{y}_{1t}$. It is plausible to assume that it is uncorrelated with lagged values of the external target, thus allowing the domestic and the external targets to be more clearly isolated. In this case, when a country's monetary authority targets a domestic variable exclusively, lagged values of the external target should be uncorrelated with the domestic target. These tests are apparently similar to those performed by Pippinger (1984) and Dutton (1984), who analyzed central bank policies under the gold standard. As I stress in Giovannini (1986), however, the interpretation of my test is dramatically different. While I concentrate on the reduced-form properties of the data, implied by the alternative structures of the international monetary system, Pippinger and Dutton intend to estimate the parameters of central banks' reaction functions. These specifications, however, are not linked to an underlying optimization problem of central banks: hence the tests of the significance of individual parameters proposed by these authors are difficult to interpret.

Tables 2.3, 2.4 and 2.5 report the results of some exploratory tests of the asymmetry hypothesis. Table 2.3 contains the results for the gold standard

Table 2.3   Test results: Gold standard

	Country		
	Britain	Germany	France
Sample	1889:12–1907:12	1892:12–1907:12	1900:10–1907:12
R^2	0.480	0.915	0.515
F-tests	0.271	0.004	0.029

Note: The entries denoted by F-test are the marginal significance levels of the null hypothesis that the coefficients of the lagged net imports of gold are not significant. The statistic is computed using the White (1980) correction of the variance–covariance matrix of disturbances.

Table 2.4   Test results: Bretton Woods

	Country			
	US	UK	Germany	France
Sample	62:2–71:4	64:2–71:4	62:2–71:4	62:2–71:4
R^2	0.516	0.594	0.185	0.163
F-tests	0.000	0.000	0.518	0.400

Note: The entries denoted by F-test are the marginal significance levels of the null hypothesis that the coefficients of the lagged ratio of reserve flows relative to high powered money are not significant. The statistic is computed using the White (1980) correction of the variance–covariance matrix of disturbances.

data (monthly). I assume that the domestic target variable for each central bank is an index of coverage of the central bank's liabilities: the proportion of the gold reserve to total deposit liabilities in the Banking Department of the Bank of England, the proportion of cash to total demand liabilities in the Reichsbank,[38] and the ratio of the gold reserve to circulation in the Bank of France. In addition, I assume that the desired value of the target variable is constant (plausibly determined by national regulations on coverage, and by banking practice). For all three countries, I test whether lagged values of net imports of gold are significantly correlated with the target variable (in first difference), beyond a set of seasonal dummies.[39] The table shows that the null hypothesis of no correlation is rejected at the 5 percent level in the

Test 2.5   Test results: EMS

	Country		
	Germany	France	Italy
Sample	80:3–88:1	80:3–88:1	80:3–87:4
R^2	0.079	0.345	0.350
F-tests	0.690	0.009	0.003

Note: As Table 2.4

case of Germany and France (the marginal significance level, the probability that the test statistic exceeds the reported value when the null hypothesis is true, is actually less than 1 percent in the case of Germany), but it is not rejected for Britain.

Table 2.4 contains the results for the Bretton Woods data (quarterly). The domestic target variable is assumed to be the domestic money-market interest rate, while the foreign target variable is the change in foreign exchange reserves relative to high-powered money.[40] As before, I include seasonal dummies in the regression. I find that past balance of payments flows are highly significantly correlated with the domestic money market rate in the United States and in the United Kingdom. This correlation is insignificant in France and West Germany.

Table 2.5 contains the results for the EMS data. The specification of the regression equations is identical to that for the Bretton Woods data. The hypothesis that lagged values of foreign reserve flows are orthogonal to the domestic target (nominal interest rate) is rejected at the 1 percent level in the case of France and Italy, but not in the case of West Germany. In summary, the test results agree with the 'centre country' hypothesis in the case of the gold standard and the EMS, but not in the case of Bretton Woods.

VI Concluding observations

The data seem to support the hypothesis of asymmetry, at least in the case of the gold standard and the EMS. Although the institutional setup in both regimes is clearly not inducing asymmetry, there are striking similarities in the use of capital controls. Furthermore, the evidence on interest rate behaviour and the statistical tests both support the asymmetric model.

In the case of Bretton Woods, the statistical model rejects the asymmetry hypothesis, and the evidence on interest rates is – at least in some cases – not as clearcut as in the case of the EMS.

In this paper I have followed the strategy of trying to uncover evidence of asymmetry without exploiting the implications of specific models of asymmetric international monetary systems, like those mentioned in Section IV. None of the factors giving rise to asymmetries described above, in my opinion, can alone fully explain all three historical experiences studied in this paper. I do believe, though, that further empirical work should help to identify which of the alternative models of an asymmetric international monetary system best fit the individual historical experiences.

Notes

1 Recent supporters of the 'asymmetry' hypothesis include Eichengreen (1987) on the gold standard, and Giavazzi and Giovannini (1989) on the European Monetary System.

2 In fact, each central bank quoted buying and selling prices for gold coins, which presumably represented the costs of minting and of administration of the bank. These buying and selling prices are also referred to as the gold points.

3 See Tew (1977) for an analysis of the IMF Articles of Agreement.

4 Countries could also declare their exchange rates 'in terms of the US dollar of the weight and fineness in effect on July 1, 1944', that is, the gold parity could be defined in terms of the US dollar. Even with this method, however, the ultimate numeraire is gold.

5 In France the conversion of banknotes into coins was at the authorities' discretion.

6 Tew (1977) page 120.

7 The constraint operated through the influence on speculators' confidence exercised by deviations between the official and free-market prices of gold.

8 Since some currencies like the pound and the drachma are not part of the EMS exchange-rate arrangements, the missing external numeraire is in practice provided by these currencies.

9 The fluctuation bands of *all* cross exchange rates, including dollar rates, would have been 2 percent on each side, had they been set in terms of gold. Hence the Bretton Woods regime provided for narrower fluctuations of the dollar, relative to the other currencies.

10 'Diversified intervention, measures of domestic monetary policy, changes in central parities, or other measures of economic policy.' (Monetary Committee, 1986).

11 See Spaventa (1982) for an illustration of the properties of the indicator of divergence. Spaventa observes that the indicator crosses the threshold less frequently for those currencies with a smaller weight in the ECU, and therefore it is not really a means of achieving symmetry in the system.

12 Few countries specified a constant ratio of circulation to reserves. As Eichengreen (1985) notes, England, among others, was on a fiduciary system, requiring full backing of note issue after a certain limit (the fiduciary issue) was reached. In Germany the Bank Act required that note circulation could not exceed a limit above three times the value of gold reserves, and if it did, the Reichsbank had to pay a 5 percent tax on the excess circulation. See US National Monetary Commission (1911).

13 See also Bloomfield (1959).

14 In the 1960s even the lowest conditionality resources, however, were not obtainable quickly enough to be usable to fend off balance-of-payments crises.

15 See Alesina and Grilli (1987) for an illustration of the effectiveness of these arrangements in avoiding speculative attacks. Credit lines for marginal intervention

mature 75 days after the end of the month following the one in which the intervention has taken place.

16 See Giavazzi and Giovannini (1989) for a dicussion.

17 Giavazzi and Giovannini (1989).

18 '...experience shows that, when severe stress comes, the gold standard is usually suspended. There is little evidence to support the view that authorities who cannot be trusted to run a nationally managed standard, can be trusted to run an international gold standard.' (Keynes, 1930, p. 267).

19 In Giavazzi and Giovannini (1989) we show that the tightening and release of controls on international trade credits by France and Italy can be explained by the occurrence of balance-of-payments difficulties, and are used very frequently by central banks. We also model the effects of controls on trade credits on the differentials between onshore and offshore rates.

20 Yeager (1966).

21 This point is shown explicitly in the next section.

22 See Dornbusch and Giovannini (1988), for example. Here I adopt the version of the model used by Barsky *et al.* (1988), who analyzed the international implications of the creation of the Federal Reserve System.

23 See Calomiris and Hubbard (1987) for a careful evaluation of the law of one price in goods and assets markets during the gold standard.

24 It can be shown that in this model a variable real exchange rate, not affected by monetary policy, is equivalent to x. Hence x can be interpreted as a general idiosyncratic shock in goods and assets markets.

25 This subdivision of the world economy, suggested to me by David Backus, facilitates the comparison with the symmetric case reported above.

26 From goods markets equilibrium, $d - f + v = i_i^* - f_i^* + v_i^*$, for all i. Summing these conditions over all i and using the condition that world reserve flows are zero, one can solve for f. To compute the world rate of inflation, substitute the expression for f into (4) and (1).

27 As Giavazzi and Giovannini (1989) stress, however, these models do not provide a justification as to why the centre-country would prefer such an arrangement over, for example, a flexible-exchange rate regime.

28 7 times upwards, 7 downwards.

29 January 10 and January 24, 1889.

30 This evidence contrasts with the findings of Eichengreen (1987). He estimated monthly bivariate VARs which included the British discount rate and the German and French rate, respectively. He found that lagged values of the British rate were significantly correlated with both the French and the German rates. I was unable to reproduce these results by reconstructing Eichengreen's sample. While my coefficient

estimates are virtually identical to his, I found in the monthly data that lagged values of the British rate were not significantly correlated with the German rate, while lagged values of the French rate were significant in the Bank Rate regression.

31 Since the French rate changed few times in this period, I left it out of my analysis.

32 See Andreades (1909), Keynes (1930) and Ford (1962) for descriptions of the 'autumnal drains' that prompted these reactions by central bankers.

33 Evidence on the timing structure of discount rates during the EMS is provided by Roubini (1988). Using quarterly data, he finds that lagged values of the German discount rate are correlated with Italian, Belgian and Danish rates, which he interprets as evidence of German leadership. Genberg, Saidi and Swoboda (1982) test the temporal precedence of US monetary policies during the Bretton Woods years: their evidence does not consistently support the hypothesis that US monetary policy changes preceded those in the rest of the world.

34 The limited use of Granger causality tests is argued in detail by Cooley and Leroy (1985).

35 Gavazzi and Giovannini (1987) show that the asymmetric behaviour of interest rates is also an implication of models where prices are sticky.

36 These data are obtained from *International Financial Statistics*.

37 See Sargent and Wallace (1976) for derivations of similar tests in the context of linear-quadratic control models.

38 Which equals the ratio of the sum of coin and Imperial treasury notes, divided by the sum of notes in circulation and other demand liabilities.

39 Since the theory does not predict that the disturbances should be i.i.d. under the null hypothesis, the test statistics are computed using the White (1980) correction for heteroskedasticity.

40 All the data are from *International Financial Statistics*. Valuation effects on foreign exchange reserves are calculated by subtracting the 'other items' line from net foreign reserves at the central bank.

References

Alesina, A. and V. Grilli. (1987) 'Avoiding Speculative Attacks on EMS Currencies: A Proposal,' Economic Growth Center Discussion Paper No. 547, Yale University.

Andreades, A. (1909) *History of the Bank of England*, London: P.S. King & Son.

Argy, V. (1981) *The Postwar International Money Crisis*, London: George Allen and Unwin.

Barro, R. (1988) 'Interest-Rate Smoothing', mimeo, Harvard University, March.

Barsky, R.B., N.G. Mankiw, J.A. Miron, and D.N. Weil (1988) 'The Worldwide Change in the Behaviour of Interest Rates and Prices in 1914.' *European Economic Review* **32**, 1123–54.

Birch, W.J. (1887) 'Presidential Address,' *Journal of the Institute of Bankers*, 503–36.

Bloomfield, A. (1959) *Monetary Policy Under the International Gold Standard: 1880–1914*, New York: Federal Reserve Bank of New York.

Calomiris, C.W. and R.G. Hubbard (1987) 'International Adjustment Under the Classical Gold Standard: Evidence for the U.S. and Britain, 1879–1914,' mimeo, Northwestern University, May.

Clark, T.A. (1984) 'Violations of the Gold Points, 1890–1908.' *Journal of Political Economy* **92**, 791–823.

Cooley, T.F. and S.F. Leroy (1985) 'Atheoretical Macroeconomics: A Critique,' *Journal of Monetary Economics* **16**, 283–308.

Dornbusch, R. and J. Frenkel (1984) 'The Gold Standard Crisis of 1847,' *Journal of International Economics* **16**, 1–27.

Dornbusch, R. and A. Giovannini (1988) 'Monetary Policy in the Open Economy' manuscript for the *Handbook of Monetary Theory*, ed. by F. Hahn and B. Friedman, February.

Dutton, J. (1984) 'The Bank of England and the Rules of the Game Under the International Gold Standard: New Evidence,' in M.D. Bordo and A. Schwartz, eds., *A Retrospective on the Classical Gold Standard 1821–1931*, Chicago: University of Chicago Press.

Eichengreen, B. (1985) 'Editor's Introduction' in B. Eichengreen (ed.), *The Gold Standard in Theory and History*, New York: Methuen.

Eichengreen, B. (1987) 'Conducting the International Orchestra: Bank of England Leadership Under the Classical Gold Standard,' *Journal of International Money and Finance* **6**, 5–29.

Ford, A.G. (1962) *The Gold Standard 1880–1914, Britain and Argentina*, Oxford: Oxford University Press.

Genberg, H., N. Saidi and A.K. Swoboda (1982) 'American and European Interest Rates and Exchange Rates: US Hegemony or Interdependence?' mimeo, International Center for Monetary and Banking Studies.

Giavazzi, F. and A. Giovannini (1986) 'The EMS and the Dollar,' *Economic Policy* **2**, 455–78.

Giavazzi, F. and A. Giovannini (1987) 'Models of the EMS: Is Europe a Greater Deutsche-Mark Area?' in R. C. Bryant and R. Portes (eds.), *Global Macroeconomics: Policy Conflict and Cooperation*, London: Macmillan.

Giavazzi, F., and A. Giovannini (1989) *Limiting Exchange Rate Flexibility: The European Monetary System*, Cambridge, MA: MIT Press, forthcoming.

Giavazzi, F. and M. Pagano (1988) 'The Advantage of Tying One's Hands: EMS Discipline and Central Bank Credibility,' *European Economic Review* **32**, 1055–82.

Giovannini, A. (1986) ' "Rules of the Game" During the International Gold Standard: England and Germany,' *Journal of International Money and Finance* **5**, 467–83.

Helpman, E. (1981) 'An Exploration in the Theory of Exchange Rate Regimes,' *Journal of Political Economy* **89**, 865–90.

Keynes, J.M. (1930) *A Treatise on Money*, London: Macmillan.

Kindleberger, C.P. (1984) *A Financial History of Western Europe*, London: George Allen and Unwin.

McCloskey, D.N. and J.R. Zecher (1976) 'How the Gold Standard Worked, 1880–1913,' in J.A. Frenkel and H.G. Johnson (eds.) *The Monetary Approach to the Balance of Payments*, London: Allen & Unwin.

Monetary Committee (1986) *Compendium of Community Monetary Texts*, Brussels: European Community.

Morgenstern, O. (1959) *International Financial Transactions and Business Cycles*, Princeton: Princeton University Press.

Mundell, R.A. (1968) *International Economics*, New York: Macmillan.

Officer, L.H. (1986) 'The Efficiency of the Dollar–Sterling Gold Standard, 1890–1908,' *Journal of Political Economy* **94**, 1038–73.

Pippinger, J. (1984) 'Bank of England Operations 1893–1913,' in M.D. Bordo and A. Schwartz, (eds.) *A Retrospective on the Classical Gold Standard 1821–1931*, Chicago: University of Chicago Press.

Roubini, N. (1988) 'Sterilization Policies, Offsetting Capital Movements and Exchange Rate Intervention Policies in the EMS,' mimeo, Harvard University.

Sargent, T.J. and N. Wallace (1976) 'Rational Expectations and the Theory of Economic Policy,' *Journal of Monetary Economics* **2**, 169–83.

Scammell, W.M. (1965). 'The Working of the Gold Standard,' *Yorkshire Bulletin of Economic and Social Research*, 32–45. Reprinted in B. Eichengreen, (eds.) *The Gold Standard in Theory and History*, New York: Methuen, 1985.

Spaventa, L. (1982) 'Algebraic Properties and Economic Improprieties of the "Indicator of Divergence" in the European Monetary System,' in R. Cooper *et al.* (eds.) *The International Monetary System Under Flexible Exchange Rates – Essays in Honor of Robert Triffin*, Cambridge, MA: Ballinger.

Spiller, P.T. and R.O. Wood (1988) 'Arbitrage During the Dollar-Sterling Gold Standard, 1899–1908: An Econometric Approach,' *Journal of Political Economy* **96**, 882–92.

Stockman, A.C. (1987) 'Real Exchange Rate Variability under Pegged and Floating Nominal Exchange Rate Systems: An Equilibrium Theory,' mimeo, University of Rochester, October.

Swoboda, A.K. (1978) 'Gold, Dollars, Euro-Dollars, and the World Money Stock under Fixed Exchange Rates,' *American Economic Review* **68**, 625–42.

Tew, B. (1977) *The Evolution of the International Monetary System 1945–77*, New York: John Wiley & Sons.

US National Monetary Commission (1910) *Statistics for Great Britain, Germany and France*, Washington, DC: Government Printing Office.

US National Monetary Commission (1911) *The Reichsbank 1876–1900*, Doc. 507, Washington, DC: Government Printing Office.

White, H. (1980) 'A Heteroskedasticity-Consistent Covariance Matrix Estimator and Direct Test for Heteroskedasticity,' *Econometrica* **48,** 817–38.

Yeager, L.B. (1966) *International Monetary Relations*, New York: Harper & Row.

Discussion

Barry Eichengreen

Academic economists and practical men – call them policymakers for want of a better term – subscribe to two different views of the operation of fixed exchange-rate systems. In the view of the academics, fixed exchange rates subject countries to the rule of market forces. Government policies influencing supplies of financial assets must be consistent with demands. Otherwise the authorities' ability to peg the domestic-currency price of foreign exchange will be undermined by the market. The point applies equally to large and small countries, except insofar as large countries have an extra degree of freedom by virtue of their ability to influence global economic conditions. Aside from this complication, which is probably of limited empirical relevance, fixed-rate regimes should be symmetrical.

Practical men perceive the world differently. Fixed-rate regimes exhibit important asymmetries. Some countries seem to be largely immune from the discipline of market forces. Their central banks acquire a reputation for leadership. The monetary authorities of other countries follow the leader. These asymmetries, in much of the literature, stem from institutional differences in the markets in which leader and follower countries interact and in the resources they command. Under the classical gold standard, for example, the Bank of England was 'conductor of the international orchestra' (Keynes's phrase) because London's exceptionally deep financial markets endowed the Bank with unrivalled command over the direction of international capital flows.

Alberto Giovannini's excellent paper brings these literatures together. It is rich in empirical evidence spanning more than a century. It makes apt use of theory, developing a model along lines familiar from the literature on international economic policy coordination. It takes institutions seriously. In order to reach generalizations about the operation of fixed-rate systems, it does not limit its attention to the most recent example of the phenomenon. Many authors pay lip service to the principle that, in order to reach general conclusions about the operating properties of regimes,

BLUEPRINTS FOR EXCHANGE RATE MANAGEMENT
0-12-497060-5
Copyright © 1989 Academic Press, Ltd
All rights of reproduction reserved

we need to subject our hypotheses to more than just one data point from the post-World War II era. Giovannini puts his foreign exchange where his mouth is. He reaches two conclusions. First, is that the data support the asymmetry hypothesis. Second, is that compared to the gold standard and the EMS there is somewhat less evidence of asymmetry under Bretton Woods. This is striking, since the literature on Bretton Woods contains even more references to asymmetries than those on the gold standard and the EMS.

Giovannini is skeptical of rules-based explanations for the asymmetric operation of the three systems. Under all three fixed exchange-rate regimes, he argues, the numeraire was set symmetrically. Countries pegged either to gold or to a basket of currencies. Fluctuation bands were symmetrical, although narrower for the dollar under Bretton Woods and wider for currencies like the lira under the EMS. To quote the paper, 'the rules of the gold standard, Bretton Woods and the EMS do not seem *per se* to induce an asymmetric working of international adjustment'.

But if not rules, then what can account for the asymmetries in the operation of the system? One possibility is differences in preferences, in conjunction with the reputations they confer. Another is institutions, in conjunction with differences in country characteristics.

Giovannini is silent on the question of which explanation is correct. I would argue that institutions and country characteristics are at the root of the asymmetries with which he is concerned. In particular, the currency denomination of reserves is a leading source of asymmetries in the operation of fixed exchange-rate regimes. The international diversification of reserves is a recent phenomenon. Under the classical gold standard, one currency, sterling, accounted for the majority of non-gold reserves. For most of the reign of the Bretton Woods system, the same was true of the dollar. In both cases, countries wishing to acquire interest-bearing reserves had to obtain claims on the reserve-currency country. Insofar as demands for foreign exchange reserves were elastic, the external constraint on the reserve-currency country did not bind. In the limit, the reserve-currency country did not have to concern itself with external balance, in contrast to the rest of the world. In other words, the targets with which policymakers were concerned were a function of the structure of the system, not merely of their preferences.

This begs the question of why institutional asymmetries like key currencies emerge in the first place. Perhaps they are no more than a reflection of preferences: central bankers choose to hold their foreign exchange reserves in the currency of a country whose policymakers have an unquestioned preference for monetary stability. But so to argue is to neglect other historical features of these arrangements. These other factors include the depth, efficiency and openness of domestic financial markets. Sterling was the dominant reserve currency of the 19th century in large part because of the attractiveness of transacting in the London financial market, which arose in turn out of London's preeminent role in international trade. Similarly, the dollar was the dominant reserve currency of the mid-20th century in large part because of the attractiveness of transacting in New York. Skeptics might respond that London and New York acquired these features precisely because of the preference of British and American policymakers for monetary stability. If they are right, the dichotomy between preferences and institutions may break down at a deeper level. Untangling this question requires delving into the origins of both institutions and preferences and attempting to determine whether they have a common source or whether one determines the other.

The empirical sections of Giovannini's paper contain three significant sets of results. First are the vector autoregressions that provide evidence on the timing of domestic and foreign discount rate changes under the gold standard. Giovannini finds that changes in the German discount rate preceded changes in the British and French rates. While consistent with a leader-follower equilibrium, these results are at odds with the model of British leadership one finds in the literature. According to Giovannini, the Reichsbank conducted the international orchestra. This is truly an EMS-style model of the gold standard!

Second, there are event studies designed to determine whether anticipated exchange-rate changes had symmetrical effects on domestic and foreign interest rates. Giovannini identifies several episodes when foreign interest rates did not respond noticeably, which he takes as evidence of asymmetry. One wonders how these results are affected by the author's neglect of country size, since the interest rates of large countries might move less than those of small countries even in an otherwise symmetrical world.

Third, there are regressions of a proxy for internal balance on a measure of external balance. If some countries were leaders and worried only about internal balance, leaving other countries to deal with external adjustment, in their equations one should find coefficients of zero on the lags of external balance. For the gold standard period, Giovannini proxies internal balance by the ratio of foreign to domestic assets of the central bank, and external balance by gold flows. Thus, his test for a positive correlation between the two variables is precisely the test of 'the rules of the game' implemented by Arthur Bloomfield (1959), Charles Goodhart (1972), John Dutton (1984) and John Pippinger (1984), among others. Giovannini finds that Germany and France played by the rules of the game, but that Britain did not. This raises a number of intriguing questions that deserve to be explored. For example, can these results be reconciled with the vector autoregressions? Are Giovannini's results consistent with those of Pippinger, who estimated reaction functions for Britain and found that, although the Bank of England violated the rules of the game in the short run, it obeyed them in the long run?

For Bretton Woods, Giovannini finds that the US and UK took both internal and external balance into account when formulating policy. For the US, this is not what advocates of the asymmetry hypothesis would expect to find. In contrast, Giovannini finds that neither Germany nor France worried about external balance. Again, these results are perplexing.

For the EMS, the results support the hypothesis of German leadership. Germany worries only about internal balance. France and Italy worry about internal balance but in addition restore external balance for themselves and, in the process, for Germany.

In conclusion, I find the results for the EMS intuitive and entirely consistent with the conventional wisdom, perhaps because the pathbreaking work of Giavazzi and Giovannini has done so much to establish that wisdom. In contrast, I find the results for Bretton Woods and the gold standard surprising, and even more difficult to reconcile with the asymmetry view than Giovannini suggests. I remain a staunch supporter of the asymmetry hypothesis, but as much on the basis of priors as on the evidence in this paper.

References

Bloomfield, Arthur (1959) *Monetary Policy under the International Gold Standard,* New York: Federal Reserve Bank of New York.

Dutton, John (1984) 'The Bank of England and the Rules of the Game under the International Gold Standard; New Evidence,' in Michael Bordo and Anna Schwartz (eds), *A Retrospective on the Classical Gold Standard*, Chicago: University of Chicago Press.

Goodhart, Charles (1972) *The Business of Banking, 1891–1914,* London: Weidenfeld and Nicolson.

Pippinger, John (1984) 'Bank of England Operations, 1893–1913,' in Michael Bordo and Anna Schwartz (eds), *A Retrospective on the Classical Gold Standard*, Chicago: University of Chicago Press.

Chapter 3

Monetary interdependence and deflation in Britain and the United States between the wars*

Stephen N. Broadberry

I Introduction

Historians have long believed that the depressed conditions of the world economy between the wars arose because of a lack of international cooperation in an increasingly interdependent world. Lewis (1949) writes that one of the key lessons of the interwar period is that 'without international cooperation we are lost'.[1] One obvious manifestation of this lack of cooperation is the chaotic state of the international monetary system. The restoration and breakdown of the gold standard have been central to many analyses which seek to account for this failure of cooperation and for its relationship to the interwar depression.[2]

As Eichengreen (1984) notes, however, economists' models have generally failed to capture adequately the importance of interdependence and non-cooperative behaviour in the 1920s and 1930s. Drawing on the recent theoretical literature, in this paper we apply a model of monetary interdependence to explain deflationary monetary policies in Britain and the US between the wars. Deflation is portrayed as a consequence of the external constraint which bound each country when it attempted to expand alone, in conjunction with the failure to act collectively to relax that external constraint.

* Helpful comments and suggestions have been received from Brian Copeland, Barry Eichengreen, Paul Turner, and seminar participants at the University of Sussex. The usual disclaimer applies.

BLUEPRINTS FOR EXCHANGE RATE MANAGEMENT
0-12-497060-5

Copyright © 1989 Academic Press, Ltd
All rights of reproduction reserved

The consequences of this failure to cooperate were evident both before and after Britain's return to gold. Because of higher inflation in Britain than in the US during the First World War, returning sterling to its prewar parity required the Bank of England to maintain a deflationary monetary policy. Given continued US commitment to the gold standard, high interest rates in London had to be matched by high interest rates in New York, so that deflationary monetary policy in Britain can be seen as limiting the freedom of action of the US monetary authorities. Hence monetary policy remained relatively tight for much of the 1920s. Had the US and Britain agreed instead to reflate cooperatively, neither would have run the risk of losing gold to the other, but in the absence of cooperation both were forced to pursue restrictive monetary policies.

Although the players changed, the problem remained the same after Britain's devaluation in 1931. The maintenance of the gold parity of the dollar required deflationary monetary policy in the US to stem gold outflows to France and the rest of the gold bloc, in the absence of a commitment by these countries to reflate cooperatively. Given the importance of the US and other gold standard countries in the world economy, expansionary monetary policy in Britain was not sufficient to prevent a severe world depression.

Following the abandonment of the gold standard by the US in 1933, both the US and the UK were able to adopt more expansionary monetary policies. The economic recovery that followed is evidence of the impact their monetary policies exercised over the world economy in the preceding years.

Kindleberger (1986) and others who have recognized the importance of monetary interdependence in the interwar slump have argued that the emergence of a single leader is the key to international financial stability. He sees Britain as unable and the US as unwilling to fulfill the leadership role. The argument here suggests, in contrast to this view, that a single leader may not be the key to financial stability. We argue that first Britain in the 1920s and then the US in the 1930s made a bid for the leadership role. But neither Britain in the first instance nor the US in the second instance was large enough in international markets to adopt reflationary initiatives on the requisite scale without running up against the external constraint. Nor was Britain in the first instance or the US in the second influential enough to lead by example (to successfully induce other countries to reflate following its lead) or to lead by force (to compel other countries to follow its lead through the exercise of political pressure). Recovery required not leadership but cooperation. Like Lewis (1949), we see international cooperation rather than the establishment of a single leader as the key to financial stability.

In the next section we examine the monetary history literature for Britain and the US between the wars, focusing on the issues arising from monetary interdependence. This is followed by an explicit model of monetary interdependence, which is applied to the interwar economy. We demonstrate that gains from cooperation were available irrespective of the international monetary regime in operation.

II Leadership and monetary policy in Britain and the US

II.1 Introduction

The issue of leadership is of central importance to understanding the international economic system between the wars. Kindleberger (1986) argues that a clear leader is needed to stabilize the international economy by maintaining an open market for distress goods, by providing stable long-term lending, by policing a stable system of exchange rates, by ensuring the coordination of macroeconomic policies and by acting as a lender of last resort.[3] He goes on to argue that the failure to establish a clear leader was the ultimate cause of the Great Depression from 1929. He sees Britain as unable and the US unwilling to fulfil the role.

In one way our view extends the Kindleberger story by encompassing the problems caused by Britain's attempt to fulfil a leadership role in the 1920s as well as the problems caused by the uncertain and temporary US leadership in the early 1930s. In another way, however, our view departs from the Kindleberger story by rejecting the assumption that leadership is necessary for stability of the international monetary system. Here, we agree with Eichengreen (1989) that even in periods of strong leadership, the system must be predicated on international cooperation. Thus we stress the importance of cooperation rather than leadership.

II.2 Monetary policy 1919–31

Deflationary monetary policy in Britain during the 1920s can only be understood in relation to the desire of the authorities to return to the gold standard at the prewar parity, despite much higher wartime inflation in Britain than in the US. Thus when the pound was floated at the end of the war there was an immediate sharp depreciation. Even before the end of the war, the Cunliffe Committee (1918) were arguing for deflationary monetary policy as a prerequisite for return to gold at the prewar parity. This was finally achieved in April 1925, when Churchill announced in his budget speech that the gold export embargo legislation due to expire at the end of 1925 was not to be renewed and was effectively suspended forthwith.[4]

The return to gold can be interpreted as an attempt by Britain to regain leadership of the international monetary system.[5] For the half century before

1914, Keynes (1930) graphically described the Bank of England as 'the conductor of the international orchestra'.[6] However, as Eichengreen (1989) notes, after the First World War, Britain no longer had sufficient market power to dominate the international economy, as other countries had obtained significant proportions of international financial and commercial transactions.

The Cunliffe Committee (1918) set out the objective of return to the prewar international monetary system and the deflationary domestic policies needed for its attainment. In addition, various gold economy measures were suggested to mitigate the effects of deflation. As Clarke (1973) notes, by restricting the use of gold primarily to international settlements, the Committee hoped to increase the scope for official administration of the gold standard.[7]

The British proposals for restoration of the gold standard were widely accepted at the Genoa Conference in 1922, attended by thirty-four countries, mostly European.[8] The US stayed away because of European insistence on discussing reparations and war debts as well as the international monetary system.[9] The gold economy measures recommended by the Cunliffe Committee were redesigned for the international monetary system to mitigate the deflationary pressure expected from the general return to gold, particularly after the violent slump of 1920–21.[10]

During the first half of the 1920s a number of countries stabilized on gold, including Britain at the prewar parity in April 1925. As Clarke (1967) shows, the Bank of England played a leading role in this process, in particular by helping to secure stabilization loans. Broadberry (1984) shows how the return to gold at the prewar parity by a number of Scandinavian countries led to a North European depression during the 1920s.

The British bid for leadership led to the adoption of a deflationary monetary policy in Britain, and this in turn set limits to monetary policy in the US. Although Friedman and Schwartz (1963) play down the role of international factors in the determination of US monetary policy during the 1920s, their interpretation strains credulity. Wicker (1965) argues strongly that international factors were of overriding importance. Even Friedman and Schwartz note how the Federal Reserve Board were swift to raise discount rates in response to the external drain of gold after the sharp rise in Bank Rate in Britain during 1919–20.[11] Wicker (1965) argues that although open market operations in 1924 and 1927 did operate counter-cyclically, they were nevertheless conducted primarily because of international conditions.

During the late 1920s, with Britain committed to the gold standard at the prewar parity, attempts were made by the Bank of England to avoid the deflationary increases in Bank Rate needed to defend sterling. As Clarke (1967) and Eichengreen (1984) note, pressure could have been removed from the pound by a reduction in discount rates abroad instead of by domestic deflation. However, such attempts at cooperation were not generally very successful.

II.3 Monetary policy 1931–33

In September 1931, after a run on the pound, Britain left the gold standard, and sterling was floated.[12] The US retained the link with gold until April 1933, and then after a short period of experimentation with gold prices, the dollar was stabilized against gold at a lower parity in February 1934.[13]

After Britain had abandoned gold in 1931, a monetary expansion was possible, and indeed a policy of low interest rates or 'cheap money' was adopted early in 1932.[14] Cheap money has often been seen as an important factor in the British recovery from 1932, particularly through its effects on housing investment.[15]

In the US, however, an expansionary monetary policy could not be adopted because of the need to maintain the gold parity of the dollar. Indeed, any threat of a gold outflow led to an immediate rise in discount rates. Discount rates had to be raised very sharply at the beginning of October 1931 to maintain the credibility of the commitment following Britain's departure from gold.[16]

As we have already seen, this interpretation of US monetary policy as being significantly influenced by external events is controversial. Friedman and Schwartz (1963) argue that after successfully conducting open market operations in relation to domestic conditions during the 1920s, the Federal Reserve Board made a terrible mistake in the early 1930s and failed to adjust the system in line with domestic needs. The reason they offer for this failure is the sudden death of Benjamin Strong, the Governor of the New York Federal Reserve Bank, leaving a power vacuum which led to inaction.

The alternative view of Wicker (1965) is that Federal Reserve policy over this period was consistently determined with respect to international conditions. When domestic and international conditions suggested the same policy, as in 1924 and 1927, both interpretations are consistent with the evidence. However, when international and domestic conditions demanded different policies, as in the early 1930s, it seems clear that international factors prevailed.

This view of commitment to the gold standard constraining US monetary policy during the Great Depression receives additional support from Meltzer (1976) and more recently from Epstein and Ferguson (1984), who find archival and statistical evidence to support the importance of external constraints on the Federal Reserve System during 1929–33.

If Federal Reserve policy was constrained by the decision to maintain the gold value of the dollar, as we have suggested, then this raises the issue of why the US did not immediately follow Britain in leaving gold and adopting an expansionary monetary policy. After all, the US had not experienced the traumatic inflation of the early 1920s that made many of the gold bloc countries so determined to resist exchange rate depreciation.[17] Our answer here is that the US was offered leadership of the international monetary system and took nineteen months to decline the offer.

It is important that the US decision to leave gold was preceded by a change of administration, since the US were not forced off gold in the manner of Britain.[18] Accepting the need for a World Economic Conference, eventually held in June 1933, the outgoing President Hoover believed that his administration had adopted all the necessary domestic measures for recovery and that international initiatives were needed.[19] Looking back, James Cox, the Democratic presidential candidate for 1920 notes that 'For a time, it seemed that America was assuming the leadership in an enterprise that held out every hope of success'.[20] However, the incoming Roosevelt administration believed instead in domestic recovery measures, and were prepared to sacrifice international responsibilities.[21]

II.4   Monetary policy 1933–38

In April 1933 the US broke the link with gold and effectively renounced any role of leadership. Both Britain and the US were thus able to adopt expansionary monetary policies. Both countries can be seen as expanding as fast as possible, given the monetary policy of the other.

The US decision to leave gold was effected through Roosevelt's acceptance in April 1933 of the Thomas amendment to the Agricultural Adjustment Act, which aimed to raise prices and stimulate recovery through monetary expansion by allowing the President to reduce the gold content of the dollar (raise the dollar price of gold).[22] After a period of experimenting with gold prices, Roosevelt fixed the price of gold at $35 an ounce in February 1934.[23]

The dollar immediately depreciated from April 1934 both against the gold bloc countries such as France and against countries such as Britain that had left gold earlier.[24] A refusal by Roosevelt to consider an early stabilization of the dollar effectively scuppered the World Economic Conference in June 1933 and the hope of a cooperative approach to monetary policy.[25]

Choudri and Kochin (1980) show that for a sample of eight European countries, the Great Depression was severest in the gold bloc, and mildest in Spain, which remained on flexible exchange rates throughout the period. Eichengreen and Sachs (1985) go a step further and show how it is possible for a series of competitive devaluations to lead to a global welfare gain. The standard argument that the gain to a devaluing country is offset by the loss of its neighbours need not hold if the devaluation is accompanied by a monetary expansion, since the reduction in interest rates stimulates activity both at home and abroad. For a sample of ten European countries, Eichengreen and Sachs show that the beggar-thy-neighbour losses of competitive devaluation outweighed the gains from the interest rate reduction. This indicates the importance of cooperation, for similar policies coordinated internationally could have avoided the competitive losses and allowed the beneficial effects of lower interest rates to be realized.

When France finally left the gold standard in September 1936, the devaluation was accompanied by the Tripartite Monetary Agreement between Britain, the US and France.[26] In practice this committed the three countries to nothing and amounted to little more than 'a declaration in favour of the international economic equivalent of motherhood'.[27] However, it did at least lead to the establishment of consultations between the three authorities over exchange rate policy.[28]

II.5   Monetary trends 1920–38

Our interpretation of interwar history attaches great importance to deflationary monetary policy in Britain and the US as a result of bids for leadership in a world of interdependence. The pattern and results of these policies can be seen in the data of Figure 3.1. The superscripts UK and US refer to Britain and the United States respectively. Data sources are given in an appendix.

The deflation originating in Britain during the 1920s and in the US during the 1930s can be clearly seen in monetary trends with the money stock (M) falling substantially in Britain during the early 1920s and even more substantially in the US during the early 1930s.

Deflation in Britain during the 1920s secured the appreciation of the sterling-dollar exchange rate (e) back to prewar parity by April 1925, while the monetary deflation in the US during the early 1930s accompanied by monetary expansion in Britain allowed a depreciation of sterling against the dollar which remained fixed against gold. With the adoption of an expansionary monetary policy by the US from the the mid-1930s the pound appreciated against the dollar back above the prewar parity.

Turning to the results of these policies, we see that during the 1920s growth of income (Y) was faster in the US than in Britain, where deflation took its toll. However, the situation was reversed in the 1930s, with the US

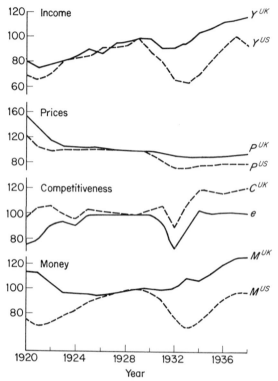

Figure 3.1   Trends in income, prices, competitiveness and money, UK and US, 1920–38

suffering from a catastrophic fall in income during the Great Depression, barely regaining the 1929 level by 1937. Britain, however, experienced substantial growth after a much smaller fall in income.

The trends in the price level (P) also bring out the contrast between the 1920s and 1930s. Britain experienced a much more deflationary 1920s, with the price level falling substantially from its post-First World War peak of 1920. During the 1930s the price level fell substantially further in the US.

The movement of the exchange rate and relative prices determines the competitiveness (C) or real exchange rate of a country. The competitiveness of Britain against the US is shown in Figure 3.1. A rise in C indicates a loss of competitiveness for Britain (or gain in competitiveness for the US). During the early 1920s Britain lost competitiveness as the pound appreciated because British prices did not fall sufficiently relative to US prices to offset the exchange rate appreciation. During the early 1930s, however, Britain's competitive position improved with the depreciation of the pound since British prices did not rise to offset the exchange rate depreciation. However, as the dollar depreciated against the pound from 1933, Britain's competitive position again deteriorated.

Competitiveness is important for economic performance because a loss of competitiveness makes it harder to sell exports and to resist imports. Thus a loss of competitiveness is likely to lead to a balance of payments deficit and/or exchange rate depreciation. Competitiveness is influenced by monetary policy which directly affects the price level and output. However, the precise effect of money on competitiveness will depend on the exchange rate regime in operation.

During the 1920s, the exchange rate target set by the British authorities implied a loss of competitiveness which was offset by the fall in prices associated with the deflationary monetary policy pursued to attain the target. During this period, an expansionary monetary policy in Britain without abandonment of the exchange rate target would have adversely affected competitiveness by raising domestic prices.

During the early 1930s with the US committed to the gold standard, a monetary expansion in the US would similarly have implied a loss of competitiveness for the US. During the mid-1930s, however, the impact of an expansionary monetary policy on competitiveness was less certain because of the floating exchange rate. During 1933–34 as the dollar depreciated sharply against the pound, US competitiveness improved with monetary expansion, but from 1934 competitiveness remained more or less unchanged with both countries reflating rapidly.

III Modelling monetary interdependence

III.1 The basic model

In this Section we outline a model of monetary interdependence and the gains from cooperation between two monetary authorities. The model is essentially a simplified version of the one used in Oudiz and Sachs (1984) for the 1980s. We consider the case of two countries, the UK and the US. Each country has two targets, real income (Y) and competitiveness (C), which is defined as the real exchange rate (eP/P^*) where e is the nominal exchange rate (foreign currency price of a unit of domestic currency), P is the domestic country's price level and P^* the other country's price level. Each country has a utility function (U) defined over the two targets:

$$U = U(Y, C) \qquad (1)$$

Utility is assumed to be increasing in real income $\left(\dfrac{\partial U}{\partial Y} > 0\right)$ and decreasing in competitiveness $\left(\dfrac{\partial U}{\partial C} < 0\right)$. The inclusion of competitiveness in the utility function can be seen as a way of combining the price and current account targets of the Oudiz and Sachs study. Each country is assumed to have one instrument to achieve the two targets. In this case the instrument is the money supply (M). An increase in the money supply is assumed to increase real income $\left(\dfrac{\partial Y}{\partial M} > 0\right)$ and worsen competitiveness $\left(\dfrac{\partial C}{\partial M} > 0\right)$. As we shall see, this trade-off between real income and competitivness plays an important role in the model.

An important distinction is between the non-cooperative and the cooperative solutions to the model. For the non-cooperative solution we use the idea of a Nash equilibrium. Each country sets its monetary policy so as to maximise its own utility, taking the other country's policy as given. At the Nash equilibrium, then, the first derivative of the utility function with respect to the money supply must be zero. Any other setting for the money supply would lower utility:

$$\frac{\partial U}{\partial M} = \frac{\partial U}{\partial Y}\cdot\frac{\partial Y}{\partial M} + \frac{\partial U}{\partial C}\cdot\frac{\partial C}{\partial M} = 0 \qquad (2)$$

Now let us write the marginal utility of income $(\partial U/\partial Y)$ as U_1 and the marginal utility of competitiveness $(\partial U/\partial C)$ as U_2. Thus we have:

$$\frac{\partial U}{\partial M} = U_1\alpha_1 + U_2\beta_1 = 0 \qquad (2')$$

where α_1 and β_1 are the monetary policy 'multipliers' $(\partial Y/\partial M)$ and $(\partial C/\partial M)$, describing how income and competitiveness change, respectively, in response to a change in the domestic money supply.

Let us now normalise the utility function by setting the marginal utility of income U_1 equal to unity:

$$\frac{\partial U}{\partial Y} = U_1 = 1 \qquad (3)$$

Then:

$$\alpha_1 + U_2\beta_1 = 0$$

and the marginal utility of competitiveness U_2 is given by:

$$U_2 = -\alpha_1/\beta_1 \qquad (4)$$

It is now necessary for the empirical application to assume a particular functional form for the utility function, such that we can retrieve the parameters from knowledge of the marginal utilities U_1 and U_2. It turns out that the following simple quadratic utility function has the required property:

$$U = -\tfrac{1}{2}(\mu Y^2 + \phi C^2) \tag{5}$$

where

$$\mu = -\frac{1}{Y_B} \tag{6}$$

$$\phi = \frac{\alpha_1}{\beta_1}\frac{1}{C_B} \tag{7}$$

Here, the subscript B refers to the baseline value of the variable, assumed a Nash equilibrium. Thus Y_B is just the value of income actually observed in a particular year. It is assumed to be a Nash equilibrium since we take it as given that the actual outcome of the interwar years resulted from the absence of cooperation. This is consistent with the pessimistic assessment of attempts at central bank cooperation in Clarke (1967) and Eichengreen (1984). Note that a Stackelberg equilibrium would not be appropriate here since neither country established leadership during this period.

Having obtained the utility function parameters μ and ϕ in equations (6) and (7), it is then possible to calculate baseline utility for Britain and the US using the utility functions (5) for each country. The optimal cooperative monetary policy can then be found by changing the money supply in Britain and the US. Changing the money supply in one country affects income and competitiveness in both countries, through the policy multipliers, and thus affects utility in both countries. Denoting baseline utility in Britain by U_B^{UK} and in the US by U_B^{US}, we characterize optimal cooperative monetary policy as maximizing the welfare gains in each country:

$$\max \cdot (U^{UK} - U_B^{UK})(U^{US} - U_B^{US}) \tag{8}$$

Thus we can investigate the welfare implications of different monetary policies in the two countries.

III.2   Exchange rate regimes

Before we move on to the empirical application, we should note the importance of the exchange rate regime. The first issue concerns the possibility of an independent monetary policy under a fixed exchange rate regime. It is a well known result that in the absence of sterilization by the central bank, an increase in the money supply cannot be sustained due to balance of payments effects. An increase in the money supply worsens the balance of payments on current account because of higher income and prices leading to higher imports and lower exports; and also worsens the capital account because of lower domestic interest rates. With a fixed exchange rate a balance of payments deficit implies an excess demand for foreign currency, which must be sold by the central bank from reserves in exchange for domestic currency. Thus the domestic money supply falls and reverses the initial increase in the money supply. However, a balance of payments deficit need not lead to a reduction in the money supply if the central bank also buys government bonds, through open market operations, since this puts money back into circulation.[29] This is known as sterilization, and as Nurkse (1944) and others have noted, such violations of the gold standard 'rules of the game' were widespread between the wars.[30]

Assuming an independent monetary policy was possible, in our model the exchange rate regime affects the policy multipliers, and thus the trade-off between an increase in output and loss of competitiveness. An increase in the money supply will be split between an increase in real output and an increase in the domestic price level. The increase in the domestic price level will obviously result in a loss of competitiveness if the exchange rate is fixed. However, if the exchange rate is allowed to depreciate, this will offset the loss of competitiveness.

The actual experience of the interwar period is a mixture of exchange rate regimes. In the period from the end of the First World War to the restoration of the Gold Standard in April 1925, the pound essentially floated freely against the dollar, without Central Bank intervention. The dollar retained convertibility at the prewar gold parity. From April 1925 to September 1931 the restored gold standard acted as a fixed exchange rate regime with the pound and the dollar at prewar parity. From September 1931 the pound was floated, but with Central Bank intervention through the Exchange Equalisation Account to influence its value. The US authorities maintained the gold value of the dollar fixed until April 1933, and then devalued against gold. The gold value of the dollar was stabilized at a lower level from February 1934. As Broadberry (1987) notes, there appears to be an asymmetry in foreign exchange markets during the period between September 1931 and 1933, with the exchange rate responding more strongly to monetary shocks originating in Britain than to monetary shocks originating in the US, since the latter were assumed to be temporary while the US adhered to the gold standard.

III.3   Fiscal policy

Economic historians have argued that the absence of a counter-cyclical fiscal expansion during the Great Depression played an important part in the deflationary environment. This case has been made by Brown (1956) for the US and by Middleton (1981) for Britain. However, we note that in general, pre-Keynesian budgetary orthodoxy prevailed between the wars, so that a large fiscal expansion was never seriously on the political agenda. In addition, we note that with fixed exchange rates, in the absence of cooperation, the fiscal authorities were as constrained as the monetary authorities. Indeed, an attempt to avoid the cuts dictated by budgetary orthodoxy in 1931 brought down the Labour government.

IV An empirical application

IV.1 Policy multipliers

We shall assume that income and the price level are both affected by domestic and foreign money supplies. Thus:

$$Y = \gamma_0 + \gamma_1 M + \gamma_2 M^* \tag{9}$$

$$P = \delta_0 + \delta_1 M + \delta_2 M^* \tag{10}$$

Since all variables are in index number form based on $1929 = 100$, the multipliers can be seen as elasticities evaluated at the 1929 levels.

An increase in the domestic money supply is split between an increase in income and an increase in the price level at home, so that the sum of the multipliers $(\gamma_1 + \delta_1)$ must be unity. This assumes that there is no change in velocity, which is determined by institutional factors. We shall make the pessimistic assumption that most of the increase in the money supply raises the price level rather than output. Thus $(\delta_1 > \gamma_1)$.

For the effects of the overseas money supply on income and the price level, we assume that these effects are roughly proportional to the shares of foreign trade in national income. Thus for Britain we assume that $\gamma_2 = 0.2\gamma_1$ and $\delta_2 = 0.2\,\delta_1$, while for America we assume that $\gamma_2 = 0.1\gamma_1$ and $\delta_2 = 0.1\delta_1$. The policy multipliers in the general case are summarized in Table 3.1. So far we have worked in terms of policy multipliers for the domestic price level rather than competitiveness. We now note that the effects on competitiveness will depend on the exchange rate regime. An increase in the domestic price level will lead to less of a deterioration in competitiveness to the extent that

Table 3.1 Policy multipliers: The general case

	γ_1	δ_1	γ_2	δ_2
UK	0.2	0.8	0.04	0.16
US	0.2	0.8	0.02	0.08

it is offset by an exchange rate depreciation. Thus exchange rate depreciation improves the trade-off between income and competitiveness.

We now derive the policy multipliers for income and competitiveness under a fixed exchange rate regime. Note that we have to assume sterilization by the Central Bank to allow the possibility of an independent monetary policy under a fixed exchange rate regime. We require multipliers of the form:

$$Y = \alpha_0 + \alpha_1 M + \alpha_2 M^* \qquad (11)$$

$$C = \beta_0 + \beta_1 M + \beta_2 M^* \qquad (12)$$

The multipliers α_1 and α_2 are given by γ_1 and γ_2 in equation (9). However, the multipliers β_1 and β_2 differ from δ_1 and δ_2 in equation (10). An increase in the domestic money supply (M) will affect both domestic (P) and foreign (P^*) prices, so that the overall effect on competitiveness (β_1) is the difference between these two effects. We can denote this overall effect by ($\delta_1 - \delta_2^*$), using the star to denote the parameter value for the foreign country. Thus for an increase in the UK money supply, ($\delta_1 \dot{M}$) is the effect of this on the UK price level, while ($\delta_2^* \dot{M}$) is the effect of this on the US price level. Since a loss of competitiveness for the UK means a gain in competitiveness for the US, then it must be true that $\beta_2 = -\beta_1^*$. The policy multipliers for the fixed exchange rate case are given in Table 3.2.

Finally, we derive policy multipliers for income and competitiveness under a flexible exchange rate regime. Again, multipliers are of the form given in equations (11) and (12), but this time the multipliers β_1 and β_2 are affected by the change in the exchange rate. We make the relatively pessimistic assumption that as an increase in the domestic money supply (M) raises relative prices (P/P^*), only half of this effect is offset by an exchange rate depreciation. Thus there is a smaller effect on competitiveness given by $\beta_1 = \frac{1}{2}(\delta_1 - \frac{1}{2}\delta_2^*)$. An increase in the UK money supply ($\dot{M}$) leads to an increase in the domestic price level of $\delta_1 \dot{M}$, and an increase in the US price level of $\frac{1}{2}\delta_2^* \dot{M}$. Since the exchange rate has fallen, overall competitiveness deteriorates only by $\frac{1}{2}(\delta_1 - \frac{1}{2}\delta_2^*) \dot{M}$. Thus there is also only a boost to US income of $\frac{1}{2}\gamma_2 \dot{M}$, so that $\alpha_2 = \frac{1}{2}\gamma_2$. As before, $\beta_2 = -\beta_1^*$. Although the smaller deterioration in competitiveness may be expected to boost domestic real income slightly, we continue to assume that $\alpha_1 = \gamma_1$ in line with the quantity

Table 3.2 Policy multipliers: Fixed exchange rates

	α_1	β_1	α_2	β_2
UK	0.2	0.72	0.04	−0.64
US	0.2	0.64	0.02	−0.72

theory restriction that the increase in real income plus the increase in the price level must equal the increase in the money supply.[31] The policy multipliers for the flexible exchange rate case are given in Table 3.3.[32]

Before we go on to consider the implication of the above policy multipliers, we should note their limitations and the reasons for the adoption of this approach. Ideally, the multipliers would come from an econometric model of the world economy between the wars, but data limitations prevent this. Indeed, data limitations are probably at their severest when it comes to international linkages.

However, in defence of the above values, we should note that pessimistic numbers have been chosen so as to bias the case against finding benefits from cooperation too easily. We have assumed that most of an increase in the money supply leads to an increase in the price level rather than an increase in real income, and we have assumed that when the exchange rate is floating, it only offsets half of any change in relative prices. This pessimistic view of the ability of governments to create prosperity does not seem to be out of line with the view of the authorities at the time.

IV.2   Monetary policy in 1926

We can view monetary policy in 1926 as working within a fixed exchange rate regime. The characteristics of the baseline for 1926 are given in Table 3.4(a). Using equations (6) and (7) we can obtain the utility function parameters μ and ϕ. Baseline utility can then be calculated using the utility function parameters and baseline values. Baseline utility is given in Table 3.4(b).

Now let us consider the effects of counterfactual changes in monetary policy in 1926. In this section we only consider counterfactuals with a fixed exchange rate, since a floating rate in 1926 was never really a serious possibility.[33] First let us examine the effects of a 10% monetary expansion in the UK. The results are shown in Table 3.4(c). Although there is a boost to real income in the UK, the beneficial effects of this are more than outweighed by the loss of competitiveness, so that overall utility in the UK is reduced. For the US, however, there is an unambiguous gain because income rises and competitiveness improves. Since the UK loses overall, such an expansion would not be adopted. The interpretation of UK monetary policy in 1926, then, is that it maximized UK utility, taking US policy as given.

Exactly analogous arguments could be used to characterize US monetary policy in 1926 as optimal given UK policy. In Table 3.4(d), an expansion by the US alone leads to a loss of utility in the US. However, in Table 3.4(e)

Table 3.3   Policy multipliers: Flexible exchange rates

	α_1	β_1	α_2	β_2
UK	0.2	0.38	0.02	-0.36
US	0.2	0.36	0.01	-0.38

Table 3.4   Monetary policy in 1926

(a) *Characteristics of baseline, 1926*

	Y_B	C_B	M_B
UK	87.2	102.0	95.2
US	91.7	98.0	93.7

(b) *Baseline utility, 1926*

	U_B
UK	29.421
US	30.462

(c) *10% UK monetary expansion*

	ΔY	ΔC	ΔU
UK	1.904	6.854	-0.043
US	0.190	-6.854	$+2.265$

(d) *10% US monetary expansion*

	ΔY	ΔC	ΔU
UK	0.375	-5.997	$+1.990$
US	1.874	5.997	-0.046

(e) *10% joint monetary expansion*

	ΔY	ΔC	ΔU
UK	2.279	0.857	$+2.068$
US	2.064	-0.857	$+2.354$

we see that if both countries expand together, most of the change in competitiveness is eliminated, so that both countries clearly gain. This is essentially the case considered by Eichengreen (1984), who notes the attempts by the Bank of England to get other central banks to lower their interest rates rather than raising its own in response to external disequilibrium.

Thus in 1926 the source of deflationary pressure in the world economy was the UK commitment to the gold standard at the prewar parity. Taking UK policy as given, the US could not have expanded more rapidly than it did.

IV.3   Monetary policy in 1932

The characteristics of the baseline in 1932 are given in Table 3.5(a). At this stage the US was in very severe depression, while the UK's competitive position had dramatically improved with the abandonment of the gold standard in September 1931. The US remained committed to gold.

Baseline utility for 1932 is calculated on the basis of the floating exchange rate parameter values for the UK but the fixed exchange rate parameters for the US. This reflects the fact that the pound was free to vary against gold while the dollar was fixed against gold. Under these circumstances, as Broadberry (1987) notes, there was an asymmetry in foreign exchange markets, with the sterling-dollar rate responding more strongly to monetary shocks originating in the UK. Monetary shocks originating in the US did not have the same effect because of the commitment to gold, which shaped expectations.

Table 3.5   Monetary policy in 1932

(a) *Characteristics of baseline, 1932*

	Y_B	C_B	M_B
UK	93.0	89.9	101.1
US	66.8	111.2	77.4

(b) *Baseline utility, 1932*

	U_B
UK	22.852
US	15.987

(c) *10% UK monetary expansion*

	ΔY	ΔC	ΔU
UK	2.022	3.842	−0.023
US	0.101	−3.842	+1.285

(d) *10% US monetary expansion*
   (without offsetting $ depreciation)

	ΔY	ΔC	ΔU
UK	0.310	−4.954	+2.848
US	1.548	4.954	−0.021

(e) *10% joint monetary expansion*
   (with offsetting $ depreciation)

	ΔY	ΔC	ΔU
US	2.332	−1.112	+2.944
UK	1.649	1.112	+1.320

Thus we can consider a counterfactual simulation with the exchange rate changing in response to a monetary expansion in the UK, but remaining fixed in response to a monetary expansion in the US. The Nash equilibrium requires that a UK monetary expansion (with offsetting £ depreciation) lowers UK utility in Table 3.5(c), while a US monetary expansion (without offsetting $ depreciation) lowers US utility in Table 3.5(d).

Note however that in Table 3.5(e), a US monetary expansion with an offsetting $ depreciation would increase US as well as UK utility. This indicates that while the US remained committed to gold, its monetary policy was individually optimal. But if the US had been prepared to abandon the gold standard in 1932, the trade-off between real income and competitiveness would have improved so that a more expansionary monetary policy would have been beneficial to the US as well as the UK.

Thus in 1932 the source of deflationary pressure in the world economy was the US commitment to the gold standard. Taking US policy as given, the UK could not have expanded more rapidly than it did.

IV.4   Monetary policy in 1935

In Table 3.6(a) we give the baseline characteristics for 1932, while baseline utility is given in Table 3.6(b). For 1935, this is calculated using the floating exchange rate policy multipliers, since symmetry was by this stage restored in foreign exchange markets, as Broadberry (1987) notes.

In Table 3.6(c) and (d) we see that further monetary expansion by one country acting alone would have lowered utility, while in Table 3.6(e) we see that a joint monetary expansion would have raised utility in both countries. Thus by 1935 both countries were expanding as fast as they could individually, but a cooperative policy would have allowed further expansion.

V   Conclusions

In this paper we bring together historical and economic accounts of the depressed condition of the world economy between the wars. Of central importance to this account is the failure of international cooperation. This is true both for the 1920s and the 1930s. During the 1920s Britain's return to the gold standard at the pre-war parity required deflationary monetary policy. Given continued US commitment to the gold standard, high interest rates in London had to be matched by high interest rates in New York, so that deflationary monetary policy in Britain can be seen as restricting the freedom of action of the US monetary authorities.

Table 3.6 Monetary policy in 1935

(a) *Characteristics of baseline, 1935*

	Y_B	C_B	M_B
UK	108.3	118.8	113.1
US	83.5	84.2	83.8

(b) *Baseline utility, 1935*

	U_B
UK	22.996
US	18.367

(c) *10% UK monetary expansion*

	ΔY	ΔC	ΔU
UK	2.262	4.298	−0.009
US	0.113	−4.298	+2.442

(d) *10% US monetary expansion*

	ΔY	ΔC	ΔU
UK	0.168	−3.107	+1.733
US	1.676	3.107	−0.012

(e) *10% joint monetary expansion*

	ΔY	ΔC	ΔU
UK	2.430	1.281	+1.783
US	1.789	−1.281	+2.517

During the 1930s the continued adherence of the US to the gold standard after Britain's departure required deflationary monetary policy in the US and other countries of the gold bloc. Given the importance of the US and these other countries in the world economy, offsetting expansionary monetary policy in Britain could not prevent a severe world depression. The situation changed in 1933 when the US broke the link with gold. Freed from the gold standard constraint, both Britain and the US were able to adopt expansionary monetary policy.

The remaining question is why Britain in the early 1920s and the US in the early 1930s adopted goals (restoring sterling to its prewar parity in the British case, remaining on the gold standard until 1933 in the US case) that had such damaging deflationary consequences. The answer, we argue, is that in each case these policies represented a bid for leadership of the international monetary system. By returning to the prewar parity, Britain hoped to regain her status as the leading international financial power, which would permit the Bank of England to set the tone for monetary policy that other central banks would follow. By remaining on the gold standard after Britain devalued, the US hoped to acquire the leadership role. The problem with this strategy was that Britain was no longer sufficiently influential, and the US was not yet sufficiently powerful, to function effectively as leader. International cooperation was the only viable alternative. The key problem for interwar monetary policy, we suggest, was not these countries' failure to lead but rather the failure of international cooperation.

Appendix: Data sources

United Kingdom

M   Money Stock (Broad Money M3) (£m).
      Source: Capie and Webber (1985), Table I.3.

P   Net National Product Deflator (1929 = 100).
      Source: Friedman and Schwartz (1982), Table 4.9.

Y   Real Net National Product (£m 1929).
      Source: Friedman and Schwartz (1982), Table 4.9.

C   Competitiveness (Real Exchange Rate).
      Source: Calculated as $e(P/P^*)$.

e   Sterling-dollar exchange rate ($ per £).
      Source: Friedman and Schwartz (1982), Table 4.9.

United States

M*   Money Stock (Broad Money) ($bn).
      Source: Friedman and Schwartz (1982), Table 4.8.

P*   Net National Product Deflator (1929 = 100).
      Source: Friedman and Schwartz (1982), Table 4.8.

Y*   Net National Product ($bn 1929).
      Source: Friedman and Schwartz (1982), Table 4.8.

All variables expressed as index numbers based on 1929 = 100.

Notes

1 Lewis (1949), p.200.

2 See, for example, Brown (1940), Nevin (1970), Clarke (1967), Kindleberger (1986), Eichengreen (1984).

3 In the political science literature this is usually called hegemony. Eichengreen (1989) provides a sceptical economist's view of hegemonic stability theories of the international monetary system.

4 Sayers (1970), p.86.

5 Sayers (1970), p.91, Moggridge (1972).

6 Keynes (1930), Vol.2, pp.306–307.

7 Clarke (1973), p.12.

8 Clarke (1973), p.5.

9 Clarke (1973), p.8.

10 Clarke (1973), p.13.

11 Friedman and Schwartz (1963), p.229.

12 The financial crisis originated in Austria with the collapse of the Creditanstalt, but soon spread to Britain. A good account of the crisis is given in Kindleberger (1986), Chapter 7.

13 Kindleberger (1986), pp.221–224.

14 Nevin (1970), p.68, Howson (1975), pp.86–89.

15 Broadberry (1986), Ch.5, and Broadberry (1987).

16 Kindleberger (1986), pp.165–166.

17 Choudri and Kochin (1980), p.567.

18 Indeed the Glass-Steagall Act of 1932, which allowed the use of government securities in addition to gold as collateral for Federal Reserve notes, made such an eventuality unlikely. See Kindleberger (1986), p.183.

19 Clarke (1973), p.25.

20 Quoted in Kindleberger (1986), p.204.

21 Clarke (1973), p.25.

22 Friedman and Schwartz (1963), p.465.

23 Kindleberger (1986), p.224.

24 Friedman and Schwartz (1963), p.465.

25 Clarke (1973), pp.36–37.

26 Kindleberger (1986), pp.255–260.

27 Clarke (1977), p.38.

28 Kindleberger (1986), p.258.

29 Strictly, for sterilization to affect the domestic money supply we require imperfect capital mobility, a stock adjustment process for money demand, or the assumption of a large country.

30 As with Wicker (1965), we do not see sterilization as completely freeing the US from the gold standard constraint during the 1920s.

31 Note that we have assumed that velocity changes permissively in response to changes in the foreign money supply but not in response to changes in the domestic money supply. This is purely a simplification which allows us to derive specific values for the multipliers.

32 Note that in terms of the Mundell-Fleming framework we are assuming that

Britain and the US were large economies in a world of less than perfect capital mobility, so that through monetary policy they could affect global interest rates.
33 As Sayers (1970) notes.

References

Broadberry, S.N. (1984) 'The North European Depression of the 1920s', *Scandinavian Economic History Review* **32,** 159–67.

Broadberry, S.N. (1986) *The British Economy Between the Wars: A Macroeconomic Survey,* Oxford: Blackwell.

Broadberry, S.N. (1987) 'Purchasing Power Parity and the Pound-Dollar Rate in the 1930s', *Economica* **54,** 69–78.

Brown, E.C. (1956) 'Fiscal Policy in the Thirties: A Reappraisal', *American Economic Review* **46,** 857–79.

Brown, W.A. (1940) *The International Gold Standard Reinterpreted 1914–1934,* New York: National Bureau of Economic Research.

Capie, F. and A. Webber (1985) *A Monetary History of the United Kingdom 1870– 1982: Vol. I: Data, Sources, Methods,* London: George Allen and Unwin.

Choudri, E. and L.A. Kochin (1980) 'The Exchange Rate and the International Transmission of Business Cycle Disturbances', *Journal of Money, Credit and Banking* **12,** 565–74.

Clarke, S.V.O. (1967) *Central Bank Cooperation 1924–1931,* New York: Federal Reserve Board of New York.

Clarke, S.V.O. (1973) 'The Reconstruction of the International Monetary System: The Attempts of 1922 and 1933', *Princeton Studies in International Finance,* No. 33.

Clarke, S.V.O. (1977). 'Exchange Rate Stabilisation in the Mid-1930s: Negotiating the Tripartite Agreement', *Princeton Studies in International Finance,* No. 41.

Cunliffe Committee (1918) *First Interim Report of the Committee on Currency and Foreign Exchange After the War,* Cd. 9182, London: HMSO.

Eichengreen, B.J. (1984). 'Central Bank Cooperation Under the Interwar Gold Standard', *Explorations in Economic History* **21,** 64–87.

Eichengreen, B.J. (1989) 'Hegemonic Stability Theories of the International Monetary System', in R.C. Bryant (ed.) *Can Nations Agree? Essays in International Cooperation.* Washington, D.C.: The Brookings Institution.

Eichengreen, B.J. and J. Sachs (1985) 'Exchange Rates and Economic Recovery in the 1930s', *Journal of Economic History* **65,** 925–46.

Epstein, G. and T. Ferguson (1984) 'Monetary Policy, Loan Liquidation and Industrial Conflict: The Federal Reserve and the Open Market Operations of 1932', *Journal of Economic History* **44,** 957–83.

Friedman, M. and A.J. Schwartz (1963) *A Monetary History of the United States 1867–1960*, Princeton, Princeton University Press for the National Bureau of Economic Research.

Friedman, M. and A.J. Schwartz (1982) *Monetary Trends in the United States and the United Kingdom*. Chicago: Chicago University Press for the National Bureau of Economic Research.

Howson, S. (1975) *Domestic Monetary Management in Britain 1919–1938,* Cambridge: Cambridge University Press.

Keynes, J.M. (1930) *A Treatise on Money*, London: Macmillan.

Kindleberger, C.P. (1986) *The World in Depression 1929–39*, 2nd Edition, Harmondsworth: Penguin.

Lewis, W.A. (1949) *Economic Survey 1919–1939*, London: George Allen and Unwin.

Meltzer, A.H. (1976) 'Monetary and Other Explanations of the Start of the Great Depression', *Journal of Monetary Economics* **2**, 455–72.

Middleton, R. (1981) 'The Constant Employment Budget and British Budgetary Policy 1929–39', *Economic History Review* **34**, 266–86.

Moggridge, D.E. (1972) *British Monetary Policy 1924–31: The Norman Conquest of $4.86*, Cambridge: Cambridge University Press.

Nevin, E. (1970) 'The Origins of Cheap Money', in Pollard, S. (editor), *The Gold Standard and Employment Policies Between the Wars*, London: Methuen.

Nurkse, R. (1944). *International Currency Experience: Lessons of the Interwar Period*, Geneva: League of Nations.

Oudiz, G. and Sachs, J. (1984) 'Macroeconomic Policy Coordination among the Industrial Economies', *Brookings Papers on Economic Activity* **1**, 1–64.

Sayers, R.S. (1970) 'The Return to Gold, 1925', in Pollard, S. (editor), *The Gold Standard and Employment Policies Between the Wars*, London: Methuen.

Wicker, E.R. (1965) 'Federal Reserve Monetary Policy, 1922–23: A Reinterpretation', *Journal of Political Economy* **73**, 325–43.

Discussion

Paul Turner

In being asked to provide comments on a paper one automatically falls into the role
of critic in that the easiest thing to do is to talk about the aspects of the paper one
disagrees with. I would like to begin by emphasizing that, although my comments
may appear to be of this kind, I found this paper extremely interesting and a very
valuable contribution to my understanding of the inter-war world economy. In
particular I found that the historical discussion in the first section of the paper put
into context a whole range of topics in a way which clearly emphasize the value of
the game-theoretic analysis which follows.

My comments relate mainly to the formal economic model presented and the use
of game-theoretic concepts to describe the possible outcomes which can arise. Turning
first to the economic model embodied in equations (9) and (10) I was a little unsure
as to why the author forces a quantity theory interpretation onto the model. Indeed
this causes some problems of interpretation. Consider a simultaneous monetary
expansion by $x\%$ in both countries. The standard quantity theory would predict
rises in price and output totalling $x\%$ in each country. However (9) and (10) imply
increases which add to something greater than $x\%$.

Now the above problem is by no means crucial to the author's argument since it
is perfectly easy to find plausible structures for which (9) and (10) constitute an
appropriate reduced form. However if the strict quantity theory is not assumed then
the justification for concentrating solely on monetary interdependence does not
follow naturally from the theory. In particular my own belief is that monetary policy
has greater effects because of the constraints it places on the adoption of counter-
cyclical fiscal policies rather than any direct impact on aggregate demand. Of course
in the inter-war period the Keynesian view of the importance of budgetary policy
was not widely accepted. Therefore it may well be that the model presented here
conforms more closely to the world that policy makers believed themselves to be
inhabiting, while a model which more closely represented the true state of the world
would be quite alien to their thinking during this period.

Turning to the analysis of policy making I found the discussion of the benefits of
coordination extremely interesting. Given that both the form of the economic model,
and the parameter values chosen, would tend to bias the results towards a low gain

BLUEPRINTS FOR EXCHANGE RATE MANAGEMENT
0-12-497060-5
Copyright © 1989 Academic Press, Ltd
All rights of reproduction reserved

from coordination, it is of especial interest to see that Tables 3.4, 3.5 and 3.6(e) all show that a coordinated expansion results in a significant gain in utility over the baseline level. In addition, despite the discussion of the Nash cooperative solution in the text, this gain is derived from consideration of the arbitrary counterfactual of a 10% expansion of both countries' money stocks. If an optimal cooperative solution were to be employed instead then the welfare gain might be still larger.

The use of 'plausible parameter values' is so widespread in this type of model that it rarely gives rise to comment. Indeed, in this case, I appreciate that estimation of a full econometric model is hardly feasible. However one way of carrying the work further might be to seek some sort of compromise solution by extracting parameter estimates from some of the existing econometric work on the inter-war period.

One way of extending the results generated by this paper further might be to make use of alternative solution concepts to capture aspects of the historical discussion in the early sections. In particular the idea of the value of a leader in the world economy might be modelled using the Stackelberg solution concept while the issue of the relative power of the two players might be captured using the generalized Nash cooperative solution. Here power is reflected in the weights put on the gains in utility in the joint welfare function. Of course the allocation of weights is somewhat arbitrary but so is the assumption of equal shares embodied in the standard Nash cooperative solution. Thus it is not difficult to see the ideas in this paper generating further interesting research.

Another way in which the interdependence of economic policy could be illustrated is by comparison of the Nash reaction functions of the two countries. Using the notation in the paper these can be derived as:

$$M = [\mu\alpha_1^2 + \phi\beta_2^2]^{-1} [-\mu\alpha_1\alpha_0 - \phi\beta_1\beta_0 - (\mu\alpha_1\alpha_2 + \phi\beta_1\beta_2)M^*]$$

Since the μ and ϕ parameters vary with the baseline levels of income and competitiveness the slopes of the reaction functions are not constant. However, given the parameter values and the baselines reported in the paper they can easily be computed for 1926, 1932 and 1935. These are reported below in Table 3A.1.

These indicate that the constraints imposed by interdependence are greater during periods of fixed exchange rates as predicted by economic theory.

In conclusion, this paper makes a strong case that lack of policy coordination constituted one of the reasons for poor inter-war macroeconomic performance. The historical evidence of imperfect coordination is well documented and the formal economic model indicates that it may have been quantitatively significant. I doubt if this will be the last paper we will see on this subject and I think that the work here will provide a useful base for further research.

Table 3A.1   Slopes of Nash reaction functions

	1926	1932	1935
UK	0.62	0.59	0.56
US	0.82	0.71	0.65

Part II

Theoretical issues

Chapter 4

Stabilization policy, fixed exchange rates and target zones

George S. Alogoskoufis*

Ministers and governors emphasized their continued interest in stable exchange rates among their currencies. Therefore they reaffirmed their commitments to pursue policies that will maintain exchange rate stability and to continue to cooperate closely on foreign exchange markets. They are continuing their study of ways of further improving the functioning of the international monetary system and the coordination process (Group of Seven Communique, 24 October 1988).

I Introduction

The international monetary system seems to be moving away from the floating exchange rates regime that characterized much of the seventies and half of the eighties, towards a system of greater exchange rate stability. Of the blueprints that have been put forward in recent years, two have received most attention. One, associated with McKinnon (1980, 1982), envisages fixed nominal exchange rates at levels consistent with purchasing power parities,

*I should like to thank the conference participants, as well as Joshua Aizenman, David Begg, John Black, Dale Henderson and Marcus Miller for their comments on an earlier version of this paper; also the participants in the Essex University Economics Seminar, the International Monetary Economics Seminar at the National Foundation of Political Science, Paris, an ESRC International Economics Study Group workshop, a CEPR Workshop on Target Zones, and the 1988 NBER Summer Institute. This paper is part of a CEPR research programme on Macroeconomic Interactions and Policy Design in an Interdependent World, supported by grants from the Ford Foundation (No. 850–1014) and the Alfred P Sloan Foundation (No. 85-12-13), whose help is gratefully acknowledged.

BLUEPRINTS FOR EXCHANGE RATE MANAGEMENT
0-12-497060-5

Copyright © 1989 Academic Press, Ltd
All rights of reproduction reserved

and coordination of monetary policies in pursuit of a world monetary stability objective. The other, associated with Williamson (1983), is also in two parts. First it envisages determination of central nominal exchange rate parities consistent with 'fundamental equilibrium' real exchange rates. Second, it suggests a wide target zone around these central parities that can be used for domestic stabilization purposes in the short run. In more recent restatements, McKinnon (1984, 1988) and Williamson (1987) have slightly modified their proposals. McKinnon now clearly suggests that the indicator for world monetary policy should be the rate of inflation of traded goods, while Williamson suggests the additional use of fiscal policy in pursuit of national nominal GDP targets.

The proposals have been widely discussed and criticized by other experts. See Dornbusch (1986, 1988), Branson (1986), Fischer (1986), Frenkel (1987) and Kenen (1987), for example. In addition, the target zones proposal has been formally evaluated with the help of multi-country econometric models by Edison, Miller and Williamson (1986), Currie and Wren-Lewis (1988), and Hughes Hallett, Holtham and Hutson (1989). The results of the first two are quite favourable. They suggest that a regime akin to the extended target zones proposal would have resulted in much greater macroeconomic stability during the late seventies and early eighties. On the other hand, the Hughes Hallett *et al.* evaluation is rather unfavourable. The two alternative proposals have also been compared in Miller and Williamson (1988), who present numerical simulations using a calibrated theoretical world macro model, based on Dornbusch's (1976) analysis. They report asymptotic variances of prices and output in the face of demand and supply shocks. The results do not distinguish very sharply between the extended McKinnon and Williamson proposals.

In this paper I use a small analytical world macromodel to attempt a comparative theoretical evaluation of these alternatives. The aim is to investigate how they compare with an optimal international monetary regime. In particular I examine two main issues: first, the circumstances under which coordination of monetary policies would obviate the need for short-run nominal exchange rate flexibility, and, second, the question of the optimal width of the band, if one were to be formally adopted. I also discuss Williamson's advocation of nominal income targets.

To keep matters as simple as possible, I assume a world economy consisting of a large number of identical small countries, producing internationally traded commodities only. Goods and assets are assumed perfect substitutes internationally.[1] Following Gray (1976), I assume that nominal wages in each country are set in advance for one period and are imperfectly indexed to the price level. Thus, transitory disturbances that were unanticipated at the time of wage setting cause a distortion in the labour market. To the extent that they cause nominal interest rates to deviate from their long-run equilibrium, they also cause a distortion in the money market. The policy authorities in each country are assumed to be concerned with minimizing a weighted average of the labour-market distortion (welfare cost of unemployment) and the money-market distortion (welfare cost of inflation). Two cases are considered. In the first, the authorities have recourse to both monetary policy and an additional policy instrument (fiscal or incomes policy), while in the second the only available instrument is monetary policy.

When both policy instruments can be utilized, the authorities in each country can achieve the first-best: the complete elimination of both distortions. Monetary policy can ensure that domestic interest rates do not respond to world interest rate shocks, by triggering the necessary changes in nominal exchange rates, while fiscal (or incomes) policy can be used to eliminate the labour market distortion.

When the only available instrument is monetary policy, countries are in a second-best situation, in which the welfare costs are positive, but minimized in the sense that the marginal welfare cost of unemployment is equal to the marginal welfare cost of inflation. This policy also implies exchange rate management, but now the exchange rate responds not only to world interest-rate shocks, but to world inflation and domestic supply shocks as well.

It is shown that the pursuit of fixed nominal income targets is a third-best policy, which can be seen as one which gives no weight to the monetary stability objective, and which involves sub-optimal reactions to supply shocks.

So much for the policies of individual countries. Optimal policies for the world economy are analogous. If all countries have recourse to both monetary and fiscal policy, there exists a first-best optimal regime, involving coordination of monetary policies so as to eliminate deviations of world interest rates from long-run equilibrium, and decentralization in the pursuit of domestic stabilization policy objectives. The result is fixed exchange rates, as individual countries will aim to keep their interest rates in line with the optimal world interest rate, and will use fiscal (or incomes) policy towards their unemployment objective. This first-best outcome is akin to the McKinnon proposal. However, it presupposes a lot of flexibility in fiscal or incomes policy worldwide. It is what Miller and Williamson (1988) have dubbed 'McKinnon with fiscal activism'. There is no need for a band or target zone, unless there is some uncertainty about the level of fundamental equilibrium exchange rates.

In the more relevant second-best case where monetary policy is the only stabilization policy instrument, the optimal regime involves coordination of monetary policies to minimize the distortions caused by worldwide (average) components of demand and supply shocks, and decentralization of exchange rate management to individual countries. The latter will opt for exchange rate changes in response only to relative supply shocks. Worldwide supply shocks are taken care of by world monetary policy, and fixed exchange rates provide the optimal response to money demand shocks. This regime requires the short-run nominal exchange rate flexibility which distinguishes the Williamson from the McKinnon proposal. However, this paper offers no rationale for having a formal band. If a band were to be put in place, it would be better to have 'soft buffers'. In any case, its optimal width should be proportional to the standard deviation of relative supply shocks.

The rest of the paper is as follows: in Section II I present a brief summary of the two proposals, stressing their similarities and differences. In Section III I present the representative country model, which serves as the basis for my analytical 'world' model, and discuss the nature of the distortions whose minimization is the aim of stabilization policy. In Section IV I investigate optimal policies for the representative small open economy. First- and second-best international monetary regimes are examined in Section V, where I discuss their relation to McKinnon's fixed exchange rate proposal and Williamson's target zones. The final section summarizes the conclusions of the analysis for the two alternative blueprints.

II   The fixed exchange rates and target zone proposals

Both proposals for international monetary reform go back a long way. The fixed exchange rate proposal of McKinnon can be discerned in his famous paper on 'optimum currency areas' (McKinnon, 1963) and a Princeton Essay of 1974. On the other hand, many of the elements of Williamson's target zones can be traced back to a celebrated (1965) Princeton Essay on the 'crawling peg'. However, in describing the proposals I shall stick to recent statements, namely McKinnon (1982, 1984, 1988) and Williamson (1983, 1986, 1987).

McKinnon first suggests fixed nominal exchange rates among the major industrialized countries, at levels consistent with approximate purchasing power parity (PPP) in internationally traded goods. Second, he proposes that in the longer run 'central banks would aim to keep constant their common (wholesale) price level in internationally tradable goods ... as a nominal anchor for the system as a whole. For this purpose, aggregate money growth, the sum of domestic credit expansions, could be targeted as an intermediate variable' (McKinnon 1988, p.93). He suggests using nominal interest rates actively to stabilize potentially volatile exchange rates, but predicts that 'With confidence in the official parities, very small changes in interest rates would attract (or repel) sufficient short term capital to equilibrate the foreign exchanges' (ibid, p.93). He proposes 'symmetrically unsterilized intervention' only as a last resort. There is no mention of internal balance or fiscal policy, and the 'transfer problem' is expected to be solved automatically, through changes in the relative price of traded to non-traded goods within each country. To quote, 'Although these relative price movements within … countries would be modest, gradual, and need not be permanent, they would be sufficient to support the transfer of saving from one highly open economy to another, as with past experiences of fixed exchange-rate regimes approximating a common currency area' (ibid, p.99).

Williamson starts with 'fundamental equilibrium exchange rates'. They are defined as those which will 'generate a current account surplus or deficit equal to the underlying capital flow over the cycle, given that the country is pursuing "internal balance" as best it can, and not restricting trade for balance of payments reasons' (Williamson, 1983, p.14). Nominal exchange rates consistent with these real rates will be set as targets, which 'should be regularly updated in the light of new data' (Williamson, 1987, p.202). The individual economies would be expected to 'conduct their macroeconomic policies … with a view to preventing exchange rates going outside a broad zone of perhaps ±10 percent around the target. The principal instrument to be used for that purpose would be monetary (interest rate) policy' (ibid, p.202). Two additional elements are 'compensatory adjustments of fiscal policy', in pursuit of national nominal GDP targets, and 'soft buffers' which would give countries the right to allow their exchange rate to drift outside the zone, when major transitory shocks occur. Williamson proposes the following assignment rules.

(1) The average level of world interest rates should be revised up (down) if aggregate growth of nominal income is threatening to exceed (fall short of) the sum of the target growth of nominal income for the participating countries.
(2) Differences in interest rates among countries should be revised when necessary to limit the deviations of currencies from their target levels.
(3) National fiscal policies should be revised to achieve national target rates of growth of nominal income (Williamson, 1987, p.204).

McKinnon's and Williamson's proposals differ in two main respects. One is the definition of 'equilibrium' exchange rates, where the former espouses PPP as a prescriptive norm, and the latter espouses a version of the Meade (1951) synthesis of the elasticities and income approaches. They also differ in the short-run exchange rate flexibility they allow around the target exchange rates, where McKinnon goes for fixed exchange rates, and Williamson for exchange rate flexibility within a broad zone, which could also have 'soft buffers'.

Their other differences are semantic rather than substantive. McKinnon goes for coordination of monetary policies in pursuit of an intermediate conditional money supply target, and Williamson opts for a conditional intermediate nominal GDP target. Each could be translated into the other if the final objective is the same, for example price stability. Williamson gives more weight to national fiscal policies, but McKinnon does not rule them out. In addition, they both agree on unsterilized symmetrical intervention as the instrument of exchange rate management.

In what follows, I shall not be concerned with the issue of the appropriate theory for medium-term equilibrium exchange rates. I shall concentrate on short-run issues, and particularly on whether, given the objectives and instruments of governments, short-run exchange rate flexibility is desirable for stabilization purposes.

III The representative country model

The representative country model I use in this paper is one of the simplest available in international macroeconomics. It is short-run in nature, and has been widely used to address questions of exchange market intervention (Aizenman and Frenkel, 1985). Such a model has important analytical and notational advantages as a building block of a world macro model. It has the minimal number of parameters required for an adequate characterization of macroeconomic interdependence through goods and asset markets, and its properties are not misleading, in the sense that they carry over to more general models of open economies.[2]

III.1 The model

Consider an open economy that produces one internationally traded commodity. In what follows all variables are expressed as percentage deviations from a constant long-run equilibrium. This allows us to concentrate on pure problems of macroeconomic stabilization.[3]

Capital will be assumed fixed in the short run, in which case, (deviations of) output are given by

$$y_j = \pi l_j + \mu_j; \quad 0 < \pi < 1 \tag{1}$$

where y_j is output, l_j is employment, and μ_j is a transitory supply shock. π is the share of labour in total output, and j indexes the individual country. Labour demand determines employment. Profit maximization under perfect competition in the goods market suggests that

$$l_j = -\lambda(w_j + \tau_j - p_j) + \lambda\mu_j; \quad \lambda = \sigma/(1 - \pi) \tag{2}$$

where w_j denotes nominal wages and p_j the price of domestic output. τ_j is the payroll tax rate, and will be considered as a potential policy instrument. λ is the elasticity of labour demand, and σ is the elasticity of substitution between labour and capital.[4]

Labour supply is assumed to be a positive function of the consumption wage, thus

$$l_j^s = \varepsilon(w_j - p_j); \quad \varepsilon > 0 \tag{3}$$

where ε is the elasticity of labour supply.

The next assumption about wage adjustment is a crucial one. Following Gray (1976) I assume that wages are negotiated before the current (previously unanticipated) shocks have been observed. *Ex post* they are only partially indexed to the price level. Thus, nominal wages are determined by

$$w_j = \theta p_j + \omega_j; \quad 0 < \theta < 1 \tag{4}$$

where θ is the degree of wage indexation, and ω_j measures the effects of a potential incomes policy. With this wage adjustment rule, and the assumption that employment is on the demand for labour curve, the labour supply function is 'notional' in the short run. Nevertheless, it is required for the calculation of the welfare cost of unemployment, the minimization of which is assumed to be one of the objectives of stabilization policy.[5]

We next turn to the demand side. There is a demand for money function, given by

$$m_j - p_j = y_j - \alpha i_j + k_j; \quad \alpha > 0 \tag{5}$$

where k_j is a transitory shock to money demand. α is the interest rate semi-elasticity of the demand for money, and i_j is the domestic nominal interest rate. Bonds are assumed perfect substitutes internationally, in which case i_j is determined by uncovered interest parity.

$$i_j = i + s_j^e = i - s_j \tag{6}$$

where s_j^e is the expected rate of future depreciation of the exchange rate, and i is the (average) world interest rate. Since all shocks to the economy are assumed transitory, the expected rate of future depreciation of the exchange rate is equal to minus the current rate of depreciation s_j. This is the 'minimal set of state variables' rational expectations solution in this model (see McCallum, 1983). The exchange rate is expected to return to its long-run equilibrium, although it temporarily overshoots because of transitory shocks.

The last element in the model is an assumption about price determination. I shall assume perfect commodity arbitrage, alias the law of one price.

$$p_j = s_j + p \tag{7}$$

where p is the average world price level. The law of one price can be seen as the limiting case of the IS curve in an open economy, as the elasticity of net exports with respect to competitiveness tends to infinity. This special assumption is made for notational simplicity, and does not affect the nature of the results of this paper.

Let me finally turn to the stochastic specification of shocks. Both supply and money demand shocks are assumed to be the sum of independent white noise processes. Thus:

$$\mu_j = \mu + \mu(j) \tag{8}$$

$$k_j = k + k(j) \tag{9}$$

where μ and k are worldwide (aggregate) shocks, and $\mu(j)$ and $k(j)$ are country-specific (relative) shocks.

III.2   Solution of the model

The solution of the model is conceptually very simple. Substituting the law of one price (7) in the wage adjustment equation (4), and then substituting for nominal wages in the labour demand curve (2), we can use the resulting expression to derive an aggregate supply curve from (1).

$$y_j = \pi\lambda(1 - \theta)(s_j + p) - \pi\lambda\omega_j - \pi\lambda\tau_j + (1 + \pi\lambda)\mu_j \tag{10}$$

Substituting the uncovered interest parity condition (6) and the law of one price (7) in the money demand function (5), and solving for output, we derive an aggregate demand curve.

$$y_j = m_j - k_j - p + \alpha i - (1 + \alpha)s_j \tag{11}$$

Under flexible exchange rates, for a small open economy, the only endogenous variable in the right hand sides of (10) and (11) is the exchange rate. Solving for the exchange rate at the intersection of the aggregate demand and aggregate supply curves, we get

$$s_j = \frac{1}{1 + \alpha + \pi\lambda(1 - \theta)}$$
$$\{m_j - k_j + \alpha i - (1 + \pi\lambda(1 - \theta))p - (1 + \pi\lambda)\mu_j + \pi\lambda\omega_j + \pi\lambda\tau_j\} \tag{12}$$

The remaining endogenous variables are easily determined, by substituting (12) in the law of one price condition, the uncovered interest parity condition, the aggregate demand (or supply) curve, the wage equation and the employment equation.

I next turn to the objectives of stabilization policy.

III.3   Welfare losses

The authorities will be assumed to have two targets, unemployment and inflation (monetary stability).

   An appealing measure of the welfare cost of unemployment in the context of this model has been proposed by Aizenman and Frenkel (1985). The welfare cost can be measured by the loss of producers' and consumers' surplus, induced by being away from labour market equilibrium. Given that labour demand and supply have been assumed log-linear, the distortion is measured by the area of a triangle whose height is the difference between equilibrium and actual employment given the realization of the shocks, and whose base is the difference between the supply and demand real wages at the actual employment level. Obviously, the area is one half of the product of base and height. From (2) and (3), equilibrium employment is given by

$$\hat{l}_j = \frac{\varepsilon\lambda}{\varepsilon+\lambda}\mu_j \qquad (13)$$

where deviations of payroll taxes τ_j have been set to zero. The difference between actual and equilibrium employment is given by

$$l_j - \hat{l}_j = \lambda(1-\theta)(s_j + p) - \lambda\omega_j - \lambda\tau_j + \frac{\lambda^2}{\varepsilon+\lambda}\mu_j \qquad (14)$$

The 'demand' and 'supply' wages at the actual level of employment can be found by inverting the labour demand and supply functions (2) and (3). Then, the welfare cost of 'unemployment', a Harberger (1971) triangle in the labour market, is given by

$$\frac{1}{2}\left[\frac{1}{\varepsilon} + \frac{1}{\lambda}\right]\left(l_j - \hat{l}_j\right)^2 =$$

$$\frac{1}{2}\left[\frac{1}{\varepsilon} + \frac{1}{\lambda}\right]\left\{\lambda(1-\theta)(s_j + p) - \lambda\omega_j - \lambda\tau_j + \frac{\lambda^2}{\varepsilon+\lambda}\mu_j\right\}^2 \qquad (15)$$

   The welfare cost of inflation seems to have been overlooked in most recent analyses of optimal exchange market intervention. As is well known, one way to incorporate it is through the distortion that arises in the money market from deviations of interest rates from long-run equilibrium interest rates (Bailey, 1956). To compute this welfare loss one needs to multiply the difference between the actual and the long-run equilibrium domestic interest rate, by half the difference between money demands at the respective interest rates, given the current output level, and the realization of the money demand shock k. This gives us,

$$\frac{1}{2}\alpha i_j^2 = \frac{1}{2}\alpha(i - s_j)^2 \tag{16}$$

as a measure of the welfare cost of inflation.

The problem of the authorities can then be seen as minimizing the following social welfare function:

$$H_j = E\left[\frac{\delta}{2}\left[\frac{1}{\varepsilon} + \frac{1}{\lambda}\right](l_j - \hat{l}_j)^2 + \frac{1 - \delta}{2}\alpha i_j^2 \,\middle|\, \Lambda\right]; \quad 0 < \delta < 1 \tag{17}$$

subject to the model, and using a subset of the set of instruments $\{m_j, \tau_j, \omega_j\}$. E is the mathematical expectations operator, Λ the information set and δ is the weight given to the welfare cost of unemployment.

IV   Optimal policies in the representative open economy

It can easily be shown that the welfare loss (17) can be completely eliminated under full information. The authorities in each country have enough independent instruments in the short run, ranging from monetary to fiscal and incomes policy. In fact, any two will suffice. Let me restrict attention to monetary and fiscal policy. A popular assignment is to use monetary policy for the inflation target, and fiscal policy for the unemployment target. The welfare cost of unemployment will be eliminated if

$$\tau_j^* = (1 - \theta)(s_j^* + p) + \frac{\lambda}{\varepsilon + \lambda}\mu_j \tag{18}$$

At the optimum, the payroll tax rate increases with inflation shocks, which because of partial wage indexation, will reduce real wages, causing a sub-optimal increase in employment. It also increases with supply shocks, since, because of the sluggishness of wages, the employment effects of the latter overshoot the equilibrium effects. (18) implies that incomes policy is not being used, so that $\omega_j = 0$. A formally equivalent policy would be to set $\tau_j = 0$, and ω_j as suggested by the right hand side of (18). This is because a change in payroll taxes operates through wage costs, exactly like an incomes policy.

The rule for optimal exchange rate depreciations is also simple. Since the objective is to keep domestic nominal interest rates constant, this implies from the uncovered interest parity condition that

$$s_j^* = i \tag{19}$$

At the optimum, the exchange rate should depreciate by the full extent of deviations of world interest rates from the long-run optimum, in order to generate expectations of a future appreciation that will maintain domestic nominal interest rates at their long-run optimum level. This rule can be expressed as a rule for the domestic money supply, by inverting the reduced form exchange rate equation (12). It would imply full accommodation of changes in nominal income, as well as money demand shocks. This would be in order to neutralize the effects of the various disturbances on domestic interest rates.

The first-best policy examined above implies a lot of activism on the fiscal or wage determination side. However, there are many reasons for which a country may be constrained not to use such policies for stabilization purposes.

First, fiscal policy is mainly used for allocative, distributional and more generally political objectives, and the authorities may be unwilling to jeopardize these objectives for the sake of stabilization policy. For example, this seemed to be the response of the British Chancellor of the Exchequer to a recent call for fiscal tightening in Britain, made in the IMF *World Economic Outlook*. He is reported as having said that:

> Britain's fiscal policy would continue to be set in a medium term framework and would not be used for short term demand management. ... Attempts at fiscal fine tuning would offset the beneficial supply side effects of cuts in tax rates (*Financial Times*, 26 September 1988).

Similar views have been expressed in other countries.

Second, depending on the details of the budgetary process, the implementation lag may be quite long for a change in tax rates. This lack of flexibility may completely undermine any usefulness of fiscal policy for stabilization purposes.

Third, with respect to incomes policy, which is a potential substitute for fiscal policy, the structure of labour market institutions in many countries is such that attempts to control wages are extremely difficult. For example, in economies with highly decentralized wage setting, this option may not even be available. In addition, many governments refuse to consider incomes policy on allocative grounds, fearing that interference with such a sensitive price may jeopardize the efficient sectoral allocation of labour.

For the above reasons, and possibly others, monetary policy may be the only available instrument for stabilization purposes. In such a case, we are naturally in a second-best situation with respect to stabilization policy. The distortions imposed by the macroeconomic shocks cannot be eliminated, as the authorities have one instrument and two targets. The loss function (17) will of course be minimized, in the sense that the marginal welfare cost of unemployment will be equal to the marginal welfare cost of inflation. Setting

$\tau_j = \omega_j = 0$, the exchange rate depreciation rule that achieves this second-best outcome is given by

$$s_j^{**} = -\frac{1}{\alpha + \delta(\psi - \alpha)}\left[\delta\psi p + \frac{\lambda\delta\psi}{(1-\theta)(\varepsilon+\lambda)}\mu_j - (1-\delta)\alpha i\right] \quad (19)$$

where $\psi = \left[\dfrac{1}{\varepsilon} + \dfrac{1}{\lambda}\right]\lambda^2(1-\theta)^2$.

The exchange rate responds to domestic supply shocks and foreign price and interest rate shocks, but not to money demand disturbances. Fixed exchange rates provide the optimal response to autonomous shifts in money demand.

It would be interesting to see how this second-best exchange rate policy differs from the exchange rate policy implicit in the pursuit of a fixed nominal income target. Assume that monetary policy is used to ensure the nominal income target,

$$p + y = 0 \quad (20)$$

Substituting (20) in the money demand function (5), and then substituting in the reduced form exchange rate equation (12), we get

$$s_j^{***} = -p - \frac{1}{1 + \pi\lambda(1-\theta)}\mu_j \quad (21)$$

(21) describes the exchange rate rule implicit in using a nominal income target. This is clearly a third-best policy as can be seen by comparing it to (19). First, the authorities are doing very little about the monetary stability objective. It is as if $\delta = 1$ in the social welfare function. Fixed nominal income targets imply sub-optimal (zero) reactions to world interest rate and price shocks (see also Alogoskoufis, 1988). Even under the assumption that $\delta = 1$, nominal income targets imply a reaction of exchange rate policy to supply shocks that is sub-optimal. In the case of $\delta = 1$, the policy in (19) is of course first-best, and is given by

$$s_j^{**} = -p - \frac{1}{(1-\theta)(\varepsilon+\lambda)}\mu_j \quad (19')$$

Comparing (19') to (21), one can see that although the reaction to world inflation is optimal, the reaction to supply shocks is not (Bean, 1983; Alogoskoufis, 1985).

For these two reasons, the rule of using monetary policy to achieve a fixed nominal GDP target is clearly sub-optimal, even when inflation carries no weight in the policymakers' objective function.

Having examined the optimal individual responses in the representative country, let us now turn to the world economy.

V Optimal arrangements for the world economy

Consider a world consisting of J identical economies of the type described in the previous two sections. To close the world model, one must specify a relation that will ensure the balance between world savings and investment. Such a relation can be obtained by postulating a world *IS* curve, which can be seen as the average of the (implicit) country-specific ones. This can be written as

$$y = - \phi(i + p) \tag{22}$$

where ϕ is the semi-elasticity of aggregate expenditure with respect to the real interest rate.

Averaging the other country-specific relations, and using the condition of world savings and investment balance (22), one can easily determine all world variables. The model of world averages is presented in Table 4.1.

In order to evaluate alternative monetary arrangements for the world economy, one must specify a world social welfare function. I will assume a Benthamite objective, which is simply the sum of the welfare costs of

Table 4.1 The model of world averages

Production Function

$$y = \pi l + \mu; \ 0 < \pi < 1 \tag{1}$$

Employment

$$l = - \lambda(w - p) + \lambda\mu; \ \lambda = \sigma/(1 - \pi) \tag{2}$$

Wage Adjustment

$$w = \theta p + \omega; \ 0 < \theta < 1 \tag{3}$$

Money Demand

$$m - p = y - \alpha i + k; \ \alpha > 0 \tag{4}$$

Savings-Investment Balance

$$y = - \phi(i + p); \ \phi > 0 \tag{5}$$

Note: The model determines y, l, p, i, and w as functions of the exogenous disturbances k and μ and the world money supply m.

individual economies. This can be written as

$$H = \Sigma_{j=1}^{J} H_j = E \Sigma_{j=1}^{J} \left[\frac{\delta}{2} \left[\frac{1}{\varepsilon} + \frac{1}{\lambda} \right] (l_j - \hat{l}_j)^2 + \frac{1-\delta}{2} \alpha i_j^2 \, | \, \Lambda \right]; \quad 0 < \delta < 1$$

$$(23)$$

V.1 Fiscal policy and the first-best world monetary system

If all countries had recourse to both monetary and fiscal policy, it is easy to show that coordination of monetary policies could achieve the objective of world monetary stability, in the sense of keeping the average world interest rate at its first-best long-run equilibrium level. Coordination of monetary policies is an essential feature of the McKinnon standard, and has also found its way into Williamson (1987) and Williamson and Miller (1987) extended target zones proposal. If world policy achieves $i^* = 0$, then decentralization of national exchange rate (monetary) and fiscal policies will result in

$$s_j^* = i^* = 0 \tag{24}$$

$$\pi_j^* = (1 - \theta)p + \frac{\lambda}{\varepsilon + \lambda} \mu_j \tag{25}$$

for all $j = 1, 2, \ldots, J$. Countries will opt for fixed exchange rates and will use their fiscal policies in pursuit of the unemployment objective. The first-best is akin to McKinnon's fixed nominal exchange rate proposal, with targeting of the world money supply (or the world price level). It is equivalent to what Miller and Williamson (1988) have dubbed 'McKinnon with fiscal activism'. In general the world price level is given by

$$p = \frac{1}{\phi + \pi\lambda(1 - \theta)} \{\phi i + \pi\lambda\tau - (1 + \pi\lambda)\mu\} \tag{26}$$

Under the first-best policy ($i^* = 0, \tau^* = (1 - \theta)p + \frac{\lambda}{\varepsilon + \lambda}\mu$), we get:

$$p^* = -\frac{1}{\phi} \left[1 + \frac{\pi\varepsilon\lambda}{\varepsilon + \lambda} \right] \mu \tag{27}$$

Thus, with the optimum arrangement, world prices of traded goods react negatively to world supply shocks. This is because supply shocks increase the equilibrium (optimal) level of world output. In order to maintain the savings investment balance with $i = 0$, the price level will have to fall, so as to generate expectations of future inflation, and therefore cause a reduction in the world real interest rate. (27) can be seen as the target inflation rate towards which world monetary policy should aim, if the world were to be on a McKinnon standard.[6]

In this first-best world monetary regime there is no need for any exchange rate flexibility. Countries will simply wish to stick to fixed exchange rates in the short run. Thus, the zone around the equilibrium exchange rate seems redundant. However, this is not the case if countries have recourse to monetary policy alone. This is the case to which we turn next.

V.2 A second-best arrangement for the world economy

For the reasons stated in Section IV, and in view of recent experience, it appears highly unlikely that the authorities in many countries would be prepared to adopt the fiscal (or incomes policy) activism required by the first-best world monetary arrangement. Thus, we have to consider the optimal (second-best) arrangements in the case where monetary policy is the only instrument available for stabilization purposes. The case is analogous to the second-best policies of individual economies. Coordination of monetary policies is used to minimize the distortions caused by the aggregate components of the supply and money demand disturbances, and decentralized exchange rate management by individual economies is used to minimize the distortions caused by the country-specific components. The second-best world interest rate rule is

$$i^{**} = -(\gamma_1/\gamma_2)\mu \tag{28}$$

where $\gamma_1 = \dfrac{\delta\psi\lambda^2(\phi + \pi\lambda(1 - \theta)) - (\varepsilon + \lambda)(1 + \pi\lambda)}{(\phi + \pi\lambda(1 - \theta))(\varepsilon + \lambda)(1 - \theta)\lambda}$,

$\gamma_2 = (1 - \delta)\alpha + \dfrac{\delta\psi\theta}{\phi\pi\lambda(1 - \theta)}$

Once world interest rates (or the money stock or the price level) are set optimally, individual countries will manage their exchange rates according to the rule

$$s_j^{**} = -\frac{\lambda}{\delta\psi(1 - \theta)(\varepsilon + \lambda)}\mu(j) \tag{29}$$

From (29), the standard deviations of nominal exchange rates in a second-best world will be proportional to the standard deviation of relative supply shocks only. The nominal exchange rate flexibility envisaged in the

Williamson proposal is essential in a second-best world, although the analysis in this paper offers no rationale for formally confining nominal exchange rate changes within a 'hard' target zone. A target zone with 'soft buffers', as envisaged in the extended Williamson proposal, might be better in this respect. In any case, if a band were to be adopted formally, its width should reflect the standard deviation of relative supply shocks.

V.3   Robustness of the results

A question that naturally arises relates to the robustness of the results to model specifications and the postulated social welfare functions.

First, the results carry over to a more general model, with traded and non-traded goods, and a more general wage adjustment equation (Alogoskoufis, 1987).

Second, the results are unaffected qualitatively if one postulates other stationary stochastic processes for the exogenous disturbances, such as AR(1) processes. The analysis is slightly more complicated and the notation necessarily heavier.

Third, the results do not change qualitatively if one replaces the law of one price condition for tradeables by a more traditional *IS* curve. Again the penalty is notational complexity, as there is at least one extra parameter (the elasticity of aggregate demand with respect to competitiveness), and potentially one extra disturbance to worry about.

Fourth, the results are robust to using inflation directly, instead of nominal interest rates in the monetary stability objective. In the latter case the world welfare objective (23) is transformed to,

$$H = \Sigma_{j=1}^{J} H_j = E \, \Sigma_{j=1}^{J} \left[\frac{\delta}{2} \left[\frac{1}{\varepsilon} + \frac{1}{\lambda} \right] (l_j - \hat{l}_j)^2 + \frac{1 - \delta}{2} (s_j + p)^2 \, | \, \Lambda \right]; \, 0 < \delta < 1$$

$$(30)$$

When fiscal policy is an option, coordination of monetary policy to achieve the world monetary stability objective will result in $p^* = 0$. The optimal world rate of inflation of traded goods will be zero. Then, decentralization of exchange rate and fiscal policies will result in

$$s^* = 0 \qquad\qquad (31)$$

$$\pi_j^* = \frac{\lambda}{\varepsilon + \lambda} \mu_j \qquad\qquad (32)$$

Again the McKinnon solution emerges with fiscal policy flexibility. Without the latter, the second-best outcome will be coordination of monetary policies to achieve the (constrained) optimal rate of inflation of traded goods, which is given by

$$p^{**} = -\frac{\xi\lambda^2}{(\xi + 1 - \delta)(\varepsilon + \lambda)}\mu \tag{33}$$

where $\xi = \delta\lambda^2(1 - \theta)^2\left[\dfrac{1}{\varepsilon} + \dfrac{1}{\lambda}\right]$.

Decentralization of exchange rate management will then result in

$$s_j^{**} = -\frac{\xi\lambda^2}{(\xi + 1 - \delta)(\varepsilon + \lambda)}\mu(j) \tag{34}$$

The second-best standard deviation of exchange rates is again proportional to the standard deviation of relative supply shocks, although the factor of proportionality is now different. The exchange rate flexibility envisaged in the Williamson proposal is necessary, and the width of the band, in case one was formally adopted, should depend on the variability of relative supply shocks.

A more extensive sensitivity analysis would of course be required for a fuller evaluation of the robustness of the results, but this exceeds the scope of any single paper. One set of circumstances for which the results are not robust relates to differences in economic structure, or differences in policy objectives among countries. This may help explain the empirical results of Hughes Hallett *et al.* (1989).

VI Conclusions

The conclusions of the analysis can be summarized as follows: First, with fiscal policy flexibility, the McKinnon proposal of monetary policy coordination geared towards the monetary stability (inflation) objective, and fixed exchange rates, is not only desirable, but also feasible, as it is incentive-compatible for every individual economy. The big if, which may also explain why it has not been adopted, is that this regime requires a great deal of fiscal policy activism, which may not be forthcoming. In such a case, the short-term nominal exchange rate flexibility envisaged in the Williamson target zones proposal is necessary. However, this paper offers no theoretical rationale for any limits on short-run exchange rate flexibility. Wide zones with 'soft buffers', as suggested by Williamson, may not be too far off the optimal world monetary arrangement, especially if the 'buffers' are made conditional on relative real shocks.

Two other elements of the target zones proposal are worth mentioning. First, the announcement of target parities. This is necessary as a guide to expectations about the future evolution of the exchange rate. Note that in deriving the rational expectations solution, I have used it as a condition to avoid 'bootstrap' solutions. The second feature is the recent addition to the proposal that envisages nominal income targets. Williamson suggests that nominal income targets should be pursued through coordinated monetary policy at the world level, and through fiscal policies at the national level. Let me deal with each element in turn.

Fixed nominal income targets at the world level are sub-optimal, for the very reason that they are suboptimal in the closed economy, namely supply shocks (Bean, 1983). On the other hand, an optimal conditional nominal income target is formally equivalent to either an optimal conditional monetary target, or an optimal conditional price-level target. In fact Williamson (1987) suggests that 'A target for nominal income growth need not ... take the naive form of a constant growth rate' (p.203). Thus, this element of the proposal does not seem too controversial.

The more controversial element is the one which suggests that 'National fiscal policies should be revised with a view to achieving national target rates of growth of nominal income' (Williamson, 1987, p.204). If fiscal policy is an option, then it can be used to affect unemployment. Of course, this can always be expressed as a conditional nominal income target. In that case, however, there is no need for short-term nominal exchange rate flexibility, and we are back to the McKinnon standard, which is the first-best international regime. On the other hand, if fiscal policy is available but is artificially constrained to aim for a fixed nominal income target, the result is a sub-optimal arrangement away from the attainable first best.

Notes

1 In a companion paper, Alogoskoufis (1987), I examine these issues in a more realistic model with both internationally traded and non-traded goods, and a more general wage adjustment equation.

2 For a survey of alternative models of stabilization policy in open economies see Marston (1985).

3 The individual country model used in this paper is similar in most respects to that of Aizenman and Frenkel (1985), where the reader is referred for more details. The present analysis differs from this in the simultaneous consideration of the monetary stability objective and in the potential use of fiscal policy.

4 More generally, τ can be seen as the deviation in the total tax wedge between the producer wage and the net consumption wage, if the latter is defined as $w - p$. This wedge can be affected not only by payroll taxes, but also by income and indirect taxes.

5 In much of the subsequent analysis, ω will be set to zero, as we shall concentrate on fiscal and monetary policy. With two targets and certainty about the parameters a third instrument is redundant, and therefore incomes policy can be seen as a substitute for fiscal policy. Note that in this model both operate through the same channel, namely through labour costs.

6 The precise nature of this policy depends on the social welfare function. If inflation entered the objective function directly, instead of nominal interest rates, then the optimal policy would imply $p = 0$, fixed exchange rates, and world nominal interest rate adjustments to ensure savings and investment balance.

References

Aizenman J. and J.A. Frenkel (1985) 'Optimal Wage Indexation, Foreign Exchange Intervention, and Monetary Policy', *American Economic Review* **75**, 402–23.

Alogoskoufis G.S. (1985) 'Monetary, Nominal Income and Exchange Rate Targets in a Small Open Economy', Discussion Paper no. 185, Birkbeck College, forthcoming *European Economic Review*.

Alogoskoufis G.S. (1987) 'On Optimal World Stabilization and the Target Zones Proposal', CEPR Discussion Paper no. 214, London.

Alogoskoufis G.S. (1988) 'On Optimal Stabilization Policy and Nominal Income Targets in an Open Economy', CEPR Discussion Paper no. 220, London.

Bailey M.J. (1956) 'The Welfare Cost of Inflationary Finance', *Journal of Political Economy* **64**, 93–110.

Bean C.R. (1983) 'Targeting Nominal Income: An Appraisal', *Economic Journal* **93**, 806–19.

Branson W.H. (1986) 'The Limits of Monetary Coordination as Exchange Rate Policy', *Brookings Papers on Economic Activity* **1**, 175–94.

Currie D. and S. Wren-Lewis (1987) 'Evaluating the Extended Target Zones Proposal for the G-3', CEPR Discussion Paper no. 221, London.

Dornbusch R. (1976) 'Expectations and Exchange Rate Dynamics', *Journal of Political Economy* **84**, 1161–76.

Dornbusch R. (1986) 'Flexible Exchange Rates and Excess Capital Mobility', *Brookings Papers on Economic Activity* **1**, 209–26.

Dornbusch R. (1988) 'Doubts about the McKinnon Standard', *Journal of Economic Perspectives* **2**, 105–12.

Edison H., M.H. Miller and J. Williamson (1986) 'On Evaluating and Extending the Target Zone Proposal', *Journal of Policy Modelling* **9**, 199–224.

Fischer S. (1986) 'Comment', *Brookings Papers on Economic Activity* **1**, 227–32.

Frenkel J. (1987) 'The International Monetary System: Should it be Reformed?' *American Economic Review, Papers and Proceedings* **77**, 205–10.

Gray J.A. (1976) 'Wage Indexation: A Macroeconomic Approach', *Journal of Monetary Economics* **2**, 221–35.

Harberger A. (1971) 'Three Basic Postulates for Applied Welfare Economics: An Interpretive Essay', *Journal of Economic Literature* **9**, 785–97.

Hughes Hallett A.J., Holtham G.H. and G.J. Hutson (1989) 'Exchange Rate Targetting as Surrogate International Cooperation', this volume.

Kenen P. (1987) 'Exchange Rate Management: What Role for Intervention?', *American Economic Review*, Papers and Proceedings **77**, 194–99.

Marston R.C. (1985) 'Stabilization Policy in Open Economies', in R. Jones and P. Kenen (eds), *Handbook of International Economics*, Amsterdam, North Holland.

McCallum B.T. (1983) 'On Non-Uniqueness in Rational Expectations Models: An Attempt at Perspective', *Journal of Monetary Economics* **11**, 139–68.

McKinnon R. I. (1963) 'Optimum Currency Areas', *American Economic Review* **53**, 717–25.

McKinnon R.I. (1974) 'A New Tripartite Monetary Agreement or a Limping Dollar Standard', *Essays in International Finance*, 106, Princeton University.

McKinnon R.I. (1980), 'Dollar Stabilization and American Monetary Policy', *American Economic Review*, Papers and Proceedings **70**, 382–87.

McKinnon R.I. (1982) 'Currency Substitution and Instability in the World Dollar Standard', *American Economic Review* **72**, 320–33.

McKinnon R.I. (1984) *An International Standard for Economic Stabilization*, Washington DC, Institute for International Economics.

McKinnon R.I. (1988) 'Monetary and Exchange Rate Policies for International Financial Stability: A Proposal', *Journal of Economic Perspectives* **2**, 83–103.

Meade J.E. (1951) *The Balance of Payments*, Oxford, Oxford University Press.

Miller M.H. and J. Williamson (1988) 'The International Monetary System: An Analysis of Alternative Regimes', *European Economic Review* **32**, 1031–54.

Williamson J. (1965) 'The Crawling Peg', *Essays in International Finance*, 50, Princeton University.

Williamson J. (1983) *The Exchange Rate System*, Washington DC, Institute for Intenational Economics.

Williamson J. (1986) 'Target Zones and the Management of the Dollar', *Brookings Papers on Economic Activity* **1**, 165–74.

Williamson J. (1987) 'Exchange Rate Management: The Role of Target Zones', *American Economic Review*, Papers and Proceedings **77**, 200–4.

Williamson J. and M.H. Miller (1987) *Targets and Indicators: A Blueprint for the International Coordination of Economic Policy*, Washington DC, Institute for International Economics.

Discussion

Neil Rankin

George Alogoskoufis's paper is a welcome attempt to study proposals for new international monetary regimes using a simple analytical model, in contrast to the ambitious and complex simulations carried out on large theoretical or econometric models. Important as the latter are, they regrettably often appear as 'black box' exercises, allowing their inputs and their outputs to be examined and discussed, but offering only a limited view of the inner mechanisms by which inputs and outputs are linked. To cut through the mass of real-world detail which the larger models faithfully reproduce, and still to yield results which have a strong claim to practical policy relevance, requires much careful judgment and ingenuity. This paper, while it inevitably leaves room for serious debate, demonstrates both these qualities, and provides a valuable complement to the simulation approach, with potential for further fruitful developments in future.

The structure of the model of an individual country which is employed is of a very basic nature, consisting of a money market, a labour market with a short-run money wage which is partially indexed to the price level, and a single output sector, the output being an internationally-traded good. Having read also the companion paper in which a non-traded goods sector is introduced, I would agree that the single-sector assumption is inessential to the conclusions. Nevertheless, this does imply that the only way in which fiscal policy affects output in the model is a pure 'supply-side' one, giving no importance to its effects on demand. Under a fixed exchange rate the real product wage is exogenous to the country by virtue of the 'law of one price', and so determines employment by picking off a particular point on the demand curve for labour. Fiscal policy works because it takes the form of an employment tax on the firm, and so is able to shift the labour demand curve up or down. Had fiscal policy taken the form of government purchases of output, or of an income tax, it would have been powerless to affect employment and output in this framework. In order to restore the more conventional effects of fiscal policy operating via aggregate demand, one would need either a non-traded-goods sector in a state of excess supply, or that the country's output be internationally differentiated, so that it would face a downward-sloping demand curve. Either of these would allow 'quantity spillovers' from the goods to the labour market, and thus a more recognizably Keynesian transmission mechanism. While I would regard this as empirically a more plausible story, I accept that it has no bearing on the general nature of the policy conclusions obtained.

The main results are that when each government has both monetary and fiscal policy available as instruments, then, given some cooperative agreement by which aggregate world monetary policy ensures a constant average world interest rate, the optimal policy for any individual country is to operate monetary policy to fix its exchange rate, in the sense of not allowing the latter to respond to country-specific random shocks; but that when only monetary policy is available, optimal policy requires that each country's exchange rate should be allowed to respond to certain types of shock. The first (the 'first-best') case is claimed to have a broad resemblance to McKinnon's proposed international monetary regime; while the second (the 'second-best') is suggested to be more consistent with the alternative, 'target zones', regime proposed by Williamson.

The first-best case appears to offer a neat theoretical justification for a new world regime in which a key feature would be fixed exchange rates. However, what it in fact proves is the case for agreeing to coordinate world monetary policy in order to achieve a constant world interest rate. The result that a fixed exchange rate is optimal is shown to be crucially dependent on this. Once such a policy has been agreed, there is no need to *agree* on fixed exchange rates in addition, because it is then in each country's own interest to fix its exchange rate. The nature of the sacrifice which individual countries are asked to make if they are to join the new regime, seems to be, not to relinquish sovereignty over their exchange rates and to negotiate over international parities, but rather to agree to control (in a way which is not made explicit in the paper) some world aggregate of money supplies. The model thus provides a justification for individual countries to adopt exchange rate targets, but at the level of international regimes, it instead provides a justification for an agreement to target the world interest rate. Given the importance of the latter, it would perhaps be desirable to make explicit in the model the means by which international liquidity is to be controlled.

An appealing feature of the fixed-rates result is its apparent robustness to a number of changes of specification. Not only does introducing non-traded goods leave it unaffected, so does substituting incomes policy for fiscal policy, and so too does redefining the welfare function to make deviations of the price level, rather than of the interest rate, the object of concern. The alternative welfare function, in fact, would seem more reasonable than the original. Inflation and unemployment are widely accepted as the arguments of similar loss functions, whereas deviations of the interest rate causing sub-optimal holdings of real money balances are harder to credit with the same practical importance.

If one were nevertheless to seek modifications under which fixing the exchange rate might cease to be optimal even in the first-best case, two in particular might be suggested. First, suppose a country-specific random shock is introduced to the uncovered interest parity condition (6), so replacing it by $i_j = i - s_j + \varepsilon_j$, where ε_j is the shock. Since, as an empirical matter, uncovered interest parity is known to hold only very imperfectly, this kind of 'stochastic risk premium' does not seem implausible. Then it is not difficult to see that, although the optimal fiscal policy rule (18), is unchanged, the exchange rate rule is now $s_j = i - \varepsilon_j$. When world monetary policy is coordinated to ensure $i = 0$, we have $s_j = -\varepsilon_j$: the exchange rate should be allowed to fluctuate to absorb the UIP shock, and should not be held constant as previously. Second, as an alternative to this, consider the case in which p_j rather than i_j is used in the welfare function, and suppose there is a country-specific random shock, η_j, in the 'law of one price'. (7) is thus replaced by $p_j = s_j + p + \eta_j$. This too would seem a realistic modification, in view of the failure of purchasing power parity in practice. The optimal exchange rate rule is now to set $s_j = -p - \eta_j$. When world monetary policy is coordinated to ensure $p = 0$ we obtain $s_j = -\eta_j$, so that again the fixed-rate rule is no longer optimal. These modifications indicate that the two arbitrage conditions are made to do a great deal of work. To the extent that they hold only approximately in practice, complete rigidity of the exchange rate is no longer optimal.

A final point concerns the device of specifying the model entirely in terms of 'deviations' of variables from some underlying equilibrium. This seems legitimate insofar as the interest is in short-run, stabilization objectives. However, it does mean that the fixed exchange rates conclusion must not be taken too literally. If the underlying equilibrium is a moving one, for example because of differing international growth rates or changing world trade patterns, then the actual optimal exchange rate may not be constant at all. As a suggestion for future research, it would be particularly interesting to see the present framework transformed into a dynamic one.

Chapter 5

Commodity price indicators: A case for discretion rather than rules*

Alison Hook and David Walton

I Introduction

Although world inflation levels have fallen dramatically in the 1980s, inflation is still one of the major concerns of policymakers in the industrialized countries. Over the last decade monetary targets have been used as intermediate objectives in the pursuit of low inflation. However, empirical evidence suggests that the relationship between money supply growth and consumer price inflation, which appeared to hold until around 1980, has now broken down. Large deviations in the velocity of money from previous patterns have meant that an upward trend in money supply growth has been accompanied by a downward trend in consumer price inflation. A number of explanations have been put forward for these changes, including deregulation, large movements in interest rates and financial innovations, but at present there is no clear understanding of how such factors combine to explain variations in velocity. Yet without stable and predictable trends in velocity, it is difficult to have faith in monetary targets as an intermediate objective.

Policymakers have increasingly come to recognize that monetary targets

* We would like to thank Marcus Miller who initiated this research and Barry Eichengreen, James Boughton, Ken Warwick and a number of paricipants at this conference for many helpful comments. We would also like to acknowledge the Parliamentary Unit at Warwick University for making Saddlepoint available and, in particular, Alan Sutherland for his help and advice. Thanks are also due to Geraldine Davis for her expert typing. The views expressed are our own and are not necessarily those of either the Foreign and Commonwealth Office or Goldman Sachs. Any errors are also our own.

BLUEPRINTS FOR EXCHANGE RATE MANAGEMENT
0-12-497060-5
Copyright © 1989 Academic Press, Ltd
All rights of reproduction reserved

need, at the very least, to be supplemented by alternative indicators of inflationary trends. The need to find additional indicators was the subject of some discussion at the Annual Meeting of the IMF/IBRD Board of Governors in September 1987, where the potential of commodity prices as an indicator attracted particular attention. In his address to the meeting, the former US Treasury Secretary, James Baker, said that a basket of commodities 'could be helpful as an early warning of potential price trends'. At the same meeting the UK Chancellor, Nigel Lawson, added that commodity prices, along with a number of other new indicators, could help to 'ensure that there is no persistent inflationary (or for that matter deflationary) bias for the group (of major industrial countries) as a whole'. Subsequently, the major seven industrialized countries have agreed to adopt a commodity price basket as an 'additional analytical instrument' to guide policymakers' monetary policy decisions.

The idea of a commodity price indicator is intuitively attractive for a number of reasons. Firstly, generalized rises in commodity prices can represent early signs of inflationary pressure. A rise in the price of raw materials, for example, will increase industrial production costs which may then be passed on to the consumer in the form of higher retail prices. Secondly a commodity price index could give a better idea of the underlying inflationary pressure facing all industrialized economies, since it is easier to measure the changes in a global commodity price basket than it is to measure the changes in the G7 total of domestically defined monetary aggregates. Finally, it is possible that commodity prices could provide an alternative nominal anchor for the international monetary system which does not depend on the ability of one country to exercise hegemony.

But are the advantages which commodity prices have over monetary or exchange rate targets sufficient to make them effective and reliable additional indicators? Manuel Johnson, the Vice-Chairman of the Federal Reserve Board, has set out three basic properties that alternative indicators should possess if they are to be a useful supplement to monetary aggregates as portents of inflationary trends:[1]

> First, useful indicators should be accurately measurable and readily available. Second, they should respond to changes in ... policy actions. And third, they should be reliably related to the ultimate goals for monetary policy.

There is no doubt that commodity prices satisfy the first property; data for a broad range of commodities are readily and continuously available. Prices are quoted on a daily basis in a variety of forms and a wide range of indices are regularly published using both consumption and trade weights. However, it may not always be true that commodity price indicators fulfil the second and third properties. In this paper we develop a theoretical model to show the links between commodity prices, inflation and monetary policy actions. We are then able to draw some inferences about the extent to which commodity prices can be used in policymaking, either as an additional indicator or more formally in the shape of a simple rule.

In Section II we examine the relationship between inflation and commodity prices in more detail and in Section III we develop a simple model of commodity price overshooting to illustrate this relationship in theoretical terms and to demonstrate how commodity prices respond to economic shocks. In particular, we show how shocks may generate commodity price movements but have no necessary implications for the growth of the money supply. Section IV examines the effects of using a simple feedback rule from commodity price movements to changes in money supply growth on output and inflation, and the final section offers some concluding observations.

II   Commodity prices and inflation

Until recently, policymakers paid relatively little attention to the role of commodity prices in the inflation process and instead focused on monetary variables and cost push factors like wages. Nevertheless, the idea that the prices of primary goods play an important causal role in inflation is not new (e.g. Kaldor, 1939). This, at first sight, appears to conflict with the evidence of a long-run declining trend in real commodity prices, on which the commodity price literature has tended to concentrate. However, this long-run effect does not necessarily mean that in the short run commodity prices will also have a negative impact on inflation, but it does suggest that if commodity prices are to be used as an inflationary indicator then they should only be used in the short run, to look for turning points in the inflation process for example. Indeed an OECD empirical study of the relationship between commodity prices and inflation undertaken by Durand and Blondal (1988) found that *changes* in commodity prices were important in determining the recent history of OECD inflation and played a greater part than commodity price *levels*. Other work has also shown the importance of rises in commodity prices for inflation, either in the major industrialized countries as a whole or for individual countries. Walton (1987) observed that the major turning points in commodity price indices led the important turning points in OECD inflation in 1973–75 and 1979–81 by about a year, and Rowlatt (1987), in her analysis of the UK inflation process, found that the major turning points in domestic inflation could also mainly be attributed to changes in the real cost of primary commodities.

The empirical evidence suggests that commodity price movements do play an important part in inflation, at least in the short run, and could therefore add a considerable body of information to guide policy decisions. If commodity prices are to be used more formally as indicators of inflation it is important to understand how changes in the prices of foodstuffs, other agricultural products and metals affect consumer and producer prices. Commodity prices obviously have a direct effect on the inflation process both as final goods (e.g. food) and as raw materials inputs into the manufacturing process. Increases in food prices will automatically raise the price of a fixed basket of consumer goods, and although some increases in raw material costs may at first be absorbed in profit margins, sooner or later finished goods prices will reflect rising raw material costs. However, commodity prices also affect the economy through other, less direct channels.

The nature of supply and demand for commodities suggests that their prices ought to be flexible as they are determined under conditions of market clearing. Although the existence of commodity price agreements, e.g. for coffee and oil, means that the flex-price assumption does not universally hold, it is still true for the majority of traded commodities and of metals in particular. Like all flex prices, commodity prices move quickly in relation to prices in other 'fixed price' markets, e.g. for labour or finished goods, and are determined partly by speculative activity. These characteristics create two channels through which changes in the prices of primary goods affect the inflation process: the *transactions* and the *speculative* effects.

The transactions effect, described by Kaldor (1976), implies that when aggregate demand is rising, the demand for commodities will also rise in order to allow output to expand. Because most commodity prices are determined under conditions of market clearing, their markets adjust much faster than finished goods markets and so the commodity price will rise immediately to reflect this higher aggregate demand. In so doing inflation rises and this will tend to choke off some of the higher aggregate demand. Thus as Kaldor observed, the combination of flexible price primary goods markets and fixed price finished goods markets means that it is the producers of primary commodities who bear much of the burden of macroeconomic adjustment, in terms of price and income volatility. Beckerman and Jenkinson (1986) produced some empirical evidence to support the hypothesis that commodity prices are one of the main channels for macroeconomic adjust-ment. They found that the correlation between wage inflation and commodity prices in the OECD was far greater than the correlation between wage inflation and unemployment. Inflation fell because lower aggregate demand fed into lower demand for commodities and then into lower wages and thus into general deflation.

The speculative channel through which commodity prices can affect inflation arises because stocks of many commodities can be held as assets. An expected rise in inflation will drive up the demand for commodities, not only through the transactions demand because output is increasing, but also because the return on holding commodities is expected to rise. This raises the demand for stocks and hence the commodity price which, because it has some of the characteristics of an asset price, will tend to overshoot its new equilibrium level. Speculation may thus exacerbate the inflationary consequences of rising aggregate demand. The overshooting mechanism which is central to much of the recent literature of commodity prices in a macroeconomic context (e.g. Frankel, 1986), is explored in more detail in the next section.

The most familiar flex price in macroeconomic literature is probably the exchange rate. The flex price similarities between commodity prices and exchange rates have led much of the macroeconomic literature on commodity prices to follow the exchange rate overshooting framework developed by Dornbusch (1976) and Buiter and Miller (1982). However, there is some debate over the possible differences between the adjustment of commodity prices and exchange rates in a macroeconomic context. In particular, it is possible that rising and falling commodity prices do not affect the economy to the same degree. For example, it may be true that firms do not pass on falling raw material costs as quickly as they pass on rising costs, thereby forcing commodity prices to fall further to achieve a deflation than they need to rise in order to achieve an inflation of the same magnitude. Moutos and Vines (1987) discuss in some detail the potential existence of other non-linearities in commodity price adjustment, associated with stock adjustment in particular. They suggest that there may be asymmetries between good and bad harvests since there is less scope for building up stocks after a bad harvest than for running down stocks after a good harvest. To allow for this behaviour would require a highly non-linear model which, although more realistic, would necessarily be much more complex than the linear model developed in the next section. Moreover, there is little empirical evidence to support the macroeconomic importance of these non-linearities.

Commodity prices also differ from exchange rates in that they can have effects on inflation at a global level. A country may try to reduce the inflation rate by allowing its exchange rate to appreciate but when the source of inflation is general, this may be matched by a beggar-thy-neighbour appreciation from other countries, thereby negating the first country's attempt at reducing inflation with the result that all countries end up pursuing excessively contractionary policies. That monetary policy might be too tight if countries do not cooperate is a result familiar from the policy co-ordination literature (e.g. Sachs, 1983). However, the global monetary tightening that results from these beggar-thy-neighbour policies will tend to reduce the transactions and speculative demand for commodities, causing their price to fall. Under these conditions commodity prices will be the channel through

which either coordinated or uncoordinated government policies may successfully reduce inflation. There may therefore be a role for commodity prices
to supplement exchange rate targets, to ensure that the global monetary
stance is neither too loose nor too tight.

In this section, we have argued that commodity prices possess one of the
desirable characteristics of an intermediate target, namely that they are
closely related to real output growth and inflation. In the next section we
develop a commodity price overshooting model to show how the adjustment
processes considered in this section may work.

III The dynamics of commodity prices

In order to analyse the macroeconomic relationship between monetary
policy, commodity prices and consumer prices, we adopt a theoretical
framework which shares many of the features of the exchange rate analysis
developed by Dornbusch (1976) and extended by Buiter and Miller (1982).
Like these exchange rate models, it is the differential adjustment speeds of
goods and asset markets which causes the complex dynamics in our
commodity price model following economic shocks. Such a framework has
also been adopted by Frankel (1986), Hook (1987), Moutos and Vines (1988),
and Walton (1988) to analyse the impact of various policy changes on
commodity prices, output and inflation.

In the model, we make the simplifying assumption that commodities are
perfect substitutes for other assets in portfolios, so that the expected capital
gain on commodity stocks equals the short-term interest rate; any differences
in expected return should be arbitraged away. Formally, we have

$$Dq = r \tag{1}$$

where q is the logarithm of commodity prices, r is the short-term nominal
interest rate, such as the rate on Treasury Bills and D is the differential
operator with respect to time, i.e. $Dx = dx/dt$. Equation (1) ignores the risk
premium and the storage cost associated with holding commodities, both of
which are likely to raise the required rate of return from holding commodities
in preference to other assets which bear a positive yield. We also ignore the
convenience yield that is generated by the transactions motive for holding
commodities. This would tend to reduce the required rate of return on
commodities, particularly when the amount of stocks held is low. In practice,
therefore, the arbitrage relationship given by Equation (1) would be expected
to be much looser than that indicated by the analogous uncovered interest
parity condition in the foreign exchange market. It seems most likely to be
a good approximation to reality when commodity stocks are high since then

the convenience yield would be close to zero and the effect of a disequilibrium between flow demand and flow supply would have only a marginal effect on the commodity price.[2] There are other possible approaches which can avoid some of the simplifications of this condition. Van Duyne (1979) and more recently Moutos and Vines (1988), for example, consider a portfolio approach, in which the different assets considered: money, commodities, foreign exchange (bonds in Moutos and Vines) are imperfect substitutes. This has the drawback, however, of introducing a third dynamic equation showing the accumulation of commodity stocks. Adopting this approach enriches the dynamics but as Moutos and Vines (1988) show, most of the qualitative properties of the model are unaffected.

The specification of the rest of the model is similar to the log-linear exchange rate model of Buiter and Miller (1982). However, we are able to ignore the exchange rate in this model by considering the OECD as a whole. In effect the OECD is treated as a closed economy. While exchange rate changes affect the evolution of inflation across different countries, at the aggregate level these are assumed to have no impact on the average level of inflation.[3] The rest of the model is described by Equations (2) to (6):

$$m - p = ky - \lambda r + \varepsilon \qquad k, \lambda > 0 \tag{2}$$

$$y = - \gamma(r - Dp) + \delta(q - p_m - c^*) \qquad \gamma, \delta > 0 \tag{3}$$

$$Dp_m = \phi y + \pi + \sigma D(q - p_m) \qquad \phi, \sigma > 0 \tag{4}$$

$$p = \alpha p_m + (1 - \alpha)q \qquad 0 < \alpha < 1 \tag{5}$$

$$\pi = Dm = \mu \tag{6}$$

The notation is as follows:

m = domestic money stock (in logs)
p_m = price index of domestic manufactured goods (in logs)
y = real output, measured from its non-inflationary level (in logs)
r = domestic short-term nominal interest rate
q = price index of commodities (in logs)
p = general price level (in logs)
c^* = equilibrium real commodity price (in logs)
ε = random velocity shock
π = trend or core rate of inflation
μ = growth of money supply
D = differential with respect to time

Equation (2) defines equilibrium in the domestic money market (the *LM* curve), where the demand for real balances depends positively on real output and negatively on the opportunity cost of holding money, measured by r. The LM curve is subject to random shocks to velocity (money demand) which may be either permanent or temporary. The level of output is demand-determined and, as shown by the IS curve in Equation (3), depends negatively on the short real interest rate and positively on a wealth effect summarized by the relative price of commodities *vis-à-vis* manufactured goods. In addition, following Walton (1988), we include a term c^* which represents the assumed equilibrium relationship between commodity prices and manufactured goods prices. As specified, this term implies that commodity prices and manufactured goods prices are cointegrated (using the terminology of Engle and Granger, 1987) or, more intuitively, that they share a common trend over time. Yet there can be no guarantee that c^* is constant over time – its evolution will be determined by exogenous supply factors such as oil prices and resource industry costs – and this is borne out by the empirical evidence of Durand and Blondal (1988). A more complete formulation of this model would include the dynamics of c^* but for short-run analysis it seems reasonable to assume that an equilibrium relationship exists between commodity and goods prices at any point in time. c^* is assumed to be unaffected by monetary factors. The inclusion of this term is designed to capture the effect of permanent real shocks to the commodity price, which will change the equilibrium relationship between p_m and q. The next section illustrates the importance of distinguishing between real and monetary shocks.

Inflation, given in Equation (4), evolves according to the state of excess demand on the economy and its augmented by the underlying core rate of inflation, π and a term $\sigma D(q - p_m)$ which acts as an 'error-correction' mechanism. The latter term helps to restore the existing equilibrium relationship between commodity prices and manufactured good prices (i.e. for a given c^*) when it has been disturbed by unanticipated changes in commodity prices. The augmentation term in this version of the model is taken to be the equal to the rate of growth of the money supply, μ. A more general formulation would allow the core rate of inflation to evolve more slowly in response to built-in trends in wages and prices but this does not add much to the qualitative results derived from this type of model. In the long run, monetary policy is assumed to be neutral. The speed of adjustment of prices is not the same in all markets, however. Asset markets can react quickly; thus current and anticipated future monetary policy actions are reflected immediately in commodity prices, set as they are in a forward-looking, efficient auction market. But the same expectations are reflected only gradually and with a lag in domestic nominal labour costs and goods prices. Accordingly, we rule out jumps in the general price level, given by Equation (5), except where they result directly from a jump in the price of commodities used as final goods.

The dynamics are conveniently summarized in terms of the two state variables l and c,

$$l = m - p_m \qquad (7)$$

$$c = q - p_m \qquad (8)$$

Real liquidity, l is a backward-looking or predetermined variable. With the price of domestic output predetermined in the short run, real liquidity can only make discrete jumps when the money stock is changed discontinuously. By contrast, real commodity prices, c, is a forward-looking or jump variable which is not at all dependent on its past history. Real commodity prices jump whenever nominal commodity prices, q, jump, given that the price of domestic output is taken to be predetermined.

The state-space representation of the model given by equations (1) to (8) may, after substituting for y and r, be expressed as two simultaneous differential equations in l and c. Thus

$$
\begin{bmatrix} Dl \\ Dc \end{bmatrix} = \frac{1}{\Delta} \begin{bmatrix} \sigma - \alpha\gamma\phi & (1-\alpha)(\alpha\gamma\phi - \sigma) - \delta(\phi\lambda + \sigma k) \\ -1 & \delta(k - \phi\lambda) + 1 - \alpha \end{bmatrix} \begin{bmatrix} l \\ c \end{bmatrix}
$$
$$
+ \frac{1}{\Delta} \begin{bmatrix} -\lambda(\alpha\gamma\phi - \sigma) & \delta(\phi\lambda + \sigma k) & \alpha\gamma\phi - \sigma \\ -\lambda & -\delta(k - \phi\lambda) & 1 \end{bmatrix} \begin{bmatrix} \mu \\ c^* \\ \varepsilon \end{bmatrix} \qquad (9)
$$

where $\Delta = \alpha\gamma(k - \phi\lambda) + \lambda(1 + \sigma)$. A necessary and sufficient condition for the stationary equilibrium of this model to be a 'saddlepoint' is that the determinant of the state matrix is negative, indicating two roots of opposite sign. This is satisfied provided $\alpha\gamma(\phi\lambda - k) - \phi - \sigma\lambda < 0$, which we assume holds true. The dynamic system, set out in (9), is shown graphically in Figure 5.1. In the following analysis, we assume that commodity prices are on the linear stable manifold, SS, associated with the negative root.

We now consider two types of shock, a change in money demand and a real disturbance, in order to illustrate the dynamics of commodity and goods prices. Our concern here is to consider shocks which generate commodity price movements but have no necessary implications for the growth of the money supply.

III.1   Adjustment to a velocity (money demand) shock

Under the assumptions of this model, the long-run effect of an autonomous unanticipated permanent 10% increase in the demand for money, with a non-accommodating monetary policy, is an equiproportionate fall in the price of commodities and manufactured goods, which increases the level of

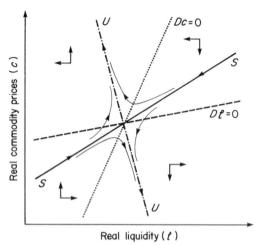

Real liquidity (l)

Figure 5.1   Saddlepoint equilibrium

real balances by 10% without changing the monetary growth rate. In Figure 5.2, this is given by a shift of $Dl = 0$ and $Dc = 0$, and the long-run equilibrium moves from point *A* to point *C*. However, in the short run because of the 'stickiness' of prices in the goods and labour markets, manufactured goods prices do not at first change. Initially, to restore equilibrium in the money market, interest rates have to rise. This leads to a fall in aggregate demand and to a decrease in the transactions demand for commodities, and therefore over time to a fall in the price of commodities and goods, thereby increasing real balances to their new level. However, the initial rise in interest rates raises the relative cost of holding commodities as an asset. This reduces the speculative demand for commodities and causes a further fall in their price. Any increase in interest rates above their long-run level requires the expectation of a rise in commodity prices if the arbitrage condition is to be satisfied. This can only be achieved if commodity prices overshoot their long-run level initially (to point *B* in Figure 5.2), and then gradually rise to their new equilibrium.

In principle, therefore, it would seem that changes in commodity prices could give additional information about inflationary trends. A common finding in all theoretical work (e.g. Frankel, 1986; Moutos and Vines, 1988; and Walton, 1988) is that in response to *all* types of monetary shock, commodity prices both overshoot and lead consumer prices. However, it is not always the case that a sudden rise in commodity prices is indicative of a subsequent rise in consumer prices. To illustrate this, we now consider the theoretical implications of a supply shock.

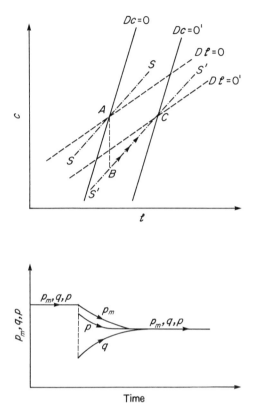

Figure 5.2 Adjustment to a velocity shock

III.2 Adjustment to a restriction in the supply of commodities

In the event of a shock which permanently restricts the supply of commodities, their equilibrium price relative to manufactured goods $(q - p_m)$ will rise to a new level of c^* (from c_0 to c_1 in Figure 5.3), in order to re-establish equilibrium in both markets for a given level of output. An exogenous increase in commodity prices will tend to depress aggregate demand by worsening the terms of trade with commodity producers and will consequently lead to deflation. In the absence of an accommodating monetary policy, commodity prices will be higher in the long run while manufactured goods prices (and the aggregate price level) will fall. To maintain equilibrium in the money market, interest rates will fall over time to ensure that the increase in real balances (l_0 to l_1 in Figure 5.3), resulting from the lower price level, is willingly held. Immediately after the supply shock interest rates will be above their new long-run equilibrium level. From the commodity price

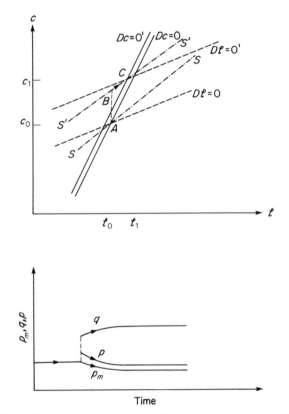

Figure 5.3   Adjustment to a restriction in the supply of commodities

arbitrage condition, this would induce the expectation of a commodity price appreciation. But although commodity prices jump (from *A* to *B* in Figure 5.3), they do not rise by the full amount of the change in the equilibrium relative price in order that there may be the rational expectation of an appreciation towards the new equilibrium price (at point *C* in Figure 5.3).

The results of these two exercises show that commodity price movements may be accompanied by changes in the general price level *with no necessary change in the growth of the money supply*. In this respect, commodity prices contain information about inflation additional to that given by monetary aggregates alone. However, depending on the source of the shock to the economic system, a rise in commodity prices could imply either a rise or a fall in the general price level. It therefore appears that unless the source of the shock is known, considerable care needs to be taken in interpreting commodity price movements.

IV   A policy role for commodities?

At present the G7 have agreed only to monitor two commodity price baskets[4] and not automatically to respond to their movements. However, given the information which they contain, there may be a case for increasing the role of commodity price indices in monetary policy. The question is, given the evidence of Sections II and III, what sort of role should this be?

At one extreme commodity price indices could be incorporated into policy in the form of a commodity standard. Supporters of such a standard argue that this type of a regime would be a more effective limit on money creation than the present fiat money system operated by the G7, and would thus help to produce international financial stability. A commodity standard would operate like the Gold Standard whereby the money price of one commodity, or more likely a weighted basket of commodities, would be fixed and governments would intervene to maintain the dollar price of the basket rather than the price of individual commodities in the basket.

However, as Garner (1985) suggests, a commodity standard may not be appropriate since it is unlikely to possess all of the characteristics which are desirable in a monetary system. An ideal monetary system should deliver long-term aggregate price stability at low resource cost, i.e. in terms of resources diverted from production, and with a minimal amount of short-run price fluctuations. Although a commodity price standard would successfully limit the creation of money, because the natural limits on commodity production would control the amount of new money which could be issued without devaluing the currency, it would not necessarily deliver long-term price stability. If there is a long-term downward trend in real commodity prices, as was suggested in Section II, then a monetary policy designed to stabilize the price of commodities will lead to an upward trend in industrial prices (this is simply the converse of the example given in Section III.2). A commodity standard would also be worse in that it would divert commodities from industrial production to the monetary system, and as such would have real resource costs. Furthermore, even if the monetary system were not disturbed by monetary shocks but by supply shocks, which only changed the relative prices of commodities in the basket, and did not represent generalized price changes, the government would still have to intervene in order to maintain the value of the whole basket.

Thus there are good arguments against adopting a commodity standard in the strict sense of the term. However, given the additional information which commodity prices contain, there may be some argument for adopting them as intermediate inflationary indicators. We have already argued in Section II that commodity prices are closely related to the main goals of macroeconomic policy, but Section III suggests that unless the reasons for commodity price movements are clear they may not be reliable indicators. In the rest of this section we look at whether, under these circumstances, movements in commodity prices should automatically be linked to monetary policy actions.

The linkage could be introduced in the form of a G7 commodity price rule. In designing such a rule, we assume that the objective of the G7 countries is to stabilize inflation and output around their steady-state levels. In line with the experience of recent years, policymakers are also assumed to follow a money supply growth rule, $Dm = \mu$. However, this does not always deliver the desired inflation outcome because of the incidence of shocks to velocity (changes in money demand) and to commodity prices. In addition to following a money supply rule, policymakers are able to observe changes in commodity prices and they now wish to use them as an 'additional analytical instrument' for operating monetary policy.

The most obvious way of choosing a commodity price rule would be to minimize some explicit objective function subject to the equations of the model in Section III. As Edison, Miller and Williamson (1987) point out, however, such explicit policy optimizations are subject to two major criticisms. The first is that rules derived in this way are only optimal with respect to particular objective function and the model chosen. The rules may well not be robust to misspecification of, and variations in, the model structure. This is important because, as indicated in Section II, these models may be non-linear. The second problem relates to the *time inconsistency* of optimal rules when the private sector has forward-looking expectations in the absence of precommitment on the part of policymakers.[5]

Both of these problems are potentially serious in the context of international policy coordination. At the national level there is likely to be disagreement between countries about the nature of the transmission mechanism between monetary actions, commodity prices and inflation. More importantly, individual countries may have differing concerns about commodity price movements depending on the relative weight of commodities in their production and trade. Japan, for example, which imports most of its raw materials, is more likely to be concerned about the implications of rising commodity prices for domestic inflation than the US, say, which tends to gain from favourable movements in the terms of trade because of its substantial exports of commodities. It is also unlikely that governments would have the ability to precommit themselves to the optimal rule unless they were prepared to adopt a fully-fledged commodity price standard.

For these reasons, we decided not to consider an explicit intertemporal optimisation problem but rather to consider simple feedback (or contingent) rules from commodity price changes to monetary policy actions. Such rules seem to be more in the spirit of recent G7 statements and are more likely to act as error correction mechanisms and be less dependent on the precise model structure. Support for simple rules is also given by Levine, Currie and Gaines (1989) in this volume. Specifically, we considered money supply rules of the following form:

$$\mu = -\beta c - \theta Dc \tag{10}$$

so that the money supply rule is modified according to both the direction and the rate of change of commodity price movements.

To illustrate the operation of the model, we chose parameter values as follows:

$$\lambda = 2, k = 1, \alpha = 0.75, \phi = \gamma = \delta = 0.5, \sigma = 0.25$$

With these values substituted into Equation (9), the system becomes

$$\begin{bmatrix} Dl \\ Dc \end{bmatrix} = \begin{bmatrix} 0.05 & -0.275 \\ -0.4 & 0.2 \end{bmatrix} \begin{bmatrix} l \\ c \end{bmatrix} + \begin{bmatrix} 0.1 & 0.25 & -0.05 \\ -0.8 & 0.0 & 0.5 \end{bmatrix} \begin{bmatrix} \mu \\ c^* \\ \varepsilon \end{bmatrix} \tag{12}$$

All simulations were conducted using 'Saddlepoint', described in Austin and Buiter (1982). To see the effects of operating a commodity price rule given by Equation (11), we simulated the two types of shocks described in Section III. In the presence of velocity shocks, the following rule was found to perform well in terms of minimizing the variance of inflation and output:

$$\mu = -0.2c - 0.35 Dc \tag{13}$$

Figure 5.4 shows the 'cost' of a 10% shock to velocity in terms of the square of output and inflation from following the rule given by Equation (13) compared to adopting no rule. In both cases real liquidity ends 10%

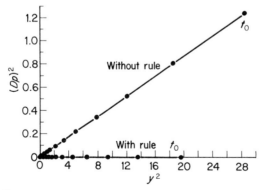

Figure 5.4 Adjustment to a velocity shock with and without a commodity price rule

higher with real commodity prices unchanged. However, the money supply rule based on information given by commodity price movements is successful at holding inflation at zero. At the same time the variability of output is reduced compared to using the rule which is not based on commodity price movements. In some ways, the rule given in Equation (10) is similiar to an interest rate rule which, from work on the assignment problem of instruments to targets (e.g. Poole, 1970), is a first-best response to velocity shocks in terms of stabilizing output. However, the major problem with simply following an interest rate rule is that there is then no nominal anchor to determine the absolute price level, a point made forcefully by Sargent and Wallace (1975). By operating a rule such as that given by (10), policymakers have the ability to neutralise velocity shocks while maintaining a nominal anchor. Table 5.1 illustrates the evolution of the main variables in response to a velocity shock both with and without the commodity price rule.

The second simulation was that of a commodity supply shock which raised the equilibrium real commodity price by 10%. In response to a jump in commodity prices, the policy reaction indicated by Equation (13) is to reduce the rate of monetary growth. This leads initially to a further drop in output from that which occurs in response to the adverse commodity supply shock. From Equation (11) the steady state rate of monetary growth is given as

Table 5.1   Responses to a 10% velocity shock

Time	l	c	y	Dp	μ
(i) *Without rule*					
0	0.0	−9.6	−5.3	−1.1	0.0
1	1.9	−7.8	−4.3	−0.9	0.0
2	3.5	−6.3	−3.5	−0.7	0.0
3	4.8	−5.1	−2.8	−0.6	0.0
4	5.8	−4.1	−2.3	−0.5	0.0
5	6.6	−3.3	−1.8	−0.4	0.0
10	8.8	−1.1	−0.6	−0.1	0.0
∞	10.0	0.0	0.0	0.0	0.0
(ii) *With rule*: $\mu = -0.2c - 0.35Dc$					
0	0.0	−8.1	−4.4	0.0	1.1
1	1.7	−6.8	−3.7	0.0	0.9
2	3.1	−5.6	−3.1	0.0	0.8
3	4.2	−4.7	−2.6	0.0	0.6
4	5.2	−3.9	−2.1	0.0	0.5
5	6.0	−3.2	−1.8	0.0	0.4
10	8.4	−1.3	−0.7	0.0	0.2
∞	10.0	0.0	0.0	0.0	0.0

$-\beta c$ which in this case is equal to -2% a year. Inflation therefore settles to a rate of -2% a year which in turn is equal to the rate of decline of commodity prices. The new equilibrium commodity price is achieved through a greater initial disinflation of manufactured goods prices than of commodity prices. As may be seen in Figure 5.5, compared with not applying the rule, the output and inflation costs are both much greater when the rule given in Equation (13) is applied. If the authorities had simply been following an interest rate rule, monetary policy would have been eased in response to the drop in output. This leads to a further sharp rise in commodity prices and a period of positive inflation. Table 5.2 illustrates the evolution of the main variables in response to a commodity supply shock both with and without the commodity price rule.

V   Conclusions

There is now a growing awareness that movements in commodity price indices may contain useful information about prospective inflation trends. The analysis in this paper suggests that commodity prices have a role in the inflation process and, perhaps more importantly, are responsive to monetary policy actions. Furthermore, we have shown how certain economic shocks can generate commodity price movements and yet have no necessary implications for the growth of the money supply. The key question is how this information might be exploited.

Essentially there are three ways in which greater use could be made of commodity prices in monetary policy decisions. At one extreme, the G7

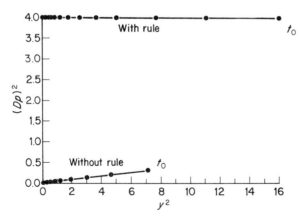

Figure 5.5 Adjustment to a commodity supply shock with and without a commodity price rule

Table 5.2   Responses to a 10% commodity supply
shock

Time	l	c	y	Dp	μ
(i) *Without rule*					
0	0.0	5.2	−2.7	−0.6	0.0
1	1.0	6.1	−2.2	−0.4	0.0
2	1.7	6.9	−1.7	−0.4	0.0
3	2.4	7.5	−1.4	−0.3	0.0
4	2.9	8.0	−1.1	−0.2	0.0
5	3.3	8.4	−0.9	−0.2	0.0
10	4.4	9.4	−0.3	−0.1	0.0
∞	5.0	10.0	0.0	0.0	0.0
(ii) *With rule:* $\mu = -0.2c - 0.35\,Dc$					
0	0.0	2.7	−4.0	−2.0	−1.0
1	1.5	3.9	−3.3	−2.0	−1.2
2	2.8	4.9	−2.8	−2.0	−1.3
3	3.8	5.8	−2.3	−2.0	−1.4
4	4.7	6.5	−1.9	−2.0	−1.5
5	5.4	7.1	−1.6	−2.0	−1.6
10	7.6	8.8	−0.6	−2.0	−1.8
∞	9.0	10.0	0.0	−2.0	−2.0

could adopt a commodity standard which would place restrictions on the independence of national monetary policies. As we indicated in Section IV, there are a number of reasons why the adoption of such a standard would be undesirable at present, and we have not pursued this line of enquiry. Alternatively, the major industrialized countries could simply monitor commodity prices in much the same way as they already follow the macroeconomic variables as indicators. This is in the spirit of the current G7 agreement. However, given both their flexibility and responsiveness to 'news', it has been suggested that commodity prices might play a more formal role in monetary policy decisions. The adoption of a rule which would call forth a policy action in response to commodity price movements is therefore a third option.

Our main concern in this paper has been to assess whether commodity price indicators are reliable enough to be given such a formal role. The tendency for commodity prices to overshoot immediately calls into question their reliability as indicators. Once governments are committed to respond to their movements, there could well be an inherent tendency for them to overreact in response to a commodity price overshoot. A more fundamental objection to the adoption of a commodity price rule, however, is that a unique rule is unlikely to exist.

Our theoretical and simulation results suggest that it is important to know the source of the change in commodity prices. For example, in Section IV we showed that modifying the money supply growth rule in response to a change in commodity prices could lead to an increase in the variability of output and inflation if supply shocks are widespread. On the other hand, a rule is likely to be effective in the case of a velocity shock, but the problem policy-makers face is that it is very difficult to know the precise nature of any particular shock to the economic system. If they did, they could take the appropriate policy action without recourse to observing commodity price movements. There is unlikely to be a unique rule, therefore, which the authorities could apply in all instances in response to any given change in commodity prices, since the source of each shock has different implications for inflation.

Many of these arguments are familiar from the 'rules versus discretion' debate which suggests that money supply rules should be adopted because they are well understood and are likely over time to enhance the anti-inflation credibility of policymakers. But our observations of commodity markets suggest that commodity price disturbances are more often derived from supply shocks rather than monetary shocks. If the world's monetary authorities were therefore to react automatically to each of these shocks, they would run the risk of introducing additional noise into monetary policy decisions, which could be counterproductive from both the point of view of stabilizing inflation and of retaining anti-inflation credibility. Sometimes, however, it may be clear that commodity prices are saying something about the underlying state of demand, and in these circumstances it would be desirable for policymakers to take appropriate policy actions. But given that it may be difficult to distinguish between different types of shock, reactions to commodity price movements call for discretion rather than rules.

Notes

1 Speech given to Conference on Dollars, Deficits and Trade, Washington, DC, sponsored by the Cato Institute, 25 February 1988.

2 One (weak) test of the plausibility of Equation (1) is to investigate whether changes in commodity prices are cointegrated with short-term interest rates. In such a regression using monthly data since 1972, the hypothesis of no cointegration was rejected at more than the 99% level.

3 This suggests a possible interesting extension to the two-country models considered by Miller (1982) and Buiter (1986) which have been used in the analysis of alternative monetary regimes by Miller and Williamson (1988). In such a model the state of

global demand would determine the evolution of world commodity prices while differences in policy would distribute the effects of commodity prices across countries via the exchange rate.

4 It was reported in the Financial Times that one contains oil and gold with weights of 50% and 5% respectively; the second contains no oil but contains gold with a 10% weight.

5 For a more complete discussion of these ideas, see the papers by Miller and Salmon, Currie and Levine, and Oudiz and Sachs in Buiter and Marston (1985).

References

Austin, G.P. and W.H. Buiter (1982) 'Saddlepoint – A Programme for Solving Continuous Time Linear Rational Expectation Models', Discussion Paper No. 39, LSE Econometrics Programme.

Beckerman, W. and T. Jenkinson (1986) 'What Stopped the Inflation? Unemployment or Commodity Prices?' *Economic Journal* **96**, 39–54.

Buiter, W.H. (1986) 'Macroeconomic Policy Design in an Interdependent World Economy', *IMF Staff Papers* **33**, 541–82.

Buiter, W.H. and R.C. Marston (eds.) (1985) *International Economic Policy Coordination*, Cambridge: Cambridge University Press.

Buiter W.H. and M.H. Miller (1982). 'Real Exchange Rate Overshooting and the Output Cost of Bringing Down Inflation', *European Economic Review* **18**, 85–123.

Dornbusch, R. (1976) 'Expectations and Exchange Rate Dynamics', *Journal of Political Economy* **84**, 1161–76.

Durand, M. and S. Blondal (1988) 'Are Commodity Prices Leading Indicators of OECD Prices?', Working Paper No. 49, OECD Department of Economics and Statistics.

Edison, H.J., M.H. Miller and J. Williamson (1987) 'On Evaluating and Extending the Target Zone Proposal', *Journal of Policy Modelling* **9**, 199–224.

Engle, R.F. and C.W.J. Granger (1987) 'Cointegration and Error Correction: Representation, Estimation and Testing', *Econometrica* **55**, 251–76.

Frankel, J.A. (1986) 'Expectations and Commodity Price Dynamics: The Overshooting Model', *American Journal of Agricultural Economics* **68**, 344–48.

Garner, C.A. (1985) 'Commodity Prices and Monetary Policy Reform', *Federal Reserve Bank of Kansas City Economic Review*, 7–21.

Hook, A.J. (1987) 'Commodity Price Overshooting – A Necessary Evil?', Mimeo, University of Warwick.

Kaldor, N. (1939) 'Speculation and Economic Stability', *Review of Economic Studies* **7**, 1–27.

Kaldor, N. (1976) 'Inflation and Recession in the World Economy', *Economic Journal* **86**, 703–14.

Levine, P., Currie, D., and J. Gaines (1988) 'The Use of Simple Rules for International Policy Agreements', this volume.

Miller, M.H. (1982) 'Differences in the Policy Mix and Consequences for Real Exchange Rates', mimeo, University of Warwick, to appear in S. Honkapohja and A. Saranto (eds.), *Raha, Inflaatio ja Talonspolitiikka, (Money, Inflation and Economic Policy)*. Helsinki: Valtion Painataskeskus (1988).

Miller, M.H. and J. Williamson (1988) 'The International Monetary System: An Analysis of Alternative Regimes', *European Economic Review*.

Moutos, T. and D. Vines (1987) 'Microeconomic and Macroeconomic Theories of Primary Commodity Prices', Mimeo, University of Glasgow.

Moutos, T. and D. Vines (1988) 'Output, Inflation and Commodity Prices', CEPR Discussion Paper No. 271.

Poole, W. (1970) 'Optimal Choice of Monetary Policy Instrument in a Simple Stochastic Macro Model', *Quarterly Journal of Economics* **84**, 197–216.

Rowlatt, P.A. (1987) 'Analysis of the Inflation Process', Working Paper No. 99, Government Economic Service.

Sachs, J. (1983) 'International Policy Coordination in a Dynamic Macroeconomic Model', NBER Working Paper No. 1166.

Sargent, T.J. and N. Wallace (1975) 'Rational Expectations, the Optimal Monetary Instrument, and the Optimal Money Supply Rate', *Journal of Political Economy* **83**, 241–54.

Van Duyne, C. (1979) 'The Macroeconomic Effects of Commodity Market Disruptions in Open Economies', *Journal of International Economics* 9, 559–82.

Walton, D. (1987) 'Focus on Commodity Prices and Inflation', *International Economics Analyst*, Goldman Sachs, November/December.

Walton, D. (1988) 'The Reliability of Commodity Prices as Leading Indicators of Inflation', *International Economics Analyst*, Goldman Sachs, April/May.

Discussion

James M. Boughton*

The first issue that must be sorted out before one can analyse the usefulness of a commodity price indicator is whether it is intended to serve as one indicator of inflationary conditions or as the basis for formulating monetary policies. Hook and Walton's emphasis on policy rules puts them into the latter camp, where the requirements for finding affirmative answers are rather high. That is, empirical support for the idea that one might be able to formulate a monetary policy rule based on observed movements in commodity prices is far more difficult to establish than is support for the idea that commodity prices contain useful and timely information about future shifts in global inflationary pressures.

The development of a commodity price indicator as an 'additional analytical instrument' (in Secretary Baker's phrase, cited by Hook and Walton) does not necessarily form the basis for a rule in any sense, any more than does the development of indicators for output growth or interest rates. It is thus important to recognize that the analysis in this paper does not bear directly on the question of the usefulness of the indicator *per se*, but rather on the question of whether the information content in commodity prices would be strong enough to move well beyond existing proposals.

The simulation exercise presented by Hook and Walton suggests that one could design a feedback rule in which monetary policy responds to changes in primary commodity prices, with the feedback parameters chosen so as to reduce the variance of inflation and output in response to money demand shocks. The problem that they note is that the rule might work quite badly in the presence of real shocks in commodity markets. This exercise, of course, is purely illustrative, but it seems likely that the conclusion would be robust if subjected to a variety of empirical tests. The basic rationale is simply that the relationship between primary commodity and other prices is not invariant with respect to the nature of the disturbance. Consequently, such a feedback rule would be of little value unless disturbances were predominantly to money demand.

There is reason to wonder whether such a rule would work even if all shocks were simple disturbances to money demand. The theoretical model developed in this

---

* I would like to thank my colleagues Andrew Crockett and Blair Rourke for helpful comments. The views expressed in this note are personal and should not be attributed to the IMF.

paper, which is an extension of a model developed by Frankel and in turn adapted from Dornbusch's model of exchange rate overshooting,[1] is dependent on the assumption that commodity and consumer prices are cointegrated. As Frankel (1986, p. 345) put it, 'in long-run equilibrium the relative price of the two commodities (i.e., primary commodities and manufactures) settles down to a given value'. In the Hook-Walton model, this condition is expressed as an error-correction process on the relative price of commodities, in equation (4). Without this assumption, the overshooting process by which commodity prices lead consumer prices may not hold, because there is no way to tie down the endogenous response of consumer prices.

Unfortunately, available evidence clearly demonstrates that commodity and consumer prices are not cointegrated. For example, it is noted in Boughton and Branson (1988) that standard commodity price indexes are integrated of order one (stable first differences), while consumer prices for the large industrial countries as a group are integrated of order two (stable second differences). Over the past thirty years through 1987, there has been a negative long-run trend in the relative price of commodities, but this trend has been interrupted for substantial periods by upward thrusts, and the true long-run tendency is highly uncertain.

There are at least two possible explanations for the apparent unboundedness of the relative price of commodities. First, it may be that combining dissimilar commodities into an index produces an aggregate for which the supply and demand functions are not well behaved. In this case, the theoretical model is inapplicable to the data. Second, there may be a stable equilibrium relative price at any moment, but ongoing structural forces may have shifted the equilibrium price in ways that are difficult to measure. For example, the production of some commodities may have been subject to small increases in productivity, relative to those observed for manufactures. For another, some commodities (notably petroleum and gold) are essentially nonrenewable and thus of increasing scarcity. These factors would contribute to a positive trend for the relative price of commodities.

On the other side, 'green revolutions' in the production of many agricultural commodities would have shifted supply curves rightward. As for demand, increasing industrialization over time, rising real global incomes, health concerns regarding a few important commodities such as coffee and sugar, and the secular development of manufactured substitutes for primary commodities (such as synthetic fabrics and fuels, or chemical sweeteners) have probably shifted the composition of demand from commodities to manufactures. Shifts such as these would have contributed to a negative trend in the relative price of commodities over the past few decades.

On balance, then, it is not surprising that commodity prices would be a poor basis for developing a policy rule: even if the theoretical model is valid, the informational requirements for interpreting such a rule would be formidable. Furthermore, it is questionable whether the simple form of rule examined by Hook and Walton would be anyone's first choice, since commodity prices are not the most obvious candidate for inclusion. For example, McCallum (1988) has tested the contribution of a feedback in which the growth rate of the monetary base in the United States is allowed to whenever nominal income departs from a targeted growth path. McCallum finds significant increases in the stability of nominal income growth in response to this feedback rule. It would be interesting to see whether the addition of other variables, such as commodity prices, would contribute further; but the notion that commodity prices would be a superior candidate to nominal income seems dubious.

The most interesting question about commodity prices is not whether they might be used to impose a rule on the conduct of monetary policy, but rather whether they have *any* useful information content that can be exploited either for forecasting or for implementing policies. Is the relative importance of flexible pricing in commodity markets empirically important enough to overcome the structural and aggregation problems just described?

This less stringent way of formulating the problem has been examined in Boughton and Branson (1988). There, empirical evaluation of conventional trade-weighted commodity price indexes, using data for G-7 countries denominated in a broad currency index, leads to several conclusions. First, as noted above, commodity and consumer prices are not cointegrated; the hypothesis that the relative price of primary commodities is bounded, or that there is a reliable long-run relationship between the level of commodity prices and the level of consumer prices, is rejected. Second, there is a tendency for changes in commodity prices to lead those in consumer prices. Notably turning points in commodity-price inflation frequently precede turning points in consumer-price inflation for the large industrial countries as a group. Third, although the inclusion of commodity prices significantly improves the in-sample fit of regressions of a multi-country consumer price index, the results may not be sufficiently stable to improve post-sample forecasts. The bottom line is that commodity prices do have a useful role to play in this context, but one must be quite careful to interpret the relationships correctly.

Note

1 For other models derived from Frankel's, see Boughton and Branson (1988) and Moutos and Vines (1988).

References

Boughton, James M. and William H. Branson (1988) 'Commodity Prices as a Leading Indicator of Inflation,' International Monetary Fund, Working Paper WP/88/87.

Frankel, Jeffrey A. (1986) 'Expectations and Commodity Price Dynamics: The Overshooting Model,' *American Journal of Agricultural Economics* **68,** 344–48.

McCallum, Bennett T. (1988) 'Robustness Properties of a Rule for Monetary Policy,' *Carnegie-Rochester Conference Series on Public Policy* **29,** (forthcoming).

Moutos, T. and D. Vines (1988) 'Output, Inflation and Commodity Prices,' University of Glasgow, Discussion Papers in Economics No. 8811.

Chapter 6

Policy assignment strategies with somewhat flexible exchange rates*

James M. Boughton

I Introduction

How can one design an approach to macroeconomic policy that will improve international economic performance in conditions where countries care about exchange rates but do not wish to adopt explicit exchange-rate objectives? Such circumstances appear to be inherently ambiguous because there is no clearly identifiable and quantifiable measure of external balance, and therefore no unequivocal way to formulate an objective function that could be maximized. To some extent, the exchange rate matters because it affects current account balances, but it may also represent a variety of other more visceral concerns, including the sectoral distribution of income and national pride; and it is linked as well to domestic balance, especially through its effect on aggregate price stability. However, none of these items is determined solely or even primarily by the exchange rate. Thus the external objective for macroeconomic policy cannot be identified solely by the exchange rate but must be extended to incorporate more fundamental concerns.

The organization of the paper is as follows. Section II examines the role of exchange rates and current account balances as alternative external objectives of macroeconomic policy. Section III then takes up the assignment problem: the question of which policies should be emphasized in efforts to

* I have benefited greatly from discussions on these issues and on earlier drafts of the paper with Max Corden, Andrew Crockett, David Currie, Michael Dooley, Robert Flood, Morris Goldstein, Jocelyn Horne, Marcus Miller, Paul Masson, Stephen Symansky, David Vines, and Geoffrey Woglom. The views expressed are mine alone and should not be interpreted as reflecting those of my colleagues or of the International Monetary Fund.

BLUEPRINTS FOR EXCHANGE RATE MANAGEMENT
0-12-497060-5
Copyright © 1989 Academic Press, Ltd
All rights of reproduction reserved

achieve external balance. This topic is elaborated further in Section IV, in which the possibilities for effective policy cooperation based on the assignment of fiscal policy to external balance are discussed. A summary of the principal conclusions is offered in Section V.

II The international objectives of macroeconomic policy

II.1 Definition of the problem

The international objectives of macroeconomic policy depend, *inter alia*, on the exchange rate regime.[1] Under a regime of pure floating, an important objective is for countries to cooperate so as to avoid 'beggar thy neighbour' policies by which one country might attempt to gain a competitive advantage by encouraging markets to depreciate the currency or to export inflation by encouraging an appreciation. At the other extreme, the limitations of the floating-rate system have led some to propose a return to a system of fixed exchange rates or to develop a set of target or reference zones.[2] In this case, the maintenance of exchange rates within the established bands would be the main proximate objective, but countries might also be supposed to wish to maintain 'external balance', in the sense of avoiding large imbalances in their external payments positions.

Between these two regimes lies a gray area encompassing what might be called 'somewhat flexible' exchange rates. That is, a distinction may be made between a pure floating-rate system in which countries choose to treat the exchange rate as a market-determined price over which they do not wish to attempt to exercise a direct influence, and a less pure but still flexible system in which the authorities wish to *influence* although not necessarily to *set* exchange rates.[3] Such a regime might evolve because countries are uncertain of their ability to control exchange rate movements, or because they do not believe that exchange rate management will necessarily secure net benefits for the general welfare. They nonetheless would like to promote exchange rate stability along with other economic objectives, at least partly in order to avoid large current account imbalances.

In this paper, it will be assumed that the international policy objective is to secure benefits both for exchange rate stability and for current account balances. Because these objectives must be consistent across countries, their achievement may require cooperation or coordination of policies. However, it may be difficult for countries to pursue exchange rate and current account objectives independently because of a shortage of available instruments. In that case, countries can either focus on exchange rates and thereby hope to move toward their current account objectives, or focus on the current account and hope to reduce the volatility of exchange rates.

It has been shown elsewhere (see Boughton *et al.*, 1986) that exchange rate adjustment is not a sufficient condition for current account adjustment, because the relationship between the two depends very much on the choice of policies for inducing changes in the exchange rate. In contrast, policies to limit current account imbalances will reduce exchange rate volatility to the extent that they limit shifts in the mix of monetary and fiscal policies. By how much volatility would be reduced is quite difficult to assess, in view of the limited empirical success of exchange rate models. The empirical question is essentially whether exchange rate movements arise primarily from policy shifts or from independent speculative shifts on the part of private investors. It will be assumed here that the extent of the reduction would be significant, but it would be inappropriate to claim much more than that.

The implication of these general considerations is that – as a convenient simplification – the current account may be taken to be the external objective, while the exchange rate may be treated as an intermediate indicator. The objective of relative exchange rate stability may be assumed to be reasonably well satisfied as long as domestic policies are circumscribed by the current account objective. It should be noted that the objective for the current account need not be the achievement of balance, but normally will involve the avoidance of excessively large imbalances, somehow defined.

The remainder of this section outlines the more specific considerations behind this way of setting up the problem. Those who are prepared to accept the assumptions as realistic may wish to skip directly to Section III.

II.2   Elaboration

In a system without official intervention in foreign exchange markets, it is not obvious that it is sensible for countries to have any external objective. The current account balance is simply the reflection of the balance of national saving and investment, and the real exchange rate is a relative price determined freely through market transactions; both represent the endogenous outcome of presumably rational decisions. On the other hand, the saving-investment balance is determined in part – and shifts in the balance may be determined in large part – by government policy decisions; to argue that those decisions should take account of their effects on intertemporal and intergenerational wealth transfers is equivalent to arguing that they should take account of their effects on the external current account balance. Furthermore, shifts in real exchange rates may be determined in large part by speculative pressures in financial markets that give rise to shifts in the sectoral distribution of wealth; such shifts also are a legitimate concern of macroeconomic policy.

If one accepts the validity of an external objective for macroeconomic policy, the next question concerns whether it should be identified as the current account or the exchange rate. When James Meade (1951) formulated the idea of external and internal balance as the fundamental objectives of macroeconomic policy, he argued that external balance was synonymous with a target for the balance of payments. Similarly, Mundell's classic (1962) article on the subject defined external balance in terms of equality between the trade balance and net capital exports at the fixed exchange parity. This work, of course, was written in the context of fixed exchange rates. The introduction of floating rates forces a reevaluation of this equation by introducing the possibility that the exchange rate – either its level or its stability – may itself be an objective rather than (or in addition to its role as) an instrument of macropolicy.

Perhaps the leading exponent of the view that the external policy objective should be the exchange rate rather than the current account is Ronald McKinnon. McKinnon (1988, p. 86) argues that floating exchange rates are 'socially inefficient because private foreign exchange traders face a huge gap in relevant information' arising from frequent, large, unanticipated fluctuations. In this view, there is no stable relationship between exchange rate changes and trade balances, but the latter constitute a separate problem to be dealt with by improvements in the stability of domestic policies rather than by international coordination.

At the other end of the spectrum, some have argued that the level of the exchange rate does not matter, or that its equilibrium level cannot be determined within a reasonable tolerance. In either case, the implication is that efforts at international coordination – if made at all – should focus essentially on the current account. For example, Genberg and Swoboda (1987) note that, for the large industrial countries, the exchange rate has the character of an intermediate variable – neither an instrument nor a target – and that it has no predictable link with the current account balance or other fundamental objectives.

A third view is that neither the exchange rate nor the current account balance should be a policy target. The exchange rate, it may be argued, is simply a relative price that should be allowed to adjust freely to reflect shifts in the balance of market supply and demand. The current account similarly reflects the outcome of differences in national preferences for savings and investment, and it should be allowed to assume whatever values are necessary. This view has been expressed, for example, by Herbert Stein (cited in Dornbusch, 1987), and by Alan Stockman (1988), and its rationale has been set out clearly by Corden (1985). It could also be argued that the Feldstein-Horioka proposition – that changes in domestic saving rates have been largely offset by shifts in domestic investment and have not led to sustained current account imbalances – makes a current account target irrelevant. However, as Caprio and Howard (1984) point out, the evidence developed by Feldstein and Horioka (1980) is consistent with the proposition that governments *have* targeted the current account. In that event, a shift in regime (such as may have occurred during the early 1980s) might be expected to lead to greater persistence of current account imbalances.

The difficulty with this third view is that there may be externalities associated with current account imbalances, as well as with exchange rate fluctuations. One potential cost of current account deficits, stressed by Feldstein (1988), among others, is that there are limits to the ability of even a reserve currency country to finance a growing external debt. Another, emphasized by Cooper (1986) and by Corden (1985), is that a current account deficit represents a transfer of income from future generations to the present; ensuring that the extent of such transfers is consistent with the collective preferences of the public, as well as that conflicts do not arise between countries, is a legitimate concern of governments. Genberg and Swoboda (1987) cite other costs, including the effects of external imbalances on aggregate demand and on protectionist pressures.

In a fourth strand of the modern literature on external balance, it is assumed that there exists a simple mapping of the current account balance into the real exchange rate; the latter then may be taken as the proximate external objective. Recent examples include Corden (1986) and Williamson and Miller (1987). Both make the important qualification that one must take the total level of employment (Corden) or output (Williamson and Miller) as fixed in order to make such a mapping. The argument then is that a shift in the *mix* of financial policies that leaves output unchanged will alter the real exchange rate in a predictable way and thereby alter the current account balance.

The differences between this school of thought and those that treat the exchange rate and the current account as largely independent arise partly out of the analytical choice of whether to hold output fixed. However, several empirical issues might also force a choice between the exchange rate and the current account as the primary indicator of external balance. First, the elasticity conditions required for depreciation to lead to a strengthening of the trade balance may not be satisfied over a reasonable time horizon. Second, if exporters are able to absorb exchange rate fluctuations through shifts in unit profit margins, these fluctuations might have only a weak effect on prices in terms of the importers' currency. Third, in view of the limited success of exchange rate models, it might be more difficult to predict the effects of macro policies on exchange rates than on current account balances. Fourth, exchange rates and current account balances might shift independently for reasons unrelated to shifts in policies.

These issues seem to lead to ambiguous conclusions about the best way to formulate the external objective. Given that countries do express interest in both exchange rates and current account positions, there is no generally accepted standard by which one could determine unequivocally which is foremost. Nonetheless, at least two observations may be advanced in support of the view that the primary focus should be on the current account. First, there is greater consensus in the professional literature about the determination of external balances than about the determination of exchange rates; therefore, the empirical basis for policy recommendations is more solid. Second, virtually the whole of the rationale for caring about exchange rates has to do with one dimension or another of international trade: if not the net balance, then its growth or its distribution. If a country had internal stability and a stable and balanced pattern of international trade, its concerns about changes in its exchange rate would be greatly diminished; however, the converse would not hold.

One may also note that the major industrial countries do, in fact, express concerns over the current account as well as over the exchange rate. For example, the Louvre Accord of February 1987, in which the large industrial countries 'agreed to cooperate closely to foster stability of exchange rates around current levels', also cited the 'serious economic and political risks' associated with large trade and current account imbalances (see *IMF Survey*, March 9, 1987).

III   The assignment of policies

III.1   General considerations

The working hypothesis for this section will be that the external objective of macroeconomic policies is represented by the current account, on the assumption that the avoidance of excessive current account imbalances would also imply a reduction in the instability of exchange rates. This hypothesis does not exclude the possibility that exchange rates could play a useful role as an intermediate target; that issue will be examined below. The remaining open question concerns the choice of policy instrument to be given the primary emphasis in discussions on the achievement of external balance.

In a static optimal-policy framework, the assignment question would not arise: one would simply solve for the values of monetary and fiscal policy settings that were consistent with both internal and external balance.[4] The question, however, is important in the context of limited policy coordination, because it is probably not realistic to expect countries to agree on mutually consistent settings for both monetary and fiscal policies. The problem, as Mundell (1960, 1962) showed, is that there may be a problem of dynamic stability if instruments are assigned to objectives over which they have relatively little influence. More particularly, as stressed recently by Genberg and Swoboda (1987), the possibility of dynamic instability is especially important in this context, because monetary policy – which has long been thought to be the natural choice to be assigned to external balance – has a relatively weak effect on current account balances.

It has been commonly accepted that monetary policy has a comparative advantage for external stability. Mundell (1962) demonstrated that in a fixed exchange-rate system with some capital mobility, the assignment of fiscal policy to external balance would be unstable. The floating-rate, two-country version of the Mundell-Fleming model (see Mundell, 1963, 1964) seemed to have similar assignment implications, because it suggested that monetary expansion in one country would lead unambiguously to a decline in output in the other country because of the appreciation of the second country's real exchange rate. More generally, the emphasis that has been placed in much of the recent literature on exchange rate stability as the key to external balance, coupled with the recognition that monetary policy has a dominant role to play in determining exchange rates, has contributed to the view that monetary policy should be assigned to the maintenance of external balance.

The idea that shifts in monetary policy by a large industrial country will give rise to significant spillover effects on other countries has not been supported by the bulk of the empirical evidence. This conclusion is especially true with respect to the effect of monetary policy on the current account: most recent evidence shows a very limited impact on current account balances with an ambiguous sign. For example, Sachs and Roubini (1987) perform a set of tests with a global simulation model and find 'a striking, and seemingly robust result of this model: monetary policy can be pursued by each region independently, without spillovers on the trade balance or level of activity in other regions'. Helkie and Hooper (1988), summarizing the results of a comparison of the properties of nine internationally linked econometric models conducted by the Brookings Institution, concluded as follows: 'an average of the simulation results suggested that a shift in US money growth would significantly affect real interest rates but would have only a negligible effect on the current account'.

Table 6.1 summarizes the results of selected recent model simulations. For this exercise, the effects of a policy change or other exogenous shock were simulated, with the magnitude of each disturbance being scaled to produce (a) a given path for the effective exchange rate of the US dollar, or (b) a given path for nominal GNP. Specifically, the top part of the table shows

Table 6.1   United States: Changes in current account balance resulting from shifts in monetary and fiscal policies (% of GNP)

Exogenous disturbance	With adaptive expectations		With forward expectations	
	3 years	5 years	3 years	5 years
A. *Scaled to a 10% nominal effective depreciation of the $*				
1. MINIMOD simulations[a]				
expansionary monetary policy	−0.1	0.1	0.1	0.6
contractionary fiscal policy	1.2	1.4	0.9	1.7
2. MULTIMOD simulations[b]				
expansionary monetary policy			0.4	0.2
contractionary fiscal policy			1.4	2.8
B *Scaled to a 10% rise in nominal GDP*				
1. MINIMOD simulations[a]				
expansionary monetary policy	−0.4	0.2	0.8	1.0
expansionary fiscal policy	−1.1	−1.8	−0.8	−2.3
2. MULTIMOD simulations[b]				
expansionary monetary policy			0.8	0.2
expansionary fiscal policy			−0.8	−0.7

[a] *Source*: Boughton *et al.* (1986), Tables 41 and 42. Data have been normalized on 1987 GNP.
[b] *Source*: Masson *et al.* (1988), Tables 11 and 12.

the changes in the US current account balance associated with a 10 percent nominal effective depreciation of the currency, assuming that the depreciation resulted from monetary expansion or from fiscal contraction. The bottom part shows the results of the same simulations, scaled for a 10 percent increase in nominal GNP. In the first set of simulations listed in each part, two versions of MINIMOD (Haas and Masson, 1986) were used, one with adaptive expectations and one with forward-looking model-consistent expectations. Simulations are also reported for MULTIMOD (Masson *et al.*, 1988).

Regardless of the choice of model or the length of time allowed for adjustment, the strengthening resulting from monetary policy actions is generally much smaller than that resulting from a shift in fiscal policy. That relation by itself would not necessarily be a problem, because countries could simply implement relatively large changes in monetary growth. The more serious problem is that the sign of the monetary effect on the current account is ambiguous.[5] Although the simulations in Table 6.1 that incorporate the assumption of model-consistent expectations find positive signs (monetary expansion strengthening the current account), other models and even other versions of the same models are less consistent. For example, the two versions of MINIMOD have opposing effects over a horizon of up to three years. Also, for the two models with forward expectations, MINIMOD shows an increasing effect from monetary policy over time, while MULTIMOD shows a decreasing effect.

There are many reasons for the weakness of the effect of monetary policy on the current account, and each of the empirical studies cited above offers some suggestions. The basic reason, however, is quite straightforward: the relative-price effects are roughly offset by the effects on the growth of domestic demand. That is, monetary expansion strengthens the current account by depreciating the real exchange rate, but it weakens it by stimulating domestic demand and thereby the demand for imports.

III.2 A two-country model

Table 6.2 sets out a simplified two-country model to illustrate the conditions under which monetary policy would have no effect on the current account balance. Genberg and Swododa (1987) set out similar models, with more of an emphasis on small-country properties and on dynamic stability; they derive conclusions similar to those in this sub-section. The model set out here is not intended to be a realistic description of the total macroeconomic response to a shift in monetary policy; the point is to write down a set of equations that is simple enough to yield an analytically transparent result. The Appendix deals in more detail with the consequences of extending the model to cover many of the analytical complications that are necessary to provide a more realistic picture. The net effect of those complications is shown there to be fairly small.

Table 6.2 A simplified two-country model (for notation see Appendix)

$q = P \cdot a + x - E \cdot m$	output identity	(1)
$q^* = P^* a^* - x + E \cdot m$		(2)
$E \cdot m = \alpha_1 P \cdot a - (\alpha_2 - m_0)E$	home-country demand for imports	(3)
$x = \alpha_1 P^* a^* + \alpha_2 E$	demand for home country's exports	(4)
$a = \alpha_5 q/P - \alpha_6 r + g$	domestic demand	(5)
$a^* = \alpha_5 q^*/P^* - \alpha_6 r + g^*$		(6)
$L/P = \alpha_7 a - \alpha_8 r$	demand for money	(7)
$L^*/P^* = \alpha_7 a^* - \alpha_8 r$		(8)
$P = \alpha_9 E$	overall price level	(9)
$P^* = -\alpha_9 E$		(10)
$K = x - E \cdot m$	current account balance	(11)

The model listed in Table 6.2 has a Keynesian structure, with domestic prices fixed and similar coefficients for each of the two identically sized countries. It is a minimal extension of the two-country, flexible-rate version of the Mundell-Fleming model (Mundell, 1964), with import and money demands assumed to depend on expenditure rather than output, and the demand for money deflated by the general price level. In addition, the equations have been written so as to make the role of import prices more explicit in the output identities and the absorption equations; these equations are derived more explicitly in the Appendix. In this model, real import demand in each country (equations 3 and 4) depends on domestic absorption and the exchange rate. In the importing country, the domestic-currency value of demand is negatively related to the exchange rate only if the price elasticity exceeds unity ($\alpha_2 > m_0$). Real absorption (equations 5 and 5) is a function of income (rather than output), the rate of interest, and the level of government expenditure. The interest rate is assumed to be equated between countries through perfect capital mobility. The demand for real money balances (equations 7 and 8) depends on absorption and the interest rate.

Overall price levels in each country vary proportionally to the exchange rate (equations 9 and 10), the coefficient depending on the share of imports in absorption. The last equation defines the current account balance, which is one of three targets (K, q, and q^*) at which the four instruments (L, L^*, g, and g^*) are aimed;[6] the implications of having an excess instrument are discussed below.

What is desired at this stage is a solution of the model for the current account balance, K, as a function of the home-country monetary instrument L, holding the other instruments fixed. This multiplier turns out to have an ambiguous sign, with the following property (starting from a position with balanced trade):

$$dK/dL \gtrless 0 \text{ as } 2\eta \gtrless 1 + 2\alpha_1,$$

where η is the price elasticity of import demand. This result, of course, is comparable to the Marshall-Lerner condition for the effectiveness of a devaluation, except that the requirement is somewhat stricter.[7] Essentially, the sum of the price elasticities must exceed unity by enough to offset the effect of monetary policy on the current account working through changes in aggregate demand.

The external effects of fiscal policy are different from those of monetary policy, because the relative price effects on the trade balance either work in the same direction as the expenditure effects or – if perverse – are weak relative to those of monetary policy.[8] Suppose that a country undertakes to strengthen its current account by reducing government spending and thereby raising domestic saving. The direct effect on expenditure demands will reduce imports. In addition, the downward pressure on interest rates will (given perfect capital mobility) contribute to a depreciation of the exchange rate; only if the price elasticities in import demands are quite low will this depreciation worsen the trade balance by enough to offset the expenditure effect.

The effect of fiscal policy on the current account in the simple model has the property that

$$dK/dg \gtrless 0 \text{ as } 2\eta \gtrless 1 + 2\alpha_1(1 - 1/\eta_l)$$

where η_l is the income elasticity of the demand for money. For $\eta_l = 1$, the requirement in this model for the standard result is simply that the Marshall-Lerner condition must hold. There does not appear to be a great deal of difference between these two inequalities, but – for price elasticities that are high enough to satisfy the Marshall-Lerner condition, but still low – the implications for the current account may be substantial. For example, using the parameters assumed in the Appendix, including a price elasticity of import demand equal to 0.75, a rise in government spending by an amount sufficient to raise nominal income by 5 percent would weaken the current account balance by about 2 percent of initial GNP; for a commensurate rise in the money stock, the strengthening of the current account would amount only to about $\frac{1}{4}$ of 1 percent (for further details, see Table 6A.2).

What is important in this scenario is not the specific model – which is deliberately simplified and obviously not realistic – or the numerical results, but rather the conclusion that one does not have to tell a very complicated story in order to conclude that the two policy instruments have quite different implications for the current account balance, relative to their effect on domestic macroeconomic targets. Even with a quite simple Mundell-Fleming extension, the effects of monetary policy on the current account may be subject to a particularly long J-curve (if the import price elasticity operates with a distributed lag) and have an ambiguous sign even in the long run.

III.3   Practical implications

The foregoing discussion suggests that, as a first approximation, macroeconomic relations among the largest industrial countries may be characterized by a model in which both monetary and fiscal policies affect exchange rates; monetary policy, however, has little or no effect on current account balances or on output in other countries, while fiscal policy has substantial effects. If exchange rates are fundamentally what countries care about, then the assignment of monetary policy to external balance – and to centre stage in discussions of policy coordination – makes sense. This type of assumption is essential in order to justify proposals such as that of McKinnon (1982, 1988), under which countries coordinate monetary policies so as to maintain exchange rates close to agreed parities. If, on the other hand, exchange rate stability is desired primarily in order to avoid destabilizing trade balances, then the picture looks rather different.

Obviously, if monetary policies have no effect on current account balances, a scheme that assigns monetary policy to maintain current accounts at target levels will fail. What is not obvious is whether a scheme that first translates current account objectives into exchange rate targets and then assigns monetary policy to those targets will also fail. Such a scheme has been proposed recently by Williamson and Miller (1987) as a means of articulating the policy requirements for maintaining target zones for exchange rates.

Recall from Section III that Williamson and Miller, as well as Corden, argue that for a given output or employment path there exists a single mapping of current account balances into real exchange rates. Given this mapping, the choice between the two external objectives boils down to a question of which one can be most easily agreed and acted upon; as a practical matter, there is little doubt that the exchange rate is the preferred choice on these grounds. Furthermore, monetary policy adjustments, if mutually consistent between countries and not constrained by other consider-ations, could easily be used to maintain exchange rates within reasonably narrow bands. The effects on real exchange rates would be subject to greater errors than those on nominal rates, but the uncertainty and the practical difficulties of implementation would probably be much smaller than in the case of fiscal policies.

With monetary policy assigned to defend the target zones, the Williamson-Miller scheme would then assign fiscal policy to maintain internal balance within each country. Given internal balance, exchange rate stability would ensure current account stability. If, over time, the initial exchange rate targets turned out to have been wrong – in the sense of leading to an undesired pattern of current account balances – then they could simply be changed by mutual agreement.

The workings of the target zone proposal are illustrated in Figure 6.1. There are two targets: the current account balance (vertical axis) and nominal income (horizontal axis); and two instruments: monetary and fiscal policy. Two schedules are drawn, with slopes reflecting the empirical finding that monetary policy does not significantly affect the current account balance. With unchanged fiscal policy, the horizontal *gg* schedule is fixed, and monetary policy affects income by shifting the *LL* schedule. With unchanged monetary policy, the *LL* schedule is fixed, and fiscal policy alters both income and external balance by shifting the *gg* schedule.[9]

Suppose that the economy is initially at point *A* and that the authorities

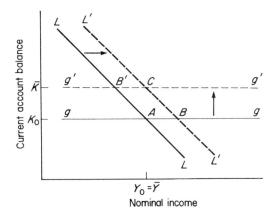

Figure 6.1   Adjustment to a current-account target.
Notation: *gg*, constant fiscal policy (fiscal expansion shifts *gg* downward); *LL*, constant monetary policy (monetary expansion shifts *LL* to the right).

seek to strengthen the current acount (from K_0 to $\bar{K}$). Under a target zone scheme, this objective would be translated into a desired depreciation of the exchange rate, and monetary policy would become more expansionary. The *LL* curve would shift to the right, and the new temporary equilibrium would be put at point *B*. At this stage, nothing would happen to the current account, but nominal income would be higher. To restore internal balance, fiscal policy would then have to be tightened. This reaction would shift the *gg* schedule upward, and the economy would reach the desired point *C*. This process is dynamically stable; a problem would arise, however, if the adjustment process – during which time it would be apparent that the monetary expansion was succeeding only in depreciating the currency while failing to strengthen the current account – took long enough to sow confusion and throw the intended policy mix off course. That is, the information requirements for such a process may be quite strict.

A more complicated scenario would ensue if the initial imbalance were on the internal side. Figure 6.2 illustrates the case in which, starting from point *A*, the objective is to raise nominal income. With monetary policy minding the exchange rate, this objective would call for fiscal expansion shifting the *gg* schedule downward to a temporary equilibrium at point *B*. Income would then be at its target level, but the current account would have weakened. Presumably at this point the exchange rate would be appreciated relative to its target zone, so monetary expansion would then be called for; this response would raise income further, and the new equilibrium would be at point *C*. Finally, fiscal policy would have to be reversed in order to restore internal balance at $\bar{Y}$.

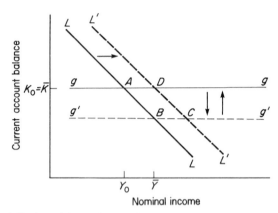

Figure 6.2   Adjustment to an income target.

The implications of these scenarios for the evaluation of the Williamson-Miller target zone scheme are as follows. In response to external imbalance, the scheme may break down because of the failure of the current account to respond to monetary policy, unless fiscal policy rescues the situation in time. In response to internal imbalance, fiscal policy will be destabilized, in the sense that any attempt to alter the level of income through fiscal policy will have to be reversed once monetary policy responds to the resulting external imbalance.

These inefficiencies are alleviated substantially if the assignment is reversed. Consider now the situation in which fiscal policy is assigned directly to the current account balance, monetary policy is aimed at nominal income, and the exchange rate is left to find its own market level. If a country wanted to strengthen its current account, as in Figure 6.1, it would first contract fiscal policy (to point B'); monetary policy would then be eased to offset the undesired decline in income. The advantage over the target zone scheme would be that one would see more clearly the effects of the policy shifts on the targeted variables.[10] If a country wanted to raise nominal income, as in Figure 6.2, it would simply ease monetary policy (to point D); fiscal policy would not have to change at all, in contrast to the temporary expansion that would be required under the target zone proposal. With policies more stable and more transparent, the likelihood of wide swings in exchange rates would be reduced.

IV   A simplified model of policy cooperation

The preceding analysis is too simplified to serve as a model of policy cooperation. To develop a more complete analysis, it is necessary both to allow for other policy objectives and to incorporate other features that might alter the relationships between instruments and targets. This section sketches some of these complications and then offers a model of international policy cooperation that is consistent with the more general framework.

Targets for macroeconomic policy in the large industrial countries may include, in addition to stability of nominal income growth and of external balance, the maintenance of a sustainable rate of economic growth and of an adequate transfer of resources to developing countries.[11] In terms of the model developed above, these two additional targets both imply that a lower level of real interest rates may be desired than would obtain at the equilibrium determined by internal and external balance. For a given level of output, the growth target requires low real interest rates in order to stimulate home investment, while the resource-transfer target requires relatively low fiscal deficits (and therefore low real interest rates) to generate the desired trade surplus vis-à-vis the rest of the world. Thus the presence of these additional targets can be expressed very simply as an objective for the level of real interest rates.[12] Because (in the absence of capital controls) each country cannot independently pursue its own agenda for real interest rates without throwing the other targets off the desired path, this type of target must be set cooperatively.

When the problem is posed in this way, one gets a different picture of the international cooperation problem compared with the game-theoretic models in the policy coordination literature. The problem is frequently stated as one of a shortage of instruments. In the simplest formulation (e.g., Hamada, 1974) there are two instruments (monetary policy in each country) and three targets (internal balance in each country, plus the common objective for external balance); coordination offers the possibility of moving closer to the global optimum. In an expanded model that includes fiscal policy (e.g., Oudiz and Sachs, 1984), there are four instruments but five targets (say, growth in each country plus the three listed above). Here, in contrast, there is a potential match involving four instruments and four targets: internal balance in each country plus the common objectives for external balance and for real interest rates. The task of policy cooperation is twofold: to reach agreement on the common objectives and on the emphasis to be given to each instrument in achieving them.

The second type of extension that should be made is to incorporate behavioural features of the economy that are thought to be important in a macroeconomic framework but that were ignored in the simple framework discussed earlier. The following are examples of possible extensions. First, flexibility of domestic prices in response to policy shifts may be introduced; this extension would break the simple dependence of the overall price level on the exchange rate. Second, one could allow the real exchange rate to affect the supply of real output directly through the gap between product and consumption real wages. Third, one could model the effect of changes in the inflation rate on real interest rates and on the real exchange rate. Fourth, the notion of fiscal policy could be expanded by allowing tax revenues to depend on the level of income. Fifth, the influence of existing stocks of debt, both internal and external, could be introduced. Sixth, there is the possibility that such debt instruments might or might not be considered to be net wealth by the private sector. Seventh, debt instruments denominated in different currencies might not be perfect substitutes, opening the possibility for sustained real interest differentials between countries. Eighth, anticipated policy shifts might have strong effects on behaviour via expectations.

Although each of these extensions is important, there is no presumption as to their net effect for any of the issues that are relevant here. Notably, it was argued on the basis of the simple model in Table 6.2 that the external effects of monetary policy appear to be quite small; would the inclusion of these extensions in the analysis significantly alter that conclusion? Judging from the empirical findings of fairly comprehensive models (as discussed in Section III), the answer would apear to be negative. This question is taken up more specifically in the Appendix, where it is shown that both an extended version of the model and the simpler Mundell-Fleming version lead to essentially similar conclusions.

Either the simple model discussed earlier or the extended model of the Appendix may be reduced to a four-equation system in which the four target variables are functions of the four instruments. Dropping the monetary policy terms that are expected to have very small values, this system has the following form:

$$Y = Y(g, g^*, L) \tag{1}$$

$$Y^* = Y^*(g, g^*, L^*) \tag{2}$$

$$K = K(g - g^*) \tag{3}$$

$$r = r(g + g^*, L + L^*) \tag{4}$$

The most striking conclusion to be drawn from this system is that the international coordination of *monetary* policy is neither necessary nor sufficient for attaining the targets; *fiscal* policy coordination, however, is necessary and – if monetary policy is aimed correctly at internal balance – sufficient as well. Suppose that fiscal policy were to be aimed instead at internal balance. Aggregate monetary policy $(L + L^*)$ could then be used to influence interest rates; it would still remain necessary, however, to coordinate that policy with the differences in fiscal stances in order to keep the current account in line.

These considerations lead to a model of medium-term policy cooperation that has these main elements:

(a) aggregate fiscal policy could be aimed at limiting the growth of demands on available savings, so that the global level of real interest rates could be kept within acceptable bounds;
(b) differences between national fiscal stances could be circumscribed as needed to maintain external balance;
(c) each country could use monetary policy independently to maintain internal balance.

To illustrate how such a programme might work, consider the effects of one country deciding to embark on an anti-inflationary policy; i.e. to try to reduce nominal income.[13] With fiscal policy constrained by cooperative agreements, this decision would call for a tightening of monetary policy, which would have the undesired side effect of raising world interest rates. Aggregate fiscal policy would then have to be changed; in general, both countries would have to move toward a more contractionary fiscal stance, and in the end the second country would also have to ease its monetary policy in order to maintain internal balance. Thus a shift in the domestic objectives of one country would constrain the policy mix to be adopted by the other country. Depending on circumstances, it might be necessary for discussions between the countries to focus on the initial setting of the objectives or on the subsequent adjustment of fiscal policies. In neither case would it be particularly helpful to bring monetary policies explicitly into the discussions.

What happens to the exchange rate in this world? In general, exchange rates would shift in response to any policy action, shift in expectations, or other disturbance. Nothing in the model as outlined would call on countries to adjust policies in direct response to such movements. The relevant empirical question concerns the extent to which the observed swings in, and volatility of, exchange rates have resulted from shifts in the mix of policies rather than from independent shifts in private portfolio preferences. This question, of course, is impossible to answer. Empirical analysis of exchange rate movements for key currencies explains, at best, no more than half of the broad swings observed in the 1980s on the basis of measured differences in macropolicies (see, for example, Boughton, 1988). Part of the remainder, however, may well be attributable to shifts in market perceptions about the stability or the sustainability of those policies. All that can be claimed is that cooperation to limit shifts in the mix of policies would contribute unambiguously to the stability of exchange rates. The extent of the reduction can be determined only through experience.

A major caveat is that fiscal policy cannot be used effectively as an

instrument for short-term policy adjustments, either for domestic or international objectives. Tanzi (1988) discusses the empirical obstacles to effective
fiscal coordination, and Polak (1988) reviews the difficulties that many
countries have experienced in implementing fiscal policy flexibility, especially
during the 1980s. Not only is it difficult for countries to agree upon and
implement fiscal changes quickly; it also is important for budgetary decisions
to be aimed at stable medium-term targets. Furthermore, agreements on the
appropriate use of fiscal policy would be complicated by the multidimension-
ality of the budgetary process; as Frenkel and Razin (1987) have shown, the
international effects of a given shift in the fiscal position may be affected
substantially by the choice of which expenditure or which tax is to be
changed.

These complications are not necessarily disadvantageous if the objectives
of international cooperation are sufficiently limited. If coordination were
directed primarily at stabilizing exchange rates, the stickiness of fiscal policies
would be a fatal blow. The objective of constraining current account
imbalances, in contrast, is a medium-term goal that is more consistent in its
time dimension with the fiscal instrument. In other words, cooperation could
be sought, not to attempt to fine tune each country's budget for external
purposes, but to circumscribe any budgetary shifts that might bring policies
between countries into conflict.

V   Conclusions

This paper has argued in favour of an assignment strategy for macroeconomic
policy in large industrial countries that would focus more on current account
balances than on exchange rates, and would emphasize fiscal policy more
than monetary policy in efforts to achieve external balance. The fundamental
problem with the exchange rate as an external objective is that the conditions
under which there would be a reliable relationship between exchange
rates and external balance are unrealistically restrictive. The steady-state
relationship between the level of the real exchange rate and the level of the
current account balance depends very much on the mix of policies that is
pursued in each country; only in circumstances in which each country is able
to maintain internal balance might the real exchange rate serve as a reliable
guide (aside from dynamic considerations) to the prospects for external
balance.

The problem with monetary policy as the instrument to be assigned to
external balance is that it may seriously aggravate the obscurity of the
international transmission process. Empirical evidence strongly suggests that
monetary policy has little effect on external balance, and this paper has

discussed some simple models that illustrate a straightforward rationale for this phenonmenon.

The limitations could be partially overcome to the extent that countries cooperate on the basis of the linkages between fiscal policies and current account balances. More specifically, a feasible model of policy cooperation might be one with the following principal elements. First, countries could seek agreement on an appropriate range for real interest rates and on an aggregate medium-term fiscal stance (covering a period of, say, two or three years) that would be broadly consistent with that rate level. This initial step is intended to limit policy conflicts concerning interest rate levels; fiscal rather than monetary policy is required for this purpose for consistency with other policy objectives. Second, agreement could be sought on at least general objectives for current account balances and on the relative stances of fiscal policy that would be consistent with those balances over the medium term. This second step would limit conflicts over what is acceptable in terms of external balance; monetary policy cannot, for the reasons discussed above, be used for this purpose. Third, each country could use monetary policy independently to pursue internal balance. By thus allowing exchange rates to float freely, while constraining current account imbalances through medium-term fiscal agreements, countries would be able simultaneously to maintain independence to pursue their own national interests while contributing indirectly to exchange rate stability.

Appendix: An expanded model of internal and external balance

This Appendix sets out an extended version of the model discussed in the text. As with the simpler version, it describes two identical economies linked by trade and capital flows. It is extended here to allow for several features (described in section 1) that may be important determinants of the international transmission of policy effects. The model, listed in Table 6A.1, is a static medium-term system; the dynamics are suppressed and all stock-flow interactions are exogenous.

1 Description of the model

The first two equations in Table 6A.1 are the income identities for the two countries, which for simplicity are assumed to constitute a closed trading system. In nominal terms, equation (1) would be written as follows:

$$P_d q = P \cdot a + P_d x - P_d^* E \cdot m,$$

where domestic output is valued at its own price (P_d), imports are valued at their own prices (P_d^*) converted into the home country's currency, and absorption is valued

Table 6A.1 An expanded two-country model

Equations

$$q \equiv a(P/P_d) + x - R \cdot m \tag{1}$$

$$q^* \equiv a^*(P^*/P^*_d) - x/R + m \tag{2}$$

$$R \cdot P_d \cdot m = \alpha_1 P \cdot a - (\alpha_2 - m_0)R \tag{3}$$

$$x = \alpha_1 P^* a^* + \alpha_2 R \tag{4}$$

$$a = \alpha_5 [P_d q + r^* E \cdot B_f^* - \alpha_3(T - rB_d) \tag{5}$$
$$- (1 - \alpha_3)(P \cdot g + rB_f)]/P - \alpha_6(1 - \alpha_4)r + I_0 + g$$

$$a^* = \alpha_5 [P_d^* q^* + rB_f/E - \alpha_3(T^* - r^* B_d^*) \tag{6}$$
$$- (1 - \alpha_3)(P^* g^* + r^* B_f^*)]/P^* - \alpha_6(1 - \alpha_4)r^* + I_0^* + g^*$$

$$L/P = \alpha_7 a - \alpha_8 r \tag{7}$$

$$L^*/P^* = \alpha_7 a^* - \alpha_8 r^* \tag{8}$$

$$P = (1 - \alpha_9)P_d + \alpha_9 P_d^* E \tag{9}$$

$$P^* = (1 - \alpha_9)P_d^* + \alpha_9 P_d/E \tag{10}$$

$$K \equiv P_d x - P_d^* E \cdot m + r^* E^* \cdot B_f^* - rB_f \tag{11}$$

$$Y \equiv P_d \cdot q + rB_d + r^* E \cdot B_f^* \tag{12}$$

$$Y^* \equiv P_d^* q^* + r^* B_d^* + rB_f/E \tag{13}$$

$$R \equiv E \cdot P_d^*/P_d \tag{14}$$

$$\Delta R = \alpha_{11}(r^* - r) \tag{15}$$

$$T = \alpha_4 Y \tag{16}$$

$$T^* = \alpha_4 Y^* \tag{17}$$

$$q = y_0 R^{\alpha_{12}} P_d^{\alpha_{10}} \tag{18}$$

$$q^* = y_0 R^{-\alpha_{12}} P_d^{*\alpha_{10}} \tag{19}$$

Table 6A1-*contd.*
Notation and initial values (stocks and flows are both expressed as ratios to initial output . Initial values are the same for both countries.)

a	1	real absorption (domestic demand)
B_d	0.48	stock of government bonds held by domestic residents
B_f	0.06	stock of government bonds held by nonresidents
E	1	nominal exchange rate (increase = depreciation)
g	0.23	government expenditure
I	0.04	net investment expenditure
K	0	current account balance
L	0.76	stock of money
m	0.12	volume of imports by the home country
P	1	overall price level
P_d	1	price level for domestically produced goods
q	1	output
R	1	real exchange rate (increase = depreciation)
r	0.043	interest rate
T	0.20	nominal tax revenue
x	0.12	volume of exports by the home country
$*$		value for the second country
α		fixed coefficients

Coefficients (derived on the basis of the assumptions described in the accompanying text, and normalized on a value of unity for real output.)

α_1	0.12	marginal propensity to import
α_2	0.12	relative price coefficient on import demand
α_3	0.667	debt neutrality coefficient ($0 \leq \alpha_3 \leq 1; 0$ = full neutrality)
α_4	0.20	marginal tax rate
α_5	0.77	marginal propensity for private expenditure
α_6	0.50	interest rate coefficient in absorption demand
α_7	0.79	scale coefficient in money demand
α_8	0.76	interest rate coefficient in money demand
α_9	0.12	average import propensity
α_{10}	1	information-cost or money-illusion effect on supply of output
a_{11}	10	effect of interest-rate differential on the real exchange rate
a_{12}	0.10	competitiveness effect on supply of output

at a weighted average of the two.

Equations (3) and (4) describe import demand equations for the two countries, with demand depending on the level of domestic demand as well as on relative prices. Note that in local-currency terms, equations (3) and (4) have the same form. Equations (5) and (6) express the demand for goods and services in each country (absorption). These last expressions are rather more complex than in the simplified version of the model, having been derived from the following subsystem:

$$c = \alpha_5 y^p \tag{20}$$

$$P \cdot y^p = P_d a + r \cdot B_d + r^* E \cdot B_f^* - T^p \tag{21}$$

$$T^p = \alpha_3 T + (1 - \alpha_3)[P \cdot g + r(B_d + B_f)] \tag{22}$$

$$I = I_0 - \alpha_6(1 - \alpha_8)r \tag{23}$$

$$a \equiv c + I + g \tag{24}$$

Equation (20) states that real consumption expenditure (c) is proportional to real permanent disposable income (y^p). The latter is defined in equation (21) as real output, plus the real interest received on residents' holdings of government debt and foreign assets, minus the perceived real value of permanent tax liabilities (T^p). Nominal permanent tax liabilities are a weighted average of actual liabilities and the (static) level of total government outlays, as described in equation (22). Under full debt neutrality ($\alpha_3 = 0$), the method of financing expenditures will not matter and people will treat outlays, rather than current taxes, as the relevant variable that must be deducted from income to derive permanent disposable income.[14] At the other extreme, where $\alpha_3 = 1$, then equations (20) and (22) constitute a standard Keynesian consumption model, except for the explicit addition of interest income to output.[15]

This subsystem is completed by equation (23), which links investment (I) to the cost of capital via the after-tax real interest rate, and equation (24), which defines absorption as the sum of its components. The solution to equations (20) through (24) is given by equation (5) of the model. Equation (6) is derived similarly for the second country.

The demand for money is decribed by equations (7) and (8), where three features are of note. First, the relevant deflator is the aggregate price level rather than the deflator for domestic output, on the hypothesis that the demand for money is a demand for purchasing power. Second, on the same grounds, the relevant scale variable is absorption rather than GNP. Third, the model contains only one interest rate in each country, ignoring shifts both in the term structure and in inflationary expectations.

Equations (9) and (10) describe aggregate price levels in each country as weighted averages of domestic and import price indexes. The weights on import prices are simply the portions of demand accounted for by imports. Next, the current account of the balance of payments is defined by equation (11), and equations (12) and (13) define nominal income. Equation (14) defines the real exchange rate as the relative price of domestic output converted by the nominal exchange rate.

Changes in the real exchange rate are generated by interest rate differentials, as shown in equation (15). In keeping with the static character of the model, the expected future change in the nominal exchange rate – which would otherwise enter equation (15) as a determinant of expected differences in yields – is assumed to be zero.

The next two equations (16 and 17) relate tax revenues to a base that includes interest income. In each country, interest income is assumed to be taxed where it is received, regardless of its source. Finally, the supply of output is captured by equations (18) and (19). Departures from the trend or potential level are generated by changes in the real exchange rate or in the domestic price level. Specifically, an appreciation of the real exchange rate will raise the supply of output by raising the real wage that is relevant to workers (W/P) relative to that which is relevant to firms (W/P_d). In addition, a rise in domestic prices will raise output to the extent that information costs are important in factor markets.[16]

2   Parameters and data

A number of assumptions have been made in order to parameterize the model for illustrative purposes. First, income elasticities for import demands, private absorption, and money demand have all been set to unity. Second, price elasticities for import demands have been set at 0.75. Third, the semi-elasticities of demand for money and for investment with respect to the interest rate have both been set at unity. For money demand, this choice approximates the steady-state elasticities estimated for major industrial countries in papers such as Boughton (1981) and Atkinson *et al.* (1984). For the investment function, the choice is purely arbitrary; however, the properties of the model are more sensitive to the ratio of these two elasticities than to their levels, and the assumption of equality has the advantage of neutrality.[17]

For the extended version of the model, the following additional assumptions have been made. First, the marginal tax rate has been set at 0.2, which is close to the average tax rate in the United States. Second, the 'debt neutrality' parameter (α_3) has been set at 2/3, which is approximately the value estimated in Carmichael (1983). Third, α_{11} has been set equal to the effect of the interest differential on the effective rate of the US dollar estimated in Boughton (1984), allowing for a two-year response. Fourth, the semi-elasticities of the supply of output with respect to the real exchange rate and the domestic price level have been set arbitrarily at 0.1 and 1, respectively.

The initial conditions for the model approximate those for the United States in the first half of the 1980s, except that it has been assumed for simplicity that each country is in initial trade balance. The values of parameters and of relevant data are listed in the table.

3   Properties of the model

In contrast to the simple model described in the paper, the solution of the full model is too complex to lead to clear analytical implications. Note, however, that this model reduces to the text model by making several simplifying assumptions. First, assume that initial debt stocks are all zero. Second, fix the level of domestic prices in each country, while retaining flexibility of output and overall prices ($\alpha_{12} = 0$ and $\alpha_{10} = \infty$). Third, assume perfect capital mobility so that interest rates must be equal in each country ($\alpha_{11} = \infty$). Fourth, assume no discounting of future tax liabilities associated with current interest receipts ($\alpha_3 = 1$). Fifth, assume all taxes are lump sum ($\alpha_4 = 0$).[18]

The properties of this simplified model are illustrated in Table 6A.2. In particular, fiscal policy is transmitted positively and monetary policy negatively to foreign output. Fiscal expansion weakens the current account, while monetary expansion strengthens it, although in the latter case the effect is quite small. As noted in Section

Table 6A.2   Simulated effects of exogenous shocks in a two-country model: Version used in text (% except as noted)

	Disturbance	
	Government spending[a]	Money stock[b]
Output		
home	1.1	5.8
abroad	5.5	−1.4
Domestic demand		
home	7.3	3.3
abroad	−0.7	1.1
Export volume	−2.7	1.5
Import volume	−0.7	1.2
Current account balance[c]	−2.0	0.3
Interest rate[d]		
home	3.5	−1.0
abroad	3.5	−1.0
Aggregate price level		
home	−4.2	2.2
abroad	4.2	−2.2
Exchange rate[e]		
nominal	−34.8	18.3
real	−34.8	18.3

[a] Effects of a rise equal to 5 percent of initial GNP.
[b] Effects of a rise equal to 5 percent of the initial stock.
[c] Change in percent of the initial value of output.
[d] Change in percentage points.
[e] An increase indicates a depreciation.

III.2 of the text, these signs are not analytically unambiguous.

The properties of the full model are illustrated in Table 6A.3. Most results are qualitatively unchanged, with two exceptions. First, both monetary and fiscal expansion now generally produce substantial price increases, because domestic as well as import prices are now allowed to respond. Second, monetary expansion now has no effect at all on the current account balance. More generally, the implication is that the elasticity requirements for monetary expansion to lead to a strengthening of the current account are more strict than in the simpler model.

Table 6A.3 Simulated effects of exogenous shocks in a two-country model: Expanded version (% except as noted)

	Disturbance	
	Government spending[a]	Money stock[b]
Output		
home	2.7	2.8
abroad	5.5	−0.9
Domestic demand		
home	7.0	1.7
abroad	1.2	0.2
Export volume	−1.2	0.8
Import volume	0.4	−0.9
Current account balance[c]	−1.8	—
Interest rate[d]		
home	9.4	−1.8
abroad	7.2	−0.9
Aggregate price level		
home	2.2	3.0
abroad	5.9	−1.1
Exchange rate[e]		
nominal	−20.8	11.4
real	−22.5	9.6

[a] Effects of a rise equal to 5 percent of initial GNP.
[b] Effects of a rise equal to 5 percent of the initial stock.
[c] Change in percent of the initial value of output.
[d] Change in percentage points.
[e] An increase indicates a depreciation.

Notes

1 For a general exposition of alternative regimes in this context, see Dornbusch and Frankel (1987). The following discussion ignores the possibility (which they discuss) of using taxes or controls to reduce capital mobility as a substitute for modifying domestic policies in order to achieve an external objective.

2 The difference between fixed rates and target zones is that the latter does not require a commitment by the authorities to buy or sell foreign exchange within the established bands. Rather, it requires a commitment to implement policies that are intended to be consistent with a market-determined exchange rate that lies within the bands. General references on target zones are Williamson (1985) and Frenkel and Goldstein (1986). Also see Currie and Wren-Lewis (1987), Edison *et al.* (1987), Krugman (1988), and Williamson and Miller (1987).

3 The term 'somewhat flexible' is chosen in preference to 'managed floating', because the latter carries the connotation of management through official intervention in foreign exchange markets. The connotation that is being sought here is one of management primarily through adjustment of domestic financial policies, as explained below.

4 It is well known that simplified strategies, such as focusing on intermediate targets or assigning specific instruments to targets, are in general not optimal ways to maximize welfare. On intermediate targets, see Friedman (1975); on the use of simple assignment rules, see Currie and Levine (1985). The assignment approach is nonetheless adopted here in deference to the desirability of simplicity as a characteristic of the design of any practical scheme for policy coordination.

5 In addition to the potentiality in the Mundell-Fleming model that expenditure effects will dominate the relative-price effect, other possibilities for a negative monetary effect on the current account have been noted. For example, Liviatan (1981) developed an extension of the Calvo and Rodriguez (1977) model in which monetary policy leads on impact to a real appreciation and a weakening of the trade balance. Kimbrough and Koray (1984) estimated the reduced form of a model in which an unanticipated monetary expansion weakens the trade balance by raising the perceived real rate of return abroad.

6 With domestic price levels fixed and with investment income ignored, nominal income and real output are equivalent targets: $P \cdot y = P_d \cdot q$, where $y \equiv$ real income.

7 Because of the symmetry of the model, the expression 2η represents the sum of the import elasticities in the two countries.

8 Fiscal policy is defined here in a very simple manner, as a change in the level of government spending for which the import content is identical to the average propensity (m_y). For a full discussion of the implications of the specification of fiscal policy, see Frenkel and Razin (1987).

9 The specification of the internal objective, though somewhat arbitrary, is not central to the issues being addressed. The justification for focusing on nominal income is that a nominal anchor is needed for macroeconomic stability, the government has greater control over nominal income growth than over the rate of

inflation, and other potential nominal anchors such as monetary growth are subject to greater uncertainty in their effects on welfare. For expositions of the rationale for this type of policy strategy, see Vines *et al.* (1983) and Currie and Levine (1985). In the absence of supply shocks, a nominal and a real target for internal balance would be equivalent, but the choice is material even in a simple two-country demand-oriented framework because policy disturbances in one country act as supply shocks on its trading partners and so cannot be ignored.

10 Frenkel (1986) makes a related argument in favour of externally-aimed fiscal policy in the context of a Mundellian model of a small open economy with a fixed exchange rate and high capital mobility.

11 A closely related approach would be to introduce a target for wealth, as in Meade and Vines (1989) and Blake *et al.* (1989). In terms of the semi-reduced form discussed below, the implications would be identical.

12 This simplification ignores possible quantitative inconsistencies between the two added targets, which in any case could be resolved only through the use of additional instruments.

13 This example does not deal with the more complicated problem of a country attempting to achieve the structural result of reducing inflation without reducing the rate of growth of real income. That outcome would normally require the introduction of an additional policy instrument, although there may be circumstances where it could be achieved by a shift in the monetary-fiscal mix.

14 These calculations implicitly assume that both outlays and revenues are perceived as following a random walk. It is also assumed that corporate profits are fully passed through to the personal sector through dividends, so that national and personal income are equivalent.

15 This practice amounts to defining output as GNP net of net interest receipts from the rest of the world. Although the choice of definition has little quantitative importance for the issues discussed here, it is conceptually helpful to analyze the role of interest rates and debt stocks separately from that of the output of goods and other services.

16 For an exposition of the first point, see Argy and Salop (1979); on the latter, which generalizes the standard 'money illusion' arguments, see Boughton and Fackler (1981).

17 Heuristically, this assumption may be described loosely as giving the *IS* and *LM* curves slopes that are equal in absolute value.

18 With two more simplifying assumptions, the model can be equivalent to the flexible-rate, two-country version of the Mundell-Fleming model (Mundell, 1964). First, let import and money demands depend on output rather than on demand. Second, let money demand be deflated by domestic rather than overall prices.

References

Argy, Victor and Joanne Salop (1979) 'Price and Output Effects of Monetary and Fiscal Policy Under Flexible Exchange Rates,' *IMF Staff Papers* **26**, 224–56.

Atkinson, Paul, Adrian Blundell-Wignall, Manuela Rondoni, and Helmut Ziegel-shmidt (1984) 'The Efficacy of Monetary Targeting: The Stability of Demand for Money in Major OECD Countries,' *OECD Economic Studies*, No. 3, 145–75.

Blake, Andrew, Martin Weale, and David Vines (1989) 'Wealth Targets, Exchange Rate Targets and Macroeconomic Policy,' in Weale *et al* (1989).

Boughton, James M. (1981) 'Recent Instability of the Demand for Money: An International Perspective,' *Southern Economic Journal* **47**, 579–97.

Boughton, James M. (1984) 'Exchange Rate Movements and Adjustment in Financial Markets: Quarterly Estimates for Major Currencies,' *IMF Staff Papers* **31**, 445–68.

Boughton, James M. (1988) 'Exchange Rates and the Term Structure of Interest Rates,' *IMF Staff Papers* **35**, 36–62.

Boughton, James M. and James S. Fackler (1981) 'The Nominal Rate of Interest, the Rate of Return on Money, and Inflationary Expectations,' *Journal of Macroeconomics* **3**, 531–45.

Boughton, James M., Richard D. Haas, Paul R. Masson and Charles Adams (1986) 'Effects of Exchange Rate Changes in Industrial Countries,' *IMF Staff Studies for the World Economic Outlook*, 115–49.

Calvo, Guillermo A., and Carlos Alfredo Rodriguez (1977) 'A Model of Exchange Rate Determination under Currency Substitution and Rational Expectations,' *Journal of Political Economy* **85**, 617–25.

Caprio, Gerard, Jr. and David H. Howard (1984) 'Domestic Saving, Current Accounts, and International Mobility,' International Finance Discussion Paper No. 244, Board of Governors of the Federal Reserve System (Washington).

Carmichael, Jeffrey (1983) 'Pitfalls in Testing the Ricardian Equivalence Theorem' (Manuscript).

Cooper, Richard N. (1986) 'Dealing with the Trade Deficit in a Floating Rate System,' *Brookings Papers on Economic Activity* **1**, 195–207.

Corden, W. Max (1985) *Inflation, Exchange Rates, and the World Economy: Lectures on International Monetary Economics*, Third Edition (Chicago: University of Chicago Press, 1985).

Corden, W. Max (1986) 'Fiscal Policies, Current Accounts and Real Exchange Rates: In Search of a Logic of International Policy Coordination,' *Weltwirtschaftliches Archiv* **122**, 423–38.

Currie, David, and Paul Levine (1985) 'Macroeconomic Policy Design in an Interdependent World,' in Willem H. Buiter and Richard C. Marston (eds), *International Economic Policy Coordination*, (Cambridge: Cambridge University Press), 228–71.

Currie, David and Simon Wren-Lewis (1987) 'Evaluating the Extended Target Zone Proposal for the G3,' CEPR Discussion Paper No. 221.

Dornbusch, Rudiger (1987) 'External Balance Correction: Depreciation or Protection?' *Brookings Papers on Economic Activity* **1**, 249–69.

Dornbusch, Rudiger, and Jeffrey Frankel (1987) 'The Flexible Exchange Rate System: Experience and Alternatives,' NBER Working Paper No. 2464.

Edison, Hali, J., Marcus H. Miller, and John Williamson (1987) 'On Evaluating and Extending the Target Zone Proposal,' *Journal of Policy Modeling* **9**, 199–224.

Feldstein, Martin (1988) 'Rethinking International Economic Coordination: a Lecture on the Occasion of the Fiftieth Anniversary of Nuffield College, Oxford,' *Oxford Economic Papers*.

Feldstein, Martin and Charles Horioka (1980) 'Domestic Saving and International Capital Flows,' *Economic Journal* **90**, 314–29.

Frenkel, Jacob A. (1986) 'International Interdependence and the Constraints on Macroeconomic Policies,' *'Weltwirschaftliches Archiv* **122**, 615–46.

Frenkel, Jacob A., and Morris Goldstein (1986) 'A Guide to Target Zones,' *IMF Staff Papers* **33**, 633–73.

Frenkel, Jacob A., and Assaf Razin (1987) *Fiscal Policies and the World Economy: An International Approach* (Cambridge, Massachusetts: MIT Press).

Friedman, B.M. (1975) 'Targets, Instruments, and Indicators of Monetary Policy,' *Journal of Monetary Economics* **1**, 443–73.

Genberg, Hans and Alexander K. Swoboda (1987) 'The Current Account and the Policy Mix Under Flexible Exchange Rates,' IMF Working Paper No. 87/70.

Haas, Richard D. and Paul R. Masson (1986) 'Minimod: Specification and Simulation Results,' *IMF Staff Papers* **33**, 722–67.

Hamada, Koichi, (1974) 'Alternative Exchange Rate Systems and the Interdependence of Monetary Policies,' in Robert Z. Aliber, editor, *National Policies and the International Financial System* (Chicago, University of Chicago Press), 13–33.

Helkie, William L, and Peter Hooper (1988) 'An Empirical Analysis of the External Deficit,' in Ralph C. Bryant, Gerald Holtham, and Peter Hooper, editors, *External Deficits and the The Dollar: The Pit and the Pendulum* (Washington: The Brookings Institution).

Kimbrough, Kent P., and Faik Koray (1984) 'Money, Output, and the Trade Balance: Theory and Evidence,' *Canadian Journal of Economics* **3**, 508–22.

Krugman, Paul R. (1988) 'Target Zones and Exchange Rate Dynamics,' NBER Working Papers No. 2481.

Liviatan, Nissan (1981) 'Monetary Expansion and Real Exchange Rate Dynamics,' *Journal of Political Economy*, **89**, 1218–27.

Masson, Paul R., Steven Symansky, Richard Haas, and Michael Dooley (1988) 'MULTIMOD: A Multi-Region Econometric Model,' *IMF Staff Studies for the World Economic Outlook*, 50–104.

McKinnon, R.I. (1982) 'Currency Substitution and Instability in the World Dollar Market,' *The American Economic Review* **72**, 320–33.

McKinnon, R.I. (1988) 'Monetary and Exchange Rate Policies for International Financial Stability: A Proposal', *The Journal of Economic Perspectives* **2**, 83–103.

Meade, James E. (1951) 'The Balance of Payments,' *The Theory of International Economic Policy*, Vol. I (Oxford: Oxford University Press).

Meade, James E. and David Vines (1989) 'Monetary Policy and Fiscal Policy: Impact Effects with a New Keynesian "Assignment" of Weapons to Targets,' in Weale *et al.*

Mundell, R. A. (1960) 'The Monetary Dynamics of International Adjustment Under Fixed and Flexible Exchange Rates,' *Quarterly Journal of Economics* **74**, 249–50.

Mundell, R.A. (1962) 'The Appropriate Use of Monetary and Fiscal Policy for Internal and External Stability,' *IMF Staff Papers* **9**.

Mundell, R.A. (1963) 'Capital Mobility and Stabilization Policy Under Fixed and Flexible Exchange Rates,' *The Canadian Journal of Economics and Political Science* **29**, 475–85.

Mundell, R.A. (1964) 'A Reply: Capital Mobility and Size,' *The Canadian Journal of Economics and Political Science* **30**, 421–28.

Oudiz, Gilles and Jeffrey Sachs (1984) 'Macroeconomic Policy Coordination Among the Industrial Economies,' *Brookings Papers on Economic Activity* **1**, 1–75.

Polak, Jacques J. (1988) 'Economic Policy Objectives and Policy-Making in the Major Industrial Countries,' prepared for the Conference on National Economic Policies and their Impact on the World Economy, Hamburg, May 1988.

Sachs, Jeffrey D. and Nouriel Roubini (1987) 'Sources of Macroeconomic Imbalances in the World Economy: A Simulation Approach,' prepared for the Third International Conference sponsored by the Institute for Monetary and Economic Studies, the Bank of Japan, Session III (May 1987).

Stockman, Alan C. (1988) 'On the Roles of International Financial Markets and their Relevance for Economic Policy,' *Journal of Money, Credit and Banking* **20**, 531–49.

Tanzi, Vito (1988) 'International Coordination of Fiscal Policies: A Review of Some Major Issues,' IMF Working Paper No. 88/70.

Vines, David, Jan Maciejowski, and James E. Meade (1983) *Stagflation, Volume 2: Demand Management* (London: Allen and Unwin Ltd.).

Weale, Martin, Andrew Blake, Nicos Christodoulakis, James Meade, and David Vines (1989) *Macroeconomic Policy, Inflation, Wealth and the Exchange Rate* (London: Unwin Hyman.).

Williamson, John (1985) *The Exchange Rate System*, Policy Analyses in International Economics, No. 5 (Washington: Institute for International Economics, Second Edition).

Williamson, John and Marcus H. Miller (1987) *Targets and Indicators: A Blueprint for the International Coordination of Economic Policy*. Policy Analyses in International Economics, No. 22 (Washington: Institute for International Economics).

Discussion

David Vines

1 Introduction

Some of these comments relate to a forthcoming book which I have written with colleagues Andrew Blake, Nicos Christodoulakis, James Meade and Martin Weale in Cambridge (Weale et al., 1989). An early version of chapters two and three of this book has appeared as Meade and Vines (1988) and Blake, Vines and Weale (1988). It will become obvious that Boughton and we are doing rather similar things.

Boughton is looking for simple rules in policy coordination rather than the outcomes of full optimal, game-theory analyses. Although the latter are often very illuminating, for certain purposes we should side with Boughton (see Weale et al., 1989, chapters 1, 6 and 11).

Let us agree to focus on nominal income as the internal demand management objective. Marcus Miller might tell us that such a focus is arbitrary: the authorities would not – he tells us – be indifferent if there were at the same time a one per cent rise in prices and a one per cent fall in output, whereas a nominal income target suggests that they would be. For a defence against his argument see Weale et al., chapter 1. It is, I think, helpful in doing this to recognize that there should be a feedthrough from y to P, of the kind missing from equations (9) and (10) of Boughton's paper. Weale et al. work out the details of all this for the one-country case, with a model which is static like Boughton's in Chapter 2. A comparison with their analysis is useful.

Let us agree that there is another objective of policy. For Boughton it is ensuring a satisfactory current account of the balance of payments. There is a long and honourable tradition of caring about the current account. But for Corden (in the recent writings referred to by Boughton) what matters is the overall accumulation of wealth, and not merely the current account of the balance of payments, which is merely a part of wealth accumulation. Weale et al. agree with Corden rather than Boughton, for reasons explained at length in chapter 1 (see also Vines, 1988). But for the moment, let us agree with Boughton, for the sake of argument.

Finally, let us agree that world real interest rates have an important effect on a single economy and that world capital accumulation is an important objective of policy. But Boughton's analysis dichotomises the problem, focusing mainly on fiscal and monetary policy for current balance and inflation control, sometimes even only in a single open economy. I am not sure that this simplification makes sense.[1] But let me provisionally agree with Boughton, again for the purposes of argument.

2 The model

We thus turn to the analytical heart of Boughton's paper, Sections III.2 and III.3. His fundamental point follows from the claim that monetary policy has very little effect on the current account. This is the case in his model because:

(a) To the extent that monetary expansion *does* depress the exchange rate, its effects on the trade balance are lagged (there may even be a *J* curve).

(b) To the extent that the exchange rate depreciation *does* cause the trade balance to improve, this effect must be strong enough to overcome the effects of monetary expansion on imports (via interest rate effects on domestic expenditures).

These two effects are the reasons for the ambiguity in the signs of $\partial K/\partial L$, which is discussed at the beginning of Section III.2. Boughton concludes that $\partial K/\partial L$ is probably small in magnitude and perhaps nearly zero. For a related discussion, see Blake, Vines and Weale (1988, p. 23, equation 31) and Weale *et al.* Chapter 3, Section 8, where we analyse a very similar sort of inequality.

Surely Boughton's fundamental point concerns the comparative advantage of monetary policy on external balance, rather than its absolute magnitude or sign. Thus I think he should analyse and describe the ratio:

$$v = \frac{(\partial K/\partial L)/(\partial K/\partial g)}{(\partial Py/\partial L)/(\partial Py/\partial g)} \tag{1}$$

If this ratio has an absolute value of less than unity, then monetary policy has a comparative advantage over internal balance. Analysis of such a ratio is the centrepiece of the analysis in Sections 6 and 7 of Blake, Vines and Weale (1988) and in all of Meade and Vines (1988) and in much of Weale *et al.* (1988). Boughton's argument about $\partial K/\partial L$, reviewed above, suggests that the magnitude of this ratio is small.

It is not immediately easy to see why *gg* is flat in Boughton's Figure 6.1. Is not Figure 6A.1 more transparent?

The lines show combinations of the instruments consistent with particular outcomes for the target variables. Both shocks *and* changes in the desired outcomes for the target variables shift the K^* and $(Py)^*$ lines. The K^* line is flat on Boughton's argument that a very large change in L would be required to compensate for the effect on K of even a small change in g. The $(Py)^*$ line is downward sloping for an obvious reason: fiscal and monetary expansions both raise nominal income; to keep nominal income constant, then, for example g must be lowered if L is raised. Boughton's policy experiments can easily be performed using shifts in only one line at a time. This is essentially what we do in the chapters referred to above.

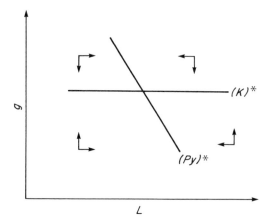

Figure 6A.1 The relationships between targets and instruments in Boughton's model: An alternative presentation

3 Policy recommendation for one country

It is clear from Figure 6A.1 and from our discussion of the ratio v in equation (1) that monetary policy certainly does not have a comparative advantage over external balance. From this Boughton concludes that fiscal policy ought to be *assigned* to external balance, and monetary policy assigned to the control of nominal income or inflation. The arrows denote this assignment. It is clearly preferable in such a set up to the opposite assignment: inspection shows how that would lead to cycles in policy adjustment. Notice that this is a strong claim amongst economists, who are used to saying that both instruments should be used to control both targets, rather than being assigned like this.

Notice that this is also very different from the equally strong claim being made by Williamson and Miller – in their 'target zone' proposals – in two distinct ways. First, here the external target is the current account and not the exchange rate. Second, for Williamson and Miller the assignment is reversed. Monetary policy for them ought to be assigned to the control of the *external* objective (for them the exchange rate) and fiscal policy ought to be used to control the internal objective (nominal income).

As to the choice of external target I suspect that both Boughton (B) and Williamson and Miller (WM) are right, and that both are wrong.

(a) If bubbles are important then an exchange rate target *does* seem important – thus I vote for Williamson and Miller in the short run.
(b) But I agree with Boughton that the current account (or more generally wealth accumulation) is relevant in the long run. Neglect of this point, as Weale *et al.* (Chapter 4) shows, can be very damaging to the target zones proposal: to take acount of it requires a 'gradually adjusting' target zone.

As to the rigid assignment of instruments to targets proposed – in quite different ways – by each of Boughton on the one hand and Williamson and Miller on the other hand, I think that this too is a mistake. In this I thus disagree with both B and WM in that I think that *both* fiscal policy and monetary policy should share in the task of controlling the internal objective (inflation or nominal income). A point which neither B or WM make is that the extent to which fiscal policy can share in this task will depend upon (i) the degree of real wage resistance (which circumscribes the ability of tax increases to damp inflation and (ii) the degree of political resistance to tax increases (which does the same thing more indirectly). This issue is thoroughly explored in Weale *et al.* and in the other papers referred to above.

I obviously also therefore disagree with both B and WM in that I think that *both* fiscal policy and monetary policy (the latter mainly via exchange rate adjustment) should be used to influence the evolution of the current account.[2] But it is clear from Boughton that, at the very least, the adjustment of the exchange rate with respect to the current account deficit will need to be slow.

The implication of the previous two paragraphs is that policies ought to be designed which link both instruments (fiscal and monetary) to the pursuit of both targets (nominal income – and we have supposed up until now – the current account). One of the most important questions then becomes finding the appropriate *emphasis* to place on each of the instruments in the control of each of the targets. This is an issue to which my colleagues and I give great attention in our forthcoming book.

It is time to suggest again that wealth accumulation rather than a current account balance should perhaps be the second objective of policy. The reason is related to an argument which was sometimes used to defend the strength of the dollar in the face of a weakening US current account in 1985, namely that if the country is investing and building up assets at home then the income from these can be used to service a current account deficit without there being any need for a policy correction. (That same argument is being used by the UK policy authorities in early 1989 to argue in a similar way for this country – see Vines, 1988.)

As a consequence of all this, my colleagues and I have been exploring the following set of policy rules:

$$
\begin{bmatrix} \Delta S \\ \Delta E^T \\ \Delta r \end{bmatrix} = \begin{bmatrix} h_{11} & h_{12} & \cdot \\ h_{21} & h_{22} & \cdot \\ \cdot & \cdot & h_{33} \end{bmatrix} \begin{bmatrix} Py-(Py)^T \\ W-W^T \\ E-E^T \end{bmatrix}
$$

where notation is as in Boughton's paper, and where the superscript T means target value, where W is wealth (which includes overseas assets accumulated through current account surpluses), where S is the tax rate, where r is the interest rate and where the h_{ik}'s are functions, some of which are lagged. Notice in particular:

(i) The exchange rate is an intermediate target and monetary policy (the interest rate) is adjusted to steer it to its desired value, as shown by the parameter h_{33}.
(ii) Fiscal and monetary policy (through adjustments in tax rates and the exchange-rate target) *share* the function of steering the economy towards the targets for Py and W: this generalizes both B and WM. As already noted large parts of our forthcoming book are taken up with exploring the question of the emphases h_{ij}

which should be put respectively on the two types of policy in the control of the two targets of policy, Py and W.

4 International implications

Although Boughton's analysis centres on policy adjustment in a single open economy, his concerns are broader than this. He wants to discuss international policy coordination in Section IV. The analysis in Section III and that sketched above are only 2×2, whereas what he really wants to recommend globally is 4×4. The four targets are: inflation in two countries, current account balance, and global capital accumulation. The four instruments are: fiscal and monetary policy in both countries. I like it, but I am not yet convinced, and more work is needed.

Notes

1 One reason for skepticism was explained in detail by Meade at a Conference in Cambridge in June 1987. If countries pursue current account targets then, if these countries inconsistently all aim for surpluses (and the world current account discrepancy will help to make them do so), this will impart an inconsistency to global policy making. By contrast, with wealth targets there is not the possibility of such inconsistency, since the current account is only one part of wealth: country A can accumulate wealth without this necessarily being at the expense of country B. Needless to say Weale *et al.* follow Meade's advice.

2 And, more generally of wealth, see Note 1.

References

Blake, Andrew, David Vines, and Martin Weale (1988) 'Wealth Targets, Exchange Rate Targets and Macroeconomic Policy', CEPR Discussion Paper No. 247.

Meade, James and David Vines (1988) 'Monetary Policy and Fiscal Policy: Impact Effects with a New Keynesian "Assignment" of Weapons to Target', CEPR Discussion Paper No. 246.

Weale, Martin, Andrew Blake, Nicos Christodoulakis, James Meade and David Vines (1989). *Macroeconomic Policy: Inflation, Wealth and the Exchange Rate.* London: Allen and Unwin.

Vines, David (1988) 'Is the Thatcher Experiment Still on Course?' mimeo, University of Glasgow.

Chapter 7

Exchange rate bands and realignments in a stationary stochastic setting*

Marcus Miller and Paul Weller

1 Introduction

As financial capital became ever more mobile and US monetary leadership progressively less credible (due, in part, to the exigencies of war finance), the Bretton Woods system of pegged-but-adjustable exchange rates became crisis-prone. Then, in the early 1970s, it finally collapsed.

In the aftermath, OECD countries were, by and large, content to allow their exchange rates to float – firmly anchored, it was hoped, by declared national money-supply targets. The UK and the US were particularly enthusiastic advocates of national monetary autonomy and floating rates (together with substantial financial deregulation); and they bore with stoic indifference the enormous changes in international competitiveness that ensued.

After a while, however, disillusionment set in. Thus, under domestic pressures for protection, the US began actively to 'manage the dollar' in 1985, and was instrumental in arranging the Louvre Accord among the G6 in February 1987. According to Funabashi (1988), this involved bilateral exchange rate bands of $\pm 5\%$ against the US dollar, although participants

* This paper was directly stimulated by Paul Krugman's stochastic treatment of currency bands. We are also grateful to Maurice Obstfeld for his comments. We are indebted to the ESRC and the Ford and Alfred P. Sloan Foundations for financial support (grants to CEPR Nos. 850–1014 and 85-12-13, respectively), and to the NBER for the opportunity to revise the paper. The research reported here is part of CEPR's research programme in International Macroeconomics.

BLUEPRINTS FOR EXCHANGE RATE MANAGEMENT
0-12-497060-5

Copyright © 1989 Academic Press, Ltd
All rights of reproduction reserved

made no explicit surrender of national monetary autonomy. The UK was a participant, and was, at that time, closely shadowing the DM. (Currently, however, there are signs of a return to floating with monetary targets.)

Concerned about their 'internal market', Europeans (other than the UK) had never been enthusiastic for generalized floating and experimented instead with regional schemes for managing their cross-rates; first the Snake and then, in 1979, the EMS. The latter has proved relatively successful in preventing big shifts in competitiveness between the member countries, but it has relied heavily on capital market controls. According to current plans, however, these controls are to be abolished; and the lessons of history and economic theory have led observers such as Padoa Schioppa (1988) to warn those planning the next phase of the EMS that they are seeking the impossible if they try to achieve free trade in goods and capital and to manage exchange rates *without* ending national monetary autonomy.

In this paper we examine this issue – the compatibility of exchange rate management and monetary autonomy – using a model with free trade, perfect capital mobility, and (adjustable) *exchange rate bands*. In particular, we examine the implication for monetary policy and exchange rates of announcing *rules for realigning* the exchange rate bands when the rate hits the edge. In a setting where there are no inherent trends in the price level, Obstfeld (1988) has recently argued that accommodation of price changes may nevertheless cause devaluation spirals. But we get different, and less startling, results from applying Krugman's (1987, 1988) analysis to a stochastic Dornbusch model. The model, and the effect of fixed exchange rate bands therein[1], is given first, before considering the implications of prospects for realignment.

II   A simple stochastic Dornbusch model

The model to be used for four equations, two static and two dynamic:

$$m - p = \kappa y - \lambda i \qquad \text{(Money Market)} \qquad (1)$$

$$y = - \gamma i - \eta v \qquad \text{(Goods Market)} \qquad (2)$$

$$dp = \phi y dt + \sigma dz \text{ or } p = \int_{-\infty}^{t} y(s)ds + z \quad \text{(Stochastic Phillips Curve)} \quad (3)$$

$$E(dx) = (i^* - i)dt \text{ or } x = E \int_{t}^{+\infty} (i(s) - i^*(s))ds + \hat{x} \quad \text{(Arbitrage)} \qquad (4)$$

where the symbols used are defined as follows:

m the domestic money stock (in logs)

p price index of domestic final product (in logs)

p^* price index of imported foreign product (in logs)

y level of domestic final production, measured from its non-inflationary level (in logs)

x the exchange rate, defined as the foreign currency price of domestic currency (in logs)

$v \equiv$ $(x + p - p^*)$ the 'real' exchange rate (in logs)

i (instantaneous) domestic nominal interest rate

i^* (instantaneous) foreign nominal interest rate

df the stochastic differential of the process f

z a scalar Brownian motion process with unit variance, so σdz is white noise

E the expectations operator

$\hat{x}$ a hat ($\hat{}$) above a variable denotes its long-run equilibrium value.

The equations are doubtless familiar (see Dornbusch, 1976, Appendix), so we can be brief. The first defines equilibrium in the domestic money market, where the demand for real balances is associated positively with output and negatively with the opportunity cost of holding money (measured by i). For simplicity, the price deflator for the money stock is that of domestic product. So long as the exchange rate is inside the band, we assume that the nominal money stock is fixed at a 'target' level: what happens at the edges of the band is *either* that the money supply is adjusted to ensure $i = i^*$, so the band is defended; *or* there is a realignment and the money stock is adjusted to a new target level.

The level of output is demand-determined and, as shown by equation (2), depends (negatively) on the real exchange rate (the relative price of domestic output) and on the domestic interest rate. Although it would doubtless be more accurate to use the 'real' interest rate here, we have stayed with Dornbusch's original formulation because it is simpler and because the fixed money supply rules out persistent inflation.

The next two equations show the contrast between the way the price of domestic production evolves and the way the exchange rate is determined. (Foreign prices are assumed to be constant throughout.) The price of domestic output is 'predetermined', i.e. it depends on its previous value except insofar as it is raised or lowered by movements in current production above or below the non-inflationary level or by white noise disturbances, σdz. Thus we have adhered to Dornbusch's formulation in ignoring terms reflecting past or future inflation, but have added a random disturbance.

The nominal exchange rate – here defined as the foreign currency price of domestic currency – is a 'forward-looking' variable which depends not at all on its previous value. As indicated to the right of equation (4), the current exchange rate is the long-run equilibrium, $\hat{x}$, 'discounted' back by the integral of expected future international interest differentials. So a future interest differential which is, on average, expected to be in favour of the domestic economy will lift the currency above equilibrium, and vice versa.

The evolution of these two 'prices' can be expressed as two simultaneous stochastic differential equations (after eliminating y and i by substitution). Thus

$$\begin{bmatrix} dp \\ E(dx) \end{bmatrix} = \frac{1}{\Delta}\begin{bmatrix} -\phi(\gamma + \lambda\eta) & -\phi\lambda\eta \\ \kappa\eta - 1 & \kappa\eta \end{bmatrix}\begin{bmatrix} pdt \\ xdt \end{bmatrix} + \frac{1}{\Delta}\begin{bmatrix} \phi\gamma & \phi\lambda\eta & 0 \\ 1 & -\kappa\eta & \Delta \end{bmatrix}\begin{bmatrix} mdt \\ p^*dt \\ i^*dt \end{bmatrix}\begin{bmatrix} + \sigma dz \\ + 0 \end{bmatrix}$$

(5)

where $\Delta = \kappa\gamma + \lambda$. Alternatively, defining variables x_0, p_0, as deviations from equilibrium, (so $x_0 = x - \hat{x}$, $p_0 = p - \hat{p}$),

$$\begin{bmatrix} dp_0 \\ E(dx_0) \end{bmatrix} = A\begin{bmatrix} p_0 dt \\ x_0 dt \end{bmatrix} + \begin{bmatrix} \sigma dz \\ 0 \end{bmatrix}$$

(6)

where A is the matrix of coefficients on the right-hand side endogenous variables in equation (5). From now on, we will work with the formulation in (6), and to simplify notation will relabel $p = p_0$, $x = x_0$.

The determinant of the matrix A (namely, $\dfrac{-\phi\eta}{\Delta}$) is negative, indicating roots of opposite sign. One solution to the stochastic system is that it lies on the linear stable manifold associated with the negative root of A, ρ_s, so

$$x = \theta_s p$$

(7)

where $\theta_s = \dfrac{1 - \kappa\eta}{\kappa\eta - \rho_s\Delta}$.

Note that the sign of θ_s depends on that of $1 - \kappa\eta$. If $\kappa\eta < 1$, and θ_s is positive, then the exchange rate is high in response to positive price disequilibria; which is also the case where the exchange rate 'overshoots' in response to monetary changes. (When $\kappa\eta > 1$ and $\theta_s < 0$, one has 'under-shooting'.)

But, where $\sigma^2 > 0$, there are many other functional relationships between x and p which satisfy equation (6); and as the problem is stationary, one can obtain an ordinary differential equation characterising these solutions, as follows. Let $x = f(p)$ be a solution. Then, by Ito's lemma,

$$dx = f'(p)\,dt + \frac{\sigma^2}{2}f''(p)\,dt$$

(8)

On taking expectations and substituting from (6), one obtains the required equation, namely

$$\left[A_2 - f'(p) A_1 \right] \left[\begin{matrix} p \\ f(p) \end{matrix} \right] = \frac{\sigma^2}{2} f''(p) \tag{9}$$

where A_1, A_2 denote the respective rows of A.

By imposing the boundary condition $f(0) = 0$, we obtain solutions which satisfy the symmetry property $f(x) = -f(-x)$. These are the appropriate ones to consider for problems with boundary conditions symmetric about equilibrium.

For the case of exchange rate 'undershooting', where the rate weakens as the price level rises relative to the money stock, we illustrate, in figure 7.1, the qualitative nature of all these trajectories[2] and indicate how the boundary conditions implied by a symmetric, *fully credible exchange rate band* serve to pin down a particular solution. The lines *SOS'* and *UOU'* represent the stable and unstable saddlepaths respectively of the deterministic system, and are also solutions to the stochastic system for suitable boundary conditions. But there are an infinity of other (non-linear) solutions passing through the origin, whose qualitative features are illustrated by the curved lines in the figure. The appropriate boundary condition requires that the trajectory be tangent to the band (so-called 'smooth pasting').[3] So the desired solution consists of the bands themselves, and the backward S-shaped curve that links them, and is shown labelled as *ABCD* in the figure. The curvature of this trajectory from *B* to *C* relative to the manifold *SOS'* exhibits what Krugman has dubbed the 'bias in the band'. (But note that as σ^2 tends to zero, the section *BC* moves close to *SOS'*, the stable eigenvector of A, coinciding with it in the limit.) Figure 7.1(b) shows the stance of monetary policy necessary to support such a band, where m^* is the target level of the money supply and the 'state-contingent' shifts of the money stock from this target level are those required to keep international interest differentials at zero at the edges of the band.

III Realignments

The boundary conditions considered above are those appropriate for fully credible currency bands where the temporary departures of the money stock from its target level reflect action taken by the monetary authorities to hold the rate at the edge of the band. But what if the consequence of the rate hitting the edge of the band was, instead, a realignment of the band itself and a simultaneous shift of the monetary target? And what if market

(a) The 'smooth-pasting' condition

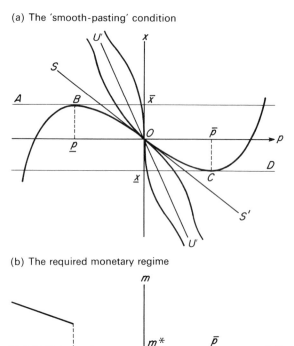

(b) The required monetary regime

Figure 7.1   A 'symmetric' currency band

participants were unsure whether there was to be a defence of the band or a realignment? In these circumstances, as Krugman has argued, different boundary conditions apply depending on the size of the possible realignment and how likely it is expected to be.

Consider, for example the rule that, 'if the rate hits the edge of the band, then the money stock target be adjusted exactly to accommodate the divergence of the price level from its equilibrium, and the centre of the exchange rate band be moved by the same percentage amount'. And suppose that market participants believe that the rule will be followed with some probability π. Also, following Krugman (1988), let us make two additional, simplifying assumptions. First, if the band is ever defended, the authorities establish full credibility. Second, if a realignment does occur, the market does not change its perception of the probability of future realignments. Then the probability π assigned to realignment (as opposed to defense) systematically affects both the size of the expected realignment itself and the trajectory for the exchange rate within the currency band.

To show this, we proceed geometrically, with the aid of Figure 7.2. In the top panel, the 45° line, PPP, is the locus of points which would preserve purchasing power parity and, as before, SOS' indicates the stable manifold of the deterministic system (which for suitable initial conditions is also a solution to the stochastic system). We concentrate for simplicity only on what happens at the bottom edge of the band. The argument is exactly symmetrical at the top. The locus ODB describes the path of the exchange rate in the presence of a fully credible band. But, where the market expects that a realignment will occur with some positive probability, the rate will follow a path such as OC. Its properties are, first, that it is a solution to (9), and so satisfies the arbitrage condition within the band; second, that when the rate hits the edge of the band at C, the *expected* change in the rate is zero; that is

$$\pi \text{ (loss on realignment)} + (1 - \pi)(\text{gain if no realignment}) = 0 \quad (10)$$

Thus, if a realignment occurs, and the money stock is increased by $\tilde{p}$ in harmony, then the rate drops instantaneously from C to E, the new equilibrium lying in the middle of the realigned band. But, if no realignment occurs, and m is held at m^*, then the rate jumps upwards to point D.

Now, as π varies from zero to one, point C moves from B to F. For if $f(p)$ is the solution to (9) in the fully credible case, then using the relationship in (10) we see that for any π, $\tilde{p}$ must solve

$$\pi(b - p) + (1 - \pi)(f(p) + b) = 0 \quad (11)$$

where b is equal to half the width of the band.

This produces a relationship between π and $\tilde{p}$ of the form

$$\pi(\tilde{p}) = \frac{f(\tilde{p}) + b}{f(\tilde{p}) + \tilde{p}} \quad (12)$$

which is illustrated in the lower panel of Figure 7.2.

There, by definition, $\pi(p_u) = 0$ and $\pi(p_l) = 1$, and it is straight-forward to confirm that $\pi' < 0$, $\pi'' > 0$ for $p_l \le p < p_u$, and that $\pi'(p_u) = 0$.

More generally, we can think of a family of solutions satisfying (10) for a class of realignment rules of which full accommodation is a special case. If we identify the realignment rule with the associated change in money supply Δm, then the following relationship must hold:

$$\pi(\tilde{p}) = \frac{f(\tilde{p}) + b}{f(\tilde{p}) - g(\tilde{p} - \Delta m) + \Delta m} \quad (13)$$

where $f(p)$ is, as before, the trajectory associated with *no* realignment but $g(p)$ is that associated with a given $\pi > 0$ and the given amount of monetary

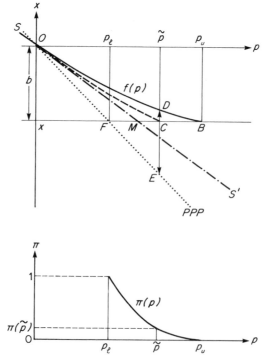

Figure 7.2 Realignments: How the hitting point ($\tilde{p}$) varies with the perceived realignment probability (π)

accommodation, Δm – see the discussion of Figure 7.4. below. So $g(p)$ is a solution to (9) which will depend upon π and Δm. A fully accommodating rule involves setting Δm equal to $\tilde{p}$, and (13) reduces to (12) since $g(0) = 0$. (It is important to point out that the relationship in (13) is not valid for arbitrary Δm. This is best illustrated by observing that if Δm is 'too large', then for some values of π there will exist no $\tilde{p}$ satisfying (13). In particular, if $\Delta m \geqslant 2p_u$, there is no value of $\tilde{p}$ that will satisfy (13) for any positive π.)

An interesting case is the hitting point at M associated with the price $\tilde{p} = \dfrac{-b}{\theta_s}$. The associated probability of realignment, π_M, will depend upon the realignment rule in the following way:

$$\pi_M = \frac{f(-b/\theta_s) + b}{f(-b/\theta_s) + b + (1 + \theta_s)\Delta m}, \quad \Delta m < -2b/\theta_s$$

This is the value of π which will exactly counteract Krugman's 'bias in the band' and ensure that the equilibrium lies along the stable manifold SOS'

(until any band is defended, at which time full credibility is established). It may be easier to see the implications of a fully accommodating realignment rule with reference to Figure 7.3 which shows what happens when the rate hits the edge in the case where $\pi = 1$. On the assumption that the market fully expects such a realignment (and the corresponding shift in the monetary target), then from a band centred on E_0 the rate will lie along the dotted line $E_H E_0 E_L$ which snakes around the 45° line of *PPP*. On reaching either end as a result of the random inflation shocks, there will be a realignment: from E_0 each of these possibilities has equal probability in the eyes of the market. If, for instance, there was a run of positive inflation shocks taking p to p_l, then the band would move down by half its width so the rate would now lie at the centre of the new band. On the assumption that the market continues to assign the same probability to future realignments, the rate will lie on the dashed line through E_L.

At first sight this result appears counterintuitive. Indeed, for the semi-stable model he analyses, Krugman (1988) argues that setting $\pi = 1$ is equivalent to a 'free float'. In our model this is not the case. If we interpret a free float as equivalent to an infinitely wide exchange rate band, the path for the exchange rate will be SOS'. But, as we show below, that is also the solution when $\pi = \pi_M \neq 1$.

The reason why, even when $\pi = 1$, there is an effect upon the path of the exchange rate, is that we have in fact introduced *thresholds* for monetary accommodation. If fundamentals fluctuate within a certain range (here $-b < p < b$), no adjustment to the money stock occurs. When p hits the trigger value b, there is an immediate increase in m, by the same amount, to a new target level which remains unchanged – until the next realignment.

Because of the discontinuous nature of monetary adjustment, the behaviour

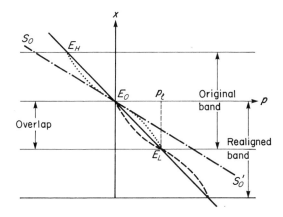

Figure 7.3   The case where realignment is expected with certainty ($\pi = 1$)

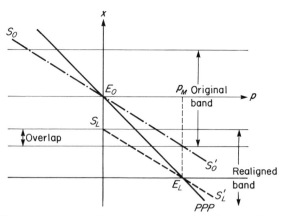

Figure 7.4 The case where realignment is expected with probability π_M

of the exchange rate betrays an element of 'hysteresis', in that its relationship
to the price level is not unique, but depends on the money stock, which is
changed from time to time (when shocks have cumulated sufficiently since
the last adjustment). It is precisely this element of hysteresis which obviates
the need for a 'smooth pasting' or tangency condition between regimes. With
a fully credible exchange rate band, switching between support and no
support regimes is triggered by the price level passing through a single
critical value. But in this case a realignment alters the trigger values for the
fundamental, and the arbitrage equation simply imposes the restriction that
there be no discontinuity in the path of the exchange rate.

Figure 7.4 illustrates the case where the probability of a realignment-with-
complete-monetary-accommodation is such as to keep the exchange rate on
$S_0 S_0'$ until it hits the edge of the band (i.e. $\pi = \pi_M$, in the notation used
above). If this happens to be the lower edge then, if a realignment occurs, as
shown, the rate jumps down to a new equilibrium on the *PPP* line, at E_L.
It then remains on the linear trajectory $S_L S_L'$ until another realignment
brings it back to E_0 or carries it further away.

IV   Underalignment and overalignment

As we have already observed, there is no necessity for a realignment to
accommodate the price level exactly. To see what happens in the case of
'overalignment' ($\Delta m > \tilde{p}$) and 'underalignment' ($\Delta m < \tilde{p}$), we shall continue
to assume that π is unchanged after any realignment. In the former case
(where the amount of monetary accommodation and the potential shift in
the exchange rate when realignment takes place are both increased) it seems

reasonably obvious that, for any given trigger price, there must be less of a risk of realigning for the arbitrage conditions to be satisfied at the edge of the band; and conversely for underalignments. The shifts in the relationship between the trigger price, $\tilde{p}$ and the risk, π, implied by changing the degree of price accommodation in either direction are shown in the lower panel of Figure 7.5, where the line CB represents the relationship already derived for the case of 100% accommodation.

In the upper panel, we sketch the implied trajectory for the exchange rate path within the band, focusing on an overalignment, expected with certainty. The requirement that the percentage change in the money stock (Δm) will be greater than the percentage deviation of prices ($\tilde{p}$) in this case is indicated by the slope of the line E_0B which has a slope greater than that of the PPP line shown there. The trajectory implied by this particular degree of overalignment, anticipated for sure, is shown labelled as E_0L and cuts the lower edge of the band to the left of the PPP line. (At point L the greater-than-proportionate shift in the money supply and the bands will for sure shift the centre of the band down to the level A, giving a new equilibrium

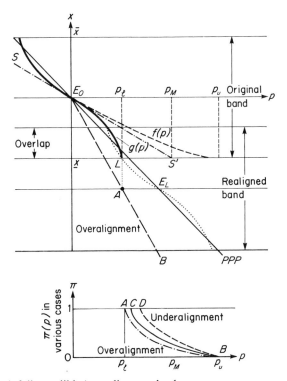

Figure 7.5 A fully credible 'overalignment' rule

on the *PPP* line at E_L; and, at point L, the exchange rate must also lie on the trajectory associated with the new equilibrium, see Figure 7.5, since the transition is expected with complete certainty.) The distance from L to the 45° line must be equal to the distance AC in the lower panel, if both measure the fall in the hitting price corresponding to the same rule for overalignment, expected for sure.

Two observations on this solution are in order. First (as has already been indicated), there is a limit to the degree of overalignment which may be anticipated with complete certainty and still generate zero expected profits. Second, we note that along trajectories which cross the *PPP* line in this type of model, the expected movement of the price level may switch away from the old equilibrium towards the new as the edge of the band is approached (see Miller and Weller, 1988b, for further discussion).

These two caveats do not, however, apply to the case of underalignments (these are not shown in the top panel), but it is reasonably clear that the hitting point for $\pi = 1$ is to the left of the *PPP* line, so the function in the bottom panel is shifted to the right for such a case. Ultimately, of course, as the degree of underalignment approaches zero, one converges to the case where the existing exchange rate band is fully credible.

IV   Conclusions

By using a stochastic approach, we have shown how it is possible to combine some measure of monetary autonomy and some management of the exchange rate while preserving free trade in both goods and financial assets. If the specific realignment rules examined here were fully believed, then the money supply would usually be fixed and the currency would float freely, except when the rate hit the edges of the band – when the money supply would jump without shocking the current spot rate. (The spot exchange rate could jump too, if the probability of realignment were less than one.) We offer this as an alternative to the 'speculative attack' treatment proposed by Obstfeld (1988) to help understand the economic implications of abolishing capital controls within the EMS. (Note, however, that there are additional parameter differences – other than in the stochastic specification – between the models used which will affect a detailed comparison of results.)

There are numerous ways in which the stochastic approach adopted here can be improved – thus the realignment probability might be revised systematically, for example (cf. Backus and Driffill, 1985) and account taken of the presence of 'noise traders' in the foreign exchange market (cf. DeLong *et al.*, 1988), to name but two. Past experience of the EMS and the pressures exerted upon it by further financial deregulation will doubtless suggest others.

Notes

1 As discussed earlier in Miller and Weller (1988a), to which the reader is referred for additional detail.

2 A formal derivation of these qualitative characteristics is provided in Miller and Weller (1988b).

3 A detailed discussion of the 'smooth pasting' condition as it applies here is given in Miller and Weller (1988a). See also Dixit (1987) for an application of these conditions in a model of entry and exit decisions by firms.

References

Backus, D. and J. Driffill (1985) 'Inflation and reputation,' *American Economic Review* **75**, 530–38.

DeLong, B., A. Shleifer, L. Summers and R. Waldman (1988) 'The economic consequences of noise traders,' NBER Working Paper, No. 2395 (October).

Dixit, A. (1987) 'Entry and exit decisions under uncertainty,' mimeo, Princeton University, and forthcoming in the *Journal of Political Economy*.

Dornbusch, R. (1976) 'Expectations and exchange rate dynamics,' *Journal of Political Economy* **84**, 1161–76.

Funabashi, Y. (1988) *Managing the Dollar: From the Plaza to the Louvre*, Washington D.C.: Institute for International Economics.

Giavazzi, F., S. Micossi and M.H. Miller (eds.) (1988) *The European Monetary System*. Cambridge: Cambridge University Press.

Krugman, P.R. (1987) 'The bias in the band: exchange rate expectations under a broad-band exchange rate regime,' mimeo, presented at Conference on the European Monetary System, and NBER Working Paper (December).

Krugman, P.R. (1988) 'Target Zones and Exchange Rate Dynamics,' NBER Working Paper No. 2481 (January).

Miller, M.H. and P. Weller (1988a) 'Target zones, currency options and monetary policy,' mimeo, University of Warwick (July).

Miller, M.H. and P. Weller (1988b) 'Solving stochastic saddlepoint systems: a qualitative treatment with economic applications,' mimeo, NBER (November), and forthcoming as a CEPR Discussion Paper.

Obstfeld, M. (1988) 'Competitiveness, realignment and speculation: the role of financial markets,' in F. Giavazzi *et al.*, (eds.) *The European Monetary System*, Cambridge: Cambridge University Press.

Padoa Schioppa, T. (1988) 'The EMS: a long-term view,' in F. Giavazzi *et al.*, (eds.) *The European Monetary System*, Cambridge: Cambridge University Press.

Discussion

John Driffill

Marcus Miller and Paul Weller have been able to extend Paul Krugman's analysis so as to characterize the dynamics of prices and exchange rates in a situation which closely models the EMS. Despite the complexity of the problem, they have been able to do it with relatively – and perhaps deceptively – simple tools. They are able to show how the probability and size of realignment affects the dynamics within the band, where there is free floating. Their analysis shows that the more likely is the band to be defended, the less is a domestic price rise associated with a depreciation of the currency inside the band, though it does not prevent the exchange rate reaching the edge and forcing the government to use its money supply policy to defend it.

They use a continuous-time stochastic model. The exchange rate is allowed to float within a band. If it reaches the edge, either it is defended by taking appropriate monetary action, or the band is shifted to accommodate partly, wholly, or more than wholly the price change which has occurred since the last realignment. They assume that the band is fully credible, or will be realigned with some given probability, and then explore the implications for exchange-rate and price dynamics, and for the monetary policy that is needed to sustain the band and realignment policy. They assume monetary policy subservient to the desired degree of exchange-rate stability. This stands in contrast to the literature on speculative attacks on managed exchange-rate regimes, where an exogenous money supply policy is assumed, typically a constantly growing money stock, and the implications for the exchange-rate regime are explored. These appear to be two complementary approaches to the analysis of monetary policy and exchange-rate regimes. But it may well be true that it is more helpful to ask directly the question: what form of money supply rule is needed to sustain a particular exchange-rate regime? as is done here, rather than to approach the question indirectly as is done in the speculative attack literature.

The model assumes that goods prices are sticky. The rate of inflation depends on the deviation of output from the equilibrium level and also on a random shock, so that the price level depends partly on cumulative past output losses (relative to equilibrium) and the value of the sum of past inflation shocks, z, which is a Brownian motion process. Thus price level shocks are exogenous and completely permanent, and are the only shocks driving the model. This particular formulation keeps the analysis tractable, and I think it is an achievement to have been able to model the evolution of exchange rates and prices when these take the form of continuous-time stochastic processes, the exchange rate being a forward-looking variable, moving between rather complicated barriers. It does however prompt the observation that while the model is an excellent vehicle for analysing exchange rate dynamics, it may be an odd model of the EMS. Why, in such a world as described here, would a government wish to keep the exchange rate floating within narrow bands, which may or may not be intermittently realigned? The shocks in the system are exogenous and permanent, and a policy of accommodating them with equiproportional money supply changes would maintain a constant real money stock, and would maintain output continuously at the equilibrium level. The domestic interest rate would equal the world rate, and the expected rate of domestic inflation and currency depreciation would be zero. The real exchange rate would be constant. From the point of view of optimal policy, this would appear to be hard to beat. By contrast, the outcome under the EMS is rather unattractive, particularly in the case where the bands are defended and never realigned. In this case, the price level is driven by a stochastic process which takes the form

$$dp = \gamma(p)dt + \sigma dz$$

where p denotes deviations from long run equilibrium. $\gamma(p)$ takes negative values, and when p lies outside the range $[-\bar{p}, \bar{p}]$ so that the exchange rate is on one edge of the band, $\gamma(p)$ is a constant. Hence p is an Ornstein-Uhlenbeck process, approximately, which, whilst it has finite variance, nevertheless has the property that any state is reached from any other state in finite time with probability one. (See Cox and Miller, 1965, page 234.) This means that starting from $p = 0$, sooner or later any specified value of p however large or small will be reached. Combined with fixed prices abroad and a bounded nominal exchange rate, this has unpleasant consequences for output.

With certain realignment, and with full accommodation, the real exchange rate will be bounded, and so also will deviations of output from equilibrium. With only uncertain realignment, or with persistent under- or over-accommodation, the possibility remains of indefinitely large or small real exchange rates occurring, and consequently unpleasant effects on output. These reflections suggest that perhaps the case in which realignments occur for sure and fully accommodate price changes is the most realistically descriptive of the EMS.

An interesting development of Miller and Weller's work may be to attempt to introduce additional sources of inflation. Those price-level shocks which are exogenous, permanent and which apply to individual countries may be best treated by allowing countries to realign. Much recent analysis of the EMS has been based on a view that many price-level 'shocks' are internally generated by macroeconomic policy or private sector agents in the EMS countries, and that the form of the exchange-rate regime which rules among them can alter the behaviour of private sector agents and governments (as in the work of Giavazzi and Giovannini, 1988). It would certainly be interesting to investigate exchange-rate and price dynamics in a model with such features.

One might note also that, in the case where realignments do not occur for sure, there is the chance that the band is defended. Then, it is assumed, the band is believed to be defended in perpetuity. This means that all such cases degenerate eventually to the no-realignment case. The phase where realignments occur is only a 'small' period of time at the start of the operation of the model. It would be interesting to ask what would happen if realignment remained a possibility whenever a currency was at the edge of a band.

Miller and Weller note in passing that they find that even with full accommodation of past inflation on realignment, devaluation spirals do not occur, whereas Obstfeld (1988) gets the opposite result. This may be because he assumes that the rate of change of prices equals a function of excess demand for goods, plus the rate of change of the goods-market-clearing price, a term which Miller and Weller do not incorporate in their model. This term makes prices in Obstfeld less sticky, since a change in the money stock can affect the price level via this term in addition to effects which are transmitted via an increase in demand.

An issue which Miller and Weller set out to examine is the compatibility of exchange-rate management and monetary autonomy. They have set out the effects of exchange-rate management in detail, but have left to the reader to decide what constitutes monetary autonomy and how much is left when the exchange rate is managed. If monetary autonomy is equated with maintaining a fixed money supply and leaving the exchange rate to float, then, when realignments are not allowed to happen, exchange-rate management makes monetary policy tighter, because higher prices are met by a smaller money supply, once the exchange rate is at the edge of the band. Price variability is reduced and output variability increased. When fully accommodating realignments happen for sure at the edge of the band, monetary policy is looser, because as prices rise, the money stock is increased (discontinuously) to accommodate them. There is more price variability and less output variability. Clearly the form taken by the loss of autonomy depends on the extent of realignment. If autonomy is equated with a money stock which accommodates price-level shocks, then exchange-rate management here tends to induce a relatively less accommodating policy: only the case of over-realignment is more accommodating.

Miller and Weller have set out a surprisingly simple method for analysing exchange rate dynamics in a stochastic model with EMS-type features. Their paper works through some possibilities and suggests many more, and will be a starting point for much further work on the topic.

References

Cox, D.R. and H.D. Miller (1965) *The Theory of Stochastic Processes*, Chapman and Hall, London.

Giavazzi, Francesco, and Alberto Giovannini (1988) 'The Role of the Exchange Rate Regime in a Disinflation: Empirical Evidence in the EMS,' in Francesco Giavazzi, Stefano Micossi, and Marcus Miller (eds), *The European Monetary System*, Cambridge University Press, Cambridge.

Obstfeld, M. (1988) 'Competitiveness, Realignment and Speculation: The Role of Financial Markets,' in Francesco Giavazzi, Stefano Micossi, and Marcus Miller (eds), *The European Monetary System*, Cambridge University Press, Cambridge.

Part III
Empirical testing

Chapter 8

A comparison of alternative regimes for international macropolicy coordination

David Currie and Simon Wren-Lewis*

I Introduction

The experience of the past decade and a half of floating exchange rates with uncoordinated macroeconomic policies has led to renewed interest in schemes or blueprints for the coordination of monetary, fiscal and exchange-rate policies between countries. Such blueprints or rules may serve to avoid the coordination failure that might otherwise arise between the macroeconomic policy stances of the major G7 countries. By formulating policy in terms of explicit rules or guidelines, such blueprints may also serve to tap the benefits of reputation and credibility in international macropolicy making.[1] Moreover, they help to avoid prolonged misalignments in exchange rates, whether by ensuring a more balanced setting of underlying macroeconomic policies or by dampening speculative bubbles in foreign exchange markets.

One such blueprint is the extended target zone proposal of Williamson and Miller (1987). In its extended form, this envisages rules for the conduct of monetary and fiscal policy to stabilize real exchange rates and nominal demand growth. In summary, this scheme takes the following form.

First, countries should determine a consistent set of real exchange-rate targets, chosen so as to ensure medium to longer-run current account equilibrium. Second, countries should choose targets for the growth of nominal demand. These targets should take account of the need to reduce

* We are grateful for the financial support of the ESRC for part of the research connected with this paper.

BLUEPRINTS FOR EXCHANGE RATE MANAGEMENT
0-12-497060-5 Copyright © 1989 Academic Press, Ltd
All rights of reproduction reserved

inflation towards zero, of the need to expand demand in the face of a fall in capacity utilization, and of the need to adjust current account balances towards equilibrium. Third, differences in interest rates between countries should be varied to limit the deviation of currencies from their target levels, aiming to keep exchange rates within a given band around the target. Fourth, the average level of world interest rates should be varied to stabilize the aggregate growth of nominal demand around the sum of national targets for nominal demand growth. Fifth, national fiscal policy should be varied with a view to achieving national targets for nominal demand growth.

An alternative set of rules reverses the assignment inherent in the Williamson-Miller blueprint by using fiscal policy primarily to achieve external current account equilibrium while monetary policy stabilizes nominal demand growth (see Boughton, 1987; IMF, 1987). This may be preferred on the grounds that monetary policy has relatively little impact on the current account, even in the medium to longer run (see Bryant *et al.*, 1988), so that considerations of comparative advantage lead to this assignment. It may also be favoured on the grounds that the political and institutional constraints on the adjustment of fiscal policy, particularly in the US and Germany, preclude its use for demand management purposes, favouring its use for longer-term structural objectives such as external equilibrium. Finally, this scheme may be attractive to those who are sceptical of the feasibility of explicit exchange-rate targeting (Frenkel, 1987); while those concerned about the vulnerability of foreign exchange markets to speculative bubbles may see greater merit in the Williamson-Miller scheme.

In previous papers (Currie and Wren-Lewis, 1987, 1988) we have used the National Institute Global Econometric Model (GEM) to evaluate the extended target zone proposal as a set of rules for this conduct of macropolicy between the G3 countries (US, Germany and Japan).[2] In summary, we found that suitably designed rules of the Williamson-Miller type would have performed better over the past decade than historical policies. The purpose of this paper is to carry out an explicit comparison of the two blueprints outlined above, namely the Williamson-Miller scheme and the alternative assignment scheme. Thus we compare their performance over the past decade, both among themselves and relative to history, as a set of rules for the G3 countries.

The plan of the paper is as follows. The next section outlines our procedure for the design of the alternative rules. Section III reports our empirical results. We use optimal control exercises on GEM to determine the feedback parameters that maximize welfare in each scheme, compare the level of welfare to historical levels, and describe the paths the world economy might have followed had either scheme been in operation. A conclusion briefly summarizes the main results.

II The design of the rules

In order to investigate the Williamson-Miller Target Zone (TZ) and alternative assignment (AA) blueprints outlined in this introduction, we must assume an explicit form for the proposed policy rules. To do so, we follow Williamson and Miller (1987) in assuming that these take the simple form of proportional-integral rules. The rules under the TZ scheme therefore have the following form:

$$d_i^* = \phi_{0i} + \phi_1 p_i - \phi_2(CU_i - CU_i^*) + \phi_3(b_i - b_i^*) \tag{1}$$

$$\Delta r_i = \alpha_1 \Delta(d_a - d_a^*) + \alpha_2(d_a - d_a^*)_{-1} + \alpha_3 \Delta(e_i - e_i^*) + \alpha_4(e_i - e_i^*)_{-1} \tag{2}$$

$$g_i = \beta_{0i} - \beta_1 \Delta(d_i - d_i^*) - \beta_2(d_i - d_i^*)_{-1} \tag{3}$$

where d is the growth in nominal domestic demand, p is the inflation rate, CU is capacity utilization, b is the current balance as a ratio of nominal GNP, r is the real interest rate, e is the real exchange rate, and g is the growth of government spending. Equation (1) represents the target for nominal domestic demand growth, depending on a country-specific constant term (representing productivity growth and inflation objectives), and terms on inflation, capacity utilization and the deviation of the balance of payments from target. Equation (2) combines the third and fourth points above, containing a response to aggregate world demand and a response to exchange rate deviations. Equation (3) requires government spending to respond to deviations of nominal domestic demand growth from its target at the national level. We assume that the parameters of the rule are the same for all countries, apart from country-specific constants, but this restriction could be relaxed. We have followed Williamson and Miller in assuming that the nominal demand target relates to nominal domestic demand growth, not nominal income. (This contrasts with our earlier work where nominal income was chosen.) This is intended to enhance the adjustment of the economy to external current account disequilibrium. (For the AA scheme below, fiscal policy is assigned specifically to current account equilibrium and so we choose nominal income growth as the relevant nominal target.)

The AA rules have a similar form but with the reverse assignment built in. Thus:

$$y_i^* = \phi_{0i} + \phi_1 p_i - \phi_2(CU_i - CU_i^*) \tag{4}$$

$$g_i = \beta_{0i} + \beta_1 \Delta(b_i - b_i^*) + \beta_2(b_i - b_i^*)_{-1} - \beta_3 \Delta(y_a - y_a^*) - \beta_4(y_a - y_a^*)_{-1} \tag{5}$$

$$\Delta r_i = \alpha_1 \Delta(y_i - y_i^*) + \alpha_2(y_i - y_i^*)_{-1} \tag{6}$$

where y_i is the growth in nominal income. Here, as discussed above, the relevant nominal growth target is assumed to relate to nominal income, rather than nominal demand, while the current account term is dropped as a target for nominal income. In our initial runs $\beta_3 = \beta_4 = 0$. However we also experimented with an enhanced scheme in which this restriction was relaxed, so that in (5) fiscal policy is allowed to respond to excessive aggregate world income growth. This is to avoid a rigid stance of fiscal policy at the world level, and is analogous to the monetary response in (2).

We assume an objective function of the form:

$$V = \sum_{i=1}^{3} w_i \{ (\overline{CU}_i - CU_i)^2 + \gamma_1 p_i^2 + \gamma_2 (g_i - \phi_{0i})^2 + \gamma_{3i} (e^* - e)^2 \} \quad (7)$$

A discounted weighted sum of this objective function, evaluated over the period 1975–86, is minimized using a quarterly discount factor of 0.99. This objective function assumes a non-linear trade-off between output and inflation. We choose $\gamma_1 = 5$, $\gamma_2 = 0.25$, $\gamma_{3i} = (0.2, 0.75, 0.4)$ where i refers to the US, Germany and Japan respectively. $\overline{CU}_i$ is set such that, at full capacity utilization and 5% inflation, 1% less output will be bought if inflation falls by more than 0.5%. At 90% utilization and 5% inflation, the trade-off is 1%/1%; while if inflation was at 10% it would be 1%/0.5% and with no inflation 1%/3%. The third term penalizes changes in government spending relative to trend; while the fourth term penalizes exchange-rate deviations. This last term (which was not included in the appraisals of our previous papers) is designed to capture the adjustment costs associated with real exchange-rate misalignments. The weights, γ_{3i}, are accordingly chosen to reflect the openness of the particular country to trade, and are such that a 10% exchange rate disequilibrium is penalized equally to a deviation of capacity utilization of 2% in Germany, 1% in Japan and 0.5% in the US. The weights, w_i, used to aggregate values of the objective function for each country are 0.4, 0.4, 0.2 for the US, Germany and Japan respectively. This roughly corresponds with GDP weights if Germany is regarded as 'representing' Europe as a whole.

To design the appropriate form of rules, the feedback rules for monetary and fiscal policy for the G3 are incorporated into the model, replacing the model's normal relationships for government expenditure and interest rates in these three countries. The parameters of the rules are chosen so as to minimize the objective function, V, defined above, evaluated over the period 1975–86. However, the feedback rules are over-parameterized. (Thus substituting the rule for nominal demand into the other two rules, we can see this: a less-accommodating nominal GDP target is equivalent to faster adjustment towards the target.) As a result, one parameter can be fixed at an arbitrary value, and we have chosen to fix the coefficient on the inflation term at two-thirds, implying that two-thirds of inflation is accommodated. The constant term in the equation for the nominal GDP growth target can be viewed as the equilibrium real growth rate of the economy. These were set at 3, 4 and 3 percent for the United States, Japan and Germany, respectively.

The target values for real exchange rates, e*, are initially set roughly equal to the average value of the actual real exchange rate over the 1970s, which also happens to be close to values recorded in 1980. This represents a significant simplification compared to the exchange rate zone proposals set out in Williamson and Miller, where target exchange rates are based on 'Fundamental Equilibrium Exchange Rates' (FEERs). As an alternative, we calculate FEERs using GEM itself, and use these calculated values for e* in the optimization exercise. CU^* is approximately equal to the average level of capacity utilization in each country. The desired values for each country's current account are discussed below.

III Optimal rules and historical paths

This section presents the results of a number of optimal control exercises carried out on GEM. Initially we consider our version of the target zone (TZ) scheme and the alternative assignment scheme (AA) under the assumption that target real exchange rates remain unchanged over the simulation period 1975–86. We then reconsider each scheme under variable exchange-rate targets designed to be consistent with long-run current account equilibrium. In both cases we look at the optimal values of the feedback parameters, the welfare implications of each scheme, and what history might have looked like if the scheme had been in operation over this period.

An optimal control exercise using GEM suggests the following parameters for the feedback rules and nominal domestic demand target in the TZ scheme, assuming fixed real exchange rate targets:

$$\phi_1 = 0.66 \quad \alpha_1 = 0.65 \quad \beta_1 = 0.5$$
$$\phi_2 = 0.54 \quad \alpha_2 = 0.03 \quad \beta_2 = 0.2$$
$$\phi_3 = 0.10 \quad \alpha_3 = 0.22$$
$$\alpha_4 = 0.02$$

The value of the parameters α_3 and α_4 imply that a sustained 1% deviation in the real exchange rate from its target value would result in an initial 0.22 point rise in the real interest rate, followed by further increases of 0.02 points per quarter thereafter. The size of the proportional control term is large, and given the model's exchange-rate equations comes near to eliminating any exchange-rate disequilibrium in some countries. Parameters α_1 and α_2 imply that a sustained 1% rise in world nominal demand above target will raise interest rates by 0.65 points in the same quarter, but increases thereafter will amount to only 0.03 points per quarter. An equivalent rise in an individual country's own demand will lead to a fall in government expenditure of 0.5% initially, followed by further falls of 0.23% per quarter. Thus although both monetary and fiscal policy are highly active as proportional controllers, in terms of integral control fiscal policy dominates. Turning to the nominal demand target itself, a 1% deviation of capacity utilization from normal levels leads to a 0.5% rise in the annual domestic demand growth target, while 1% extra inflation raises the *nominal* growth target by only 0.66%. A current account surplus worth 1% of GNP raises the target by only 0.1%.

Table 8.1 shows the value of the objective function under these feedback rules compared to history. There is no necessary reason why welfare should improve under these schemes, as they represent a significant departure from unconstrained optimization of instruments period by period. In the case of the TZ scheme, however, the welfare gain is positive and significant, and is worth about 2% off average inflation over the period. All three countries share in this benefit, although the largest gains occur in Germany. The table also shows that these gains are *not* mainly due to the presence of real exchange-rate disequilibrium in the objective function. While the US real exchange rate does stay closer to target, the opposite occurs in Japan and West Germany. (We discuss the reasons for this below.) Instead the welfare improvement stems mainly from a redistribution in activity over time, with the 1980–81 recession being replaced by a more moderate and sustained deflation throughout the period. (A similar conclusion was reached in our earlier work, where exchange-rate disequilibrium did not appear in the

Table 8.1   Objective function values

	Constant exchange-rate target				Variable targets		
	History	TZ	AA	EAA		History	TZ	EAA
Total	21,928	18,929	21,397	20,574		21,689	18,602	20,641
US	24,704	23,473	24,470	23,652		23,803	22,564	22,925
Germany	18,499	13,159	15,376	15,134		18,864	13,851	15,498
Japan	23,233	21,382	27,294	25,299		23,111	20,178	26,358
Exchange rate contribution								
Total	1,796	1,736	2,165	2,248		1,558	1,247	2,194
US	1,756	351	1,050	1,182		856	292	530
Germany	1,913	2,384	1,048	1,406		2,279	1,936	1,458
Japan	1,643	2,849	6,630	6,066		1,521	1,780	6,994

objective function. The terms in the change in government expenditure in the objective function are relatively insignificant in all cases.)

Tables 8.2–8.19 show the path of various key variables under this TZ regime compared to history. History itself is characterized by two major events which dominate these exercises. The first is the sharp tightening of global monetary policy around 1980, initiated by the United States. Although this was partly a response to the second oil price shock, domestic demand had been on average above target in all three countries in the second half of the 1970s. The second major event was the appreciation in the dollar that

Table 8.2   United States inflation, 1975–86 (% p.a.)

Year	History	Constant exchange-rate target			Variable target (TZ)
		TZ	AA	EAA	
1975	7.7	8.2	8.2	8.2	8.5
1976	5.7	6.4	6.4	6.0	6.8
1977	6.4	6.6	6.5	5.9	6.7
1978	7.0	6.6	6.2	5.7	6.3
1979	8.8	7.7	7.8	7.2	6.7
1980	10.3	9.7	10.0	9.5	9.2
1981	8.9	9.7	8.8	8.7	9.3
1982	5.5	8.2	6.8	7.1	8.1
1983	4.0	7.8	6.3	6.8	7.9
1984	3.7	6.7	4.9	5.1	6.1
1985	3.4	5.9	3.2	3.2	5.2
1986	2.2	4.5	1.1	0.3	4.3

Table 8.3   United States capital utilization, 1975–86 (1980 = 100)

Year	History	Constant exchange-rate target			Variable target (TZ)
		TZ	AA	EAA	
1975	91	93	93	93	96
1976	96	96	99	97	98
1977	100	98	101	98	99
1978	104	100	101	99	99
1979	105	102	103	100	101
1980	99	101	98	98	99
1981	98	103	103	100	100
1982	88	96	93	93	96
1983	91	98	94	94	98
1984	98	102	94	97	99
1985	96	100	90	93	98
1986	94	97	91	92	96

Table 8.4   United States real exchange rates, 1975–86 (1980 = 100)[a]

| | | Constant exchange-rate target | | | Variable targets | |
Year	History	TZ	AA	EAA	TZ	FEER
1975	105	108	108	108	107	99
1976	100	103	98	98	101	99
1977	101	105	95	96	101	100
1978	107	108	98	100	104	100
1979	105	103	100	101	97	99
1980	100	95	96	97	91	98
1981	90	92	85	88	91	96
1982	84	94	83	90	95	94
1983	81	95	88	91	93	93
1984	77	91	88	84	86	92
1985	76	89	87	78	87	92
1986	93	96	96	87	95	92

[a] Increase implies a gain in competitiveness and a depreciation.

Table 8.5   United States real interest rates, 1975–86 (% p.a.)

| | | Constant exchange-rate target | | | Variable target |
Year	History	TZ	AA	EAA	(TZ)
1975	−1.4	−1.1	−1.6	−1.2	−1.8
1976	−0.4	1.3	2.6	1.5	−0.1
1977	−0.8	1.4	3.2	1.6	0.4
1978	1.2	3.0	3.7	2.3	2.3
1979	2.4	3.5	4.7	2.4	3.3
1980	2.8	1.3	2.6	1.0	1.1
1981	7.0	0.5	6.5	4.1	0.3
1982	6.7	−1.3	2.0	0.4	−0.8
1983	5.0	−0.4	1.5	1.4	0.5
1984	6.7	−0.8	1.9	2.8	−0.3
1985	4.7	−2.5	−0.6	1.0	−2.1
1986	4.3	−1.9	−0.5	0.9	−1.1

began in 1980 and continued until 1983–84. GEM suggests that this appreciation was partly a direct consequence of the US interest rate hike, but a substantial proportion of the appreciation remains unexplained by the model's exchange rate equations. One consequence of this appreciation is of course the growing US current account deficit from 1983, and associated surpluses in Japan and Germany.

Under the TZ scheme, the global level of real interest rates rises relative to history in the early years of the simulation in an attempt to reduce global

Table 8.6   **United States government expenditure, 1975–86 (1982 $ billion)**

		Constant exchange-rate target			Variable target
Year	History	TZ	AA	EAA	(TZ)
1975	581	605	599	599	630
1976	580	608	641	611	616
1977	589	612	657	605	608
1978	604	611	647	587	595
1979	609	604	650	572	590
1980	621	612	638	572	610
1981	630	597	655	592	578
1982	642	620	667	616	639
1983	649	629	633	616	641
1984	678	607	569	594	598
1985	727	606	520	593	602
1986	755	616	491	581	630

Table 8.7   **United States current account balance, 1975–86 (% GNP)**

		Constant exchange-rate target			Variable target	FEER target
Year	History	TZ	AA	EAA	(TZ)	balance
1975	1.1	0.9	1.0	1.0	0.8	0.0
1976	0.3	0.2	0.4	0.4	0.1	0.0
1977	−0.8	−0.6	−0.4	−0.3	−0.6	0.0
1978	−0.7	−0.3	−0.5	−0.4	−0.4	0.0
1979	−0.1	0.5	−0.5	−0.3	0.2	−0.2
1980	0.1	0.2	−0.5	−0.3	−0.4	−0.4
1981	0.3	−0.4	−0.3	−0.1	−1.2	−0.6
1982	−0.3	−1.2	−1.1	−1.0	−1.9	−0.8
1983	−1.3	−1.5	−2.2	−1.7	−1.6	−0.8
1984	−2.8	−1.9	−2.7	−1.9	−1.7	−0.8
1985	−3.0	−1.8	−1.9	−1.5	−2.1	−0.8
1986	−3.3	−1.8	−1.9	−2.0	−2.4	−0.8

inflation. Fiscal policy is also more restrictive in Japan and Germany over this period, but the low level of utilization in the US produces the opposite result there. The most notable feature of the TZ simulation, however, is the absence of the US interest rate hike in 1980. To the extent that this policy represents an attempt to 'export inflation', it is ruled out of court under the TZ regime. In fact the opposite occurs, with US real rates becoming negative in 1980. This reflects an attempt to keep the US real exchange rate unchanged in the face of the autonomous tendency for the dollar to appreciate that

Table 8.8   German inflation, 1975–86 (% p.a.)

Year	History	Constant exchange-rate target TZ	AA	EAA	Variable target (TZ)
1975	5.8	5.4	5.3	5.4	5.8
1976	4.2	3.1	4.6	4.4	3.9
1977	3.5	1.3	4.6	3.6	2.2
1978	2.8	0.5	3.8	2.6	1.9
1979	3.8	2.2	4.4	3.1	3.7
1980	5.6	4.5	5.1	4.1	5.9
1981	6.0	5.3	5.4	4.7	5.9
1982	4.7	4.0	4.7	3.3	4.2
1983	3.2	3.7	3.4	2.5	4.7
1984	2.5	3.5	2.5	2.5	5.1
1985	2.0	3.6	1.9	3.0	4.4
1986	−0.4	2.9	0.6	1.5	2.8

Table 8.9   German capacity utilization, 1975–86 (1980 = 100)

Year	History	Constant exchange-rate target TZ	AA	EAA	Variable target (TZ)
1975	101	101	102	102	101
1976	105	102	105	104	102
1977	104	101	103	102	101
1978	102	99	100	99	100
1979	104	101	102	100	100
1980	100	100	98	97	98
1981	95	98	94	94	97
1982	89	95	91	91	96
1983	87	93	92	91	94
1984	87	92	90	89	93
1985	89	94	91	90	95
1986	88	94	90	91	95

began around that time. (We explore below what might happen if the target real exchange rate also appreciated over this period.) This attempt is partially successful, and so the subsequent rise in the US current account deficit is reduced.

Over the period as a whole, there is an interesting shift from a contractionary monetary policy at the global level to a contractionary fiscal policy. As real exchange-rate differentials can only shift interest-rate differentials, this shift reflects the relative size of the integral control parameters β_2 and α_3 on the feedback rules. One reason why GEM prefers fiscal to monetary policy

Table 8.10   German real exchange rates, 1975–86 (1980 = 100)

Year	History	Constant exchange-rate target			Variable targets	
		TZ	AA	EAA	TZ	FEER
1975	104	102	100	102	102	105
1976	102	98	104	104	101	105
1977	99	91	103	102	96	105
1978	97	90	107	99	97	104
1979	97	90	101	100	100	103
1980	100	93	102	97	103	101
1981	108	99	109	102	104	100
1982	107	92	104	95	95	100
1983	106	96	101	94	100	100
1984	111	100	99	98	108	100
1985	113	111	109	114	112	100
1986	104	108	99	104	106	103

Table 8.11   German real interest rates, 1975–86 (% p.a.)

Year	History	Constant exchange-rate target			Variable target (TZ)
		TZ	AA	EAA	
1975	−0.8	2.3	1.4	1.5	0.8
1976	−0.1	4.8	4.8	3.9	2.4
1977	0.9	2.4	4.4	3.2	−0.2
1978	1.0	1.9	4.8	3.6	−0.9
1979	2.9	2.6	6.6	4.5	0.9
1980	3.9	2.2	4.5	2.9	1.9
1981	6.2	3.7	1.3	0.7	3.4
1982	4.2	−0.4	0.9	0.5	−1.0
1983	2.6	1.3	1.3	0.6	0.8
1984	3.5	3.0	−0.6	−1.6	4.6
1985	3.5	5.0	−2.9	−2.9	7.5
1986	5.1	4.7	−1.6	−0.3	6.7

as an integral controller for demand may be the fact that whereas fiscal policy multipliers are fairly similar across countries, GEM suggests that interest rates have a much larger effect on domestic demand in the US and Japan compared to Europe. Any attempt to deflate global demand by raising the average level of interest rates may therefore lead to damaging changes in the distribution of economic activity between countries.

At the individual country level, a feature of the TZ simulation worth noting is the shift towards fiscal expansion in Germany from 1982. This is mainly because policy in Germany is judged to have been sub-optimal in

Table 8.12   German government consumption, 1975–86 (1980 DM billion)

Year	History	Constant exchange-rate target			Variable target (TZ)
		TZ	AA	EAA	
1975	65.8	65.8	67.6	67.5	66.3
1976	66.7	65.8	68.6	66.8	64.2
1977	67.6	67.2	68.1	66.2	65.5
1978	70.2	69.4	69.6	67.6	67.2
1979	72.6	69.4	71.5	67.9	63.6
1980	74.4	70.2	70.9	67.7	69.3
1981	75.8	73.4	69.8	67.5	77.1
1982	75.2	77.3	73.5	72.4	80.8
1983	75.4	80.9	78.4	76.6	87.8
1984	77.2	85.4	81.7	76.7	94.3
1985	78.8	90.9	84.4	76.8	101.6

Table 8.13   German current account balance, 1975–86 (% GNP)

Year	History	Constant exchange-rate target			Variable target (TZ)	FEER target balance
		TZ	AA	EAA		
1975	1.0	1.3	1.0	0.5	1.1	0.5
1976	0.6	1.4	−0.2	0.2	1.3	0.5
1977	0.8	1.8	0.2	0.9	1.4	0.5
1978	1.4	1.6	0.4	0.9	1.0	0.5
1979	−0.7	−0.7	0.3	0.7	−0.9	0.5
1980	−1.9	−2.1	−0.4	−0.3	−2.0	0.5
1981	−0.8	−1.0	0.5	0.6	0.0	0.5
1982	0.6	0.5	1.0	1.3	0.8	0.5
1983	0.6	−1.6	0.7	0.1	−2.0	0.5
1984	1.3	−1.0	1.4	0.3	−2.3	0.5
1985	2.5	−2.4	−0.5	−1.8	−2.0	0.5
1986	4.2	−1.5	1.8	2.0	−0.6	0.5

the mid-eighties, with too much activity being sacrificed for zero inflation. Experiments not reported here suggest that the relative weight given to inflation in the objective function has to be substantially higher in Germany than elsewhere to justify German macro policy over this period. As a result of the expansion in German activity, it moves into current account deficit in 1983. To prevent this leading to a movement in the real exchange rate away from the target, German interest-rate differentials have to rise.

We have already observed that the TZ regime fails to increase the stability of Japanese and German real exchange rates. At first sight this may

Table 8.14   Japanese inflation, 1975–86 (% p.a.)

Year	History	Constant exchange-rate target			Variable target (TZ)
		TZ	AA	EAA	
1975	11.2	12.8	13.4	13.3	12.8
1976	8.5	9.0	10.5	10.5	8.8
1977	7.0	7.2	8.2	8.4	6.2
1978	4.6	4.9	5.9	6.1	4.2
1979	3.4	3.0	5.7	5.7	2.8
1980	6.6	5.6	8.7	8.4	5.6
1981	4.7	5.5	5.0	5.9	5.7
1982	2.7	4.0	3.9	5.3	4.6
1983	1.4	4.6	3.0	4.2	5.4
1984	2.1	5.4	2.7	3.4	6.1
1985	2.2	5.1	2.8	3.3	5.4
1986	0.6	4.1	0.8	1.3	4.5

Table 8.15   Japanese capacity utilization, 1975–86 (1980 = 100)

Year	History	Constant exchange-rate target			Variable target (TZ)
		TZ	AA	EAA	
1975	95	97	99	99	98
1976	100	101	107	106	101
1977	99	98	108	106	98
1978	99	98	109	107	98
1979	101	99	109	108	98
1980	100	103	104	108	98
1981	96	100	99	104	98
1982	91	99	98	100	100
1983	89	99	99	102	103
1984	93	103	103	106	103
1985	92	102	98	102	103
1986	87	99	91	97	103

seem surprising given the emphasis on exchange-rate targets. However the simulation results show that the increase in instability occurs mainly in the 1970s, and so is not associated with the dollar's appreciation. Over this period it is likely that the governments concerned were in fact using monetary policy to manage the exchange rate. (See Wren-Lewis, 1987 for some evidence on this.) These results can be interpreted as suggesting that they did this rather more effectively than would be achieved by our optimized feedback rules. One reason for this is that the feedback rule imposes the same interest rate response to exchange-rate disequilibrium across countries and across time.

Table 8.16   Japanese real exchange rates, 1975–86 (1980 = 100)

Year	History	Constant exchange-rate target			Variable targets	
		TZ	AA	EAA	TZ	FEER
1975	109	121	126	125	118	102
1976	107	115	123	122	109	99
1977	100	112	111	116	102	96
1978	87	102	92	99	88	96
1979	100	114	109	118	105	99
1980	100	105	111	111	101	102
1981	97	96	107	103	97	105
1982	112	102	116	116	105	108
1983	107	100	101	105	107	110
1984	105	103	85	92	113	110
1985	108	107	85	92	116	110
1986	88	95	76	85	98	109

Table 8.17   Japanese real interest rates, 1975–86 (% p.a.)

Year	History	Constant exchange-rate target			Variable target (TZ)
		TZ	AA	EAA	
1975	−1.4	−2.8	−6.3	−5.9	−3.7
1976	−1.2	0.2	−1.9	−2.6	0.5
1977	−1.2	−0.2	1.2	−1.3	0.8
1978	0.6	−1.4	4.1	1.0	−1.1
1979	2.5	3.0	5.6	2.1	2.8
1980	4.1	1.4	3.9	2.9	2.2
1981	2.7	−0.2	4.1	2.8	−0.4
1982	4.1	−1.1	4.7	3.1	−2.5
1983	5.2	−0.2	5.9	4.7	−1.8
1984	4.3	1.2	7.0	5.7	0.6
1985	4.3	2.0	5.7	5.7	2.2
1986	4.4	−1.0	3.6	4.9	2.7

Turning to the AA type scheme, optimization produced the following parameters for the feedback rules and nominal GDP target:

$$\phi_1 = 0.66 \quad \alpha_1 = 0.52 \quad \beta_1 = 0.8$$
$$\phi_2 = 0.43 \quad \alpha_2 = 0.08 \quad \beta_2 = 1.6$$

A sustained current account surplus of 1% leads to an initial 0.8% rise in government expenditure, followed by more substantial increase of 1.6% per quarter. Both terms are therefore powerful. A 1% increase in nominal GDP

Table 8.18 Japanese government consumption, 1975–86 1980 (Yen billion)

Year	History	Constant exchange-rate target TZ	AA	EAA	Variable target (TZ)
1975	4.8	4.7	4.6	4.7	4.7
1976	5.0	4.8	4.8	4.6	4.7
1977	5.2	4.8	5.4	4.9	5.1
1978	5.4	5.0	6.4	5.5	5.4
1979	5.7	5.1	6.7	5.6	5.4
1980	5.9	5.1	5.8	5.3	5.4
1981	6.2	5.1	6.0	5.5	5.6
1982	6.3	5.2	6.3	5.7	5.4
1983	6.5	5.2	6.6	6.0	5.2
1984	6.6	5.2	6.9	6.3	4.9
1985	6.8	5.3	7.0	6.7	4.9
1986	7.2	5.3	7.4	7.4	4.8

Table 8.19 Japanese current account balance, 1975–86 (% GNP)

Year	History	Constant exchange-rate target TZ	AA	EAA	Variable target (TZ)	FEER target balance
1975	−0.1	−0.5	−0.7	−0.7	−0.5	0.0
1976	0.7	1.2	1.3	1.1	1.1	0.0
1977	1.6	2.2	2.2	2.2	1.8	0.0
1978	1.8	2.9	2.7	3.2	1.9	0.3
1979	−0.9	0.5	−1.7	−1.0	−0.5	0.5
1980	−1.1	−0.1	−1.0	−0.5	−0.7	0.8
1981	0.5	1.4	1.4	1.0	0.4	1.0
1982	0.7	0.6	1.2	0.9	0.2	1.3
1983	1.8	0.9	1.7	1.8	0.7	1.5
1984	2.7	1.6	1.3	1.7	2.2	1.5
1985	3.7	3.2	1.4	1.9	4.3	1.5
1986	4.1	4.1	1.6	2.8	5.4	1.5

growth above target leads to an initial 0.5 point increase in interest rates, followed by smaller increases of under 0.1 points per quarter.

Table 8.1 shows that welfare is only slightly better than history under this scheme. The distribution of gains is also more uneven, with Japan actually worse off. This is largely due to substantial exchange-rate disequilibrium compared to history. Tables 8.2–8.19 immediately show the reason for this. To combat a growing current account deficit, fiscal policy in the US becomes sharply contractionary from 1983. To prevent this deflating US demand too severely, US real interest rates fall over the same period. This produces a widening of the interest-rate differential in favour of Japan, leading to a growing appreciation in the Yen.

The simulation of the AA rules also produces a sharp contrast with the TZ scheme before this period. While US and average world real interest rates do not rise in 1980 under the TZ regime, the opposite is the case in the AA simulation. Indeed real rates become significantly positive well before 1980. This follows directly from the fact that only monetary policy can be used to deflate the global levels of demand, and that nominal demand targets are generally exceeded in the 1970s. Excess demand at the global level will not lead to significant individual current account deficits, and so fiscal policy will remain unchanged.

In view of the advantages mentioned earlier of fiscal compared to monetary deflation, we looked at an extension of the AA regime, where *global* demand disequilibrium can influence the level of fiscal policy in each country. This 'enhanced' AA type regime (hereafter EAA) involves the following feedback parameters generated by optimization on GEM:

$$\phi_1 = 0.66 \quad \alpha_1 = 0.53 \quad \beta_1 = 0.6$$
$$\phi_2 = 0.34 \quad \alpha_2 = 0.06 \quad \beta_2 = 1.1$$
$$\beta_3 = 0.5$$
$$\beta_4 = 0.1$$

The response of fiscal policy to current account imbalance is reduced a little, but now there is a significant response to global demand imbalances. Excess global demand of 1% will decrease government expenditure growth in each country by 0.5% in the short run, and a further 0.1% thereafter. The welfare gain compared to history is now more substantial, although still below that in TZ. The fiscal-monetary mix during the 1970s does shift in the expected direction in EAA compared to AA.

The use of monetary rather than fiscal policy as a means of targeting demand still creates problems at the individual country level in both AA and EAA. Under both schemes Japanese demand in the 1970s is excessive, and well above historical values. In 1974 Japanese inflation was extremely high, and real interest rates were around −7% at the end of the year. The feedback rules under AA and EAA bring real rates back to positive values, but at too slow a rate to deflate demand over the period. The actual rise in real rates in 1975 was extremely rapid. The increase in real rates is also faster under the TZ scheme, because the Yen was far too competitive in 1975. In addition deflation occurs under the TZ through fiscal policy, but because the current account recorded a surplus of over 1% of GNP 1976 to 1978 fiscal policy is at best neutral under the AA schemes.

We have already noted that German policy was too deflationary in the 1980s according to our objective function's parameters. Under the AA scheme this leads to a fall in real interest rates to negative values in 1984 and 1985, and in fact in 1985 nominal rates are virtually zero. Even in these somewhat implausible circumstances, the effects of monetary policy are insufficient to raise activity more than marginally. This is partly because the fall in interest-rate differentials leads to a DM depreciation which, because of the J curve, leads to a current account deficit and therefore a *deflationary* fiscal policy.

This raises two general problems with the AA scheme which are not specific to this particular conjecture. Firstly, it is plausible to suppose that in many countries (most of Europe in GEM) the most powerful effects of interest rates on demand operate through the exchange rate. If the current account is also subject to a J curve, this effect will initially be counteracted by fiscal policy under the AA rules. Secondly, reflationary action through easier monetary policy may be constrained in a world where inflation is very low or zero, simply because there is a floor to nominal rates.

The experiments shown so far have assumed constant values for target real exchange rates. The TZ proposal advocated by Williamson and others, on the other hand, lays considerable stress on the calculation of Fundamental Equilibrium Exchange Rates (FEERs). These are the real exchange rates consistent with long-run current account equilibrium. The calculation of these rates is naturally model-specific, which is partly why we have not simply taken Williamson's calculations on board. In the remainder of this section we reconsider the TZ and AA schemes assuming one possible set of FEERs derived in part from GEM itself.

An obvious prior question to calculating FEERs is what constitutes current account equilibrium. Here we have done no more than make some very crude assumptions, which are shown in Tables 8.7, 8.13 and 8.19. We have taken Germany to be a capital exporter throughout the period, so that their current account target is a constant 0.5% of GNP. We have assumed that Japan only became a capital exporter in 1978, and their equilibrium current account/GNP ratio rises from 0.25% to 1.5% by 1983. This is roughly matched in *value* terms by a gradual movement in the US deficit from an initial target of 0 to 0.75% of GNP by 1982. This equal and opposite movement in the US and Japanese current account positions is designed to reflect changes in the preferences of Japanese financial institutions over this period.

These changes will obviously be one factor influencing FEER calculations. The two other key developments are changes in oil prices and trends in trade performance. A rise in oil prices weakens Japan's relative trade position, because oil forms a relatively large proportion of its imports. In contrast, German imports are mainly manufactures. On the other hand Japanese exporters have shown a persistent tendency to gain market share over time, which implies a steady decline over time in the level of competitiveness required to achieve current account balance. (The fact that Japanese trend growth is high is counteracted by a relatively low import propensity.)

The actual calculations to compute FEERs using GEM are far too numerous to describe here. There are also many judgements involved, so the series shown in Tables 8.4, 8.10 and 8.16, should certainly not be taken as definitive. Their main features are as follows. A small trend rise in US competitiveness would normally be required, but this is more than offset by the change to current account deficit described above. The German FEER appreciates around 1980 following the oil price rise, but begins to depreciate in 1986. The FEER for Japan initially appreciates, but then depreciates reflecting the oil price rise and the move to current account surplus.

The optimization exercises described above involved current account targets similar to those used in the FEER calculations. As a result, using the FEERs will only influence the EAA scheme indirectly by changing the objective function. In fact the parameters, given below, are very similar to those already described:

$$\phi_1 = 0.66 \quad \alpha_1 = 0.56 \quad \beta_1 = 0.6$$
$$\phi_2 = 0.32 \quad \alpha_2 = 0.06 \quad \beta_2 = 1.1$$
$$\beta_3 = 0.3$$
$$\beta_4 = 0.1$$

As Table 5.1 shows, welfare continues to improve under EAA, but the gain is relatively small (worth about 0.5% off average inflation). Changes to the optimal TZ parameters are more substantial:

$$\phi_1 = 0.66 \quad \alpha_1 = 0.70 \quad \beta_1 = 1.5$$
$$\phi_2 = 1.35 \quad \alpha_2 = 0.11 \quad \beta_2 = 0.4$$
$$\phi_3 = 1.39 \quad \alpha_3 = 0.24$$
$$\alpha_4 = 0.05$$

All the parameters have increased, suggesting that the FEERs allow a generally more interventionist policy. Substantial increases have occurred in the integral control parameters in both elements of the interest rate feedback rule, while both integral and proportional controllers in the fiscal policy reaction function have risen substantially. Finally the nominal demand target is much more responsive to output disequilbrium relative to inflation than before, and also to deviations from the current account target. This last result is particularly interesting because it brings in an important element from the IMF scheme, namely national fiscal policy responding to current account disequilibrium.

This more activist policy continues to lead to a substantial welfare gain relative to history (worth about 2% off average inflation). Real exchange-rate stability (relative to FEERs) is now improved in both US and Germany, and the small deterioration in Japan is more than accounted for by events at the beginning of the simulation period. The larger feedback parameters in the fiscal rule coupled with the much greater importance of output disequilibrium has a noticeable effect in smoothing the path of capacity utilization in all three countries.

The broad pattern of events in this simulation is similar to TZ under fixed exchange-rate targets. US real interest rates still fall to negative values in the 1980s: the reduced degree of exchange-rate disequilibrium implied by the appreciating FEER over this period is offset by larger feedback parameters. Fiscal policy is strongly contractionary in the US and Japan, but expansionary in Germany. Thus introducing these estimated FEERs has influenced the vigour with which policy is pursued, but not its overall direction.

IV Conclusions

We have examined two alternative schemes for international policy cooperation using simulations of the National Institute Global Econometric Model over the period 1975–86. The first is based on the Extended Target Zone proposal advocated by Williamson and Miller (1987), where monetary policy is designed in part to avoid real exchange-rate disequilibrium, while fiscal policy stabilizes domestic demand. The second, alternative scheme uses interest rates to stabilize national income, while fiscal policy is assigned to controlling the current account.

Both schemes improved welfare compared to history over this period, but the gains associated with the target zone proposal were generally larger and more substantial. The superior performance of the target zone scheme appears to stem from two main sources. Firstly allowing monetary policy to respond to exchange-rate disequilibrium not only helped improve welfare directly (given the presence of the real exchange rate in our objective function), but on occasion over this period it also provided useful advance information about potential developments in demand and inflation. Secondly our model suggested that fiscal policy had a comparative advantage over monetary policy in directly controlling demand at a national level.

This conclusion needs to be qualified in at least two important respects. Firstly, the superior performance of the target zone proposal depends in part on the presence of real exchange-rate disequilibrium in the objective function, and although this term can be justified on distributional grounds its importance is clearly controversial. Secondly both our model, because of the absence of wealth effects, and the historical period we are using, with the 'overhang' of the US deficit, may understate the importance of the current account as an indicator for policy.

The performance of the target zone scheme will also depend on the real exchange-rate targets adopted. Recent problems associated with the 'Louvre Accord' can be interpreted as illustrating the dangers of adopting the wrong targets, or at least targets inconsistent with other aspects of macro policy. Our experiments with alternative paths for real exchange-rate targets suggested that although the welfare improving properties of the target zone scheme were fairly robust, the optimal values of feedback parameters were much more sensitive.

Notes

1 Currie, Levine and Vidalis (1987) find that these benefits may well be considerable.

2 In this exercise, the other European countries (with the exception of the UK) are tied closely to Germany through the EMS, so that Germany acts in many ways as a proxy for continental Europe as a whole.

References

Boughton, J. (1987) 'Eclectic Approaches to Policy Coordination', paper presented to the CEPR Conference on Exchange Rate Regimes, Money GDP Targets and Macroeconomic Policy, Cambridge, July.

Bryant, R.D., D. Henderson, G. Holtham, P. Hooper and S. Symansky (1988) *Empirical Macroeconomics for Interdependent Economies*, Washington: Brookings Institution.

Bryant, R.C. and R. Portes (1987) *Global Macroeconomics: Policy Conflict and Cooperation*, Macmillan, London.

Currie, D., P. Levine and N. Vidalis (1987) 'International Cooperation and Regulation in an Empirical Two-Bloc Model', in Bryant and Portes (1987).

Currie, D. and S. Wren-Lewis (1987) 'Evaluating the Extended Target Zone Proposal for the G3', CEPR Discussion Paper No. 221.

Currie, D. and S. Wren-Lewis (1988) 'Conflict and Cooperation in International Macroeconomic Policy Making', in A. Britton (ed) *Policymaking with Macroeconomic Models*, Aldershot: Gower.

Frenkel, J.A. (1987) 'The International Monetary System: Should it be reformed?', *American Economic Review* (Supp).

IMF (1987) *World Economic Outlook*, April and October.

Williamson, J. and M. Miller (1987) 'Targets and Indicators: A Blueprint for the International Coordination of Economic Policy', Institute for International Economics, Washington.

Wren-Lewis, S. (1987) 'Introducing Exchange Rate Equations with a World Economic Model', *National Institute Economic Review*, No. 119.

Discussion

John Williamson

This paper seems to me a most useful addition to the emerging literature that uses multicountry macroeconometric models to evaluate the performance of suggested international monetary regimes. It is particularly welcome to find a paper of this ilk in which the authors spell out the intuitive reasons for their findings with such care and clarity. I am naturally gratified by the results, which suggest not only that the Williamson-Miller 'blueprint' would have improved on historical performance but also that it would have performed substantially better than the 'alternative assignment' of Genberg and Swoboda (1987) and Boughton (1988).

In these comments I shall do two things. The first is examine whether my pleasure at these results might be misplaced. The second is explain why I am not surprised at the finding that the blueprint outperformed the alternative assignment.

1 Robustness

The model employed in this study strikes me as generally appropriate to the task in hand, and the use made of it is highly sophisticated. I nevertheless see three areas where the approach pursued could be subjected to criticisms that might question the conclusions reached.

One problem is that an exercise of this type must suffer from a built-in bias toward endorsing alternative policy regimes relative to history, inasmuch as the parameters of the alternative policy reaction functions are optimized in the light of historical data. Hence the only fair test of a policy regime must be its ability to out-perform history out-of-sample, just as econometric equations ultimately have to be tested by their out-of-sample performance. I presume that such tests can and will be undertaken before long, but, until their results are available, it is proper to treat the comparisons reported in this paper with a measure of reserve.

A second problem has been raised by Frenkel, Goldstein and Masson (1988a, 1988b), and responded to by Miller, Weller, and Williamson (1988). The charge of FGM was that models like GEM incorporate backward-looking expectations, and that this was critically important for the finding that manipulation of the short-term interest rate is an efficient way of managing the exchange rate. Their own model incorporated rational expectations and concluded that a change in the short-term interest rate would have minimal impact on the exchange rate, whose level would instead be dominated by investors' perfect knowledge of the path of *future* interest rates. Hence they argued that the conclusion that interest rates could be used to manage exchange rates was subject to the Lucas Critique. Miller *et al.* did not deny that the absence of forward-looking expectations in GEM could create a problem of that nature, but they showed that the presence of target zones and a credible commitment to preventing deviations from them could be expected to limit 'noise' from bubbles and fads. Failure to recognize that a regime change to exchange-rate targeting might have that effect means that the FGM conclusion is also subject to the Lucas Critique. Whether on balance the Lucas Critique works for or against the viability of exchange-rate targeting has not yet been addressed systematically, but my own expectation is that it will on balance be positive.

The third problem is that the current balance is not included in the objective function. This seems odd inasmuch as the alternative assignment that the authors are comparing to the blueprint is quite unambiguously aimed at limiting the deviations of the current balance from target. It could therefore be argued that a fair comparison must ask whether the inferior performance of the alternative assignment in stabilizing an objective function comprising capacity utilization, inflation, growth, and exchange rates might be offset by better stabilization of the current account. Using a traditional criterion, the sum of the squared annual deviations of the current account from target, the answer is that the alternative assignment outperforms the blueprint in Germany and Japan but not the United States (Table 8A.1). Both regimes also outperform history, though not particularly impressively. If one looks

Table 8A.1   Measures of current balance performance

	Sum of squared annual deviations from target	Cumulative deviation from target, 1975–86
United States		
Blueprint	15.5	−7.9
Alternative assignment	22.7	−10.6
History	32.1	−10.5
Germany		
Blueprint	27.2	−3.7
Alternative assignment	8.7	6.2
History	35.0	9.6
Japan		
Blueprint	47.9	18.0
Alternative assignment	30.7	11.4
History	50.1	14.5

Source: Currie and Wren-Lewis (1989, tables 7, 13 and 19).

at the cumulative divergence from target over the whole period, the blueprint does better in two cases out of three, the exception being Japan. Presumably, however, the results might have come out more favourable to the alternative assignment had the current balance been included in the objective function used to choose the optimal feedback parameters.

2 Rationale

I do not believe the superior performance of the blueprint, at least as measured by an objective function that excludes the current balance, to be an accident. I also believe that it is absolutely right to exclude any short-term measure of current balance from the objective function. The reason is that there are virtually no welfare costs to short-run current account imbalances: a deficit one year that is offset by a surplus a year or two later has no enduring effects on consumption, investment, inflation, or any other variable of welfare significance. On the contrary, short-run variations in the current account provide a valuable shock absorber: it is only when they cumulate over the medium term that one need be troubled with the sustainability and optimality of borrowing from or lending to the rest of the world. This is an enormously important asymmetry in comparison to 'internal balance': today's unemployed cannot make up work undone today tomorrow, while reversing rather than stopping this year's inflation next year would compound rather than undo many of the costs of inflation. Hence internal balance needs to be sought as continuously as possible, while external balance is important only in the medium term.[1]

Thus, even if the alternative assignment were unambiguously more effective in preserving short-run external balance, I would not regard that as a significant argument in its favour. It in fact enjoys no such superiority, perhaps because of the errant signals that the J-curve may produce (a temporary worsening of the current account following a depreciation resulting from monetary easing adopted to combat a recession induces perverse fiscal tightening). On the contrary, in the medium term in which current account imbalances matter, the blueprint seems to do rather better than the alternative assignment. And it achieves that while giving proper priority to maintaining internal balance and avoiding misalignments (which I certainly believe deserve their place in the objective function, for reasons perhaps spelled out most persuasively by Krugman, 1988). No one has yet established any systematic errant signals generated by the blueprint.[2] This does not particularly surprise me, since in designing the blueprint we aimed to avoid originality and instead to draw on eclectic mainstream macroeconomic theory as it has evolved from Keynes via monetarism and the Lucas Critique down to the present day. The paper of Currie and Wren-Lewis gives me no reason to think that we failed.

Notes

1 It is therefore quite wrong to describe the blueprint as proposing to use monetary policy to pursue external balance and fiscal policy to pursue internal balance, as has

sometimes been done.

2 Perhaps the closest is the implausibly large fiscal expansion required of Germany, but this may simply reflect the rather high supply-side rate of growth, 3 percent per year, that the authors assume.

References

Boughton, James M. (1988) 'Policy Assignment Strategies with Somewhat Flexible Exchange Rates', IMF Working Paper 88/40.

Currie, David and Simon Wren-Lewis (1989) 'A Comparison of Alternative Regimes for International Macropolicy Coordination', this volume.

Frenkel, Jacob A., Morris Goldstein and Paul R. Masson (1988a) 'International Economic Policy Coordination: Rationale, Mechanisms, and Effects', paper presented to the NBER conference on International Policy Coordination and Exchange Rate Fluctuations at Kiawah Island, October.

Frenkel, Jacob A., Morris Goldstein and Paul R. Masson (1988b) 'Simulating the Effects of Some Simple Coordinated versus Uncoordinated Policy Rules', paper presented to the Brookings/CEPR/IMF conference on Macroeconomic Policies in an Interdependent World, Washington, December.

Genberg, Hans, and Alexander Swoboda (1987) 'The Current Account and the Policy Mix Under Flexible Exchange Rates', IMF Working Paper 87/70.

Krugman, Paul R. (1988) *Exchange Rate Instability*, London: MIT Press.

Miller, Marcus, Paul Weller, and John Williamson (1988). 'The Stabilizing Properties of Target Zones', paper presented to the Brookings/CEPR/IMF conference on Macroeconomic Policies in an Interdependent World, Washington, December.

Chapter 9

Exchange-rate regimes and policy coordination*

Patrick Minford

There has been much discussion recently of how fixing exchange rates – a form of automatic coordination – may assist economic performance (William-son and Miller, 1988, for example, on target zones, and on the EMS, for example Giavazzi and Pagano, 1988, Giovannini, 1988, Giavazzi and Giovannini, 1986, Melitz, 1985); equally, there is an ongoing strand of literature on how monetarily independent, floating exchange-rate governments may gain or lose from coordination. This paper aims to add to the empirical material available on these issues. In choosing a monetary system, as here, one may consider various criteria of performance. Three such criteria seem relevant. First, the stabilizing properties of the system; critics of both fixed and floating regimes have pointed to destabilizing properties in the face of shocks from the natural and policy environment. Second, the capacity of the system to promote price level discipline is of interest; this has been particularly central to the EMS debate. Third, there is the lowering of monetary transactions costs; in arguing for European Monetary Union, many have made use of this point, linking it to 1992, the date set for achieving a more truly common market in Europe. The issues raised in this paper can thus be recast as whether monetary coordination in its various forms improves performance in any of these three dimensions.

*I am grateful to Eric Nowell for carrying out the many simulations of the Liverpool Model; and, for comments on earlier drafts of this paper, to David Currie, Alberto Giovannini, Peter Kenen, Norbert Kloten, Massimo Russo, Hans-Eckart Scharrer, Simon Wren-Lewis, Charles Wyplosz, and to the participants in the EMS working group at the 1988 Draeger Foundation Malente Symposium, especially Drs. Bofinger and Fest. Matthew Canzoneri commented extensively on the ideas here, suggesting important improvements, and particular thanks go to him. I cannot escape responsibility for remaining errors.

BLUEPRINTS FOR EXCHANGE RATE MANAGEMENT
0-12-497060-5
Copyright © 1989 Academic Press, Ltd
All rights of reproduction reserved

The first part asks how if at all 'pure' fixed and floating-rate regimes differ. Clearly, these regimes do differ importantly in the constraints they place on monetary policy (also on money-financed fiscal policy therefore). This first part assumes artificially that policy under both regimes is non-responsive and pre-committed. But the second part relaxes this assumption for floating, whose main attraction after all has been the freedom to carry out independent and perhaps discretionary monetary policy. In this part the stabilizing properties of floating with a variety of independent and coordinated monetary policies is compared with those of fixed rates (assumed to force rigorous monetary dependence) in response to a number of shocks.

It is not possible in this part to bring evidence to bear on the question of price discipline or transaction costs; the former involves too complex a assessment of the political economy of policy behaviour, while too little evidence is available on the latter. However, the final part turns to the behaviour of a particular form of 'fixity', the EMS – a crucial practical element in the coordination debate, in which there is evidence on disciplinary effects and where the possibility of monetary union makes transactions costs a central policy issue. The behaviour of economies in response to monetary policy shocks within the EMS is examined under differing assumptions about accompanying policies – especially the presence or not of exchange controls – and compared with behaviour under floating. A number of curious features of this regime emerge, from which tentative conclusions are drawn.

Throughout this paper the Liverpool world model (Minford et al., 1986) is used as the empirical framework. Key features of this model, which has been estimated largely on annual data, are rational expectations, perfect capital mobility, and wealth effects on consumption; markets clear continuously in an annual framework subject to a range of nominal contracts (especially bonds and wages, though the latter have a maximum maturity of one year). The latter feature distinguishes it from 'disequilibrium' rational expectations models with a high degree of nominal rigidity such as Taylor (1986), MSG2 (Ishii, McKibbin and Sachs, 1985) and Minimod (Haas and Masson, 1986) – for more detailed comparisons emphasizing this distinction, see the recent Brookings volume (Bryant et al., 1988).

I   Fixed and floating rates: How do they differ?

According to a view widely held in the early 1970s and still highly influential, floating exchange rates would to a very large extent insulate the floating economy against foreign shocks; hence fixed rates would be a mechanism for propagating and dissipating shocks across borders besides disciplining monetary policy. This view is neatly encapsulated in the Mundell-Fleming

(Fleming, 1962; Mundell, 1963) model of a small open economy, which underlies a great deal of applied work in international macroeconomics.

In the model, portfolio capital is perfectly mobile, so domestic interest rates, r, are equal to foreign interest rates, r_f, plus expected depreciation of the exchange rate (and a risk premium which we treat as exogenous and will ignore); this gives us a horizontal FF curve in r, y(domestic income) space. The curve shifts up or down with expected depreciation. Domestic prices are sticky, responding to excess demand for output; treat them as fixed in the short run, so that their behaviour is only relevant in pushing the economy to its long-run (vertical Phillips curve) position. Complete the short-run model with a standard IS and LM curve. The LM curve is treated as in a closed economy (the effect of the exchange rate on domestic prices being neglected). The IS curve is modified for the open economy by the effect of the real exchange rate (competitiveness) and world output/trade on net export volumes. Expected depreciation, finally, is assumed to be zero under fixed rates (implying occasional parity changes are unanticipated) and also under floating (implying static expectations). Figure 9.1 illustrates.

The main point is now quickly made. Under fixed rates, the LM curve adjusts (as indicated by the arrows) to the IS-FF intersection through reserve changes which shift the money supply instantaneously under perfect capital mobility, sterilization being useless. Any foreign shocks, which alter foreign ouptut, y_f, prices, p_f, or interest rates, r_f, will impact on our economy. A rise in y_f or p_f shifts IS to the right along the FF curve. A fall in r_f shifts FF down the IS curve. (As for domestic policy, the well-known Mundell-Fleming result that fiscal policy is effective, monetary policy impotent is immediate.)

But under floating, it is now the IS curve which adjusts, as the exchange rate rises or falls to clear the foreign exchange market, to the $LM-FF$ intersection. y_f and p_f now no longer impact on y. As for r_f, a fall in it in

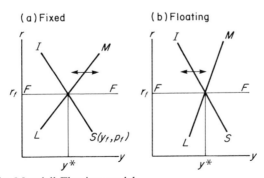

Figure 9.1 The Mundell-Fleming model

response to foreign monetary stimulus will still have an impact on y but it will be perverse and contractionary; and, if as drawn here and usually assumed the interest-elasticity of domestic money is small (or if it is neutralized by accommodation of domestic money), it can be ignored. In this case, insulation is effectively total. (Domestic policy exhibits the Mundell-Fleming reversal of fiscal/monetary roles; fiscal is now impotent, monetary policy effective.)

For completeness, we should note that in the long run the Phillips curve drives y back to y^*; under fixed rates, this occurs as changing p changes competitiveness shifting the *IS*, and under floating changing p shifts the *LM* curve.

If Mundell-Fleming insulation were correct, then fixed and floating rates should have different output-stabilizing responses to shocks. One might suppose in fact that floating would be the more stabilizing since world output variance would be the sum of the variances of independent shocks under floating while under fixed it would be this sum plus the variances of the spillover effects.

The influence of this model can be judged by its subsequent lineage. It was taken over, with the addition of regressive expectations (which also turned out to be rational), by Dornbusch (1976), whose model in turn has been widely used in construction of floating-rate models. For example, a very recent international model of Taylor (1986), is exactly of this type – like Mundell-Fleming models with rational expectations in Dornbusch and overlapping wage contacts to give price steadiness.

The paradox is that the Mundell-Fleming insulation property does not appear to tally with the facts of the floating-rate system. The evidence is clear that under floating rates economies are if anything vibrating more closely together than under fixed rates (e.g. Camen, 1987). There are a number of possible answers to this paradox. One is that the Mundell-Fleming model is wrong on insulation. Another possibility suggested by Swoboda (1983) and Genberg *et al.* (1989) is that there have been *common* (not country-specific) shocks under floating – insulation is then irrelevant, though possibly still correct.

Minford (1988) argued for the first view, on the grounds that the insulating properties of the Mundell-Fleming model are an artefact of the simplifying assumptions made in the exposition above. The key simplification seems to be that on expectations. Recent models in the Mundell-Fleming lineage have tended to adopt rational expectations. This, combined with the well-known slowness of net exports to respond to exchange rates, implies that the *FF* curve moves substantially and rapidly in response to shocks; consequently when y_f or p_f move the *IS* curve, the *FF* curve adjusts in the short run. A further modification, which turns out to be important once the *FF* curve is liberated by this expectations mechanism, is the sensitivity of domestic prices to the exchange rate; this enables the *LM* curve to move in the short run. A rise in r_f, which causes a depreciation of the spot exchange rate, will therefore now raise domestic prices and shift the *LM* curve to the left, reducing *y* in a normally-signed spillover.

It turns out that floating adds an extra set of feedbacks, namely via the nominal exchange rate and money demands, but in so doing does not alter the basic structure of interdependence between the other variables in the model; it is as if in cinematic terms a filter of unknown type were placed in front of a camera lens. (Appendix 2 sets out a stylized two-country model with details of this.) It is not possible *a priori* to say in this case which way the extra feedbacks will modify the interdependencies (the filter lens modifies the colours of the picture); it is an empirical matter. However, the paper examined two models: the Taylor model, which is New Keynesian, and the Liverpool model, which is New Classical, and found that in both there was surprisingly little difference between interdependence under fixed and floating rates (such a result was reported by Taylor, 1986, for his model) – see Tables 9.1 and 9.2.

Table 9.1 Taylor model: Comparisons of fixed and floating exchange rates

	Floating	Fixed	Comment
(a) *US money shock (permanent rise of 3% in money supply level):* Year 1 effects (%)			
y: US	0.84	0.89	n.c.
ROW	0.05	1.1	Spillover larger under Fix
p: US	0.40	0.40	n.c.
ROW	−0.03	0.45	Spillover larger under Fix
(b) *US fiscal shock (permanent rise in govt spending by 1% of GNP):* Year 1 effects			
y: US	1.2	1.45	n.c.
ROW	0.22	−1.0	Changed direction of spillover
P: US	0.48	0.41	n.c.
ROW	0.20	−0.25	Changed direction of spillover
(c) *Supply shocks everywhere (stochastic wage shocks)* *(Full period 87.1–89.4, standard deviation, % difference)*			
y: US	0.94	0.84	n.c.
ROW	0.64	2.93	Spillover larger under Fix
P: US	2.52	2.51	n.c.
ROW	0.81	0.88	n.c.

Table 9.2 Liverpool model: Year 1 response to foreign shocks under fixed and floating exchange rates

(a) *Supply shocks*

	US supply shock (10% temporary 1-year fall in US output supply)		Non-US supply shocks** (10% temporary 1-year rise in real exchange rates)	
y	*Floating*	*Fixed*	*Floating*	*Fixed*
US	(−5.3)*	(−5.5)*	−0.40	−0.34
Ca	−0.8	−0.8	−0.05	−0.78
Ja	−0.5	−0.4	−0.08	−0.03
Ger	−2.1	−2.3	−0.36	−0.24
Fr	−1.6	−1.8	−0.21	−0.16
It	−1.1	−1.3	−0.16	−0.15
UK	−1.3	−1.3	−0.20	−0.18
Average	−1.23	−1.35	−0.23	−0.23
p				
US	(3.2)*	(3.3)*	0.43	0.28
Ca	0.2	0.6	0.50	0.27
Ja	0.4	1.2	0.41	0.41
Ger	2.1	0.8	0.29	0.33
Fr	0.7	0.6	0.28	0.29
It	3.3	0.6	1.07	0.43
UK	0.8	0.7	0.10	0.32
Average	1.2	0.8	0.45	0.33

* US response to own supply shock.
** Each entry shows average response to shock in non-US foreign countries
(i.e. excluding US and own country).

Given an absence of Mundell-Fleming insulation and considerable similarity of interdependence across exchange-rate regimes, one might well expect the stabilizing properties of the two regimes to be similar also. By contrast, a number of economists have gone to the other extreme and argued that – because of exchange rate 'overshooting' – floating is less stabilizing than fixed rates.

We now therefore turn to a systematic comparison of these relative stabilizing properties, using the Liverpool model.

II Stabilizing properties of fixed and floating regimes in the face of non-policy shocks

Canzoneri and Minford (1988) set up a policy coordination problem for governments of the US and 'Europe', where they had to decide how much

Table 9.2 Continued

(b) *Monetary shocks*

	US monetary shock (2% once for all rise in money supply)		Non-US supply shocks**	
y	*Floating*	*Fixed*	*Floating*	*Fixed*
US	(0.58)*	(1.0)*	0.06	0.35
Ca	0.05	0.27	−0.06	−0.02
Ja	0.05	0.48	0.004	0.14
Ger	0.25	0.71	0.08	−0.01
Fr	0.18	0.91	0.03	0.26
It	0.13	0.56	0.03	0.25
UK	0.15	0.24	0.04	0.02
Average	0.13	0.53	0.03	0.14
p				
US	(1.65)*	(1.17)*	−0.08	0.01
Ca	− 0.23	0.43	−0.40	0.10
Ja	− 0.21	0.83	−0.27	0.19
Ger	− 0.24	0.65	−0.05	0.14
Fr	− 0.13	0.70	−0.12	0.18
It	− 0.48	1.28	−0.44	0.39
UK	− 0.10	0.61	−0.07	0.14
Average	− 0.23	0.75	−0.20	0.16

* US response to own shock.
** Under Floating, each country raises money supply by 2% once for all; under Fixed, each devalues (trade-weighted basis) by 2% once for all. Each entry shows average response to shock in non-US foreign countries (i.e. excluding own and US shocks).

to deflate (using a single balanced monetary/fiscal instrument) in the face of a severe inherited inflation, output being supposed to be at its natural rate. The Nash and coordinated strategies from this problem are assumed here to be carried over for other shocks. That is, the reduced form rules relating the monetary/fiscal instrument to output and prices at home and abroad are assumed to apply whatever the shock.

Technically, as the derivation note in Appendix 1 shows, this is correct, if the linear and other approximations there are accurate. However, this is unlikely to be the case.

One experiment consists in setting up rule of thumb responses – using the Canzoneri-Minford parameters based on the model – that actual governments might adopt with the resources at their disposal and given the constraints of international negotiation. We suppose that governments respond continuously to events with these rule-of-thumb reactions. They respond continuously to events, rather than with a single response to our postulated shocks,

Table 9.2   Continued

(c) *Fiscal shocks*

US fiscal shock (1% of GDP rise in government spending for 5 years)   Non-US fiscal shock** (i.e. 1% of GDP rise in government spending for 5 years)

y	Floating	Fixed	Floating	Fixed
US	(0.45)*	(0.68)*	0.00	0.23
Ca	0.16	− 0.17	0.12	0.05
Ja	0.00	0.02	0.04	0.25
Ger	0.05	− 0.30	0.15	0.24
Fr	0.10	0.16	0.12	0.41
It	0.02	0.15	0.08	0.31
UK	− 0.01	− 0.04	0.02	0.11
Average	0.05	0.03	0.08	0.23
p				
US	(0.45)*	(0.56)*	0.45	0.09
Ca	0.55	0.15	0.15	0.17
Ja	0.45	0.30	0.09	0.35
Ger	− 0.12	0.22	−0.16	0.25
Fr	0.14	0.25	−0.01	0.29
It	− 0.04	0.47	−0.23	0.59
UK	0.04	0.22	−0.02	0.25
Average	0.17	0.27	0.04	0.28

* US response to own shock
** Each entry shows average response to shock in non-US foreign countries (i.e. excluding US and own country).

because we suppose that they cannot locate the source of the shock or know whether it is repeated or not.

This is not what sophisticated, fully informed governments would do, but governments are neither sophisticated nor fully informed. In effect we have placed two handicaps on them. First, the approximation from using the linear multipliers. Second, the absence of knowledge of the shocks.

We also proceed conceptually as in Canzoneri-Minford in defining the limits of strategic behaviour. There is no attempt to use the dynamics of policy and policies once adopted are followed through, it being implicitly assumed that there are penalties (perhaps electoral) on reneging. Again, governments as they are can be argued to behave in this rather simplistic way; getting policy roughly facing in the right direction is presumably difficult enough without fine-tuning its dynamics, and playing clever with policy reversal does appear to carry electoral risks.

On this basis, four regimes are now compared: fixed and floating, each with no policy reactions to shocks, and floating with these rule-of-thumb Nash and Cooperative macro-policy reactions. Under fixed, we could also have looked at policy reactions by the reserve-currency country or by all countries; but this was not done because it is not clear what would be a plausible activist regime for that country. Hence, there is scope for a number of fixed-rate regimes, along the lines perhaps of Williamson and Miller.

Obviously, too, the floating regimes considered are but a subset of the possibilities. The exercise is therefore intended to be illustrative of the stabilising properties of different exchange rate regimes and activist attempts to improve on them.

Three shocks are considered, all of them global: a one-year fall in output supply (by 10%), a one-year rise in consumption (by 5%), and a permanent rise in real oil prices (by 25%). These three are sufficient to make our negative illustrative points.

These points that emerge are not really new, but may perhaps have been lost sight of in the new age of high-technology policy optimization. They are:

(1) The relative stabilizing properties of (pure) fixed and floating rates depend on the shock and the country. Thus, Tables 9.3 and 9.4 of results show that for consumption shocks, both Europe and the US are better off under floating, while for oil shocks, Europe is better off under floating, the US under fixed. But for output supply shocks, both are better off under fixed.

Table 9.3 Welfare losses (squared % output gap equivalent) from various shocks under different regimes

Regime	Fixed	Floating	Floating-Nash	Floating-cooperative
Shocks: 1-year output supply fall				
US	5.4	6.9	6.5	5.4
Europe	1.3	1.4	1.0	0.8
1-year Consumption Rise				
US	0.023	0.015	0.857	0.683
Europe	0.622	0.495	0.380	0.573
Permanent Oil Price Rise				
US	0.74	4.47	3.34	2.66
Europe	0.45	0.16	0.30	0.36

Table 9.4   Background figures for welfare losses

Regime		Fixed	Floating	Floating-Nash	Floating-cooperative
Shocks: 1-year Output Labour Supply					
US:	y	2.3	2.6	2.4	2.2
	p	3.0	4.0	8.6	7.5
	π	0.5	0.5	1.4	1.2
Europe:	y	1.0	1.2	1.0	0.8
	p	3.7	4.6	6.1	7.1
	π	0.8	0.3	0.1	0.5
1-year Consumption Rise					
US:	y	0.15	0.12	0.19	0.17
	p	0.52	0.54	1.64	1.27
	π	0.01	0.04	1.49	1.33
Europe:	y	0.78	0.70	0.62	0.68
	p	1.01	0.45	0.36	0.57
	π	0.23	0.11	0.11	0.52
Permanent Oil Price Rise					
US:	y	0.4	1.0	0.9	0.8
	p	3.7	3.0	6.3	6.5
	π	0.5	0.4	0.5	0.5
Europe:	y	0.6	0.4	0.5	0.5
	p	5.5	1.4	2.3	6.1
	π	0.6	0.1	0.4	0.5

Notes: y = output gap (%) average absolute; p = price level (%) deviation from base; π = long-run expected inflation rate (%) p.a. over years 1–4.

(2) Strategic non-cooperative activism does not guarantee an improvement in stability/welfare over nil-reaction policies. The tables show a couple of cases where it worsens matters; for the US with the consumption shock, and for Europe with the oil price shock.

(3) Cooperative activism does not guarantee an improvement over strategic non-cooperative activism. The tables show two cases of worsening (for Europe with the consumption shock and with the oil price shock).

This first point is explained by our discussion in the first part, emphasizing the extra monetary belt put on in floating and its differences across countries.

The second is a familiar and obvious possibility; 'retaliation' can make mutual strategic action counter-productive.

The third point is a little surprising until one reflects on the restrictions in our simulations, deliberately introduced as real-world handicaps on government policy. First, the welfare weights in the cooperative solution (probably the most important thing that would vary from shock to shock) may well be a factor. One player can always lose in cooperation when there are no side payments. Here the rules that give satisfactory weights for our calibrated case may not work for all the others. Secondly, the rules of thumb may just not be accurate enough; the approximation of effects of the shock by the effects inclusive of those from policy reaction may work better for some shocks than for others, as may the approximation of assuming continuous policy response to those effects instead of the one-off policy re-setting that is truly appropriate.

What is of interest is that even in a limited set of fairly routine shocks, selected at random, these particular possibilities should occur. The may be considered somewhat discouraging to the effort of finding superior stabiliz-ation rules in a world of diverse shocks and governments working with crude rules of thumb. This points towards the simplest, fixed-policy behaviour as a reasonable choice; as for the choice between fixed and floating rates, it suggests the choice should be made on grounds other than stabilization. Further work may of course do better for stabilization rules; but governments are likely to require a high degree of robustness to shocks and to crudeness of calibration before they will shift to a new system of policy management.

III   The European Monetary System: What is wrong with it?

The European Monetary System (EMS) is a supplement to domestic monetary systems. Quite how it works depends on the countries involved. For example, the Netherlands treats the DM–Guilder link as effectively fixed. Italy and France by contrast allow devaluations periodically, after discussions with EMS partners, principally West Germany.

The Netherlands uses the EMS as a device for pegging its prices (at German levels) and for minimizing transactions costs in foreign trade, much of which is with Germany. It is happy to relinquish any freedom to use domestic monetary policy to stabilize its economy; any stabilization that occurs comes from German monetary decisions. This is a sort of European Monetary Union, though asymmetrical in this case.

Britain has a fully floating system, apart from the usual temporary central bank intervention and some recent experimentation after the Louvre Accord with a shadow EMS link to the Dm. In this floating system prices are set domestically, there are significant transactions costs in foreign trade with EEC partners, and money can be used domestically to stabilize ouput.

This section attempts to evaluate these three options – EMS with adjustable rates, EMU, and floating. I begin with some general characterization of all three regimes; then discuss some model simulations of behaviour under two of them, EMS and floating. Finally, I discuss possible policy preferences in relation to these results.

III.1   How do these regimes behave?

As argued above and in Minford (1988) fixed and floating-rate systems differ little in their transmission of real shocks. As for monetary shocks, though the direction of impact of foreign monetary shocks is altered, floating does not clearly insulate against these shocks, because the exchange rate tends to move sharply in response. So fixed rates eliminate any domestic monetary variance and foreign monetary variance dominates, while floating provides a mixture of domestic and foreign monetary variance, whose combination may be greater or less for prices or output depending on model structure and the variance-covariance structure of the shocks.

This suggests that abstracting from transitional costs a country will be attracted to a fully fixed system if the dominant foreign money in it exhibits low variance; in this case it is unlikely that the floating variance combination will be as low. This seems to be the position of the Netherlands.

What then of EMS in less than fully fixed systems? Here we face a problem of evaluating the system behaviour. It turns out that behaviour depends crucially on the parameters of flexibility, that is how large are the parity changes and the margins around parity, and how long the parity must be held.

At the one extreme where the margins are wide, the parity may be adjusted in small steps, and may be adjusted frequently, the system is indistinguishable from free floating. Clearly, in the early days of for example the Italian association with EMS, this was the regime it followed. But nowadays such a regime is seen as pointless formality.

What can happen when the limits are set more tightly? In effect there is a clash between two monetary systems. Monetary growth may be set independently over the medium term and yet exchange rates are not allowed to respond to this monetary divergence except discretely. The central problem of the EMS is seen here as this clash between the domestic drive for monetary independence and the discipline of the EMS. The domestic drive is motivated by the desire either to reflate or to deflate in a way that the dominant partner does not wish; in the simulations here we will assume the former, which is the relevant one given the stance of the dominant Bundesbank.

How do people expect this clash to be resolved? We may distinguish two polar cases: perfect capital mobility without exchange controls (so that uncovered interest parity prevails) and fully effective exchange controls where the central bank can use sterilized intervention to fix the exchange rate while setting interest rates via monetary policy. Under perfect capital mobility by contrast during the period when the exchange rate is being pegged temporarily, the central bank cannot fix the money supply as well; it has to let money supply adjust to whatever the exchange-rate peg dictates.

To model both these two regimes we have to modify our usual wage equation, which is not set up for policy conflict and sudden switches of regime. It seems likely that faced with the prospect of a sudden devaluation/price jump of uncertain timing, unions would take precautionary action to raise contracted wages in advance of the expected price jump. Another reason for pre-emptive action would be overlaps in contract periods. The model assumes that in normal times of smooth price behaviour this is of no importance, because such devices as bonus variation could iron out temporary anomalies in the contract as other workers get ahead or behind. But for extreme jumps such as those here these devices would be inadequate and we could expect the contract to reflect the likely overlap; as Taylor has shown this creates a serially correlated pattern of wage movements in response to a shock in expected prices, starting from the quarter of the shock. We capture this here in the annual model by putting an immediate reaction of wages to the current year's shock change in next year's prices.

Together these factors argue for a special adjustment of current wages in response to the prospect of future devaluation. The adjustment we make for illustrative purposes is equal to one half of the delayed price adjustment (= the long-term devaluation) required by the monetary expansion. So for example, when later we simulate a monetary expansion of 4% per annum for two years (8% overall), devaluation being permitted only in the second year, then wages are adjusted upwards in the first year by 4% (0.5 × 8%).

The effect of this anticipatory movement in wages is to push up prices rather faster than the exchange-rate peg would normally permit; consequently, the real exchange rate tends to be pushed up, very much a feature of the EMS experience of those other countries, notably France and Italy, whose underlying inflation has exceeded Germany's.

Otherwise, the model's set-up is quickly described under the two EMS regimes. Without exchange controls, the model is solved as if on fixed rates (money supply temporarily endogenous) when the floating exchange rate hits the EMS limit; otherwise it solves in the standard floating mode with money supply exogenous. With exchange controls, the model is solved with money supply exogenous throughout; but when the exchange rate hits the limit, it is fixed and the uncovered interest parity condition suspended. Interest rates are then set by the interaction of money demand (prices being set by the exchange rate and wages) and money supply.

The key difference between the two regimes is in the behaviour of interest rates (which then impacts elsewhere in the model). Under no controls, interest rates must rise sharply in response to the prospect of devaluation, as dictated by uncovered interest parity. This is obviously deflationary. It is this that creates pressure for exchange controls in this partially flexible EMS system. The authorities may be compelled, in Tobin's phrase, to throw sand in the machinery of international arbitrage.

If they do, then interest rates will be kept low by the monetary expansion, permitting more reflationary impact; the resulting speculation against the currency is simply frustrated by the controls. The catch is that real interest rates are held below going world rates, causing a micro-distortion of the domestic capital market, subsidizing capital investment and taxing saving. If the policy becomes systematic, this could cause a serious cost.

The simulations are shown for floating, EMS-no-controls, and EMS-with-controls in Figures 9.2–9.5. In all cases, the country is assumed to pursue a policy of temporary reflation, two years of 4% money growth and fiscal expansion to match (8% in total by year 2, regardless of intervention in year 1 in the no-controls case).

Under floating, Figure 9.2, this reflation has the familiar effects. Prices rise, the exchange rate falls, both rather sharply, and the real exchange rate falls, as real wages are depressed by the unexpected inflation. Output rises, with net exports stimulated by higher competitiveness and domestic demand stimulated by lower real interest rates, with lower real financial wealth restraining this effect (in some cases offsetting it).

The EMS without controls, Figures 9.3–9.5, bottom half, upsets this familiar scene. Now wages and prices rise, though not so much as in floating because they are restrained by the exchange rate limits. The real exchange rate actually rises because prices are pushed up relative to the exchange rate depreciation by the anticipatory wage pressure. Interest rates, real and nominal, rise, because of the need to maintain uncovered arbitrage, with nominal and real exchange rates expected to fall next year. Output falls as net exports are hit by the lower competitiveness and domestic demand both by the higher real interest rate and by the drop in real financial wealth. The picture is of a reflation frustrated, even reversed, on real variables yet having much of the inflationary effects on nominal variables; the mechanism of frustration is the exchange rate and its sympethetic link with interest rates.

The EMS with exchange controls, Figure 9.3–9.5, top half, can at least cut this link. Interest rates now move in line with domestic monetary conditions only, so with this reflation they fall. This fall takes out some of the reversing force on output, so that output falls less than in the no-control case. However, the price paid is that long-term interest rates are pushed below the international cost of capital, the opportunity cost for the economy.

A stylized representation of the model's operation is given in Figure 9.6,

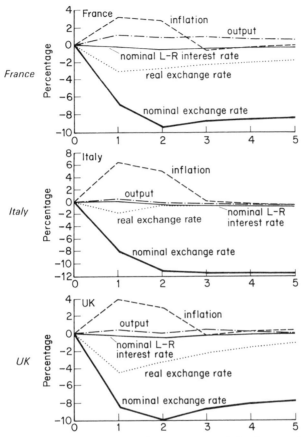

Figure 9.2 Effect of a 4% p.a. increase in money growth for 2 years, floating exchange rate (% differences from base)

which may be set beside the essentially similar but stochastic ('smooth-pasted') and smaller model of Miller and Weller (1989). The figure indicates that under floating a monetary reflation shock causes the real exchange rate to fall and thereafter to move along the saddlepath to equilibrium from below. Under EMS the same shock forces the real exchange rate upwards, and then onto the saddlepath which now approaches equilibrium from above. Hence the EMS alters both the model's impact effects and the location of its dynamic path (it does not alter its eigenvalues).

The evidence suggests superficially – Figure 9.7 shows recent behaviour of some key variables for the three countries dealt with here – that the EMS may have had some effects of this type. Output growth appears to have been

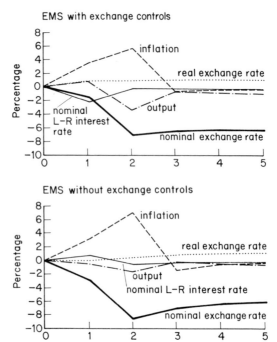

Figure 9.3   UK: Effects under EMS of a 4% p.a. increase in money growth for 2 years, devaluation allowed in year 2 (% differences from base)

slowed, the real exchange rate boosted and inflation differentials against Germany not eliminated, under the EMS regime. Interest rates are harder to see a story in; this may reflect chronic but not systematic controls.

What this illustrates is that the EMS prevents exchange rate volatility in the short term, but that it does so at a cost in loss of output and with controls a resource cost of capital protection. Thus it acts as a discipline against governments wishing to reflate, as simulated here, via monetary expansion (an essentially Keynesian policy), by attending such reflation with unpleasant side-effects.

We now turn to a discussion of the policy choices that may be made by governments in Europe.

III.2   The political choices

What might cause a government to embrace such an unsatisfactory system as the partially-flexible EMS? The reason appears to be political. Both in France and Italy there have been difficulties with achieving genuine monetary control.

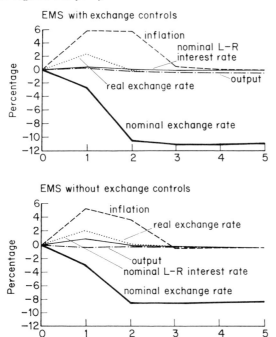

Figure 9.4 Italy: Effects under EMS of a 4% p.a. increase in money growth for 2 years, devaluation allowed in year 2 (% differences from base)

In France, the traditional method of monetary control was the direct allocation of credit. Monetary aggregates were targeted by M. Barre under the Barre Plan; but the central feature was credit control and in any case only limited success was achieved in bringing inflation down.

Subsequently, M. Mitterrand pursued expansionary policies and faced a sharply depreciating franc. He changed his mind on the appropriateness of expansion, but had difficulty in persuading his socialist party followers of the rightness of this change of course. Furthermore in an increasingly deregulated financial world credit controls were not longer viable as a method of monetary control. In these circumstances a political commitment to Europe could be made into a commitment to adhere to the disciplines of the EMS; partial monetary control through the exchange rate was better than politically embarrassing and economically unviable domestic control of credit. So much easier to blame the awkwardness of the German ally within a necessary treaty. No doubt too the fact that tougher anti-inflation policy was needed to avoid devaluations against the spirit of France's EMS commitment, itself influenced M. Mitterrand.

In Italy, the story involves the daring of the Banca d'Italia, for long

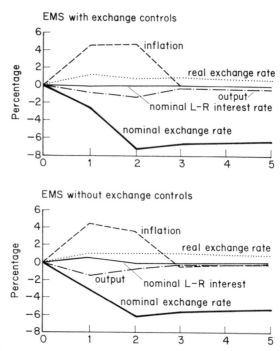

Figure 9.5 France: Effects under EMS of a 4% p.a. increase in money growth for 2 years, devaluation allowed in year 2 (% differences from base)

concerned at steady double-digit inflation. With reasons I cannot properly understand it persuaded the governing coalition that the EMS arrangement had to be a serious one, not the previous wide-margin *de facto* floating system. Perhaps the government too was aiming for lower inflation and thought that the lead should be taken by the central bank and also the blame as scapegoat should it prove politically too unpopular. Since that time the Banca d'Italia has not looked back, citing the EMS as the reason for an unprecedented tightening of Italian monetary conditions, which has indeed brought inflation down to less than 5%. The politicians meanwhile have been unable to cut the budget deficit, so that public debt has escalated in real terms and relative to GDP. Hence in Italy the central bank has indeed played Sargent and Wallace's (1981) game of chicken with the politicians.

These interpretations of French and Italian political economy are offered more to provoke accurate analysis from those much better placed than I to know, than as a scholarly account (though the account appears to be consistent with for example Sachs and Wyplosz, 1986, and Giovannini, 1988).

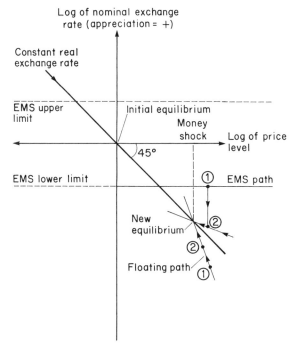

Figure 9.6 Stylized illustration of model's path for monetary reflation under floating and EMS

The fact remains that two countries not noted for strong independent anti-inflationary policy did embrace the EMS as a means to reduce inflation.

In the work adopting this type of interpretation, cited above, stress has been placed on the EMS as a discipline with credibility, whereas domestic monetary policy could not command credibility. This is a plausible argument. To have an incentive for following through on its counter-inflationary plans, a government must face some penalty for deviation, greater than the reward to cheating by an inflationary burst along the Phillips curve. The EMS provides such a penalty – a period of over-valuation until a devaluation is finally permitted under the rules. By contrast such a penalty is hard to devise under a politicized monetary policy.

An alternative line of justification for the EMS is that in a second-best world where governments cannot voluntarily coordinate macro policies the EMS ensures an approach towards the coordinated away from the free-for-all (Nash) solution. This line has been taken by Melitz (1985) for example. The idea is that the EMS prevents the beggar-my-neighbour tactics both of devaluation for growth and appreciation for counter-inflation policy.

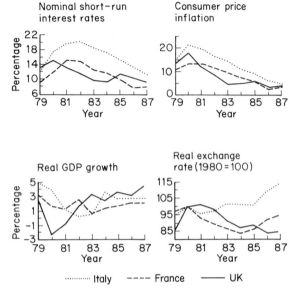

Figure 9.7   Key variables in France, Italy and UK, 1979–87

First-best coordination would limit the externalities (side-effects on neigh-bours) of both tactics; hence the usefulness of EMS, even if it does not get to the first-best point. This analysis is offered normatively but it can also be seen as an explanation of why governments may have entered the EMS.

There are three main problems with the argument. First why should governments be prevented from pursuing first-best coordination if it is truly in their interests? The reasoning is crucial but not cogently displayed.

Secondly, the coordinated solution has not been demonstrated to be closer to the EMS outcome than the Nash; even suppose coordination does involve constant real exchange rates (*no* beggar-my-neighbour), EMS fails to provide this. Its mechanism as we have seen guarantees over-valuation for the inflationary partner.

Thirdly, discretionary coordination will not necessarily bring welfare gains; Rogoff's well-known (1985) example involves two governments exploiting the Phillips curve jointly, whereas separately they are restrained by the balance of payments deterioration involved. The result is that under coordination the public expects this discretionary joint action so that it produces more inflation without more output. This is also a possibility under the EMS, if it truly makes governments more coordinated. Of course, precisely the problems of credible penalties in a single state, which the existence of a foreign treaty such as EMS can solve, arise under a coordinated

EMS; for what foreign mechanism would now exist to produce penalties to prevent such use of discretion?

To be fair to this line of argument for EMS, it is not envisaged that such discretionary coordination is possible; indeed that is why the EMS is a surrogate mechanism. Furthermore, the first-best coordinated policy is intended to be designed with a mechanism to ensure follow-through. It remains the case that coordination may not provide gains over competition in policy. Practical illustrations are tax reform and the reduction in inflation; in both cases the example of success in other countries put pressure on home politicians to match that success.

There are analogies with industrial competition. We know that competition often wastes resources, causing industrial excess capacity for example. Yet it guarantees progress to the lowest-cost outcome, yielding long-term gains. Similarly, too much stress on the short-term waste in macro policy may frustrate the long-term progress to a stable-price world.

In short, coordination appears to be a flawed justification for EMS. However, EMS does appear to have been used implicitly or explicitly by French and Italian politicians as a monetary means of discipline, so that they could match the success in controlling inflation of other economies.

III.3 The position of Britain

Up to now Britain has stayed out of the EMS, except in a recent Dm-shadowing experiment since the Louvre Accord. And even that experiment has now been brought to an effective end at least for the time being.

If we accept the reasoning just sketched for French and Italian participation, then the British refusal to join can be explained in similar terms. Mrs Thatcher's government has sunk a good deal of political capital into the creation of counter-inflationary credibility without resort to foreign entanglements. The Medium Term Financial Strategy has to be seen in these terms. This sets out targets for the PSBR, money growth (the monetary base, M0), and money GDP; the implication is that if the government fails to meet these counter-inflationary targets systematically, it will by its own admission have failed in its objectives.

Politically, this is a serious hostage to fortune, designed to penalize deviation from the plan in terms of lost votes – the ultimate deterrent in a democracy. Of course, the reverse side of the coin is that it rewards the government for adherence, since it is clearly seen to have achieved its objectives.

Hence we see here a deliberate political choice, to make the conquest of inflation an overtly domestic policy act, chosen and executed by the governing party. No foreign scapegoats are sought, nor any foreigners to share the credit. It follows obviously enough that the EMS has no contribution to make.

When this lack of political attractiveness is set side by side with the economic problems of EMS described earlier, the decision is entirely explained. Batchelor (1987) has argued that the trade-off for temporary exchange-rate stability of interest-rate and price instability is an unfavourable one because it is easy for the firms involved to hedge exchange risk whereas households are less easily placed to hedge interest-rate and price risks. This may well be so; in truth we have little empirical evidence on the relative seriousness of these types of uncertainty. But politically, interest-rate and price variability is more sensitive than exchange-rate variability, which would seem to bear out Batchelor's view. Also likely to weigh in the eyes of the politicians involved is the need for exchange controls. Again, the seriousness of the distortions created is not known empirically. But that there will be some is a good reason for not re-introducing them.

After exchange controls were abolished in 1979, the return on capital in Britain rose from more than 4% below the going international rate to equal or above it – see Figure 9.8. Other factors were of course at work. Nevertheless, a significant change can be reasonably attributed to the abolition of exchange controls.

It is reasonable to suppose that under EMS the UK would have a similar need to stop capital going overseas since its inflation rate is systematically higher than West Germany's (at present there is temporary sterling strength but that is because monetary policy is being tightened sharply and incompatibly with EMS). On this basis one could roughly estimate the distortion of exchange controls by the square formula of consumer surplus. If for example the capital-output ratio is 3.0, the semi-log interest elasticity of the capital

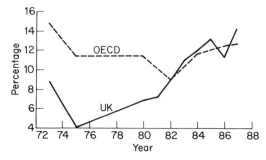

Figure 9.8 Return on capital: net operating surplus as % of net capital stock, 1973–87. The OECD figures are an average of the US, Germany, France and Canada. *Source*: *Bank of England Quarterly Bulletin*, Aug. 1988, p. 381.

stock is 1.0, and the effect on capital return is 0.04 p.a., then the loss as a fraction of annual GDP is (0.04^2 × 3 × 1 = 0.0048), or 0.5% of GDP; this would have a present value discounted at a real rate of 5% less real growth of 3%, of 24% of one year's GDP, no trivial loss. Certainly, such a hypothetical calculation fits with the impression that the discipline of the international capital markets has had something to do with the sharpening up of British productivity since 1979.

III.4 Where now?

We began by noting the criteria for judging a monetary system. The defects of EMS stem from its merely partial fixity; such partialness is however inevitable when countries are joining without compatible policies. Imagine instead a world in which policies have evolved to compatibility at zero inflation; now no longer an incredible vision. Suppose too that in such a world governments have forsworn the use of monetary policy for stabilizing output by exploiting the Phillips curve, because such use would involve time-inconsistency, penalized in the new policy environment.

It then becomes attractive to make the gains of transactions cost minimiz-ation, by fixing exchange rates in an EMU; this becomes particularly relevant in the context of moves to the single EEC market. We would then have a system, whose mechanics have to be worked out, meeting all our criteria; pegging prices and minimizing transaction costs while forswearing stabiliz-ation policy. Some mechanism relating the European monetary base to the price level while deregulating financial intermediaries could prove an attractive operating procedure which would allow the needs of trade and credit to be met flexibly without inflationary risk. Alternatively, and perhaps more attractively still, EMU could emerge from competition between national currencies and even others such as the ECU; each could co-exist, with competition enforcing effective sameness, price stability, and mutual fixity.

But that is to anticipate another debate – on what precise form EMU might take. This paper concludes with the observation that EMU, not the EMS half-way-house of partial fixity, is what is likely to prove interesting to politicians, certainly those in Britain, for the next phase of the European monetary effort.

Appendix 1: Derivation of Nash and cooperative rules

Following Canzoneri and Minford (1988):

$$U = -x^2 - u(\pi^2)$$

$$U^* = -x^{*2} - u^*(\pi^{*2})$$

$$x = x_0 + p_1 g + p_2 g^*$$

$$x^* = x_0^* + p_1^* g^* + p_2^* g$$

$$\pi = \pi_0 + g$$

$$\pi^* = \pi_0^* + g^*$$

Where:

x = output gap (%)
π = long-run expected inflation (% p.a.)
g = macro instrument (% p.a. growth in money/fiscal deficit as % of GDP)
p_i = own/spillover effects
* denotes Europe, unstarred variables US
0-subscript denotes inherited stock effect

1. *Nash case* (N-subscript denotes Nash)

$$\begin{bmatrix} p_1^2 + u & p_1 p_2 \\ p_1^* p_2^* & p_1^{*2} + u^* \end{bmatrix} \begin{bmatrix} g_N \\ g_N^* \end{bmatrix} = \begin{bmatrix} -p_1 x_0 & -u\pi_0 \\ -p_1^* x_0^* & -u^* \pi_0^* \end{bmatrix}$$

Solve for g_N, g_N^* in terms of x_0, x_0^*, π_0, π_0^*. Approximate these by x_t, x_t^*, π_t, π_t^*, i.e. actual values.

2. *Cooperative case* (C-subscript denotes cooperative)

$$\begin{bmatrix} (p_1^2 + u) + \left(\frac{1-\lambda}{\lambda}\right)p_2^{*2} & p_1 p_2 + \left(\frac{1-\lambda}{\lambda}\right)p_1^* p_2^* \\ p_1 p_2 + \left(\frac{1-\lambda}{\lambda}\right)p_1^* p_2^* & \left(\frac{1-\lambda}{\lambda}\right)(p_1^{*2} + u^*) + p_2^2 \end{bmatrix} \begin{bmatrix} g_C \\ g_C^* \end{bmatrix} =$$

$$\begin{bmatrix} -(p_1 x_0 + u\pi_0) & -\left(\frac{1-\lambda}{\lambda}\right)p_2^* x_0^* \\ -p_2 x_0 & -\left(\frac{1-\lambda}{\lambda}\right)(p_1^* x_0^* + u^* \pi_0^*) \end{bmatrix}$$

Solve for g_C, g_C^* analogously with Nash case. λ is the weight on the US.

Values from Canzoneri and Minford:

$p_1 = 0.41$	$p_2 = 0.50$	$u = 0.37$
(US own effect)	(Europe spillover to US)	
$p_1^* = 0.59$	$p_2^* = 0.11$	$u^* = 0.41$
(Europe own effect)	(US spillover to Europe)	

The resulting rules are:

Nash:

US: $g_t = -0.784x_t - 0.707\pi_t + 0.305x_t^* + 0.212\pi_t^*$
Europe (same rule followed by Germany, France, Italy and UK)
$g_t^* = 0.055x_t + 0.053\pi_t - 0.799x_t^* - 0.557\pi_t^*$

Cooperative:

US: $g_t = -0.581x_t - 0.766\pi_t + 0.089\ x_t^* + 0.220\pi_t^*$
Europe (same rule for each of 4 countries):
$g_t^* = -0.346x_t + 0.199\pi_t - 0.608x_t^* - 0.464\pi_t^*$

Appendix 2: A stylized two-country model: The nature of interdependence under fixed and floating rates

Leaving on one side the money market, our two countries will each have a goods market supply equation (1) and demand equation (2), and there will be a common foreign exchange market clearing condition, given by uncovered interest parity (UIP–5); write this last in terms of real interest rates and the real exchange rate, RXR, assume that the current RXR is observable, and assume approximate monotonic first-order saddle-path dynamics. Then (5) gives us a simple direct relationship between the real interest differential and RXR. We examine only impact effects in this model so all variables are to be considered as 'surprises', deviations from the previous period's expectation. Notice that all the effects on trade are subsumed into the demand curve for goods; this demand curve also has prices entering because of real balance effects on spending. All variables are logs except interest rates (fraction p.a.) and RXR (fractional deviation from a base date). So we have:

(Home – goods)

$$y = e_1 p + e_2 RXR \ldots \text{(supply)} \tag{1}$$

$$y = -\kappa_1 r - \kappa_2 RXR - \kappa_3 p + \kappa_4 y_f \ldots \text{(demand)} \tag{2}$$

(Abroad – goods)

$$y_f = S_1 p_f - S_2 RXR \ldots \text{(supply)} \tag{3}$$

$$y_f = -d_1 r_f + d_2 RXR - d_3 p_f + d_4 y \ldots \text{(demand)} \tag{4}$$

(Foreign exchange – UIP)

$$r = r_f + \alpha RXR \tag{5}$$

The '…' indicates omitted exogenous variables and lagged terms. Substitution of (5) into (2) to eliminate r allows us to write both demand curves as functions of f_f, RXR, own prices, and the other country's income. The goods market is illustrated in Figure 9A.1.

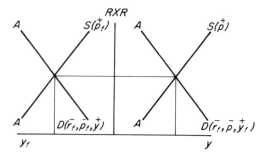

Figure 9A.1 Two-country goods markets

The system to this point has 7 endogenous variables $(y, y_f, p, p_f, r, r_f,$ and $RXR)$ but only 5 equations. To close it we must of course add the monetary sector.

We choose to represent this by three more equations. (Throughout, the nominal and real interest rates will be equated, assuming for convenience that expected inflation is equal or close to zero.)

First, a world LM curve; world supply of money is equated with world demand for money (a weighted average of the two countries' demands). World supply is a weighted average of the two countries' supplies under floating; under fixed it may be determined by the reserve-currency country (i.e. under Bretton Woods, the US essentially), but other rules relating money supply to intervention are conceivable. We will discuss this important issue further below.

Second, we have a world *differential* LM curve; this difference between the two countries' money supplies is equated with the difference between their money demands. Under fixed rates, this equation is satisfied by reserve movements which alter money supplies endogenously; any inequality gives rise to a (tiny) interest differential which causes 'infinite' reserve movements until money supplies have altered to eliminate the offending inequality.

Finally, we introduce the definition of the real exchange rate as the nominal rate, S, plus the price differential, $p - p_f$; S is the price of the *home* currency, so a rise is an appreciation. So we have:

$$m_w = wm + (1 - w)m_f = -wf_1r - (1 - w)m_1r_f + wp + (1 - w)p_f$$
$$+ wf_2y + (1 - w)m_2y_f \qquad (6)$$

$$(m - m_f) = -f_1r - m_1r_f + p - p_f + f_2y - m_2y_f \qquad (7)$$

$$RXR = S + p - p_f \qquad (8)$$

Now consider how to close the *fixed* rate system. $m - m_f$ is recursively fixed by (7); so we can ignore (7) and $m - m_f$. S is exogenous in (8). We can therefore rewrite (8) as

$$p = p_f + RXR - S \qquad (9)$$

This indicates the well-known property that, other than real (or 'fixed' nominal) exchange rate movements, prices at home are determined by foreign prices.

We can now substitute for p on our home goods markets from (9). We can also think of (6), world money markets, determining r_f, the ROW interest rate, subject to numerous feedbacks from p_f, y, y_f and RXR.

Now figure 9A.2 represents our fixed-rate world. p_f and RXR move around until $AS = AD$ at home and abroad. Notice that the new home AS and AD curves are now flatter than before because RXR enters p.

If we now turn to floating, we can treat S as recursively determined by (8); it enters in no earlier equation. However, p is now determined by (7) as

$$p = (m - m_f) + p_f + f_1 \alpha RXR + (f_1 + m_1)r_f - f_2 y + m_2 y_f \qquad (10)$$

This equation now gives us the familiar floating independence of monetary policy to fix the home price level. The first three terms in (10) correspond to the first three terms in (9). $(m - m_f)$ is the analogue of $- S$; monetary excess corresponds under floating to a depreciation under fixed. However the coefficient in RXR is not in general equal to unity because it reflects money demand (f_1) and system dynamics (α). The remaining three terms are determined by an extra set of relationships, those of money demand interacting with the system dynamics. This extra set is the added filter mentioned above, whose effect is to complicate interactions in a way that *a priori* we cannot assess. We can merely note the parallelism of structure; substituting for p from (10) gives us Figure 9A.3 under floating.

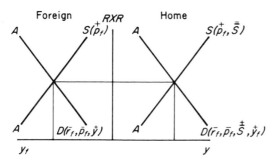

Figure 9A.2 Two-country goods markets – fixed rates

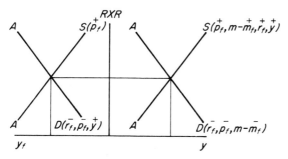

Figure 9A.3 Two-country goods markets – floating rates

The slope of the AD curve which, for given p, was

$$\frac{\partial y}{\partial RXR} = -(\kappa_1 \alpha + \kappa_2)$$

now becomes probably flatter at

$$\frac{\partial y}{\partial RXR} = \frac{(\kappa_1 \alpha + \kappa_2 + \kappa_3 f_1 \alpha)}{(1 - \kappa_3 f_2)}$$

Though we assume it does not, it may even flip over and slope up if the real balance effects are powerful (κ_3). Note too that the sign on the coefficient of y_f, $(\kappa_4 - \kappa_3 m_2)/(1 - \kappa_3 f_2)$ is now indeterminate, because of the real balance effect. The AS curve slope changes from

$$\frac{\partial y}{\partial RXR} = e_2 \quad \text{to} \quad \frac{e_2 + e_1 f_1}{1 + e_1 f_2}$$

which may go flatter or steeper. Finally notice the extra terms now in aggregate supply compared with the fixed rate case.

In short, floating *complicates* but it does not add to or subtract from interdependence.

References

Batchelor, R.A. (1987) 'Monetary indicators and operating targets – some recent issues in the UK', in P. Minford (ed.), *Monetarism and Macroeconomics*, International Economic Association, Readings 26, London.

Bryant, R., D. Henderson, G. Holtham, P. Hooper, and S. Symansky (1988) *Empirical Macroeconomics for Interdependent Economies*, Brookings Institution, two volumes.

Camen, U. (1987) 'Analysis of world business cycles,' mimeo, June, University of Geneva.

Canzoneri, M., and P. Minford (1989) 'When international policy coordination matters: an empirical analysis,' *Applied Economics* **20**, 1137–54.

Dornbusch, R. (1976) 'Expectations and exchange rate dynamics', *Journal of Political Economy* **84**, 1161–76.

Fleming, M.J. (1962) 'Domestic financial policies under fixed and flexible exchange rates,' *IMF Staff Papers* **9**, 369–79.

Genberg, H., M. Salemi, and A. Swoboda (1989) 'The relative importance of foreign and domestic disturbances for aggregate fluctuations in the open economy: Switzerland 1964–81' forthcoming, *Journal of Monetary Economics*.

Giavazzi, F., and A. Giovannini (1986) 'EMS and the Dollar', *Economic Policy*, **2**.

Giavazzi, F., and M. Pagano (1988) 'The advantage of tying one's hands: EMS discipline and Central Bank credibility', *European Economic Review* **32**, 1055–75.

Giovannini, A. (1988) 'Capital controls and public finance – the experience in Italy', in F. Giavazzi and L. Spaventa (eds.) *High Public Debt: The Italian Experience*, Cambridge University Press.

Haas, R.D., and P.R. Masson (1986) 'MINIMOD: Specification and simulation results,' *IMF Staff Papers* **33**, 722–67.

Ishii, N., W. McKibbin and J. Sachs (1985). 'Macroeconomic interdependence of Japan and the US: some simulation results,' *Journal of Policy Modeling* **7**, 533–72.

Melitz, J. (1985) 'The welfare case for the European Monetary System,' *Journal of International Money and Finance* **4**, 485–506.

Miller, M. and P. Weller (1989) 'Exchange rate bands and realignments in a stationary stochastic setting', this volume.

Minford, P. (1988) 'Do floating exchange rates insulate?', forthcoming in M. Taylor (ed.), *Studies of International Cooperation*, Macmillan.

Minford, P., P. Agenor and E. Nowell (1986) 'A new classical econometric model of the world economy,' *Economic Modelling* **3**, 154–74.

Mundell, R. (1963) 'Flexible exchange rates and employment policy,' *Canadian Journal of Economics and Political Science* **27**, 509–17.

Rogoff, K. (1985) 'Can international monetary policy coordination be counterproductive?', *Journal of International Economics* **18**, 199–217.

Sachs, J. and C. Wyplosz (1986), 'The economic consequences of President Mitterrand', *Economic Policy* **2**, 261–322.

Sargent, T. and N. Wallace (1981) 'Some unpleasant monetarist arithmetic', *Quarterly Review*, Fall, Reserve Bank of Minneapolis, 1–17.

Swoboda, A. (1983) 'Exchange rate regimes and US-European policy inter-dependence,' *IMF Staff Papers* **30**, 75–102.

Taylor, J. (1986) 'An econometric evaluation of international monetary policy rules: fixed versus flexible exchange rates', mimeo, October, Stanford University.

Williamson, J., and M. Miller (1988) 'The international monetary system: an analysis of alternative regimes,' *European Economic Review* **32**, 1031–48.

Discussion

Simon Wren-Lewis

Most of the world econometric models currently being maintained and developed in the UK are at least in part developments of work Patrick Minford completed with Mike Beenstock at the Treasury in the early 1970s. One of these is the Liverpool Model, which is particularly interesting, having changed substantially from its early origins. For these reasons we should have high expectations of a paper on this subject by Patrick using the Liverpool Model. I must admit that I was disappointed to find these expectations unfulfilled, partly because I felt the model itself was underutilized in the analysis.

This criticism is not meant to apply to the first part of the paper, which is necessarily entirely theoretical. The author attacks the Mundell-Fleming model as a paradigm for open economy macroeconomics, arguing that it is misleading in two key respects. It neglects the crucial exchange-rate dynamics implied by rational expectations and the open arbitrage condition, and it ignores the important role of the exchange rate in determining domestic prices. I agree that for these reasons Mundell-Fleming is not a good place from which to start an analysis of fixed versus floating exchange rates.

The second part of the paper uses the Liverpool Model to compare fixed and floating exchange-rate regimes. Both regimes are compared with no policy response, and under floating two additional regimes are analysed where policy reaction functions are used based on Nash and Cooperative solutions. The model is subjected to some shocks, and the stabilizing properties of each regime are tabulated in a fairly simplistic manner. No regime absolutely dominates in terms of its stabilizing properties. The conclusion is then drawn that therefore policy makers are likely to (or should) prefer fixed policy behaviour, and that issues of stabilization are not crucial to the fixed versus floating choice.

In my view this conclusion simply does not follow. No policy regime is ever likely to completely dominate all others for all shocks on all key variables. But some regimes may be generally better than others. What is required is a more comprehensive and systematic study, preferably with some analysis of the relative importance of key variables (e.g. a loss function) and the likely (relative) size of shocks (ideally using the stochastic properties of the model itself). The results given in the paper do not preclude one regime turning out to be distinctly superior to the others in this average sense, and in these circumstances it would seem sensible for governments to prefer this regime on stabilization grounds.

As far as the analysis of cooperation versus non-cooperation under floating is concerned, there is an important limitation in the analysis. Only one instrument is used; fiscal policy financed in a 'balanced' way. Much of the policy conflict that arises under floating rates occurs when fiscal and monetary policy are used in opposite ways; in particular when one country tries to 'export inflation' by raising interest rates but supports domestic activity by an expansionary fiscal policy (e.g. the United States in the early eighties). The gains to cooperation may therefore be greater when these two policy instruments are involved.

The EMS is a complex combination of fixed and floating rates. The final part of the paper attempts to use model simulations to argue that the benefits of the EMS are political rather than economic, and that it plays a self-discipline role. The monetary authorities of, say, France and Italy may not be able to control (hold down) monetary growth directly, but because this growth is above that in West Germany, the EMS produces a temporary real exchange rate appreciation which brings with it a temporary output loss, and this loss represents a political cost to those who encourage excessive monetary growth.

This argument requires that output is lower under the EMS than under pure floating, and this is what the simulations suggest. However the wage equation in the model had to be modified, in an admittedly *ad hoc* way. In these circumstances it is important to know just how sensitive the results are to the particular assumptions made, so some sensitivity analysis would have been useful. The political argument also needs to be more sophisticated. Some justification is required as to why groups should encourage 'excessive' monetary growth when it appears to bring only costs and no benefits.

This is not to imply that the author's argument is false, but simply that more analysis is required. The same can be said for the (alternative?) proposition that the EMS represents an approximation to policy cooperation, which is superior to the Nash outcome. As the paper notes, this proposition has not been demonstrated to be true, or false. This is where analysis using an econometric model is required, and it is a pity that the author did not attempt this, although the technical problems involved should not be underestimated. The simulations presented do not give us much of a guide as to what the results of such a study might be. In my view the results of such an analysis are crucial to the debate about the benefits, or otherwise, of the EMS and UK membership of it.

Chapter 10

Exchange-rate targetting as surrogate international cooperation

Andrew Hughes Hallett, Gerald Holtham and Gary Hutson

No hay atajo sin trabajo (Spanish proverb)[1]

I Introduction

International policy coordination in macroeconomics has generally been restricted to the joint targetting of exchange rates. The targetting of exchange rates may be justified on a number of grounds.

One ground is that foreign exchange markets may be subject to excess volatility or speculative bubbles; these may either be undesirable in themselves, if economic agents value stability of exchange rates, or they may lead to resource misallocation if agents cannot distinguish justified from excessive movements. A second possibility is that multilateral exchange-rate targetting, on the basis of international agreement, constitutes a form of policy precommitment that makes it easier for governments to follow optimal time-consistent policies. An international agreement implies greater penalties on time-inconsistent policies which move the exchange rate outside zones fixed by the agreement; that makes the time-consistent policies more credible and thereby harnesses private sector expectations to advantage. Related to this possibility is a third possible ground for exchange-rate targetting; that international commitments to exchange-rate stability may make it more

BLUEPRINTS FOR EXCHANGE RATE MANAGEMENT
0-12-497060-5

Copyright © 1989 Academic Press, Ltd
All rights of reproduction reserved

for governments to make policy errors. Pressure from international agents, for example, can be used to offset that from domestic pressure groups.

Yet the most appealing argument for exchange-rate targetting is that it could replicate the effects of a more thorough-going coordination of macroeconomic policies. This possibility was noted by Oudiz and Sachs (1984) in their seminal article on the gains from policy cooperation. They argued that one reason for cooperation was that, under flexible exchange rates, there was a temptation to use monetary and fiscal policy to move exchange rates in one's favour. With symmetry across countries in economies and objectives, these efforts were unsuccessful but there was excessive deflation or inflation, depending on whether, at any time, there was a tendency to competitive appreciation or depreciation.[2] Oudiz and Sachs concluded: 'new rules for target exchange rate zones might be instituted ... within which countries pursue independent policies. A constrained noncooperative equilibrium might then come very close to the optimal cooperative equilibrium.'

This is an attractive conjecture, given the much lower transactions costs, information costs and political difficulty, implicit in achieving agreement on one variable compared with a bargain across the whole set of policy variables. This paper explores the Oudiz-Sachs conjecture, using methods broadly similar to theirs.

We use an empirical multi-country model, the MCM model of the Federal Reserve Board, which does not impose similarity or symmetry across countries. A Nash equilibrium is identified for a five-country game, assigning plausible but arbitrary objective functions to the authorities of each country. We ask, first, whether agreement on virtually any exchange rate path realizes some of the gains to cooperation, or whether those gains are dependent on identifying a particular path or set of paths. This question is examined by introducing common target exchange-rate paths into the objective function for each country and repeating the Nash game. Welfare is then re-evaluated. Losses due to the exchange rate deviating from its target path are not counted, as the exchange rate is viewed as a purely instrumental or intermediate target and has a zero weight in objective functions used to compute the original, benchmark Nash equilibrium. We also compare these results with cases where governments 'disagree' and target somewhat different (i.e. incompatible) exchange-rate paths.

Second, to the extent that gains can be increased by identifying 'better', if not optimal, exchange rate paths, we explore various simple, though model-dependent, procedures for identifying such paths.

Thirdly we ask, for the 'best' exchange-rate path we can find, how hard countries should try to achieve that path. In our framework, this entails asking what weight the agreed exchange-rate path should be assigned in the objective functions of the governments of participating countries. This question, however, has an obvious analogue in terms of the widths of target zones for exchange rates on which governments agree. The greater the relative weight governments assign to hitting the agreed exchange-rate path, in our framework, the smaller will be misses and the narrower will be the implied target zone.

Finally, for the best agreed exchange-rate path we can find, and given the most appropriate weight, we ask what proportion of the total potential gains to cooperation are achieved by a joint targetting of exchange rates.

Our results can be summarized briefly as follows. Generally, for countries to target an agreed exchange-rate path, in addition to pursuing their ultimate policy goals, does not lead to a welfare improvement relative to a non-cooperative Nash equilibrium. For the vast majority of exchange-rate paths, the welfare loss occasioned by governments setting themselves an extra (albeit joint) target, without the benefit of an additional instrument, outweighs the gains arising from the elimination of competitive appreciation or depreciation. The level of welfare attained also turns out to be sensitive to the exchange-rate path chosen. Getting the agreed target path 'wrong' is frequently more damaging than is moderate disagreement about what the target path should be.

Identifying a welfare-enhancing common target path for the exchange rate is not easy, in the absence of relevant theory, or analytical expressions for the gains to cooperation in a general framework. We investigate a number of *ad hoc* procedures and find only one that results in a path which, when it is jointly targetted, leads to an improvement on the unrestricted Nash game, although this does not rule out further improvements if better procedures can be found or these rules can be refined.

The optimal degree of commitment to the targetting scheme (the width of the target zone), however, turns out to be a very fraught issue. While targetting more and more closely on the agreed exchange-rate path (analogous to narrowing the divergence bands of the exchange-rate target zone) can result in larger and larger gains in global welfare, distributional strains quickly become evident, with individual countries getting progressively worse results, in terms of their own welfare, than they achieved in Nash equilibrium.

That result caused us to limit the weight on the exchange-rate target in countries' objective functions. For the best path we could find, and also searching over utility weights, the gains from exchange-rate targetting were modest. The present exercise, using the Federal Reserve Board's MCM model and a set of plausible but arbitrary objective functions for five countries, showed that a fully cooperative equilibrium resulted in a gain of 4% in welfare terms (equivalent to 1.9% extra growth in 'World' GNP) compared to the Nash equilibrium. That is very much in line with earlier estimates for the case where exchange rates were excluded from the objective functions (Hughes Hallett, 1986a,b; Canzoneri and Minford, 1986) – a little above the Oudiz-Sachs (1984) estimates, but below the Currie et al. (1987) results. Joint targetting of the cooperative exchange-rate path in the context of a Nash game, on the other hand, led to up to 22% of those gains being realized, i.e. exchange-rate targetting led to a welfare improvement of just 0.75%.

No great claims can be made for the generality of these results; they are specific to the model used. The model, furthermore, does not embody model-consistent expectations so that our exercise is open to the Lucas critique. By changing the policy rules they follow, governments can, in principle, change the constraints they face. If that is an empirically important source of further gains to cooperation (which is still unclear) we miss those gains. With those qualifications in mind, our results do not support the conjecture that an exchange-rate-constrained non-cooperative equilibrium could come very close to the cooperative equilibrium. Only a small proportion of the potential gains to cooperation is actually realized. Perhaps more important, a great deal of exploration and care is needed to identify an exchange-rate path which affords even those gains and, what is more, the route taken will be entirely model-specific. So, although exchange rate targetting may constitute a simple policy rule for operational purposes, it is far from simple to design and the gains from doing so are very modest.

II   Design of the exercise

II.1   Optimal non-cooperative policies

This chapter considers a world of five interdependent trading economies each possessing two policy instruments – fiscal and monetary – indicated by aggregate government expenditures and the growth in the money stock (usually specified as $M1$) respectively.

The non-cooperative outcome studied is the simple Nash equilibrium. Take the case of 2 countries. Define y_t^A as the vector of deviations of country A's targets from their ideal values at time t; y_t^{Ad}. Then $y^{A'} = (y_1^{A'} \ldots y_T^{A'})$ is the vector of deviations over the decision periods $1 \ldots T$. Similarly, let $x^{A'} = (x_1^{A'} \ldots x_T^{A'})$ be the vector of deviations of country A's instruments from their ideal values.

We can now define a loss function:

$$w^A = (y^{A'}C^A y^A + x^{A'}E^A x^A) \tag{1}$$

where C^A and E^A are positive definite symmetric matrices. This loss function will be minimized subject to a set of linear constraints:

$$y^A = R_{AA}x^A + R_{AB}x^B + s^A \tag{2}$$

where R_{AA} and R_{AB} are matrices containing submatrices of dynamic multipliers, and s^A represents the sum of non-controllable (exogenous and potentially random) influences on y^A. If the instrument values of the other player, B, are treated as given, the first order conditions yield a set of linear reaction functions:

$$x^A = -(R'_{AA}C^A R_{AA} + E^A)^{-1}R'_{AA}C^A(R_{AB}x^B + s^A) \tag{3}$$

Meanwhile, country B will have a loss function $w^B = (y^{B'}C^B y^B + x^{B'}E^B x^B)$ and face the constraints $y^B = R_{BA}x^A + R_{BB}x^B + s^B$. Hence a reaction function for B, analogous to (3), can be solved simultaneously with (3) to yield the Nash equilibrium values x^A and x^B. This equilibrium is, in general, not optimal even among the set of possible non-cooperative outcomes. But it is an equilibrium in the sense that, if each player presumes the other policy maker will continue what he is currently doing, then no-one has any incentive to change policy instruments. It is therefore widely used in the analysis of static, one-period games. The alternative is to use a conjectural variations approach (Hughes Hallett, 1986a, and summarized in Appendix 2 to this paper), but in the absence of any preassigned 'rules of the game' it is not clear which equilibrium concept should be used. The Nash concept is adopted here as the conventional one, and the one used by the majority of other studies of policy coordination.

II.2   Cooperative policy making

Cooperative outcomes can be calculated by minimizing the 'collective' loss function:

$$w = \alpha w^A + (1 - \alpha)w^B \quad 0 < \alpha < 1 \tag{4}$$

subject to the constraints represented by (2) and its counterpart for y^B.

The extension of both this cooperative and the non-cooperative decision-making framework to the case where there are 5 interdependent countries is straightforward, and it is summarized in Hughes Hallett (1987).

II.3   The MCM econometric model

The model used is the Federal Reserve Board's MCM model, a linked system of 5 quarterly national macroeconometric models of the United States, Canada, West Germany, Japan and the United Kingdom. The country models are linked to each other by equations modelling trade in goods, services, investment income flows and exchange rates. MCM is a representative model which has been used for empirical analyses of different exchange-rate mechanisms, for example the target zone evaluation exercises. A detailed description of its specification, its properties and a full listing have already been published by Edison, Marquez and Tryon (1987). A comparison of its coordination properties with other models is in Holtham and Hughes Hallett (1987).

III   Policy objectives

In line with previous studies, we take real output growth (GNP), inflation, the current account balance and the central government budget deficit in each country to be the targets of policy. It is assumed that policy makers in each country will aim for growth in the 3–4% per annum range, inflation rates of approximately 1–2% per annum, balance in the current account, and substantially reduced budget deficits. The detailed numerical description of these targets of policy will be found – for each country – in Appendix 1.

The policy instruments to be investigated are fiscal (central government expenditures) and monetary (as indicated by the rate of growth of the national money stocks). Large fluctuations in interest rates are generally perceived to be undesirable because of adverse effects on domestic variables, the exchange rate and international competitiveness. For that reason, short-term interest rates have been included in the list of target variables. The idea is that policy makers will thereby be constrained in their use of their monetary instrument if interest rates would otherwise move too much. This also eliminates the risk of negative nominal interest rates.

Note that exchange rates themselves are not treated as either a target or instrument of policy in the base case scenarios. Obviously, where exchange-rate agreements are being tested for their ability to induce cooperative gains, an exchange-rate target must be set and some controlling mechanism introduced (usually by setting suitable target paths) in order to simulate the agreement's provisions. A variety of target paths is then specified (see Table 10.1) to establish: the sensitivity of economic performance to different exchange rate agreements; the scope for improving performance by attempting to control exchange rates in this way; and the importance of getting agreement on the direction in which to steer exchange rates. To the extent that outcomes are indeed sensitive to the exchange-rate path selected as a target, the question arises: how should we design target paths (and control fluctuations in the exchange rates themselves) in such a way as to secure cooperative type gains? We explore a number of policy design rules which specify how those target paths should be chosen.

Other constraints on policy instruments are as follows. It is assumed that policy makers aim to maintain government spending as a constant proportion of GNP (except in the US where it should fall to clear the budget deficit by 1992, in line with the Gramm-Rudman targets) and also a constant growth rate in money supply. However, Canada's money supply has been endogenized so that Canadian interest rates follow US rates. The precise numerical specification of these various ideal values is set out in Appendix 1.

The relative priorities (objective function weights, C^i, E^i for $i = 1 \ldots 5$) used in these exercises are also set out in Appendix 1. These weights represent a 'plausible' specification of national preferences, normalized for convenience on the priority for growth in the US. The weights specify that a 1% (or percentage point) deviation from the ideal path in any variable would be penalized equally. Growth in Germany and Japan is given a somewhat higher priority, but this is offset in the case of Germany by a higher penalty on inflation. The two US deficits are given priorities which increase over time, so it becomes more important to clear these deficits the longer they remain uncorrected.

All the policy values reported in subsequent sections are 'open loop' values computed using the initial (1986) information set. They therefore represent the policy options as they would appear when policy makers have to choose their fundamental strategy – and whether to go for some kind of exchange-rate agreement in particular. For the purpose of that calculation the exogenous variables underlying these calculations are set at (extrapolations of) the OECD's official forecasts for 1986–92, as made in 1986. We do not examine what revisions would be made as new information and the scale of model errors become known. In practice, of course, sequential revisions would be made to the selected strategy, conditional on that new information.

IV   The target exchange-rate paths

(i)   The first step in evaluating the ability of exchange-rate agreements to realize some of the gains from coordinated policy making is to analyse the dependence of economic performance on exchange-rate management by examining how that performance is affected by setting different exchange-rate parities or rates of appreciation and depreciation (the target paths).

Secondly, we examine how performance varies with the degree of commitment to exchange-rate management (the relative priority given to the exchange-rate targets).

We therefore began by conducting a sensitivity analysis of the performance of the 5 economies in the MCM model across 9 different sets of exchange-rate parities. In principle, each country could choose its own set of parities from any one of the 9 possibilities, without reference to (or agreement with) its trading partners, since these parities are just target paths to be aimed at rather than achieved exactly. It is therefore quite possible (although not necessarily sensible) to have each country aiming at a different target path. The foreign exchange market will of course yield one set of compromise exchange rate *outcomes* in each period, and if the disagreements between target paths were substantial the losses could be large just because countries had wasted policy effort by pulling in vain in mutually incompatible directions.

Since this is just a sensitivity analysis we provide no justification for the targets chosen. The idea is simply to see how far performance is dependent on the specification of exchange-rate parities, and whether improved perform-ance depends more on securing agreement on those parities or on setting the right parity 'levels' even if there is some disagreement on their precise values. However, 5 countries with 9 sets of target paths to choose from implies a sensitivity analysis of over 59,000 cases which is clearly unmanageable. But since the main problem for our 5 countries in the later 1980s has been the US trade deficit (German and Japanese surpluses) and the depreciation of the dollar needed to clear that deficit, we can simplify things by considering '(dis)agreements' between the US and non-US countries over the choice of target paths. That leaves only 81 cases to consider.[3]

(ii) The policy period studied here starts with an overvalued US dollar which, against its main trading partners, stood at the following values in 1985: $/C\$ = 0.73, $/£ = 1.28, DM/$ = 2.94, Y/$ = 244. The target paths specify various steady depreciations of the US dollar over the first three years (1986–88), and then constant exchange-rates *vis-à-vis* the dollar for 1989–92 inclusive. In each case the dollar depreciation is calculated as a weighted average of the appreciations of the four non-US countries against the dollar, with the following weights: C\$0.165, £0.215, DM0.375 and Y0.245. These are the 'trade-weights' employed in the construction of the MCM model.

Table 10.1 sets out the numerical values of the 9 sets of exchange rate parities used here. They range from dollar depreciations of 11% p.a. for three years to 30% p.a. for three years with, in each case, no further depreciations. Up to 1988, the dollar has actually depreciated about as fast as scheme A3 – the middle of the range. These target paths correspond to £/$ rates of 1.50–2.60, with the 1988 cross-rates fixed at values of DM/£ = 3.10 and Y/£ = 222.5 (actual values in June 1988). Canada, however, is targetted to appreciate by 4.37% p.a. (1986–88) in every scheme, to reach a rate of $/C$ = 0.83 for 1989–92. This reflects the special relationships in Canadian–US trade.

V Partially coordinated decision making: Selecting target paths or zones

To the extent that some target paths for exchange rates can produce better results than others, we need to provide procedures for selecting welfare-enhancing target paths in a systematic manner. No general theoretical principles exist in operational form to guide this process.

We have investigated three different schemes for identifying and setting welfare-enhancing exchange-rate paths. In each case, countries are obliged to aim at one agreed target path for the exchange-rate variables. To arrive at that agreed set of paths involves some (implicit) bargaining between countries. The bargaining in establishing the joint target exchange-rate path is the cooperative element in our decision-making process. Thereafter, beyond obeying the rules of the game by targetting the agreed exchange-rate path with an agreed degree of commitment, countries are assumed to serve their own interests and to play a (modified) Nash game. The degree of coordination is therefore incomplete. All three schemes involve a limited degree of explicit agreement in order to get some of the gains available from full-blown coordination. Each has a different rationale but their theoretical foundations are limited. We cannot prove that any of them is optimal.

V.1 Targetting the cooperative equilibrium exchange rate (CEER)

Recall that in fully cooperative equilibrium, an exchange-rate path will be determined, which is the outcome of the full set of cooperative policies, in deriving which each country implicitly takes its own objectives and those of other countries into account (Hamada, 1976). That exchange-rate path is, by construction, consistent with fully optimal policies. If the exchange rate, as such, does not appear in objective functions at this stage, there is no conflict between the exchange-rate path that emerges from cooperation and the governments' targets.

A reasonable conjecture appears to be the following. If a cooperative solution is simulated and the exchange-rate path implied by that solution is identified, that path can be used as a joint target in a modified Nash game to realize some of the potential cooperative gains. Some of the gains to cooperation may be due to the fact that countries playing a Nash game attempt to manipulate exchange rates to their own advantage. These efforts may be substantially offsetting and, therefore, self-defeating. Cooperation eliminates the element of fruitless competition. However, if countries give some weight to attempting to hit some agreed exchange-rate path, by definition, they will be moderating any fruitless struggle over exchange rates. A risk is that if the exchange rate is chosen at random it is unlikely to be consistent with countries' other objectives, and therefore attempting to maintain it could reduce welfare. This risk would appear to be minimal in the case of the CEER, which is consistent with a set of Pareto-optimal outcomes. *A priori*, it seems that jointly targetting a CEER will probably be welfare-enhancing relative to the unrestricted Nash equilibrium, as long as exchange-rate competition is a feature of the Nash.

Of course we do not know that an exchange rate which is optimal given unrestricted cooperation will also be optimal, or even nearly optimal, for the case of partial cooperation, but there is no obviously better exchange-rate path to consider. The use of a CEER is the first of the *ad hoc* exchange-rate rules we evaluate. However, two drawbacks to the approach are also evident *a priori*.

Firstly, it involves simulating a cooperative game, which countries are assumed to be unable to play, for some reason. For the resulting CEER to command assent as a target, countries must jointly have some faith in the economic model used to simulate cooperation and be prepared to accept the characterization of their own preferences embodied in specified utility functions. It may be thought that, if they had indeed arrived at such a pitch of agreement, there would be little preventing them from implementing the cooperative solution itself. At any rate, the very evident model dependency and specificity of the CEER, and its somewhat abstract method of generation, would be a considerable drawback in practice.

Secondly, the fully cooperative equilibrium is not in general unique. There is, in general, a set of such equilibria, each member of which is Pareto-optimal but which is characterized by a different distribution of the gains to cooperation (some of these equilibria were examined in Hughes Hallett, 1986b). The one which emerges from a simulation will depend on the bargaining process hypothesized. Choice of an explicit bargaining model, or merely making unmotivated assumptions about how cooperation gains are to be distributed, can generate a unique solution and a particular CEER. When that CEER is plugged back into government objective functions and the Nash game played, even granted some gains relative to the original unrestricted Nash, there is no assurance that the distribution of those gains will reflect the distribution in the full cooperative equilibrium. Indeed, it is perfectly possible that, while each country would benefit individually from a full cooperation, one or more may fail to do so when the CEER from that hypothetical cooperation is used to guide a Nash game. At best, a tedious iteration may be needed, examining not one CEER but many, to find one which, when used as a target path, is Pareto-superior without the need to invoke a Hicks-Scitovsky compensation principle. (That was in fact necessary here.) Such an iteration may be needed *a fortiori* if the outcome of the modified Nash game has to have an acceptable distribution of gains. At worst, it may be that no CEER exists which produces results in the modified Nash game which strictly dominate the unrestricted Nash equilibrium. We cannot produce a proof of dominance at the present time.

V.2 The Lagrange rule

Notice that the conjectural variations solution defined by equation (B4), Appendix 2, could also have been obtained by minimizing w^A subject to:

$$y^A = G^A_* x^A + d^A \tag{5}$$

independently of w^B and the constraints on y^B; and x^B may be similarly obtained from w^B and transformed constraints on y^B, independent of w^A and y^A. The jointly dependent decision problems have been split into two disjoint optimizations involving transformed constraint sets of the same format as in the single-player case; G^A_* and d^A have replaced R_{AA} and s^A respectively. Adopting the single player framework for minimizing w^A subject to (5), we find[4]

$$\partial w^A / \partial z^{Ad} = \mu^{A*'} H^A \quad \text{or} \quad \partial w^A / \partial y^{Ad} = \mu^{A*'} \tag{6}$$

where μ^A is the Lagrange multiplier vector in the minimization, $H^A = [I :- G^A_*]$ and $z^{Ad'} = (y^{Ad'}, x^{Ad})$ is the set of all ideal values. Similarly, $\partial w^B / \partial y^{Bd} = \mu^{B*'}$. This as far as conjectural variations solution is concerned, *both* countries can improve on their best non-cooperative outcomes if the Lagrange multiplier values corresponding to their shared exchange rate variable in any period have opposite signs. In one such element of μ^{*A} is negative and the corresponding element of μ^{*B} is positive, then both countries will gain if A raises its ideal parity value ($dy^{Ad} > 0$ so $dw^A < 0$) and B reduces its ideal value ($dy^{Bd} < 0$ so $dw^B < 0$) before repeating their non-cooperative solution procedures. We have now defined an iterative process, from an arbitrary start, in which both countries adjust their target-path values in every period where the corresponding Lagrange multipliers in the current non-cooperative solution have opposite signs. They should go on doing this until μ^{A*} and μ^{B*} have identical signs throughout and no further improvements can be generated in w^A and w^B.

It should be remembered that this rule is derived from (6), which is valid for conjectural variations solutions. If the same rule is applied to the conventional Nash solution, as we do below, it will be an approximation – although that should not be a problem so long as the differences between Nash and conjectural variations solutions are fairly small. This procedure should be viewed as an arbitrary rule which would be simulated, not played out in real time, in order to identify an exchange-rate target which was welfare-enhancing. However, Lagrange multipliers also have the interpretation of shadow prices, or the reduction in overall cost for given relaxation in a constraint. Thus, where the multipliers have opposite signs for two countries, it indicates that the current exchange rate is holding one country's perform-ance back by being too high – a reduction would improve its welfare – while the other country's performance is being held back by a rate which is too low. Hence they could 'trade' policies to their mutual advantage by making adjustments that resulted in a different exchange rate. Reducing the extent to which the exchange-rate constrains both countries means that more effort can be expended on reaching other target variables.

V.3   The ARMA updating rule

Economic theory suggests that each country should set its exchange-rate target path as that path which, in the long run, will ensure zero excess demand for its currency – the so-called fundamental equilibrium exchange-rate (FEER) path.[5] While this must be the correct specification for long-run (equilibrium) economic management, it is by no means clear that the same path is ideal for short-run (disequilibrium) problems. In addition, there are difficulties associated with the numerical evaluation of FEERs.

Equilibrium exchange paths must, in practice, be evaluated as the mean stochastic simulation of the model, solved forward under the restriction of balance-of-payments equilibrium for some suitable date. Thus any FEERs used will be model-dependent. Whether this imposes serious uncertainty on the policy calculations would have to be determined by sensitivity analysis and the ability of risk-averse decision rules to reduce the impact of that uncertainty. Since we do not have FEERs for the MCM model, that sensitivity analysis must be left to a later paper. However, the effect of varying the target paths, reported in Table 10A.1, suggests that this will be a problem to worry about.

Secondly, FEERs computed by model projection will of course be conditional on the policy trajectories used in those projections. There is a logical difficulty in assigning policy values to make projections, and then using those projections to generate improvements in those policy values. If historical or current policy values are used, then the projection path as an *ideal* (target) path denies that there is any policy problem to be solved. If not current or historical values, what policy values should be used? We need to pick a target path which includes any desirable policy changes, and policy changes which reflect a suitable target path – so target paths and policy interventions have to be chosen jointly.

Thirdly, there is no reason to suppose that model projections would normally generate a suitably stable path to aim at. They supply no incentive to smooth the natural dynamics of the target variables, and they imply that the sole function of intervention is to eliminate the impacts of unanticipated shocks on the economy. This may be adequate for a long-term equilibrium path, but it is seldom appropriate for steering short-term movements. In fact, if the projected ideal path is cyclical, it may prove very expensive to intervene in such a way as to track those fluctuations, pushing the economy first one way and then another.

Finally, and most important, if either the variables conditioning the model's projections or the model's estimated parameters have large variances, then interventions designed to track those projections can actually end up by increasing the target fluctuations. Given the perceived unreliability of empirical models this must be a very serious possibility. Hence whatever the theoretical superiority of model projections for generating equilibrium or target stabilization paths, that superiority can be totally wiped out by poor models or poor exogenous information. This problem was cited by Just *et al.* (1978) as the major drawback of using model projections as the target stabilization path. This criticism also applies to CEER paths, computed with an empirical model.

All these difficulties point to the need to choose target paths and policies jointly and also to incorporate some updating mechanism (suitably 'smoothed' if necessary) which allows those target paths to react to new information and hence reduce the impact of uncertainty and the dependence on particular model projections. A simple way of doing that, taken from earlier work on commodity market stabilization,[6] is to use the ARMA updating rule:

$$y_t^{Ad} = c_t + d_1 y_{t-1}^{Ad} + d_2 y_{t-1}^{A}. \tag{7}$$

This mechanism contains: (i) preassigned elements, c_t, describing some fundamental economic relationship (e.g. FEER projections); (ii) updating elements, $d_2 y_{t-1}^{A}$, to revise the ideal path as shocks or information innovations cause the targets to deviate from their projected values; and (iii) smoothing elements, $d_1 y_{t-1}^{Ad}$, to damp any large fluctuations induced by the preassigned elements or random shocks.[7] Setting $d_1 = (1 - d_2)$, we can insert (7) into (1) – and search for the best value of d_1 as part of the overall optimization procedure. Generalizing to all variables we can now write:

$$y^{Ad} = c + Dy^{Ad} + Fy^A \tag{8}$$

where

$$D = \begin{bmatrix} 0 \ldots\ldots\ldots 0 \\ D_1 \\ 0 \\ \\ 0 \ldots 0 \quad D_1 \quad 0 \end{bmatrix}, \quad F = \begin{bmatrix} 0 \ldots\ldots\ldots 0 \\ F_1 \\ 0 \\ \\ 0 \ldots 0 \quad F_1 \quad 0 \end{bmatrix}, \quad \text{and} \quad c' = (c_1^{*'}, c_2' \ldots c_T')$$

with $c_1^* = c_1 + D_1 y_0^{Ad} + F_1 y_0^A$ a quantity known from the start. This implies D_1 is a null matrix except for a diagonal element d_1 in the position corresponding to the exchange rate, and F_1 has $1 - d_1$ in that position. Then:

$$y^{Ad} = g + Gy^A \quad \text{with} \quad (G:g) = (I - D)^{-1}(F:c) \tag{9}$$

which can be substituted into (1) with the result that

$$w^A = \tfrac{1}{2} \hat{y}^{A'}(I - G)'C(I - G)\hat{y}^A + x^{A'}E^A x^A \tag{10}$$

where $\hat{y}^A = y^A - h$ and $h = (I - G)^{-1}g$. The optimal decisions, for this reformulated objective and the original model, are therefore given simply by transforming the objective function parameters according to (10), and its equivalent for w^B, before making the usual calculations for x^A and x^B.

The elements of agreement in this scheme are just as remote as in the Lagrange rule. The ARMA scheme does not, in itself, imply any cooperation, it is purely a rule for selecting the target paths. However, the predetermined parts, c_t, could be obtained from any partially cooperative rule for setting those paths. Secondly, each country must pick its ARMA rule (equivalent d_1 value) to give some gain over the original Nash solution which is reproduced by setting $d_1 = 1$. That is equivalent to some (unspecified) cooperative arrangement.

This ARMA scheme is not of the same type as the other two rules. Indeed it should be used in conjunction with them (they are a means of providing values for the predetermined elements c_t and y_0^{Ad}). Alternatively, it could be used with any arbitrary FEER estimate, whereupon its performance would depend on the appropriateness of the estimated FEER and the need to adjust that estimate in the light of past performance and new information.

VI   The sensitivity analysis results

Table 10B.1 in the Appendix contains the objective function values, for all 5 countries, under some of the 81 different agreement and disagreement scenarios which can be constructed from Table 10.1. (The full 81 sets of results are reproduced in Hughes Hallett *et al.*, 1989.) For convenience, four representative cases are summarized in the columns of Table 10.2 headed 'non-cooperative'. The corresponding policy variable values are reported, as average outcomes over the period 1986–92, in Table 10.3. Comparisons in Tables 10.2 and 10B.1 are between different situations in which an exchange-rate path is always being targetted. We are considering the sensitivity of the results to a range of different target paths – taking the losses due to missing the target exchange rate into account in the objective function evaluations.

VI.1   Agreement on target paths

Schemes A0–A8 show distinct and significant variations in the performance indicators as the target paths are changed. The results for all countries, except Canada, improve quite sharply as one moves from a mild US dollar depreciation over the 1986–88 period to a stronger depreciation. But if that depreciation becomes too strong their performance worsens again. For example, moving from an 11% p.a. depreciation (system A0) to the 24% p.a. depreciation case (A6) yields gains of 57% for the UK, 18% for Germany, 23% for Japan, and 7% for the US. Only Canada fails to gain – understandably, since overwhelming dependence on US trade means the best outcome is one which the US dollar depreciation is minimized (A0). But moving from A6 to the stronger 30% p.a. depreciation (A8) makes *all* countries worse off again – significantly for Japan and the US, only slightly for the others. The significance of these performance gains is underlined by the fact that the only differences among A0–A8 are in the target dollar depreciation rate for 1986–88, i.e. for just one target in a minority of years. All other objectives and constraints are unchanged. Hence the design of an exchange rate agreement is *extremely* important. The best results in this case came from the A6 scheme, yielding an average dollar depreciation of 9.6% p.a. over 1986–92 (see Table 10.3) – or 67% overall, which is similar to what has been observed and to the 72% overall target depreciation. The actual outcomes for A6 also show that depreciation to be concentrated, with a 66% fall in the dollar during 1986–88. We take A6 as a point of comparison in what follows.

The remaining target outcomes are satisfactory under the A6 scheme. Japan, Germany, UK and Canada average rates of growth of 3% over the

Table 10.1 Exchange-rate target systems

	CDN	UK	GER	JAP	US (calculated as a trade-weighted average of the other four)
1985 historical values	$/C$ 0.73	$/E 1.28	$/DM (DM/$) 0.34 (2.94)	$/Y (Y/$) 0.004 (244)	
Agreement					
A0 1988 level	0.83	1.50	0.48 (2.07)	0.007 (148)	
% change each year for 86–88	4.37	5.43	12.47	18.03	−10.98
A1 1988 level	0.83	1.60	0.52 (1.94)	0.007 (139)	
% change each year	4.372	7.72	14.91	20.60	−13.02
A2 1988 level	0.83	1.70	0.55 (1.82)	0.008 (131)	
% change each year	4.37	9.92	17.26	32.05	−14.98
A3 1988 level	0.83	1.80	0.58 (1.72)	0.008 (124)	
% change each year	4.37	12.04	19.47	25.43	−16.84
A4 1988 level	0.83	1.90	0.61 (1.63)	0.009 (117)	
% change each year	4.37	14.07	21.69	27.71	−18.67
A5 1988 level	0.83	2.00	0.64 (1.55)	0.009 (111)	
% change each year	4.37	16.04	23.79	29.91	−20.42
A6 1988 level	0.83	2.20	0.71 (1.41)	0.010 (101)	
% change each year	4.37	19.79	27.79	34.10	−23.75
A7 1988 level	0.83	2.40	0.77 (1.29)	0.011 (93)	
% change each year	4.37	23.31	31.55	38.05	−26.88
A8 1988 level	0.83	2.60	0.839 (1.19)	0.012 (86)	
% change each year	4.37	26.66	35.10	41.70	−29.86

Note: These derived changes are for each year 1986–88 inclusive, and zero thereafter.

Table 10.2   A summary of objective function values: Exchange rates are an explicit target

	Non-cooperative				Exchange-rate Targetting Rules		Standard Cooperative, A6
						ARMA with $d = 0.95$ on CEER	
	A0	A6	D60	D06	CEER	Lagrange Rule: A0 Start Rule:	
CDN	35.80	38.79	36.36	38.36	37.44	38.02	39.95	38.39
UK	52.93	22.59	22.06	60.08	18.55	18.35	24.46	20.84
GER	196.11	160.58	157.16	204.64	141.25	141.80	166.22	148.76
JAP	82.49	63.50	62.01	90.53	26.77	26.92	71.76	58.70
USA	232.60	216.55	233.35	220.42	207.01	207.48	219.06	206.85

Key: A0, agreement on exchange-rate targets (system A0); A6, agreement on exchange-rate targets (system A6); D60, disagreement on exchange-rate targets (US = A0, ROW = A6); D06, disagreement on exchange-rate targets (US = A6, ROW = A0). Cooperation involves $\alpha_i = 0.25$(CDN), 0.15(UK), 0.12(GER), 0.15(JAP), 0.33(US).

period, and these are fairly steady (except they tend to slow down for Germany, but speed up in Japan). The US, however, only manages to average 1.9% growth. The inflation rates are all fairly low; from 2.5% p.a. for Canada down to 1.25% for Germany.

The trade balances show some more substantial improvements. The US trade deficit drops steadily from $122 billion in 1986 to $13 billion in 1992. The Japanese surplus falls less dramatically, halving from 14 trillion yen in 1986 to 6 trillion in 1992, while the German surplus falls from DM 67 billion in 1986 to DM 14.5 billion. Unfortunately, similar improvements are not found for the budget deficits. The US budget deficit remains stubbornly fixed at about $75 billion – that is lower than its current level, but without any tendency to fall further. Germany and Japan likewise have fairly steady budget deficits (Germany's increases to 1989 and then flattens out), while the UK develops a substantial surplus after 1989. Finally, short-term interest rates rise slowly throughout, to finish at 4% in Germany, Japan and the US, and somewhat higher than that in the UK and Canada.

As far as the instruments are concerned, US government expenditure remains nearly constant at 19% of GDP; hence, with the slow growth, the budget deficit fails to improve much despite the Gramm-Rudman target. Monetary policy, however, tightens progressively. These two movements make it more difficult to achieve the dollar depreciations needed to clear the trade deficit – the burden of policy adjustment is therefore thrown onto the other countries. In fact both Germany and Japan fail to increase their

Hughes Hallett, Holtham and Hutson

Table 10.3 Optimized policies and their expected outcomes with different exchange-rate target paths in a non-cooperative game: Average values for 1986–92 inclusive

(a) Exchange rate target System: A0

	CDN	UK	GER	JAP	USA
$G\dot{N}P$	2.92	3.06	3.29	3.16	1.88
$\dot{P}$	2.65	2.64	1.68	1.28	2.13
CB	−8.08	−6.24	39.29	8.71	−73.29
GDEF	11.61	−6.49	40.49	9.91	88.96
ER	0.78	9.89	11.89	14.43	−8.77
RS	6.16	7.49	2.71	3.13	2.81
G	19.31	19.41	21.73	9.18	18.85
$\dot{M}$	5.00	3.52	4.62	4.45	3.79

(b) Exchange rate target system: A6

	CDN	UK	GER	JAP	USA
$G\dot{N}P$	2.91	3.06	3.25	3.16	1.88
$\dot{P}$	2.77	2.60	1.57	1.33	2.18
CB	−8.07	−6.58	38.05	8.59	−71.81
GDEF	11.40	−3.94	42.43	11.04	85.41
ER	0.69	11.02	12.91	15.23	−9.60
RS	6.07	7.62	2.88	3.24	2.72
G	19.28	19.63	21.78	9.50	18.79
$\dot{M}$	5.00	3.16	4.19	4.38	3.94

Agreement on exchange rate targets

(c) Exchange rate targets: US = A0, ROW = A6

	CDN	UK	GER	JAP	USA
$G\dot{N}P$	2.91	3.03	3.24	3.17	1.87
$\dot{P}$	2.69	2.67	1.62	1.37	2.19
CB	−8.16	−6.30	38.24	8.62	−73.70
GDEF	11.89	−3.73	42.27	10.94	89.48
ER	0.76	10.44	12.53	14.70	−9.32
RS	6.21	7.68	2.94	3.26	2.88
G	19.33	19.63	21.74	9.46	19.06
$\dot{M}$	5.00	3.12	4.11	4.29	5.37

(d) Exchange rate targets: US = A6, ROW = A0

	CDN	UK	GER	JAP	USA
$G\dot{N}P$	2.93	3.10	3.31	3.15	1.89
$\dot{P}$	2.72	2.57	1.64	1.27	2.13
CB	−7.98	−6.52	39.10	8.68	−72.39
GDEF	11.12	−6.70	40.53	10.00	84.90
ER	0.71	10.48	12.27	14.95	−9.05
RS	6.03	7.43	2.65	3.12	2.65
G	19.27	19.41	21.77	9.23	18.95
$\dot{M}$	5.00	3.56	4.71	4.54	6.17

Disagreement on exchange rate targets

government expenditures as a percentage of GDP, although Germany does allow its money supply to grow faster after 1989 and Japan produces a small increase in government expenditures in 1988–89. The picture is not a lot different for the UK and Canada. The dollar depreciations are therefore almost entirely generated by interest-rate changes. The interest-rate differentials *all* move against the dollar, with US short-term rates falling to a level equal or below those elsewhere.

VI.2   Disagreements over the exchange-rate targets

We now turn to the question of whether precise agreement about the exchange-rate targets is important relative to the issue of setting the appropriate target paths. The chances of successful exchange-rate management will be much higher if mild disagreements do not incur serious losses.

Table 10B.1 and the summary in Table 10.2 show the consequences of a series of increasingly severe disagreements. They range from cases where the US and non-US countries aim for dollar depreciations which differ by no more than 2% p.a. to cases where those aims differ by 19% p.a. over the period 1986–88. For example, 'D_{60}' in Table 10.B1 means the non-US countries aim at the target path defined by scheme A6, while the US aims at the A0 path (a 2% p.a. difference). But 'D_{08}' means the US goes for the larger dollar depreciation of A8 while the other countries aim for the mild depreciation of A0 (a 19% p.a. difference). In each case, the non-US countries maintain a fixed set of targets for their cross-rates. This constraint was imposed in order to simplify matters, and is not intended to be realistic.

The A6 rows shows the losses which would be caused if the US disagreed with an A6 target position adopted by the non-US countries. The A6 column shows the consequences of the other countries disagreeing with an A6 target path adopted by the US. In each case, the further from the diagonal, the greater the disagreement. The importance of selecting suitable target paths (rather than securing precise agreement as such) is shown by repeating these row and column comparisons about different agreement cases or, better, by comparing the losses from the disagreements about one agreement case to the losses (or gains) in changing from one agreement case to another.

The results in Table 10B.1 shows that even the larger disagreements about a well chosen target path generally cause smaller losses than occur when agreements are secured on a less suitable target path – the objective function values are more sensitive to variations in the 'agreed' target paths than they are to equivalent-sized disagreements about a given path. There will therefore be a band about the exchange-rate target path within which countries can permit their policies to create deviations without incurring serious losses, whereas a close agreement based on rather different target paths would imply larger losses. In other words, good results can be obtained if policies are designed to keep exchange rates within some target zone provided that zone is constructed around suitable parities. So what is important here is the choice of target paths and the fact that they must be chosen jointly with the policies needed to support them – *not* the width of the zone or agreement on the precise numerical values of the exchange rate/policy package.

To illustrate, take the case where the non-US countries adopt A6 as a target path, but the US goes for smaller dollar depreciations. All the non-US countries are made somewhat better off while the US is made rather worse off – as should be expected. But the four milder disagreements (D_{62} to D_{65}) still leave the US, and indeed the UK, Germany and Japan, better off than they would be under an agreement based on the corresponding US target paths (i.e. under agreements on A2 to A5). If, on the other hand, the US wants larger dollar depreciations than in A6, *all* countries become worse off. But, once again, all countries (except the US) are still better off with these disagreements than if they had agreed with the US's target paths. Notice also that all these disagreements (i.e. D_{60} to D_{68}) involve rather small losses for any country – about 5% for the UK, 3.5% for Germany, 4% for Japan, and 7% for the US. These losses are *much* smaller than the comparable losses noted in the previous subsection, when the agreed paths were changed from A6 to A0 or A8.

Suppose now that the US picks the A6 target path but the other countries disagree. If the non-US countries want smaller dollar depreciations than the US, then both they and the US lose out compared to an agreement on A6. But if they want more depreciation than the US, they lose while the US gains. In this latter case, disagreements still do better than would agreements on lower or higher depreciation paths. But in the former case the non-US countries would lose, and the US gain, compared to what they could have achieved if they had persuaded the US to agree with them when they decided to aim for smaller depreciations. All this is as expected – but, once again, allowing disagreements within a certain band around an agreed set of targets would cause *smaller* losses than changing that agreed set by the same amount.[8]

Finally, however, the consequences of disagreement become more serious when they occur around an inappropriate set of target paths than when they appear around a good set – the band of permitted disagreement narrows, and the need for a well policed exchange-rate regime increases, as the target paths become less well chosen. This can be seen comparing the disagreement losses for A0 against those for A6 (when the US decides to disagree), or the losses for A8 against A6 (when the others decided to disagree). So somebody is always worse off, and the implied target zone narrows, as the central parities become more in need of realignment.

The distribution of the losses from disagreement is complicated. It is clearly more serious for the US if it decides to deviate from the target path chosen by the others, than if the others disagree with the path chosen by the US – but the opposite holds for German, Japanese and UK losses. But it is less clear why the more extreme the disagreement, where the US tries to limit the dollar depreciations (bottom left), the worse for the US and the better for the others – and vice versa where the others attempt to limit the depreciations. Finally, Canada is the odd man out throughout this table, reflecting its special trade relationship with the US. Canada's welfare follows that of the US rather than that of the other countries, with which it has been grouped.

VI.3   The sensitivity of the policy variables

Different exchange-rate agreements imply only small changes in the settings of the policy variables. Comparing A0 to A6 (Table 10.3), we find that average growth rates are hardly affected by aiming for smaller dollar depreciations, whereas inflation is marginally lower in the US and Japan and higher in Germany. Current balances are more affected – being more out of balance – and the budget deficits are larger in the US but smaller elsewhere. Fiscal policy is slightly looser and monetary policy tighter in the US than elsewhere (with a corresponding narrowing of interest-rate differentials). Those interest-rate differentials become much wider with disagreement.

VII   Exchange-rate stability as an objective and as an intermediate target

The objective function changes discussed in subsections VI.1 and VI.2 above are largely the result of changing the contribution of the exchange-rate components in the objective function evaluations. Any alteration in the exchange-rate target values will affect the objective function values directly, as well as indirectly via their impacts on other policy variables. We therefore have to make a clear distinction between the case where exchange rates are targets in their own right, such as when policy makers value exchange-rate stability for itself, and the case where exchange rates are merely instrumental in obtaining better results for the other targets. In the latter case, exchange rates may constitute an intermediate target but have no other significance. The correct comparison then is the objective function values *net* of any losses due to the exchange-rate variables, and a benchmark of the non-cooperative (or cooperative) equilibrium without any exchange-rate targetting, i.e. when exchange rates do not enter the problem at *either* the optimization *or* the evaluation stage. It would be incorrect to allow the target paths themselves to make a direct contribution to the objective function evaluations in these comparisons.

On the other hand, Kindleberger (1981), among others, has argued that exchange-rate stability is a public good and therefore a target in its own right.[9] In that case comparisons should be made on the basis of objective function values which include the exchange-rate components. If stability is the aim, any one of these exercises can be taken as the benchmark since fluctuations about the target path are the problem; the precise values taken by that path are unimportant, so long as they are understood in advance. To distinguish intermediate targetting from the stability case, Tables 10.4 and 10B.2 provide the objective function evaluations net of exchange-rate terms, corresponding to Tables 10.2 and 10B.1. The benchmark calculations for this case (where there is no intermediate targetting), objective function and policy values respectively, appear in Tables 10.5 and 10.6.

An interesting point here is that the differences between objective function

Table 10.4   Objective function values with exchange-rate components omitted (policy values computed as in Tables 10.2 and 10.3)

	Non-cooperative				Standard Cooperative
	A0	A6	D60	DO6	
CND	33.94	37.02	34.52	36.57	36.29
UK	21.90	18.49	18.39	22.76	18.21
GER	146.55	143.89	141.39	149.75	138.01
JAP	27.50	29.25	27.35	29.67	33.09
USA	211.89	208.25	209.38	211.04	201.82

Table 10.5   Objective function values for case where exchange rates are not targets

	Nash	Cooperative
CDN	38.06	36.27
UK	17.70	16.92
GER	141.92	135.52
JAP	26.20	24.32
USA	206.66	200.16
Total	430.55	416.19

The bargaining weights used in the cooperative solution were:
α_1(CDN) = 0.2, α_2(UK) = 0.22, α_3(GER) = 0.1, α_4(JAP) = 0.22, α_5(US) = 0.26.

Table 10.6 Optimal policies when the exchange rate is excluded from the optimization process: Average values for 1986–92

	No cooperation					Cooperation				
	CDN	UK	GER	JAP	USA	CDN	UK	GER	JAP	USA
$G\dot{N}P$	2.92	3.06	3.26	3.21	1.90	3.09	3.13	3.17	3.37	2.00
$\dot{P}$	2.83	2.52	1.55	1.39	2.23	3.06	2.73	1.18	1.61	2.18
CB	-8.09	-6.58	37.40	8.63	-71.47	-8.50	-5.97	33.66	8.72	-71.90
$CDEF$	11.54	-2.87	43.31	11.41	85.57	12.63	-1.87	48.50	10.97	88.08
ER	0.66	11.40	13.17	15.27	-9.84	0.50	10.63	14.12	14.55	-10.07
RS	6.13	7.71	2.99	3.30	2.77	6.42	7.92	3.46	3.43	2.95
G	19.30	19.73	21.80	9.60	18.80	19.47	19.91	21.85	9.53	18.86
$\dot{M}$	5.00	2.91	3.96	4.38	3.95	5.00	2.92	2.73	4.35	3.71

The bargaining weights used in the Cooperative Solution are given below Table 10.5.

values are much smaller across Table 10B.2 than across 10B.1, although the pattern of those differences is unchanged. In other words, the argument that it is more important to pick suitable target paths than to ensure exact agreement on some path holds chiefly because it is harder to achieve an inappropriate target path than an appropriate one, so greater exchange-rate losses are generated. However, the fact that the losses in Table 10B.2 are all roughly equal may be due to the relatively low weight put on the exchange-rate terms in the objective functions, compared to GNP growth and inflation. Hence the exchange-rate path chosen has a relatively small impact on the other (non-exchange-rate) policy variables.

VIII   Targetting arbitrary exchange-rate paths *vs* no targetting

The most notable feature of the outcomes in Tables 10B.2 and 10.4 is that they are all worse than the benchmark Nash equilibrium reported in Table 10.5, Canada excepted. Moreover, increasing the weight on the exchange-rate terms *never* made the results better than the benchmark Nash case; raising it did improve the average performance a little, while making certain countries worse off, but increasing it beyond a factor of 3 leads to an overall deterioration (Table 10.9).[10] Thus attempting to steer an exchange rate along different arbitrary paths has introduced an extra constraint (conflict) into the problem which makes it more difficult to achieve the other objectives and hence worsens their performance. If exchange-rate stability is a target in itself, that worsening performance can be compensated for by greater stability, though it matters which target path is chosen. But if the exchange rate is just an intermediate target, then the worsening performance of the target variables following an exchange-rate agreement is a dead loss. In other words, if intermediate targetting is to work, *international* coordination must bring gains greater than the losses due to introducing an additional target which is not automatically consistent with other targets.

In fact a comparison of Tables 10.6 and 10.3, parts (a) and (b), shows where that worse performance appears. Fiscal and monetary policy turn out to be slightly more expansive in the no-targetting case (Table 10.6). Similarly, interest rate differentials are larger, the dollar depreciates further, trade is more balanced everywhere and US growth and inflation are higher in the absence of targetting. Thus although the impacts of exchange-rate targetting may be minor, they clearly do constrain the other policy targets unfavourably.

The international policy conflicts transmitted by exchange rates are evidently dominated by internal conflicts between other targets, and inter-mediate targetting becomes ineffective. It is therefore very difficult to find an exchange-rate path which actually does generate gains for everyone over the benchmark Nash solution in Table 10.5. If such a path does in fact exist, its design requires a great deal of fine tuning. This is demonstrated in the following section. Nevertheless, there are also international policy conflicts in our 5-country game, and hence gains to be had from explicit cooperation – the figures in Table 10.5 show welfare gains ranging from 3% for the US to 7% for Japan. It is just that the *net* spillover effects cannot be controlled by targetting an arbitrary exchange-rate path. Moreover, the unequal distribution of losses between Tables 10.4 and 10.5 (compare non-cooperative A6 to the benchmark Nash solution in Table 10.5) suggests that it will be significantly easier to design an exchange-rate agreement which benefits some countries but not all.

IX   Partial cooperation by exchange-rate targetting

How far can any of our suggested procedures for choosing exchange-rate target paths improve on the arbitrary paths used for the sensitivity analysis in Tables 10B.1 and 10B.2, and how large a proportion of the potential gains from complete coordination could be captured by the exchange-rate agreements which they imply?

Table 10.7 shows the objective function values achieved and the exchange-rate targets used by our three target path selection rules – the CEER rule, the Lagrange rule, and the ARMA updating rule. The policy values yielded by these rules are summarized in Table 10.8. The CEER rule simply takes the optimized exchange rate outcomes of the cooperative exercise described in Tables 10.5 and 10.6 (i.e. with *no* exchange rate targetting) as target values in the standard non-cooperative policy problem. The Lagrange rule proceeds as described in Section III from a non-cooperative A0 start. Two ARMA updating rules are given, one updating the CEER target path and one updating the A6 target path.

IX.1   The CEER rule

It is clear from Table 10.7 that none of these rules actually dominates the benchmark Nash solution in Table 10.5. So, strictly speaking, the minimum condition for setting up an exchange-rate agreement is not met – although the CEER rule comes very close to it. On the other hand, all four rules in Table 10.7 do better than the best of the target paths used in the sensitivity analysis above (non-cooperative A6 in Table 10.4) – so we have at least improved on that arbitrary selection of target paths. Moreover, the CEER rule only fails to dominate the benchmark solution with small losses for the

Hughes Hallett, Holtham and Hutson

Table 10.7   Effects of various exchange-rate targetting rules

(a) *Objective function values (exchange-rate components omitted)*

Country	CEER	Lagrange	ARMA with $d = 0.95$ based on CEER	ARMA National d values[a]
CDN	37.41	37.93	38.22	38.15
UK	17.89	17.94	17.73	17.61
GER	140.74	141.59	140.14	140.07
JAP	26.06	26.49	26.42	26.47
USA	206.87	206.76	206.49	206.10
Total	428.97	430.71	429.01	428.40

(b) *The average exchange-rate targets for 1986–8 (% change per annum)*

Country	CEER	Lagrange	ARMA on CEER
CDN	2.15	2.02	2.19
UK	19.56	20.79	21.94
GER	30.20	30.48	30.29
JAP	29.56	30.84	31.68
USA	−21.82	−23.79	−22.37

[a] The values were: $d(CDN) = 0.05$, $d(UK) = 0.70$, $d(GER) = 0.95$, $d(JAP) = 0.95$, $d(US) = 0.70$.

UK and US; the other three countries show significant gains. The welfare gains/losses are $+1.6\%$ for Canada; -1.1% for UK; $+0.9\%$ for Germany; $+0.5\%$ for Japan; and -0.1% for the US. The distribution of gains *vs* losses is as expected since the only exchange-rate target path being chosen is (in effect) the US dollar *vs* a trade-weighted index of the other currencies. Thus where dominance fails either the US or the others will suffer (the US in this case). The UK losses are less easily explained.

The difficulty with these results is therefore one of distribution, rather than the gains as such. Overall, the rule has made an improvement over the non-cooperative rule with no exchange rate targetting (Table 10.5); the weighted sum of objective function values is lower in the CEER rule. However, there may be several reasons why strict dominance has not been achieved. As pointed out in Section III, the bargains (α_i values) which are appropriate for complete cooperation may not be appropriate or acceptable for a limited bargain. In that sense the CEER generated at the first stage would not be suitable as a target path in the final calculations. It may also be that partial cooperation is sensitive to the intensity or seriousness with which the exchange-rate mechanism is being used. Or it might be that no dominating partial cooperation solution (based on any CEER) exists. It appears that the latter is probably true, since an extensive search found no alternative underlying bargain (α_i values) which would yield strict dominance. Alternative bargains on the CEER were able to bring the US back to its unrestrained Nash outcome, but the UK showed a loss throughout and the other countries' gains were reduced. The benchmark Nash equilibrium was not bettered.

Varying the degree of commitment to exchange-rate targetting (as indexed by the associated objective function weight) corresponds to altering the width of a target zone and hence the amount by which policy corrections are triggered. In this case it confirmed the distributional consequences of designing a simple policy rule; increasing the intensity of targetting exaggerated the gains and losses while increasing the degree of overall (or world) gain (see Table 10.9). However, the incremental changes here are all unimportant. Moreover, intermediate targetting becomes counterproductive when the incremental cost of tracking the intermediate target exceeds the incremental gains in the other targets. This happens quite early here; when the weight on the exchange-rate target passes 0.3, the overall performance of the rule starts to deteriorate again. More significantly, nowhere in this sequence do the UK or the US actually register gains; varying the precision or zone width in targetting does not secure dominance.

IX.2 The Lagrange rule

According to Table 10.7, the Lagrange rule performs worse than the CEER rule – every country is slightly worse off. Nevertheless, Canada and Germany do better with the Lagrange rule than under the benchmark Nash solution, whereas the US's loss (over that benchmark) is smaller than it was in the CEER case. The upshot is that, at a 'world' level, we have effectively reproduced the benchmark Nash performance but with gains for Germany, Canada, and the US (and losses for UK and Japan). Once again the drawback of exchange-rate targetting is shown to be the difficulty of controlling the distribution of gains, as well as the difficulty in creating those gains.

The Lagrange rule's performance is in fact probably better than appears from Table 10.7. It has been operated to achieve equality of signs in the Lagrange multipliers across all countries and time periods, but these multipliers are all specific for dollar *vs* domestic currency exchange rates. Each country is therefore making a series of 2-way comparisons. If that restriction were lifted, and each country were to make 5-way comparisons (i.e. they were to identify target cross-rates, as well as dollar rates), the results might improve on those from the CEER method. (But then we could target CEER cross-rates too; Hughes Hallett *et al.*, 1988.)[11] Secondly, the Lagrange rule is not dependent on selecting a particular bargaining equilibrium as the CEER is, nor does it require a formal model solution to estimate any FEERs.

Thirdly, since the rule works on signs not numerical values, the sensitivity to information/model errors may not be all that high. It is nevertheless an appropriate and model-based method.

IX.3   The ARMA rule

The best of the ARMA paths, with CEER values for predetermined elements, turned out to have $d = 0.95$. (We searched the interval 0.1 to 1.0.) This is an updating mechanism which would react only slowly to new information.

The ARMA performance, in 'world' terms, was scarcely different from the CEER rule itself (not surprisingly since $d = 1.0$ reproduces the CEER results), but it has secured gains for the US over the benchmark Nash solution which was not possible within the CEER scheme. Moreover, making the exchange rate targets *more* responsive to new information (reducing d to below 0.8) also allows gains for the UK – but at the cost of making Canada and Japan worse off than in the absence of exchange-rate targetting. The UK, US and Germany, for example, can make further gains by determining their *own* responsiveness in the setting of exchange-rate target paths (Table 10.7(b), last column). In this the UK and US targets become fairly flexible, but German and Japanese targets fixed, in response to developments elsewhere.

Thus the ARMA procedure reverses the pattern of results from the CEER scheme by increasing the degree of flexibility in the US and exchange-rate target paths. It is clear that any exchange-rate agreement should have some revision mechanism built into it, and it will pay to pick the degree of responsiveness as part of the policy design.

We have noted that these ARMA rules are designed as a revision mechanism for setting target paths. They are not a cooperation-inducing device as such. Their value will be in protecting any gains, which the predetermined target path may have managed to induce, from inevitable model and information errors. Moreover, if it is unclear what values the target path should take, or if disagreement over those values is likely, the ARMA scheme will allow the targets to adapt in the light of path results.

IX.4   The policy values

No great changes appear in the average policy values (Table 10.8) compared to those in the benchmark Nash solution (Table 10.6). This confirms that exchange-rate targetting has its impact on the timing of changes, not their size. Small differences do appear in the exchange-rate movements and in the interest-rate differentials. Almost all the exchange-rate changes appear in

Table 10.8 Policy values under exchange-rate targetting

	CEER Rule					Lagrange Rule					ARMA Rule				
	CDN	UK	GER	JAP	USA	CDN	UK	GER	JAP	USA	CDN	UK	GER	JAP	USA
$G\dot{N}P$	2.90	3.05	3.24	3.21	1.88	2.91	3.06	3.24	3.22	1.88	2.92	3.04	3.24	3.20	1.90
$\dot{P}$	2.82	2.53	1.52	1.39	2.20	2.81	2.54	1.52	1.40	2.20	2.74	2.46	1.49	1.39	2.24
CB	-8.07	-6.56	37.54	8.60	-71.50	-8.05	-6.64	37.59	8.58	-71.40	-8.02	-6.66	37.10	8.68	-70.89
$GDEF$	11.47	-3.28	43.15	11.29	85.31	11.37	-3.19	43.06	11.36	84.53	11.34	-2.41	43.76	11.28	84.48
ER	0.65	11.03	13.15	15.24	-9.80	0.67	11.40	13.21	15.35	-9.84	0.80	11.85	13.56	15.53	-10.16
RS	6.09	7.68	2.96	3.29	2.74	6.06	7.67	2.94	3.28	2.72	6.05	7.73	3.03	3.30	2.71
G	19.28	19.69	21.78	9.57	18.81	19.28	19.70	21.79	9.60	18.78	19.29	19.76	21.56	9.56	18.77
$\dot{M}$	5.00	2.97	3.99	4.41	4.27	5.00	3.00	4.03	4.46	3.98	5.00	2.77	2.32	4.40	4.04

1986–88; Table 10.7(b) shows that CEER demands (and gets) somewhat smaller dollar depreciations than the other two rules.

IX.5   When exchange-rate stability is a target in itself

The results for these different rules when policy makers do care about the exchange rate itself have been included in Table 10.2. These results only refer to the case where exchange-rate stability about some given (known) path, rather than the path itself, is the explicit target.

Evidently, the CEER rule is still slightly better than the Lagrange rule. Secondly, both the CEER and Lagrange rules dominate the non-cooperative A6 results, which we have taken to be the arbitrary standard of comparison. The degree of dominance, and the fact that it holds everywhere, shows selecting target paths carefully is important when stability is the objective. The gainers are principally Japan and Germany, and the US to a smaller extent. Thus exchange-rate stability is particularly important for the G3 countries (especially Japan, as we might have expected from Section VIII.3). The Lagrange rule also does well, despite a relatively unfavourable starting point. It may therefore have the advantage of robustness to poor information.

X   The coordination gains from exchange-rate targetting

In this exercise, the gains from targetting exchange rates have been small, hard to get and badly distributed relative to the non-cooperative, no-targetting case. Full cooperation, however, yielded some significant gains. On a 'world sum' basis, the welfare gains in Table 10.5 are 17.3 units or 4%; and for the individual countries they range from 7.2% for Japan to 3.1% for the US (Table 10.10). In terms of annual growth rate equivalents, these gains are worth 0.7%, 0.5%, 1%, 0.4% and 1.3% respectively. These figures are right in the middle of the range of previous estimates and represent worthwhile if unspectacular gains.

The results are much less promising under exchange-rate targetting; gains are only available for certain countries and they are small. Under the CEER rule, Canada, Germany and Japan make welfare gains of between 1.6% and 0.6% – a quarter or less of their fully cooperative gains – while the US and UK make losses of up to 1%. However, on a 'world' basis, the sum of loss function values has fallen 1.58 units, or 9.1% of the fully coordinated gains. Hence partial coordination has yielded a welfare gain of just 0.4% overall. Although this may seem a very small figure it is worth an extra 0.5% on the 'world' GNP growth rate. If we increase the importance attached to

Table 10.9 The objective function values with varying degrees of commitment to exchange-rate targetting: The CEER rule

	Degree of Commitment (Objective Function Weight on Exchange-rate Target)				
	0.01	0.05	0.1	0.15	0.3
CDN	37.99	37.75	37.41	37.05	35.88
UK	17.71	17.79	17.89	18.04	19.29
GER	141.88	141.36	140.74	140.06	137.79
JAP	26.19	26.14	26.06	25.99	26.09
USA	206.88	206.76	206.87	206.99	207.56
Total	430.46	429.79	428.97	428.13	426.61

Table 10.10 Welfare gains under partial coordination (% gains/losses in welfare units, compared to the no-targetting, no-cooperation outcomes)

		Exchange-rate Targetting Rules			
	Nash Bargain Full Cooperation	CEER Rule (weight 0.1)	CEER Rule (weight 0.3)	ARMA Rule on CEER	ARMA Rule National d values
CDN	4.9	+1.6	+5.7	−0.4	−0.2
UK	4.4	−1.1	−9.0	−0.1	+5.1
GER	4.5	+0.8	+2.9	+1.3	+1.3
JAP	7.2	+0.6	+0.4	−0.8	−1.0
USA	3.1	−0.1	−0.4	+0.1	+0.3
'World'	4.0	+0.4	+0.9	+0.3	+0.5

exchange-rate targetting, we can more than double these gains to 22% of the fully cooperative figure (Table 10.9). That is an increase of 0.9% in welfare units. But this can only be done at the cost of making the UK and US even worse off (for the UK the loss is 9% in welfare units). Thus it is doubtful if these gains can really be called coordination gains, and it is even less likely that the UK would accept such a loss just to make its partners somewhat better off.

The relatively poor performance of all these targetting rules, in terms of capturing the gains available from full cooperation, is illustrated in Figure 10.1, which shows a large gap between full and partial coordination compared to the small gap between partial coordination and no exchange-rate targetting at all. We have in fact been unable to find an exchange-rate targetting scheme which strictly dominates the benchmark Nash solution, although generating some gains on a 'worldwide' basis is not difficult. Table 10.10 shows that either the UK and US lose out under the CEER rules, or Canada and Japan

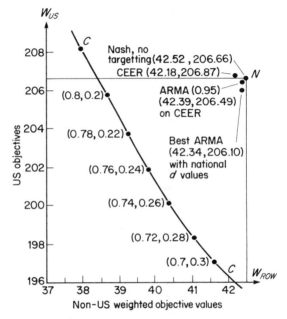

Figure 10.1 Dominant coordination and partial coordination

N = Nash with no exchange rate targetting.

C = Cooperative bargaining outcomes for different weights for US vs non-US
  [e.g. $(0.7, 0.3)$ is $\alpha_{04} = 0.7$ and $\alpha_{US} = 0.3$],
  where CDN, UK, GER, JAP outcomes are weighted 0.27, 0.3, 0.13, 0.3 to make
  W_{04}.

$W = \alpha_{04} W_{04} + \alpha_{US} W_{US}$ is the cooperative criterion. (The 0.7, 0.3 bargain does not
  dominate for Canada; the other bargains dominate Nash for all 5 countries
  simultaneously)

lose under the ARMA rules. This suggests a mixed rule – part CEER and
part ARMA – but the attempt to exploit the benefits of each rule also
involves mixing the disadvantages of both, and the results are worse than
either rule taken alone.

XI Conclusions

(a) On the basis of these results, the prospects for improving policy
coordination by exchange-rate management look to be rather poor. The
gains were small, hard to get, and badly distributed relative to unrestricted
non-cooperative policies.[12] That last point raises doubts as to whether an
exchange-rate targetting scheme would actually be sustainable, at least at a

G5 country level. Exchange-rate targetting in a G5 or G7 context therefore raises quite different problems from the 2-country case because of the distributional constraints and smaller margins in some countries.

(b) The small gains may seem to conflict with earlier work which suggested that exchange-rate targetting would bring significant improvements (e.g. Edison, Miller and Williamson, 1987; Currie and Wren-Lewis, 1988). However, previous work has compared the targetting results to history or to some baseline simulation involving historical policies, not to the non-cooperative policies of a Nash game. Exchange-rate targetting may therefore yield gains over historical policies because they were poorly designed. That underlines the need to improve the effectiveness of existing fiscal and monetary policies – perhaps through an assignment scheme. Increased policy effectiveness and policy specialization are of course the two standard reasons why policy coordination brings gains (Hughes Hallett, 1986a).

(c) Our finding has been that gains over efficient non-cooperative policies without any targetting will not be realized unless the targetting scheme is very carefully designed: simple exchange-rate rules are not simple to construct. Casual methods are therefore unlikely to be successful. Intensive staff work would be needed for partial cooperation – just as much as in the case of full cooperation, though the benefits would be less. Exchange-rate target rules may nevertheless be helpful if they tend to prevent governments adopting inappropriate domestic policies or as a means of providing external stability. The latter property will be important if foreign trade is thought to be subject to hysteresis, or if large and persistent misalignments imply large welfare losses but the costs of moderate misalignments are small.

(d) We found that the choice of exchange-rate target paths was more important than securing precise agreement on those paths or on the policies needed to track them. An exchange-rate management scheme can therefore be implemented in the form of target zones, but the choice of parities (or reference levels) is more important to the success of the scheme than the width of the band. Moreover, those parities should be revised in the light of past outcomes and new information. Finally, the proponents of target zones must pay careful attention to the distributional consequences of their policies in an asymmetric multi-country world. If, as here, there are some gainers and some losers, it will be necessary for each country to target the value of each of the currencies it faces rather than just operate with a single indicator currency. The policy intervention rules will become more complicated, being contingent on the particular combination of movements in each of the target zones which a country faces.

(e) There appears to have been an assumption in much of the literature that exchange-rate management will automatically bring policy improvements – based on the analysis behind the Oudiz-Sachs conjecture, quoted at the start.

But there is, so far as we know, no demonstration that exchange-rate targetting will generally bring policy coordination gains. While the logic of the conjecture is not in doubt, its practical importance may be restricted to a particular situation: one where economies and policy preferences are similar. An overwhelming common priority, such as the need to reduce inflation in the early 1980s (when Oudiz and Sachs wrote), may also be a precondition for competitive appreciations (or depreciations) to be a dominant tendency. Even then there is no guarantee that exchange-rate management would not just transfer competitive behaviour to other *linked* variables (e.g. reserves). In a world of more than two countries with asymmetric preferences and asymmetric spillovers, the tendency to competitive exchange-rate policies dwindles and, with it, the gains to cooperating on exchange-rate targets. If this is true, as our results suggest, then theoretical analysis is needed to show exactly when exchange-rate targetting can and cannot be helpful.

Appendix 1: The MCM model structure

The Multicountry Model (MCM) is essentially five single-country models linked together by bilateral trade equations. Each model contains four domestic agents: consumers, firms, commercial banks, and the government (fiscal and monetary authorities). There are four markets in the model: domestic output, labour, money, and bonds. Nominal wages are sticky, so that the amount of labour employed is variable and output can adjust to meet aggregate demand. The aggregate supply curve is given by producers, who set prices at a markup over variable cost. In contrast to the goods market, asset markets are perfectly competitive, and agents are assumed to be risk-neutral. Short- and long-term securities are assumed to be perfect substitutes. Foreign and home currency bonds are also assumed to be perfect substitutes, so the open interest parity holds in the foreign-exchange market. Expectations about future variables are adaptive. A full description and equation listing of this model will be found in Edison, Marquez and Tryon (1987).

The baseline trajectories used for linearizing the model in the multiplier calculations is just the baseline simulation (central projection) of the MCM model described in Edison *et al.* (1987). The 1986 and early 1987 figures are historical, but for the second half of 1987–92, forecasts obtained from the OECD *Economic Outlook* (1986) are used as far as they go and those figures extrapolated on where no forecasts have been published. This baseline gives the kind of model-free projection of the main aggregates which would be available to policy makers at the start of the exercise.

Appendix 2: A conjectural variations equilibrium

Here we outline an alternative to the Nash equilibrium, a conjectural variations (CV) equilibrium, elements of which provide a foundation for one of the restricted

Table 10A.1   The ideal policy values, 1986-92

	Policy Variable	Canada	UK	Germany	Japan	US
Targets	$G\dot{N}P$	4.0	4.0	4.0	4.0	4.0
	$\dot{P}$	2.0	2.0	1.0	1.0	2.0
	CB	0.0	0.0	0.0	0.0	0.0
	$GDEF$	10.0	3.0	15.0	5.0	75.0
Instruments	G	20.0	20.0	20.0	9.0	$20.0/18.0^a$
	$\dot{M}$	5.0	3.0	3.0	3.0	3.0
Intermediate	RS	7.0	7.5	3.0	3.0	5.0
Targets	ER	See Table 10.1 for Schemes A0 to A8				

Key:
GṄP   = real gross national product (% growth p.a.).
Ṗ   = anual % increase in consumer price index.
CB   = current account balance (billions of domestic currency, trillions for Japan.
GDEF = central government budget deficit (units as for CB).
G   = government current expenditures as % of GNP.
Ṁ   = rate of growth of money stock (M1).
RS   = nominal short-term interest rate (%).
^{a} The annual figures are 20.0, 19.6, 19.2, 18.9, 18.6, 18.3, 18.0.

Table 10A.2   The ideal objective function weights, 1986-92

	Policy Variable	Canada	UK	Germany	Japan	US
Targets	$G\dot{N}P$	1.0	1.0	2.0	2.0	1.0
	$\dot{P}$	1.0	1.0	2.0	1.0	1.0
	CB	0.08	0.05	0.01	0.01	$0.0035/0.01^a$
	$GDEF$	0.01	0.01	0.01	0.01	$0.0035/0.01^a$
Instruments	G	1.0	1.0	1.0	1.0	2.0
	$\dot{H}$	1.0	1.0	1.0	1.0	1.0
Intermediate	RS	1.0	1.0	1.0	1.0	1.0
Targets	ER	0.1	0.1	0.1	0.1	0.1

^{a} The annual figures are: 0.0035, 0.005, 0.007, 0.01, 0.01, 0.01.

cooperation schemes discussed in Section V.

In a CV process policy makers believe that their opponents will change policy as a result of their own policy changes. Player A would now conceive of his policy problem as finding the values of x^A such that:

$$\partial w^A/\partial x^A + [(\partial y^A/\partial x^B)(\partial x^B/\partial x^A) + \partial y^A/\partial x^A)]'\partial w^A/\partial y^A = 0 \qquad (B1)$$

Of course, equation (B1) depends on the values of x^B, and player A must recognize that his rival will simultaneously be choosing x^B to satisfy the first-order conditions

Table 10B.1 Objective function values under alternative exchange-rate target paths when stability is an explicit objective

Scheme:	A_0	D_{06}	D_{08}
CDN	35.8	38.4	39.8
UK	52.9	60.1	63.8
GER	196.1	204.6	208.9
JAP	82.5	90.5	94.6
USA	232.6	220.4	230.9
	D_{60}	A_6	D_{68}
CDN	36.4	38.8	40.2
UK	22.1	22.6	23.2
GER	157.2	160.6	162.5
JAP	62.0	63.5	64.4
USA	233.3	216.6	224.8
	D_{80}	D_{86}	A_8
CDN	36.7	39.1	40.4
UK	27.9	25.2	24.3
GER	161.1	162.1	162.8
JAP	78.9	77.2	76.7
USA	233.9	214.9	222.2

(for x^B) corresponding to (B1). Solving this pair of first-order conditions will then lead to a conjectural-variations equilibrium which is not unique, but which in general has a solution which is Pareto-superior to the simple Nash equilibrium. Let $\partial x^B / \partial x^A$ be estimated by D_j^B and $\partial x^A / \partial x^B$ by D_j^A at step j. Then (B1) implies:

$$\begin{bmatrix} I & -D_{j+1}^A \\ -D_{j+1}^B & I \end{bmatrix} \begin{bmatrix} x_{j+1}^A \\ x_{j+1}^B \end{bmatrix} = \begin{bmatrix} F_{j+1}^A s^A \\ F_{j+1}^B s^B \end{bmatrix} \qquad (B2)$$

where $F_{j+1}^A = -(G_j^{A'} C^A R_{AA} + E^A)^{-1} G_j^{A'} C^A$ and $G_j^A = R_{AA} + R_{AB} D_j^B$, with $D_{j+1}^A = F_{j+1}^A R_{AB} \neq D_j^A$. We need to check that these iterations do provide gains for one or both countries, and in the absence of that restriction the steps at (B2) may fail to converge or provide a unique solution. This can be done by replacing D_{j+1}^i with $\gamma_i D_{j+1}^i + (1 - \gamma_i) D_j^i$ where $0 \leq \gamma_i \leq 1$ is chosen (at each step) so as to force x_{j+1}^A and x_{j+1}^B 'downhill', i.e. so that $w^i(x_{j+1}^A, x_{j+1}^B) \leq w^i(x_j^A, x_j^A)$ for $i = A, B$. That modification introduces a directed search in which at least one country is better off (and neither worse off) at each step. An exhaustive search will then identify the equilibrium decisions (x^{A*}, x^{B*}) as defined by the joint minima specified above. Moreover, this solution procedure explicitly recognizes that it is only sensible for a player to alter his conjectures about an opponent's reactions in a way which is Pareto-improving for both players, since otherwise the opponent simply will not react in the way conjectured. In this context one cannot expect any sovereign government to adjust its responses *unilaterally* against its own interests. This solution procedure is therefore constrained to be incentive-compatible to other

Table 10B.2 Objective function values under
alternative exchange-rate target paths: The intermediate targetting case

Scheme:	A_0	D_{06}	D_{08}
CDN	33.9	36.6	38.1
UK	21.9	22.7	23.3
GER	146.6	149.7	151.4
JAP	27.4	29.7	30.8
USA	211.9	211.0	211.8

	D_{60}	A_6	D_{68}
CDN	34.5	37.0	38.5
UK	18.4	18.5	18.6
GER	141.4	143.8	143.2
JAP	27.4	29.2	30.2
USA	209.4	208.2	208.8

	D_{80}	D_{86}	A_8
CDN	34.8	37.2	38.7
UK	18.8	18.5	18.5
GER	141.1	143.2	144.4
JAP	28.4	30.2	31.1
USA	208.2	206.9	207.4

non-cooperative solutions – if Pareto improvements over the Nash solutions cannot be found, the search terminates at the Nash solution.

Another expression for x^A_{j+1} can be obtained from (B2) by inverting the left-hand matrix. Multiplying out and rearranging yields

$$x^A_{j+1} = -[G^{A'}_j C^A\{G^A_j + R_{AB}(D^B_{j+1} - D^B_j)\} + E^A]^{-1} G^{A'}_j C^A(s^A + R_{AB}F^B_{j+1}s^B) \text{ (B3)}$$

and similarly for x^B_{j+1}. This implies that when the search process terminates, *either* because (B2) itself terminates (i.e. consistent conjectures) *or* because no further Pareto-improvements can be found (i.e. $\gamma_i = 0$, so $D^i_{j+1} = D^i_j$ for $i = A, B$), then (B3) implies decision values given by

$$x^* = -[G^{A'}_* C^A G^A_* + E^A]^{-1} G^{A'}_* C^A d^A \tag{B4}$$

where G^A_* is the terminal value of G^A_j defined in (B2), and $d^A = s^A + R_{AB}F^B_* s^B$ is also evaluated at G_*.

The Nash concept is adopted in the body of the paper as the conventional one, used by the majority of other empirical studies of policy coordination. It is obvious from (3) that the Nash equilibrium is a special case of the conjectural-variations framework (B2) in which $j = 0$ and $D^A_0 = D^B_0 = 0$.

Notes

1 Translation: There is no short cut without toil.

2 This coordination argument is also used in Sachs (1986) to justify the kind of exchange-rate agreement schemes sought following the Plaza agreement of 1985.

3 The problem here is one of trying to agree on what you should do, not on how you should do it. Agreement on target paths might be more likely than agreement on, say, the model.

4 Hughes Hallett and Rees (1983, p. 220).

5 See Williamson and Miller (1987).

6 Hughes Hallett (1984), Ghosh *et al.* (1987).

7 The Group of Thirty Report (1988) stresses the need for 'periodic base exchange rate adjustments in relation to fundamental economic relationships'. This ARMA rule is one way to do that, given suitable values for c_t.

8 Strictly speaking this is only true for the non-US countries if they want a faster dollar depreciation than the US does. But it is true for the US whichever way the disagreement goes.

9 Additional reasons for this are that unconstrained foreign exchange markets do not reach equilibrium rapidly, and large or persistent misalignments may well have damaging consequences (Group of Thirty, 1988).

10 This result of course just reflects the fact that there normally is an optimal degree of commitment to an intermediate target (Rogoff, 1985). The Group of Thirty Report (1988) notes that the degree of commitment will be an important part of the design of an exchange-rate agreement.

11 Schemes in which each country targets its CEER cross-rates as well as its own indicator (dollar) exchange rate do in fact dominate the unrestricted Nash outcomes of Table 10.5, although not by much. This reveals that countries would have to operate several bilateral target zones simultaneously, rather than one zone in an indicator currency. Policy rules would no longer be simple, since the interventions triggered by deviations from any given zone would have to vary with what was happening in each of the other zones.

12 There is of course the possibility that these results are entirely model-dependent. We have therefore repeated the calculations reported in this paper on the GEM econometric model (see Currie and Wren-Lewis, 1988), and on a sample of 4 models from the Brookings model comparison seminar (see Holtham and Hughes Hallett, 1987). We obtained essentially the same results. In particular, the key result that varying the exchange-rate targets had little impact on the outcomes of intermediate targetting (equivalent to Table 10B.2), but quite a lot of impact on stability (equivalent to Table 10A.1), and that intermediate targetting was effectively unable to better unrestricted Nash outcomes (as in Table 10.5), were all replicated (Hughes Hallett *et al.*, 1988).

References

Canzoneri, M.B. and P. Minford (1986) 'When International Policy Coordination Matters: An Empirical Analysis', CEPR Discussion Paper No. 119.

Currie, D.A. and S. Wren-Lewis (1988) 'Evaluating the Extended Target Zone Proposal for the G3', CEPR Discussion Paper No. 221.

Currie, D.A., P. Levine and N. Vadalis (1987) 'International Cooperation and Reputation in an Empirical Two-Bloc Model', in R.C. Bryant and R. Portes (eds), *Global Macroeconomics: Policy Conflict and Cooperation*, Macmillan, London.

Edison, H., M.H. Miller and J. Williamson (1987) 'On Evaluating and Extending the Target Zone Proposal', *Journal of Policy Modelling* **9**, 199–224.

Edison, H., J. Marquez and R. Tryon (1987) 'The Structure and Properties of the Federal Reserve Board Multicountry Model', *Economic Modelling* **4**, 155–315.

Ghosh, S., C.L. Gilbert and A.J. Hughes Hallett (1987) *Stabilising Speculative Commodity Markets*, Oxford University Press, Oxford/New York.

Group of Thirty (1988) *International Macroeconomic Policy Coordination*, Group of Thirty, New York and London.

Hamada, K. (1976) 'A Strategic Analysis of Monetary Interdependence', *Journal of Political Economy* **84**, 677–700.

Holtham, G. and A.J. Hughes Hallett (1987) 'International Policy Cooperation and Model Uncertainty' in Bryant and Portes, *op cit.*

Hughes Hallett, A.J. (1984) 'Optimal Stockpiling in a High Risk Commodity Market', *Journal of Economic Dynamics and Control* **8**, 211–38.

Hughes Hallett, A.J. (1986a) 'Autonomy and the Choice of Policy in Asymmetrically Dependent Economies', *Oxford Economic Papers* **38**, 516–44.

Hughes Hallett, A.J. (1986b) 'International Policy Design and the Sustainability of Policy Bargains', *Journal of Economic Dynamics and Control* **10**, 467–94.

Hughes Hallett, A.J. (1987) 'The Impact of Interdependence on Economic Policy Design: The Case of the US, EEC and Japan', *Economic Modelling* **4**, 377–96.

Hughes Hallett, A.J. and H.J.B. Rees (1983) *Quantitative Economic Policies and Interactive Planning*, Cambridge University Press, Cambridge/New York.

Hughes Hallett, A.J., G. Holtham and G. Hutson (1989) 'Exchange Rate Targetting as a Surrogate for International Policy Coordination', Discussion Paper, Centre for Economic Policy Research, London (forthcoming).

Just, R., E. Lutz, A. Schmitz and S. Turnovsky (1978). 'The Distribution of Welfare Gains from Pure Stabilisation: An International Perspective', *Journal of International Economics* **8**, 551–63.

Kindleberger, C.P. (1981) *International Money*, Allen and Unwin, London.

Oudiz, G. and J. Sachs (1984) 'Macroeconomic Policy Coordination Among the Industrial Economies', *Brookings Papers on Economic Activity* **1**, 1–64.

Rogoff, K. (1985) 'The Optimal Degree of Commitment to an Intermediate Monetary Target', *Journal of Political Economy* **92**, 1169–89.

Sachs, J. (1986) 'The Uneasy Case for Greater Exchange Rate Coordination', *American Economic Review* (Papers and Proceedings) **76**, 336–41.

Williamson, J. and M.H. Miller (1987) 'Targets and Indicators: A Blueprint for the International Coordination of Economic Policy', Institute for International Economics, Washington.

Discussion

Paul Levine

The general theme which motivates this paper is the idea of the political attractiveness of *limited international agreements* which focus only on a small number of macroeconomic variables. From this it follows that cooperation could take the form of a constrained non-cooperative equilibrium. In the case examined by the paper, the agreed constraint is that exchange rates follow some agreed paths.

The general method is to allow countries to optimize independently, but to require them to penalize deviations of their own exchange rate from the agreed target paths. This introduces an extra term in each country's welfare loss with a large weight. Having computed the non-cooperative equilibrium, the true welfare loss for each country is evaluated dropping this extra term. Then if this welfare loss is lower for all countries than in the unconstrained non-cooperative equilibrium, exchange-rate targetting is an effective and sustainable form of cooperation.

Much of the paper is concerned with various ways of evaluating the target exchange-rate paths. The main conclusion is that using MCM – the multi-country model of the Federal Reserve Board – the gains from exchange-rate cooperation 'were small, hard to get and badly distributed'.

The problem examined in the paper is closely related to a number of issues in the recent macroeconomics literature. For example, Rogoff (1985) argues that it can be beneficial for society to elect a 'conservative' government which does not share their welfare criteria but puts a greater weight on inflation stabilization relative to output stabilization. Rogoff uses a closed economy model, but Laskar (1987) in a two-bloc model of open economies shows that it may, in fact, be beneficial to have 'anticonservative' government. This result is confirmed by Levine (1987) on an empirically based two-bloc model.

In all these studies, including Hughes Hallett *et al.*, governments in effect adopt the 'wrong' welfare criteria. However, when the non-cooperative equilibria are evaluated, the outcome judged using the correct criteria can be Pareto-superior. To put this another way, in the 'second-best' world of non-cooperative (Nash) games it may benefit players not to choose the same welfare criteria that they would in a 'first-best' cooperative situation.

The methodology adopted by the paper is quite general and can be applied to other forms of limited agreements such as nominal-income or money-stock targetting. Comparisons of these different 'regimes' would be interesting.

The technical meat of the paper lies in the choice of the exchange-rate target paths. The paths that come out of the cooperative outcome (CEER) do seem the most obvious candidates. But the lessons from second-best studies also suggest they will not be optimal. The main motive for choosing the alternative up-dating rule seems to be that it allows for 'target paths to react to new information and hence reduce the impact of uncertainty'. However, unanticipated shocks or changes to the model are not part of the exercise, so it comes as no surprise that up-dating does not significantly improve upon the CEER.

On the empirical result, that exchange-rate management does not appear to be a particularly effective management form of surrogate cooperation, I feel this may be unduly pessimistic for the following reason. The possible gains from limited agreements such as exchange-rate targetting must depend from the outset on the potential (maximum) gains from full cooperation. In Currie, Levine and Vidalis (1987) and Levine, Currie and Gaines (this volume) we find that in a two-bloc model with rational expectations, if governments try to exploit a reputation for precommitment but do so without cooperation, then this can greatly exacerbate the beggar-my-neighbour character of monetary policy. Thus the gains from cooperation (with reputation for precommitment) are correspondingly higher.

In the version of MCM used by Hughes Hallett *et al.*, expectations are backward-looking. If instead a rational expectations version were employed, one might well obtain far better results for exchange-rate targetting (and for other forms of limited agreement).

References

Currie, D., P. Levine and N. Vidalis (1987) 'International Cooperation and Reputation in an Empirical Two-Bloc Model,' in Bryant, R. C. and R. Portes (eds.), *Global Macroeconomics: Policy Conflict and Cooperation*, Macmillan, London.

Laskar, D. (1987) 'Conservative Central Bankers in a Two-Country World,' CEPRE-MAP, mimeo.

Levine, P. (1987) 'Three Themes from Game Theory and International Macroeconomic Policy Formation,' *Richerche Economiche* **41**, 392–418.

Rogoff, K. (1985) 'The Optimal Degree of Commitment to an Intermediate Monetary Target', *Quarterly Journal of Economics* **100**, 1169–89.

Chapter 11

The use of simple rules for international policy agreements

Paul Levine, David Currie and Jessica Gaines*

I Introduction

In recent years, appreciable advances have been made in the application of dynamic game theory to the design of macroeconomic policies for open, interdependent economies (see, for example, the papers in Buiter and Marston, 1985, and Bryant and Portes, 1987). Whereas the earlier literature (for example, Hamada, 1979; Cooper, 1985) analysed issues of international policy cooperation in the context of games between governments, the more recent literature has recognized the central role played by private agents making rational forward expectations about future policy moves. This literature therefore places at centre stage issues of reputation and credibility in policy making, and it has integrated the analysis of reputation in a single economy context (see, for example, Barro and Gordon, 1983) with the literature on international cooperation (Levine and Currie, 1987a). This analysis has permitted a more convincing analysis of the sustainability of cooperation and reputation in policy design.

In previous work by the authors, these developments have been applied to an empirically based international model to analyse the gains from cooperation and reputation in international macropolicy. Using Minilink, a reduced two-bloc version of the OECD Interlink model, Currie, Levine and Vidalis (1987) examined four separate policy regimes: cooperation with

*Financial support from the ESRC (grant number B01250012) is gratefully acknowledged.

BLUEPRINTS FOR EXCHANGE RATE MANAGEMENT
0-12-497060-5
Copyright © 1989 Academic Press, Ltd
All rights of reproduction reserved

reputation (CR), cooperation without reputation (CNR), non-cooperation with reputation (NCR) and non-cooperation without reputation (NCNR). They found that the benefits from cooperation and reputation were largely joint, in that reputation without cooperation was counterproductive, as was cooperation without reputation. These benefits were appreciable, particularly in the face of permanent disturbances to the system. Moreover, the analysis suggested that cooperative reputational policies were sustainable in a fairly wide range of circumstances.

A difficulty with this previous work is that the policies considered are all exceedingly complex, involving high-order dynamic feedback rules for the policy instruments. This feature is unfortunate as it can be convincingly argued that policy rules which might appeal to policy makers and be made credible in the eyes of the private sector should, in fact, be simple. The argument for simplicity carries particular force in the international sphere where the need to monitor policy commitments applies to both the private sector and the countries or blocs entering into agreements. These arguments led the authors in earlier work to examine the design of simple policy rules (see Currie and Levine, 1985a). However, the earlier work examined solely the efficacy of simply policy designs, and did not address questions of their sustainability. It shared that deficiency with other work on simple policy rules.

The purpose of this paper is to develop a methodology for analysing the sustainability of simple rules and to apply the methodology empirically to Minilink. In this, the paper parallels for simple rules the analysis carried out by Currie, Levine and Vidalis (1987) for complex, optimal rules. The methodology has general applicability, and future work will be concerned to apply it to a systematic appraisal of blueprints for international policy coordination, such as the target zone proposal of Williamson and Miller (1987).

The plan of the paper is as follows. Section II sets out the details of Minilink, the model to which our methodology is applied. This empirically based model was derived as a reduced representation of earlier writings of the OECD Interlink model, and therefore suffers from not including recent improvements in the specification of the parent model, as well as from approximation errors. Future work will seek to apply our methodology to more completely specified and more soundly based empirical models. Section III, together with Appendix 2, sets out the analytics of the design of simple rules. Section IV describes techniques for analysing the sustainability of simple rules. Section V reports the results of applying these techniques to Minilink, and Section VI briefly concludes.

A number of themes run through the paper. First, we address a number of objections to the use of flexible feedback rules for purposes of macroeconomic stabilization. Thus we address explicitly the time-inconsistency problem, the scope for beggar-my-neighbour policies in the international sphere, and the objection that effective stabilization rules are necessarily too complex to be realistically implemented. In future work, we will address the issues raised by model uncertainty. Secondly, we examine the scope for using agreements in the form of simple rules as a surrogate for more far-reaching agreement on international policy coordination. Finally, we highlight the possibility that simplicity in policy design may improve the sustainability and credibility of the associated macroeconomic policies.

II   Minilink in a stochastic environment

The two-bloc (US and rest of the world) stochastic version of Minilink is described by the following equations. Unstarred variables refer to the US and starred variables to the rest of the world (ROW). (See Masson, Blundell-Wignall and Richardson, 1984, for a full description of the model and the method used to construct the reduced representation from the full Interlink model.)

$$q_t = c_1 \rho_t + c_2 g_t + 2c_3 \bar{r} a_{t-1} + c_4 \eta_t + c_5 q_t^* + ad_t \tag{1}$$

$$q_t^* = c_1^* \rho_t^* + c_2^* g_t^* - 2c_3^* \bar{r} a_{t-1} + c_4^* \eta_t^* + c_5^* q_t + ad_t^* \tag{2}$$

$$\eta_t = c_{41} \eta_{t-1} + c_{42} \eta_{t-2} + c_{43} er_t \tag{3}$$

$$\eta_t^* = c_{41}^* \eta_{t-1}^* + c_{42}^* \eta_{t-2}^* + c_{43}^* er_t \tag{4}$$

$$er_t = e_t + p_t - p_t^* \tag{5}$$

$$\rho_t = c_{11} \rho_{t-1} + c_{12} rl_t \tag{6}$$

$$\rho_t^* = c_{11}^* \rho_{t-1}^* + c_{12}^* rl_t^* \tag{7}$$

$$\Delta p_t = d_3 \pi_t + (1 - d_3)(\Delta p_t^* - \Delta e_t) + d_2(q_t + as_t) \tag{8}$$

$$\Delta p_t^* = d_3^* \pi_t^* + (1 - d_3^*)(\Delta p_t + \Delta e_t) + d_2^*(q_t^* + as_t^*) \tag{9}$$

$$\Delta \pi_t = d_1(\Delta p_{t-1} - \pi_{t-1}) \tag{10}$$

$$\Delta \pi_t^* = d_1^*(\Delta p_{t-1}^* - \pi_{t-1}^*) \tag{11}$$

$$ca_t = \Delta a_t = b_1 \zeta_t + b_2 q_t^* + b_3 q_t \tag{12}$$

$$\zeta_t = b_{13} \zeta_{t-1} + b_{14} \zeta_{t-2} + b_{11} er_t + b_{12} er_{t-1} \tag{13}$$

$$rl_t = c_{13} rl_{t+1,t}^e + (1 - c_{13}) r_t \tag{14}$$

$$rl_t^* = c_{13}^* + rl_{t+1,t}^{*e} + (1 - c_{13}^*)r_t^* \tag{15}$$

$$er_{t+1,t}^e = er_t + \tfrac{1}{2}(r_t^* - r_t) \tag{16}$$

$$ad_t = \mu_d ad_{t-1} + \varepsilon_{1t} \tag{17}$$

$$ad_t^* = \mu_d^* ad_{t-1}^* + \varepsilon_{2t} \tag{18}$$

$$as_t = \mu_s as_{t-1} + \varepsilon_{3t} \tag{19}$$

$$as_t^* = \mu_s^* as_{t-1}^* + \varepsilon_{4t} \tag{20}$$

where q is real GDP, ρ is a distributed lag of the expected real long-term interest rate rl, g is real government expenditure, a is the real stock of the net foreign assets of the US, ca is the US current account balance as a proportion of a, η and ζ are distinct distributed lags of the real exchange rate er, e is the nominal exchange rate, π is the expected rate of inflation, p is the price level, r is the short-term expected real rate of interest, $\bar{r}$ denotes the mean level of r, and 'ad' and 'as' are aggregate demand and supply shocks respectively.

All variables except the rates of interest are in logarithms and measured as deviations about the long-term trend. Starred variables denote equivalents for the ROW. The model is a semi-annual one and rates of interest are measured on an annual basis.

Equations (1) and (2) specify real output to depend on real government expenditure, real net interest income ($\bar{r}a$), real foreign output and distributed lags of the expected real long-term rate of interest and real exchange rates. These lag structures are given by (3), (4), (6) and (7). Equation (5) defines the real exchange rate. (8) and (9) give inflation as determined by expectations-augmented Phillips curves with components for imported inflation (Δp_t denotes $p_t - p_{t-1}$). Inflation expectations are formed adaptively as given in (10) and (11). Equation (12) determines the accumulation of net foreign assets in terms of domestic and foreign output and a distributed lag of the real exchange rate, given by (13). Equations (14), (15) and (16) specify the arbitrage conditions between long-term, short-term domestic and short-term foreign bonds. Expectations are assumed to be model-consistent in these equations. Finally, (17) to (20) specify first-order autoregressive processes for aggregate demand and aggregate supply shocks where ε_{it} is independently distributed with zero mean and constant variance. In general we allow for contemporaneous correlation between different shocks and specify $\mathrm{cov}(\varepsilon_t) = \Sigma$ where $\varepsilon_\varepsilon^T = [\varepsilon_{1t}\varepsilon_{2t}\varepsilon_{3t}\varepsilon_{4t}]$.

Parameter values are as given in Table 11A.1, Appendix 1. In addition, we ignore wealth effects in (1) and (2) for reasons discussed in Currie, Levine and Vidalis (1987).

In the regimes which follow we assume an objective function for each country of the form $E_0(W_0)$ where

$$W_0 = \sum_{t=0}^{\infty} \lambda^t [a(\Delta p - \hat{\Delta p})^2 + b(q - \hat{q})^2 + c(g_t - \hat{g})^2 + d(r_t - \hat{r})^2] \quad (21)$$

where $E_0(.)$ denotes expectations formed at time $t = 0$. Thus we penalize deviations of inflation and output (targets) and of the real short-term interest rate and government spending (instruments) from their desired levels $\hat{\Delta p}$, $\hat{q}$, $\hat{r}$ and $\hat{g}$ relative to the long-term trends. Weights chosen for the results are $a = b = 0.01$, $c = d = 0.005$ and $\lambda = 0.97$, which correspond to the exercises reported in Currie, Levine and Vidalis (1987).

By adding relationships $\Delta \hat{p}_{t+1} = \Delta \hat{p}_t = \Delta \hat{p}$ (assumed to be the same for both blocs), etc, to those above the model may be set up in state–space form:

$$\begin{bmatrix} z_{t+1} \\ x^e_{t+1,t} \end{bmatrix} = A \begin{bmatrix} z_t \\ x_t \end{bmatrix} + B \begin{bmatrix} w_t \\ w^*_t \end{bmatrix} + \begin{bmatrix} u_t \\ 0 \end{bmatrix} \quad (22)$$

$$y_t = C \begin{bmatrix} z_t \\ x_t \end{bmatrix} + D \begin{bmatrix} w_t \\ w^*_t \end{bmatrix} \quad (23)$$

where

$$z_t^T = [\Delta \hat{p}_{t-1}\, \hat{q}_{t-1}\, c\hat{a}_{t-1}\, \hat{g}_{t-1}\, \hat{r}_{t-1}\, ad_{t-1}\, ad^*_{t-1}\, as_{t-1}\, as^*_{t-1}$$

$$\eta^*_{t-1}\, \eta_{t-2}\, \eta^*_{t-1}\, \eta_{t-2}\, \rho_{t-1}\, \rho^*_1\, \pi_{t-1}\, \pi^*_{t-1}\, \Delta p_{t-1}\, \Delta p^*_{t-1}\, \zeta_{t-1}\, \zeta_{t-2}\, er_{t-1}]$$

is the vector of predetermined variables, $x_t^T = [rl_t\, rl^*_t\, er_t]$ is the vector of non-predetermined variables, $y_t^T = [q_t\, q^*_t\, ca_t]$ is a vector of outputs, $u_t^T = [\varepsilon_t^T 0]$, $w_t^T = [g_t\, r_t]$ are the instruments of the US and $w_t^{*T} = [g^*_t\, r^*_t]$ those of the ROW. Then (21) may be written as $E_0(W_0)$ where

$$W_0 = \sum_{t=0}^{\infty} \lambda^t [y_t^T Q_1 y_t + w_t^T Q_2 w_t] \quad (24)$$

Equations (22) to (24) express the model and welfare loss function in a form for which the general solution procedures of Appendix 2 apply.

The solutions to the rational expectations model under various forms of control all assume *full information*. By full information we mean that agents have knowledge of all current variables in the state vector $[z_t^T\, x_t^T]$ but not the disturbances up to and including the current period (however, see Pearlman, Currie and Levine, 1986, for a treatment of models where information is limited to a sub-set of economic variables).

III   Complex, optimal *vs* simple, sub-optimal rules

In order to assess the role for feedback rules, whether simple or not, it is useful to distinguish between *open-loop policies* and *feedback* or *state-contingent rules*. With open-loop policies, the current and future values of the policy instruments are specified at time $t = 0$, the beginning of the policy-maker's planning horizon. They are trajectories which depend only on information available at $t = 0$. For example, in the Minilink model of the previous section, the optimal open-loop paths for instruments g_t and r_t will depend on desired levels for target variables $\Delta \hat{p}$, q, desired levels for instruments $\hat{g}$ and $\hat{r}$ and any initial displacements of other state variables in z_t in (22). Denoting the vector of instruments by w_t, an open-loop policy formulated at the time $t = 0$ can then be written ($w_t : t = 0, 1, 2 \dots$).

Feedback or state-contingent rules specify the values of policy variables w_t as functions of information available at time t. In an uncertain world, these enable the policy maker to determine future policy at time t as contingent on realizations of random disturbances in periods $0, 1, 2, \dots, t - 1$. Feedback rules are, in effect, correction mechanisms which enable the policy maker to adjust policy in the event of a series of unanticipated shocks.

In the state–space representation (22), let the optimal open-loop trajectories of state variables, instruments and outputs be denoted by $\bar{z}_t$, $\bar{x}_t$, $\bar{w}_t$, $\bar{w}_t^*$ and $\bar{y}_t$. Write $z_t = \bar{z}_t + \tilde{z}_t$ where $\tilde{z}_t$ is the stochastic component of z_t arising from disturbances u_t which are unanticipated at the beginning of the planning period. Similarly, define $\tilde{z}_t$, $\tilde{x}_t$, $\tilde{w}_t$, $\tilde{w}_t^*$ and $\tilde{y}_t$. Then the welfare loss may be written

$$E_0(W_0) = \bar{W}_0 + E_0(\tilde{W}_0) \tag{25}$$

where

$$\bar{W}_0 = \tfrac{1}{2} \sum_{t=0}^{\infty} \lambda^t [\bar{y}_t^T Q_1 \bar{y}_t + \bar{w}_t^T Q_2 \bar{w}_t] \tag{26}$$

$$E_0(\tilde{W}_0) = \tfrac{1}{2} \sum_{t=0}^{\infty} \lambda^t [\tilde{y}_t^T Q_1 \tilde{y}_t + \tilde{w}_t^T Q_2 \tilde{w}_t] \tag{27}$$

and

$$\begin{bmatrix} z_{t+1} \\ \bar{x}_{t+1,t}^e \end{bmatrix} = \begin{bmatrix} \bar{z}_{t+1} \\ \bar{x}_{t+1} \end{bmatrix} = A \begin{bmatrix} \bar{z}_t \\ \bar{x}_t \end{bmatrix} + B \begin{bmatrix} \bar{w}_t \\ \bar{w}_t^* \end{bmatrix} \tag{28}$$

$$\begin{bmatrix} \tilde{z}_{t+1} \\ \tilde{x}_{t+1,t}^e \end{bmatrix} = A \begin{bmatrix} \tilde{z}_t \\ \tilde{x}_t \end{bmatrix} + B \begin{bmatrix} \tilde{w}_t \\ \tilde{w}_t^* \end{bmatrix} + \begin{bmatrix} u_t \\ 0 \end{bmatrix} \tag{29}$$

with $\bar{z}_0$ given and $\tilde{z}_0 = 0$.

The optimization problem can now be seen to decompose very conveniently into the minimization of $\bar{W}_0$ given by (26) subject to (28) and, quite separately, the minimization of $E_0(\tilde{W}_0)$ given by (27) subject to (29). The first, purely deterministic problem gives rise to an open-loop, expected trajectory for instruments and economic variables described by the model. The second, purely stochastic problem provides a feedback rule that will stabilize the system about its open-loop trajectory in the face of unanticipated, random shocks u_t.

The broad outlines of our analysis may be summarized in terms of the matrix of policies below. Horizontally we depict the choice between cooperation and non-cooperation between governments. Vertically we depict the choice between reputational policies and non-reputational policies. The matrix yields four distinct policy sets. Within each cell, we assume that governments determine policy by an explicit optimization procedure, maximizing a specified welfare function as described above.

		Relations between Governments	
		Cooperation (C)	Non-Cooperation (NC)
Relations between Governments and Private Sector	Reputation	CR	NCR
	Non-reputation	CNR	NCNR

In the Appendix the four regimes cooperation, non-cooperation, with and without reputation (CR, CNR, NCR,NCNR) are described in detail for two types of rule, fully *optimal* and *simple* rules. In CR-OPT, CNR-OPT, NCR-OPT and NCNR-OPT it is assumed that each country pursues optimal, unconstrained rules (insofar as an absence of cooperation and/or reputation may permit). For example, for the CR-OPT regime the feedback rule takes the form

$$\begin{bmatrix} w_t \\ w_t^* \end{bmatrix} = \begin{bmatrix} g_t \\ g_t^* \\ r_t \\ r_t^* \end{bmatrix} = G \begin{bmatrix} z_t \\ p_{2t} \end{bmatrix} \tag{30}$$

where z_t as given in (22) is the vector of predetermined variables at time t and p_{2t} is a weighted sum of lagged predetermined variables with declining weights and with lags extending back to time $t = 0$. G is a matrix of fixed coefficients (see (A9) in Appendix 2).

Alternatively (30) may be expressed as a sum of open-loop plus feedback components of policy, i.e.

$$w_t = \bar{w}_t + \tilde{w}_t = \bar{w}_t + G \begin{bmatrix} \tilde{z}_t \\ \tilde{p}_{2t} \end{bmatrix} \tag{31}$$

where $(\bar{w}_t : t = 0, 1, 2, \ldots)$ is the open-loop policy or expected policy which would be adhered to in the absence of unanticipated shocks and the second term in (31) is the feedback component which stabilizes the system as random shocks occur. The regime may be implemented in either form (30) or (31).

Reputational policies CR-OPT and NCR-OPT correspond to the full optimal rule (or, in the terms of Barro and Gordon, 1983, the *ideal rule*). Such policies are frequently regarded as time-inconsistent in that an incentive to renege emerges with the mere lapse of time; we take up this issue later. Non-reputational policies CNR-OPT and NCNR-OPT correspond to the backward dynamic programming optimization solution which leads to a time-consistent solution. Under cooperation, the two governments jointly adopt a Pareto-efficient policy, the choice of policy being determined in the bargaining process. We model this by assuming that the two governments maximize a weighted average of their individual objective functions, the weights being determined by relative bargaining strengths. For non-cooperative policies each government maxmimizes its own objective function, taking as given the policy rule of the other government.

It should be stressed that within the framework of the stated optimization problem (a linear model, quadratic welfare loss function and an infinite time horizon), the matrix of feedback coefficients, G, is constant and independent of either the initial displacement z_0 or the covariance matrix of the disturbance term, $\text{cov}(u_t) = \Sigma$. Policies implemented as (30) or (31) then provide feedback rules which give optimal protection for *all* transitory shocks z_0 and *all* stochastic shocks u_t. In other words, the optimal feedback rule is a 'horse for all courses', a property referred to as *certainty equivalence*.

An obvious objection to (30) or (31) is that the rule is exceedingly complex. It has been argued that rules should, by contrast, be simple on the grounds of practical implementation, intuitive appeal to policy makers (not to mention their advisors) and the need for easy monitoring by a sceptical private sector (see, for example, Currie and Levine, 1985b; Taylor, 1985; Vines, Maciejowski and Meade, 1983; Edison, Miller and Williamson, 1987; Currie and Wren-Lewis, 1988). This last point, relating essentially to the credibility problem, assumes a greater importance in the international context where there is the additional need for policy makers to be able easily to monitor each other's adherence to agreed policies.

To some extent the complexity of (30) originates from the reputational aspect of the policy. Rules CNR-OPT and NCNR-OPT, without reputation, are less complicated proportional rules of the form

$$\begin{bmatrix} w_t \\ w_t^* \end{bmatrix} = Gz_t \tag{32}$$

see (A42) in Appendix 2). Nevertheless, for Minilink, (32) is still a very high-order controller so that confining interest to non-reputational rules does not dispose of the need for simple policy design.

In the paper we shall be considering simple, proportional-integral rules of the general form

$$\begin{bmatrix} \Delta(w_t - \bar{w}_t) \\ \Delta(w_t^* - \bar{w}_t^*) \end{bmatrix} = G \begin{bmatrix} \Delta(y_t - \bar{y}_t) \\ y_t - \bar{y}_t \end{bmatrix} \tag{33}$$

where constraints are placed on the elements of G to give the rules a particular assignment of instruments to targets. Open-loop paths $\bar{w}_t$, $\bar{w}_t^*$, $\bar{y}_t$, can be chosen as the deterministic solutions in the four regimes CR-OPT, CNR-OPT, NCR-OPT and NCNR-OPT. This leaves (33) as a *stabilization rule* which will correct for random disturbances which displace the economy away from its open-loop path. The corresponding simple rule regimes are denoted by CR-SIM, CNR-SIM, NCR-SIM and NCNR-SIM.

One of the costs of simplicity is that simple rules are sub-optimal. This is due to the fact that the rule is constrained to take the form (33) and there are further constraints on the elements of G. Another more troublesome consequence of imposing simplicity is that the rules which emerge do not satisfy the certainty equivalence property. Following the solution procedure (iii) in Appendix 2, the 'quasi-optimal' simple rules (i.e. optimal rules given the simplicity constraints) can be shown to depend on $\Sigma = \text{cov}(u_t)$, i.e. $G = f(\Sigma)$ at the optimum.

So far we have confined the simple rule to stabilization policy leaving the open-loop path to be fully optimal. Suppose instead we wish to express the policy *entirely* as a rule as in (30) for CR-OPT. We can write:

$$\begin{bmatrix} \Delta\bar{w}_t \\ \Delta\bar{w}_t^* \end{bmatrix} = \bar{G} \begin{bmatrix} \Delta\bar{y}_t \\ \bar{y}_t \end{bmatrix}; \quad \begin{bmatrix} \Delta\tilde{w}_t \\ \Delta\tilde{w}_t^* \end{bmatrix} = \tilde{G} \begin{bmatrix} \Delta\tilde{y}_t \\ \tilde{y}_t \end{bmatrix} \tag{34}$$

However, unlike CR-OPT, we now find that for simple rules $\bar{G} = f(z_0 z_0^T)$ and $\tilde{G} = f(\Sigma)$ where $f(.)$ has the same functional form for $\bar{G}$ and $\tilde{G}$. It follows from this result that the deterministic and stochastic components of policy only have the same feedback form if $z_0 z_0^T = \Sigma$, which is a very restrictive assumption.

Suppose we nevertheless wish to express the policy entirely as a simple rule

$$\begin{bmatrix} \Delta w_t \\ \Delta w_t^* \end{bmatrix} = G \begin{bmatrix} \Delta y_t \\ y_t \end{bmatrix} \tag{35}$$

Then it can be shown (Appendix 2) that $G = f(z_0 z_0^T + \Sigma/(1 - \lambda))$ at the optimum and thus (35) represents a compromise rule which handles both the open-loop and stochastic problems but neither in an optimal fashion. Another type of simple rule found in the literature takes the form

$$\begin{bmatrix} \Delta w_t \\ \Delta w_t^* \end{bmatrix} = G \begin{bmatrix} \Delta y_t \\ y_t - y^e \end{bmatrix} \tag{36}$$

where y^e is a feasible long-run equilibrium of the system imposed from the outset (Edison, Miller and Williamson, 1987; Currie and Wren-Lewis, 1988). This is a special case of (33) where $\bar{w}_t = \bar{w}_t^* = 0$, $\bar{y}_t = y^e$ for all t. By augmenting the state vector with y^e, (36) can be expressed in the form (35). The long-run equilibrium y^e may then be chosen to be the long-run values of the optimal policy which will bring the performance of (36) closer to the optimal feedback rule.

In the results that follow we shall confine the feedback rule to stabilization policy only with $G = f(\Sigma)$ with Σ given. Thus the rules are designed on the understanding that the covariance matrix of disturbance Σ can be estimated as part of the estimation of the model's exogenous process. However, we shall also investigate whether they can be used for the entire open-loop plus feedback policy as in (35) and (36).

Results for two simple rules are reported. In rule 1 both fiscal and monetary policy are assigned to output and inflation targets for each country. The full proportional-integral rule takes the form

$$\Delta g_t = \alpha_1 \Delta q_{t-1} + \alpha_2 \Delta inf_{t-1} + \alpha_3 q_{t-1} + \alpha_4 inf_{t-1} \tag{37a}$$

$$\Delta t_t = \beta_1 \Delta q_{t-1} + \beta_2 \Delta inf_{t-1} + \beta_3 q_{t-1} + \beta_4 inf_{t-1} \tag{37b}$$

for the US with a similar rule for the ROW where $inf_t = \Delta p_t$. An initial exercise reports a set of rules consisting of proportional control only ($\alpha_3 = \alpha_4 = \beta_3 = \beta_4 = 0$). For CR-SIM, an additional constraint of imposing equal coefficients is also investigated.

Rule 2 is a fixed real exchange rate regime. Its general form is

$$\Delta g_t = \alpha_1 \Delta q_{t-1} + \alpha_2 \Delta inf_{t-1} + \alpha_3 q_{t-1} + \alpha_4 inf_{t-1} \tag{38a}$$

$$r_t = -\beta er_t; \quad r_t^* = \beta er_t \tag{38b}$$

with a similar rule for the fiscal policy of the ROW. Rules (38b) along with the uncovered interest rate parity condition (16) simply have the effect of fixing the real exchange rate er_t at its long-run equilibrium (i.e. $er_t = 0$ measured in terms of deviations from the given baseline). The coefficient β therefore plays no role and the focus of interest is on fiscal policy and coefficient values in (38a).

IV   The sustainability of cooperative rules

There are two aspects of the 'sustainability' or 'incentive compatibility' problem to consider. The first arises from the familiar time-inconsistency property of optimal policies where expectations are forward-looking and model-consistent. The optimal policy formulated at the beginning of the planning period then becomes sub-optimal with the mere passage of time. Rational agents with full information on the policy maker's optimization problem can anticipate that an incentive to renege will occur and the optimal policy will therefore lack credibility. Time-consistent policies exist and do not suffer from the credibility problem; but they can be severely sub-optimal.

The question then is whether the policy makers' precommitment to the optimal or 'ideal' policy can be made credible. Following the seminal work of Barro and Gordon (1983), generalized by Currie and Levine (1987) and Levine (1988), the basic approach is to assume that if governments renege on the private sector then they will suffer a loss of reputation for further precommitment.[1] Their choice of policies after reneging will then be confined to those which are 'non-reputational' (i.e. time-consistent). In effect the private sector is assumed to operate a 'punishment' mechanism by believing only in a time-consistent policy following reneging. Whether an incentive to renege exists can then be assessed by comparing the welfare loss under the ideal policy with that after a switch to the non-reputational policy.

The second aspect of sustainability concerns the incentives of governments to renege on cooperative agreements with each other. An incentive exists because the cooperative bargain is not a non-cooperative equilibrium. In other words, each country's side of the agreement does not constitute a best reply to the other country's policy.

Agreements between countries can be made sustainable in a similar way to that for time-inconsistent policies by assuming governments operate a punishment or 'trigger' strategy of switching to a non-cooperative equilibrium in the event of either party reneging. This may be perceived as a conscious 'strategy' or a spontaneous eventual outcome of a breakdown of cooperation. As before, the sustainability of cooperation then requires a comparison of the welfare loss under cooperation with that under the non-cooperative alternatives.

Before considering the details of the analysis for simple rules, we first review the case of optimal rules.

IV.1   The sustainability of the optimal, cooperative rule with reputation (CR-OPT)

Let us abstract from the open-loop component of policy and focus only on the stabilization or stochastic problem. Consider the world economy in stochastic equilibrium with the expected values of all variables at equilibrium values (i.e. in the notation of Section III, $\bar{z}_t = \bar{x}_t = \bar{w}_t = w_t^* = \bar{y}_t = 0$). Under regime CR-OPT the feedback rule takes the form of equation (30) and from (A15) in Appendix 2 the expected welfare loss from time t onwards or 'cost-to-go' when the economy is subjected to a sequence of random shocks is given by

$$E_t(W_t^c) = -\tfrac{1}{2} \operatorname{tr}(N_{11}(z_t z_t^T + \Sigma/(1 - \lambda)) + N_{22} p_{2t} p_{2t}^T) \qquad (39)$$

where N_{11} and N_{22} are negative-definite matrices. The vector of predetermined variables z_t and costate variables p_{2t} in (39) are now stochastic deviations about their long-run equilibrium values.

Consider now the incentive for the two governments to continue to cooperate with each other but collectively to renege on the private sector. Assuming this is accompanied by a loss of reputation we need then to compare the cost-to-go under CR-OPT with that under CNR-OPT. From (A45) in Appendix 2 the latter is given by

$$E_t(W_t^c) = \tfrac{1}{2} \operatorname{tr}(S(z_t z_t^T + \Sigma/(1 - \lambda))) \qquad (40)$$

where S is the positive definite solution to the Riccati equation. In (40) stochastic deviations z_t are those generated under regime CR-OPT.

The sustainability of CR-OPT against collective reneging to CNR-OPT requires that the cost-to-go under CR-OPT is always less than that under CNR-OPT for all possible stochastic realizations of z_t and p_{2t} under CR-OPT. From (39) and (40) sustainability then requires, as both a necessary and sufficient condition, that

$$-\operatorname{tr}(N_{22} p_{2t} p_{2t}^T + (S + N_{11}) z_t z_t^T) < \operatorname{tr}((S + N_{11}) \Sigma/(1 - \lambda)) \qquad (41)$$

for all z_t and p_{2t} in stochastic equilibrium. Since N_{22} is negative-definite, the first term on the left-hand side of (41) is positive and constitutes the possible 'temptation' (Barro and Gordon, 1983) or gains from reoptimization. Since $S + N_{11}$ is positive-definite (see Appendix 2), the remaining terms constitute the 'enforcement' or cost of reneging which arises from being constrained to pursue a non-reputational policy CNR-OPT. The term $\operatorname{tr}((S + N_{11}) z_t z_t^T)$ is the enforcement in absence of any future random shocks. The term on the right-hand side is the added enforcement when the effect of future shocks is taken into account. As $\lambda \to 1$, this last term approaches infinity and so enhances the prospects of sustainability. In fact for *bounded* disturbances we can see from (41) that there will always be some discount factor λ which, when sufficiently close to unity, will ensure sustainability.[2]

For *unbounded* disturbances, which we assume in this paper, there will inevitably be some combination of random shocks for which temptation exceeds enforcement and sustainability therefore breaks down. If we can show, however, that the probability of this happening is extremely small, then its effect on private sector expectations of future policy is negligible and can be ignored. The rational expectations equilibrium in which the rule CR-OPT is believed with probability one then constitutes an approximate equilibrium.

In the results reported later in the paper a frequency distribution of the left-hand side of (41) is generated. In stochastic equilibrium the asymptotic covariance matrix of $\begin{bmatrix} z_t \\ p_{2t} \end{bmatrix}$, V, can be shown to satisfy a Lyapunov equation given by (A50) in Appendix 2. Using a NAG library subroutine, random values for $\begin{bmatrix} z_t \\ p_{2t} \end{bmatrix}$ are generated where

$$\begin{bmatrix} z_t \\ p_{2t} \end{bmatrix} \sim N(0, V) \tag{42}$$

Then for each realization of $\begin{bmatrix} z_t \\ p_{2t} \end{bmatrix}$, the stochastic expression on the left-hand side of (41) is calculated generating its frequency distribution.

Figures 11.1(a) and (b) show two hypothetical cases. In Figure 11.1(a) most of the distribution of the left-hand side of (41) lies well to the left of its critical value given by $\mathrm{tr}((S + N_{11})\Sigma/(1 - \lambda))$. Sustainability holds approximately in this case. In Figure 11.1(b) a large proportion of the distribution lies to the right of the critical value and sustainability almost certainly breaks down.

In a similar way the incentive for governments to renege on each other can be examined. In this case we need to compare the cost-to-go under CR-OPT with that under NCR-OPT or NCNR-OPT for each country separately.

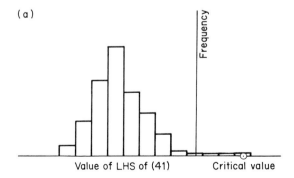

Figure 11.1(a) Approximate sustainability holds

(b)

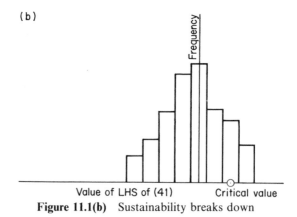

Value of LHS of (41)   Critical value

Figure 11.1(b)   Sustainability breaks down

The comparison of CR-OPT with NCR-OPT is appropriate if reputation is retained although cooperation has broken down. If reneging on a cooperative agreement with the other country destroys a policy maker's reputation for precommitment, then the CR-OPT and NCNR-OPT comparison is appropriate. The details of the analysis are as before.

IV.2   The sustainability of simple, cooperative rules with reputation (CR-SIM)

Consider a simple, proportional-integral rule of the form

$$\begin{bmatrix} \Delta(w_t - \bar{w}_t) \\ \Delta(w_t^* - \bar{w}_t^*) \end{bmatrix} = G \begin{bmatrix} \Delta(y_t - \bar{y}_t) \\ y_t - \bar{y}_t \end{bmatrix} \tag{43'}$$

where $G = f(\Sigma)$ and $\bar{w}_t$, $\bar{w}_t^*$ and $\bar{y}_t$ are optimal open-loop trajectories (i.e. the deterministic solutions of CR-OPT). The first question to address is the precise meaning of precommitment when policy is constrained to be of this simple form. There are three elements to the notion of precommitment to a particular simple rule:

(i)   The assignment of instruments to targets. This takes the form of constraints on the elements of G such as assigning some elements to be zero.

(ii)   The open-loop trajectories $\bar{w}_t$, w_t^* and $\bar{y}_t$ as chosen at the outset.

(iii) The precise values of the elements of G given the constraints implied by (i).

Reneging on a simple rule can consist of reneging on any combination of (i) to (iii). We continue to assume that the private sector operates a punishment mechanism of only believing in non-reputational rules after reneging. Similarly governments operate a trigger strategy of proceeding to non-cooperative equilibria after a cooperative agreement has been violated. The difference is that now policy makers are restricted to simple rules for their stabilization policies.

As before consider the economies in stochastic equilibrium. Consider the incentive to renege from CR-SIM to a simple, cooperative but non-reputational rule CNR-SIM. From Appendix 2, equation (A23), the cost-to-go under CR-SIM is given by

$$E_t(W_t^c) = \tfrac{1}{2} \operatorname{tr}\left(V^{CR-SIM}(z_t z_t^T + \Sigma/(1 - \lambda))\right) \tag{43}$$

where V^{CR-SIM} is a positive definite solution to the Lyapunov equation.

Suppose the policy makers renege to some new simple rule of the form (43′) with possibly different assignments of instruments to targets, a new optimal open-loop trajectory and new elements for G. The policy makers in other words renege on all three elements (i)–(iii) described above. Given the punishment mechanism of the private sector reneging must be confined to non-reputational policies only. The cost-to-go following reneging is then

$$E_t(W_t^c) = \tfrac{1}{2} \operatorname{tr}\left(S z_t z_t^T + V^{CNR-SIM}\Sigma/(1 - \lambda)\right) \tag{44}$$

where S is as given in CNR-OPT and $V^{CNR-SIM}$ is the Lyapunov matrix for the non-reputational, simple rules (see Appendix 2 for details). The first term in (44) arises from the once-and-for-all calculation of a new non-reputational open-loop component of policy; the second term arises from the new feedback rule designed to deal with all future shocks.

The sustainability condition now becomes

$$\operatorname{tr}\left((V^{CR-SIM} - S)z_t z_t^T\right) < \operatorname{tr}\left((V^{CR-SIM} - V^{CNR-SIM})\Sigma/(1 - \lambda)\right) \tag{45}$$

by an analogous argument to that preceding (41). If policy is confined to *simple rules only*, with no open-loop component, then S in (44) and (45) must be replaced by $V^{CNR-SIM}$. Then the condition is

$$\operatorname{tr}\left((V^{CR-SIM} - V^{CNR-SIM})z_t z_t^T\right) < \operatorname{tr}\left((V^{CR-SIM} - V^{CNR-SIM})/\Sigma/(1 - \lambda)\right) \tag{46}$$

Similarly, the incentive to renege from CR-SIM to the other two regimes NCR-SIM and NCNR-SIM can be examined. Conditions analogous to (45) and (46) are obtained for both countries depending on whether policy is conducted in terms of optimal open-loop paths plus simple rules or in terms of rules only.

V   Results

V.1   Cooperation using simple rules

We first consider the performance of the four policy regimes CR-SIM, CNR-SIM, NCR-SIM and NCNR-SIM constructed in the form of particular feedback rules. We are particularly interested in first, the comparison of CR-SIM with CR-OPT which indicates the cost of simplicity in formulating rules for cooperation; second, the performance of NCR-SIM which indicates the scope for using simple rules as a surrogate for full international policy coordination.

All the simple rules reported focus on the stabilization problem only, where it is assumed the covariance matrix Σ of the disturbances is known. Regarding ε, we consider two extreme cases. The first is where disturbances are uncorrelated with equal variances set to unity, i.e. Σ is the unit matrix. The second case is where disturbances are perfectly correlated with unit variance, i.e.

$$\Sigma = \begin{bmatrix} 1 & \cdots & 1 \\ \vdots & & \vdots \\ 1 & \cdots & 1 \end{bmatrix}$$

We first consider simple *proportional* rules of the form

$$g_t = \alpha_1 q_{t-1} + \alpha_2 inf_{t-1}; \qquad g_t^* = \alpha_1^* q_{t-1}^* + \alpha_2^* inf_{t-1}^* \qquad (47a)$$

$$r_t = \beta_1 q_{t-1} + \beta_2 inf_{t-1}; \qquad r_t^* = \beta_1^* q_{t-1}^* + \beta_2^* inf_{t-1}^* \qquad (47b)$$

Table 11.1 shows the resulting 'quasi-optimal' rules with respect to parameters α_i, α_i^*, β_i, β_i^* of the form (47) for each of the four policy regimes CR-SIM, CNR-SIM, NCR-SIM, NCNR-SIM.[3] Table 11.3 gives the corresponding expected welfare losses which are compared with those for optimal rules in Table 11.2.

For regime CR-SIM we compare results for symmetrical rules ($\alpha_1 = \alpha_1^*$ etc.) with those where α_i, α_i^*, β_i and β_i^* are allowed to vary freely. It turns out that the underlying symmetry in the 2-bloc model together with the symmetry of the shocks results in the symmetry constraint having only a small effect (Table 11.1). For this reason we confine ourselves to symmetrical rules only for the non-reputational cooperative regime CNR-SIM. Non-cooperative regimes are computed without any symmetry constraint, but again the basic symmetry of the model results in approximately symmetrical outcomes.

The most striking feature of Tables 11.2 and 11.3 is that the rules, although

Table 11.1 Simple proportional rules 1a and 1b

$$g_t = \alpha_1 q_{t-1} + \alpha_2 inf_{t-1}; \quad g_t^* = \alpha_1^* q_{t-1}^* + \alpha_2^* inf_{t-1}^*$$
$$r_t = \beta_1 q_{t-1} + \beta_2 inf_{t-1}; \quad r_t^* = \beta_1^* q_{t-1}^* + \beta_2^* inf_{t-1}^*$$

	α_1	α_1^*	α_2	α_2^*	β_1	β_1^*	β_2	β_2^*
$\Sigma = \begin{bmatrix} 1 & \dots & 0 \\ & & \\ 0 & \dots & 1 \end{bmatrix}$; *Rules 1a*								
CR-SIM (symmetrical)	−0.54	−0.54	−0.48	−0.48	0.36	0.36	0.87	0.87
CR-SIM (asymmetrical)	−0.52	−0.54	−0.48	−0.47	0.42	0.31	0.86	0.87
CNR-SIM (symmetrical)	−0.60	−0.60	−0.54	−0.54	0.001	0.001	0.001	0.001
NCR-SIM	−0.43	−0.44	−0.35	−0.29	0.54	0.46	1.95	2.12
NCNR-SIM	−0.57	−0.58	−0.51	−0.53	0.001	0.001	0.001	0.001
$\Sigma = \begin{bmatrix} 1 & \dots & 1 \\ \vdots & & \vdots \\ 1 & \dots & 1 \end{bmatrix}$; *Rules 1b*								
CR-SIM (symmetrical)	−0.70	−0.70	−0.48	−0.48	0.08	0.08	0.95	0.95
CR-SIM (asymmetrical)	−0.69	−0.71	−0.49	−0.47	0.16	0.00	0.95	0.95
CNR-SIM (symmetrical)	−0.76	−0.76	−0.59	−0.59	0.001	0.001	0.001	0.001
NCR-SIM	−0.59	−0.60	−0.40	−0.36	0.29	0.17	2.17	2.35
NCNR-SIM	−0.67	−0.67	−0.50	−0.50	0.001	0.001	0.001	0.001

Table 11.2 Comparison of welfare losses under optimal rules

	No Control	CR-OPT	CNR-OPT	NCR-OPT	NCNR-OPT
$\Sigma = \begin{bmatrix} 1 & 0 \\ 0 & 1 \end{bmatrix}$					
Average	142	72	88	115	90
US	140	69	87	125	90
ROW	144	74	88	120	91
$\Sigma = \begin{bmatrix} 1 & \dots & 1 \\ 1 & \dots & 1 \end{bmatrix}$					
Average	242	143	175	248	173
US	239	142	177	255	173
ROW	244	144	174	252	172

Table 11.3 Comparison of welfare losses under simple rules

	No Control	CR-SIM		CNR-SIM	NCR-SIM	NCNR-SIM
		symmetrical	asymmetrical	symmetrical only		
$\Sigma = \begin{bmatrix} 1 & 0 \\ 0 & 1 \end{bmatrix}$						
Average	142	81	81	116	89	116
US	140	81	80	115	89	115
ROW	144	82	82	117	88	117
$\Sigma = \begin{bmatrix} 1 & \cdots & 1 \\ 1 & \cdots & 1 \end{bmatrix}$						
Average	242	150	150	187	177	189
US	239	151	150	187	181	191
ROW	244	148	149	187	172	186

extremely simple, yield cooperative outcomes reasonably close to the full optimal role. The gains from full optimal control, comparing 'no control' with CR-OPT, are 49 and 41% for uncorrelated and correlated shocks respectively. For CR-SIM these become 43 and 38% respectively. The costs of simplicity, when designing a cooperative rule with reputation, are not great assuming Σ is known.

However, when policy makers are restricted to non-reputational rules the costs of simplicity (in the form of rules (5.1)) become rather more substantial. To understand this result it is useful to consider an adjustment process which proceeds from CR-SIM to CNR-SIM with rules constrained to be of the form (47). This is shown in Table 11.4(a).

The regime CNR-SIM is characterized as a Nash equilibrium where policy-makers must take private sector forward-looking behaviour as given (in the sense described in Section 7 of Appendix 2) in calculating their optimal rules. In Table 11.4(a) a Cournot-adjustment process out of equilibrium is described. In the first iteration policy makers surprise the private sector, and with the private sector still believing in CNR-SIM the real exchange rate

Table 11.4(a)   Cournot-adjustment from CR-SIM to CNR-SIM

Player responding	Iteration	α_1	α_2	β_1	β_2	Welfare loss (average)
Regime						
CNR-SIM	0	−0.54	−0.48	0.36	0.36	81
US/ROW	1	−0.54	−0.46	0.001	0.001	74
Private Sector	2	−0.54	−0.46	0.001	0.001	116
US/ROW	3	−0.60	−0.54	0.001	0.001	116
Private Sector	4	−0.60	−0.54	0.001	0.001	116
US/ROW	5	−0.60	−0.54	0.001	0.001	116

and long-term interest rates remain frozen. Then given these private sector expectations, the optimal response of the two blocs acting collectively is to switch off monetary policy almost completely. (A minimal form of monetary control is necessary to keep the model on a uniquely determined saddlepath solution.) This lowers the welfare loss to 74. But in iteration 2 the private sector wakes up to what is happening and welfare deteriorates to a loss of 116. From that point the two policy makers, constrained by assumption to the particular simple rule, are locked into a Nash game where only fiscal policy is available. Further iterations result in only negligible changes to the best simple rule of the prescribed form.

Similarly, we describe a Cournot-adjustment from NCR-SIM to NCNR-SIM in Table 11.4(b). Now there are three players to consider. In iteration 1 the US can improve its position at the expense of the ROW provided the private sector continues to believe in NCR-SIM. In iteration 2 the ROW optimizes given the most recent revision of the US with the private sector believing in the rules in iteration 1. In iteration 3 the private sector assumes the rules in iteration 2 will operate indefinitely and the welfare gains from changing NCR-SIM disappear. Again both countries are now restricted to a Nash game with minimal monetary control and with an outcome very similar to CNR-SIM.

Now consider the gains from cooperation for the two blocs. For fully optimal rules with reputation these gains are substantial, as a comparison of CR-OPT and NCR-OPT in Table 11.2 reveals. Indeed for correlated shocks NCR-OPT yields worse results than no control for the two blocs aggregated together. When policy makers are restricted to simple rules of the form (47) with reputation, the relative gains from cooperation are considerably less. This result is of some significance if simple rules of a particular form are seen *in themselves* as a form of cooperation. In other words, suppose policy makers agree that policy must be conducted in the

Table 11.4(b) Cournot-adjustment from NCR-SIM to NCNR-SIM

Player responding	Iteration	α_1	α_2	β_1	β_2	α_1^*	α_2^*	β_1^*	α_2^*	Welfare loss US	Welfare loss ROW
Regime NCR-SIM	0	−0.43	−0.35	0.54	1.35	−0.44	−0.29	0.46	2.12	89	88
US/ROW	1	−0.44	0.29	0.001	0.001	−0.44	−0.29	0.46	2.12	66	90
ROW	2	−0.44	0.29	0.001	0.001	−0.40	−0.13	0.001	0.001	92	54
Private Sector	3	−0.44	0.29	0.001	0.001	−0.40	−0.13	0.001	0.001	116	117
US	4	−0.57	−0.51	0.001	0.001	−0.40	−0.13	0.001	0.001	115	116
ROW	5	−0.57	−0.51	0.001	0.001	−0.58	−0.53	0.001	0.001	115	117
Private Sector	6	−0.57	−0.51	0.001	0.001	−0.58	−0.53	0.001	0.001	115	117
US	7	−0.57	−0.51	0.001	0.001	−0.58	−0.53	0.001	0.001	115	117
ROW	8	−0.57	−0.51	0.001	0.001	−0.58	−0.53	0.001	0.001	115	117

form of rules (47) but that the feedback coefficients are left to the two blocs to be determined in an independent fashion. Our results suggest that this could be a reasonable 'second-best' form of cooperation; for comparing CR-OPT (the 'first-best' solution) with NCR-SIM, the gains from control drop from 49 to 37% for uncorrelated shocks and from 43 to 27% for correlated shocks.

It should be stressed that the best simple rules are only best with respect to a particular assumption about, or an estimate of, the covariance matrix of disturbances Σ. Quasi-optimal simple rules do not satisfy the property of certainty equivalence. For example, if only a single demand or supply shock actually occurs, then the rules CR-SIM reported in Table 11.1 are no longer the best rules of that form. This property is demonstrated in Tables 11.5(a) and (b) where the outcomes following single deterministic demand and supply shocks, and various combinations, are reported. There are now some cases where the performance of NCR-SIM is actually better than CR-SIM, namely for rule 1b (designed for correlated shocks), following single demand shocks in either bloc and for the bloc experiencing the shock.

Up to this point we have only considered persistent shocks which are AR(1) processes of the form (17) to (20) with $\mu_d = \mu_d^* = \mu_s = \mu_s^* = 0.9$. To assess the robustness of the simple rules further, we present simulations of permanent deterministic shocks in Tables 11.5(c) and (d) (i.e. $u_d = \mu_d^* = \mu_s = \mu_s^* = 1.0$). Again although CR-SIM rules 1a and 1b perform well compared with no control and non-reputational regimes, the superiority of NCR-SIM, rule 1b in the face of demand shocks is even more apparent. Comparing these results with those for optimal rules (Table 11.5(e)) strengthens the conclusion reached above, that 'cooperation' in the form of a commitment to a particular form of simple rule (47) (leaving feedback coefficients to be determined non-cooperatively) can be quite effective.

Turning to the full proportional-integral (P–I) rule of the form (37), the results of CR-SIM (symmetrical case) are shown in Table 11.6. The addition of integral control improves the outcome for uncorrelated shocks by a further 5% reduction in the welfare loss for both blocs. For correlated shocks the improvement is negligible. In view of the rather small improvement resulting from the addition of integral control we have not pursued P–I rules further in this paper.

Finally, we present results for the alternative rules 2 where real exchange rates are held fixed by monetary rules $r_t = -\beta e r_t$ and $r_t^* = \beta e r_t$. In effect these rules constitute a 'threat' which never occurs given the uncovered interest rate parity assumption of Minilink. Monetary policy is never operational, and real short-term and long-term interest rates and the real exchange rate remain at their long-run equilibria. There is now no time-inconsistency problem and CR-SIM is identical to CNR-SIM and

Table 11.5(a) Deterministic persistent shock: Rule 1a welfare losses

	No Control	CR-SIM	CNR-SIM	NCR-SIM	NCNR-SIM
$ad_0 = 1$					
Average	1.63	0.94	1.36	0.98	1.36
US	3.18	1.66	2.68	1.66	2.68
ROW	0.09	0.23	0.04	0.31	6.04
$ad_0^* = 1$					
Average	1.67	0.99	1.39	1.01	1.39
US	0.10	0.25	0.05	0.32	0.05
ROW	3.24	1.73	2.73	1.70	2.73
$as_0 = 1$					
Average	0.38	0.26	0.35	0.34	0.35
US	0.75	0.44	0.70	0.55	0.70
ROW	0.00	0.09	0.00	0.14	0.00
$as_0^* = 1$					
Average	0.40	0.24	0.38	0.31	0.38
US	0.00	0.09	0.00	0.14	0.00
ROW	0.80	0.39	0.76	0.49	0.76
$ad_0 = ad_0^* = 1$					
Average	4.40	3.02	3.47	3.17	3.47
US	4.42	3.04	3.49	3.12	3.49
ROW	4.37	3.01	3.45	3.13	3.46
$as_0 = as_0^* = 1$					
Average	0.85	0.63	0.74	0.85	0.74
US	0.82	0.63	0.71	0.87	0.71
ROW	0.88	0.63	0.76	0.83	0.76
$as_0 = as_0^* = ad_0 = ad_0^* = 1$					
Average	7.25	4.60	5.64	5.27	5.66
US	7.18	4.64	5.59	5.43	5.59
ROW	7.31	4.56	5.70	5.11	5.72

NCR-SIM to NCNR-SIM. The results for CR-SIM and NCR-SIM (proportional rules only) are shown in Table 11.7.

These results for both the rules and the welfare outcomes are very similar to those for the non-reputational rules of the previous type where monetary policy was minimal. The difference now is that the real exchange rate remains

Table 11.5(b) Deterministic persistent shock: Rule 1b welfare losses

	No Control	CR-SIM	CNR-SIM	NCR-SIM	NCNR-SIM
$ad_0 = 1$					
Average	1.63	0.96	1.38	0.95	1.36
US	3.18	1.72	2.71	1.63	2.68
ROW	0.09	0.21	0.04	0.28	0.04
$ad_0^* = 1$					
Average	1.67	1.00	1.40	0.99	1.31
US	0.10	0.22	0.05	0.28	0.05
ROW	3.24	1.77	2.75	1.69	2.73
$as_0 = 1$					
Average	0.38	0.31	0.35	0.31	0.35
US	0.75	0.48	0.71	0.64	0.70
ROW	0.00	0.15	0.00	0.19	0.00
$as_0^* = 1$					
Average	0.40	0.28	0.38	0.37	0.38
US	0.00	0.15	0.00	0.18	0.00
ROW	0.80	0.41	0.76	0.57	0.75
$ad_0 = ad_0^* = 1$					
Average	4.40	2.97	3.47	3.01	3.47
US	4.42	3.00	3.49	3.02	3.48
ROW	4.37	2.94	3.45	2.99	3.45
$as_0 = as_0^* = 1$					
Average	0.86	0.66	0.73	1.00	0.74
US	0.82	0.66	0.71	1.02	0.71
ROW	0.88	0.66	0.76	0.98	0.77
$as_0 = as_0^* = ad_0 = ad_0^* = 1$					
Average	7.25	4.49	5.66	5.30	5.63
US	7.18	4.54	5.56	5.44	5.57
ROW	7.31	4.45	5.67	5.17	5.69

at its long-run equilibrium for rule 2, whereas for rule 1 the minimal monetary rules are sufficient to give significant initial jumps in the face of asymmetrical shocks. On average since the covariance matrix Σ is symmetrical this feature of rule 1 cancels out and we are left with non-reputational rules which are almost identical to those of type 2.

Table 11.5(c)   Deterministic permanent shock: Rule 1a welfare losses

	No Control	CR-SIM	CNR-SIM	NCR-SIM	NCNR-SIM
$ad_0 = 1$					
Average	15.61	5.33	10.28	4.95	10.38
US	13.78	6.06	8.51	5.78	8.33
ROW	17.44	4.60	12.05	4.12	12.43
$ad_0^* = 1$					
Average	15.38	5.33	10.11	4.84	10.14
US	17.53	4.53	11.52	4.01	11.28
ROW	13.23	6.13	8.70	5.67	9.01
$as_0 = 1$					
Average	11.47	5.75	9.51	6.25	9.62
US	9.18	8.89	8.90	9.95	8.85
ROW	13.75	2.61	10.12	2.56	10.38
$as_0^* = 1$					
Average	10.78	5.15	8.81	5.63	8.70
US	13.12	2.41	9.29	2.57	9.04
ROW	8.44	7.88	8.34	8.70	8.37
$ad_0 = ad_0^* = 1$					
Average	60.14	20.10	38.88	18.16	39.16
US	61.39	20.36	38.78	18.64	37.96
ROW	58.88	19.84	38.97	17.68	40.36
$as_0 = as_0^* = 1$					
Average	26.89	14.12	21.13	15.57	21.25
US	27.16	14.38	20.79	16.31	20.31
ROW	25.61	13.87	21.47	14.83	22.19
$as_0 = as_0^* = ad_0 = ad_0^* = 1$					
Average	150.22	52.05	101.08	51.01	101.85
US	153.11	53.19	100.21	53.97	97.60
ROW	147.32	50.92	101.94	48.05	106.09

V.2   The sustainability of regime CR-SIM

Consider first the sustainability of the simple cooperative rule when faced
with an incentive to renege collectively on the private sector. This requires
a comparison of CR-SIM with CNR-SIM if the blocs are constrained to

Table 11.5(d) Deterministic permanent shock: Rule 1b welfare losses

	No Control	CR-SIM	CNR-SIM	NCR-SIM	NCNR-SIM
$ad_0 = 1$					
Average	15.61	5.45	10.07	4.85	10.28
US	13.78	6.61	8.31	5.82	8.24
ROW	17.44	4.28	11.83	3.88	12.32
$ad_0^* = 1$					
Average	15.38	5.45	9.88	4.78	10.03
US	17.53	4.21	11.29	3.69	11.15
ROW	13.23	6.70	8.48	5.87	8.90
$as_0 = 1$					
Average	11.47	6.74	9.85	7.17	9.95
US	9.18	9.32	9.01	11.04	8.94
ROW	13.75	4.16	10.69	3.30	10.95
$as_0^* = 1$					
Average	10.78	5.96	9.13	6.46	9.01
US	13.12	3.83	9.81	3.22	9.57
ROW	8.44	8.09	8.46	9.70	8.45
$ad_0 = ad_0^* = 1$					
Average	60.14	20.40	37.98	17.62	38.72
US	61.39	20.64	37.89	17.90	37.51
ROW	58.88	20.16	38.07	17.33	39.94
$ad_0 = as_0^* = 1$					
Average	26.89	14.67	21.03	17.37	21.41
US	27.16	14.58	20.68	18.10	20.49
ROW	26.61	13.96	21.37	16.64	22.33
$as_0 = as_0^* = ad_0 = ad_0^* = 1$					
Average	150.22	50.64	98.99	52.14	101.33
US	153.11	51.71	98.14	54.87	97.14
ROW	147.32	49.56	99.85	49.41	105.52

pursue simple rules and with CNR-OPT if they are not. For all the results reported in Tables 11.8(a) and (b), 1,000 stochastic simulations of the sustainability condition were undertaken. For the switch from CR-SIM to CNR-OPT the tables indicate that an incentive to renege exists for only 1% of cases for uncorrelated shocks and 5% for correlated shocks. With the

Table 11.5(e)   Deterministic permanent shock: Optimal rule welfare losses

	No Control	CR-SIM	CNR-SIM	NCR-SIM	NCNR-SIM
$ad_0 = 1$					
Average	15.61	4.55	8.89	8.40	8.13
US	13.78	4.91	8.65	8.60	7.66
ROW	17.44	4.18	9.13	8.20	8.60
$ad_0^* = 1$					
Average	15.38	4.56	8.70	9.95	8.00
US	17.53	4.11	8.21	7.86	7.61
ROW	13.23	5.00	9.20	8.04	8.39
$as_0 = 1$					
Average	11.47	5.36	6.80	6.82	6.50
US	9.18	9.37	9.81	11.06	9.13
ROW	13.75	1.35	3.80	2.59	3.86
$as_0^* = 1$					
Average	10.78	4.84	6.29	6.27	5.98
US	13.12	1.47	3.66	2.67	3.63
ROW	8.44	8.21	8.93	9.87	8.32
$ad_0 = ad_0^* = 1$					
Average	60.14	17.1	34.0	31.5	31.1
US	61.39	17.3	32.9	32.2	29.8
ROW	58.88	16.8	35.0	30.9	32.3
$as_0 = as_0^* = 1$					
Average	26.89	13.5	18.8	19.5	17.3
US	27.16	14.3	19.1	20.1	17.5
ROW	26.61	12.7	18.5	18.5	17.1
$as_0 = as_0^* = ad_0 = ad_0^* = 1$					
Average	150.22	46.5	87.4	84.0	78.5
US	153.11	49.1	86.8	87.3	77.2
ROW	147.32	44.0	87.9	80.7	79.7

simplicity constraint these values drop to 0 and 2–4% respectively, the latter figure depending on whether reneging involves a recalculation of the open-loop component of policy or not.

Sustainability for the two blocs as a whole does not then appear to be a major problem. There is a small probability that a particular combination

Table 11.6 Proportional-integral CR rule (symmetrical)

$\Delta g_t = \alpha_1 \Delta q_{t-1} + \alpha_2 \Delta \pi_{t-1} + \alpha_3 q_{t-1} + \alpha_4 \pi_{t-1}$

$\Delta r_t = \beta_1 \Delta q_{t-1} + \beta_2 \Delta \pi_{t-1} + \beta_3 q_{t-1} + \beta_4 \pi_{t-1}$

	α_1	α_2	α_3	α_4	β_1	β_2	β_3	β_4	Welfare loss US	Welfare loss ROW
$\Sigma = \begin{bmatrix} 1 & 0 \\ 0 & 1 \end{bmatrix}$	−0.54	−0.45	−0.006	0.0	0.16	0.38	0.028	0.015	77.37	149.8
$\Sigma = \begin{bmatrix} 1 & \cdots & 1 \\ 1 & \cdots & 1 \end{bmatrix}$	−0.69	−0.45	−0.04	0.00	0.07	0.94	0.0	0.07	149.2	149.8

Table 11.7 Simple proportional rules 2a and 2b

	α_1	α_1^*	α_2	α_2^*	β	Welfare loss US	Welfare loss ROW
$\Sigma = \begin{bmatrix} 1 & \cdots & 0 \\ : & & : \\ 0 & \cdots & 1 \end{bmatrix}$; Rule 2a							
CR-SIM (symmetrical)	−0.60	−0.60	−0.54	−0.54	−1.0	117	120
NCR-SIM	−0.58	−0.59	−0.52	−0.54	−1.0	117	120
$\Sigma = \begin{bmatrix} 1 & \cdots & 1 \\ : & & : \\ 1 & \cdots & 1 \end{bmatrix}$; Rule 2b							
CR-SIM (symmetrical)	−0.76	−0.76	−0.59	−0.50	−1.0	185	189
NCR-SIM	−0.67	−0.67	−0.50	−0.50	−1.0	186	190

of shocks will create an incentive to renege. This will influence private sector expectations, a feature which may be modelled more formally. But as long as the probability of a policy switch remains small, the reported outcomes for CR-SIM which assume credibility (with probability unity) are approximately correct. Another feature of the results reported is that the sustainability of the simple cooperative rule is more likely than that of CR-OPT (a result obtained in Levine, 1988).

Table 11.8(a) **Sustainability in stochastic equilibrium: Uncorrelated disturbances**

Regime 1	Regime 2	Country	Cases where sustainability holds (%)
CR-OPT	CNR-OPT	aggregate	97
CR-SIM	NCR-SIM	1	99
	(with O.L. component)	2	99
CR-SIM	NCR-SIM	1	100
	(feedback rule only)	2	100
CR-SIM	CNR-OPT	aggregate	99
CR-SIM	NCNR-OPT	1	89
		2	90
CR-SIM	CNR-SIM	aggregate	100
	(with O.L. component)		
CR-SIM	CNR-SIM	aggregate	100
	(feedback rule only)		
CR-SIM	NCNR-SIM	1	100
	(with O.L. component)	2	99
CR-SIM	NCNR-SIM	1	96
	(feedback rule only)	2	98

Table 11.8(b) **Sustainability in stochastic equilibrium: Correlated disturbances**

Regime 1	Regime 2	Country	Cases where sustainability holds (%)
CR-OPT	CNR-OPT	aggregate	92
CR-SIM	NCR-SIM	1	99
	(with O.L. Component)	2	100
CR-SIM	NCR-SIM	1	100
	(feedback rule only)	2	100
CR-SIM	CNR-OPT	aggregate	95
CR-SIM	NCNR-OPT	1	83
		2	91
CR-SIM	CNR-SIM	aggregate	96
	(with O.L. component)		
CR-SIM	CNR-SIM	aggregate	98
	(feedback rule only)		
CR-SIM	NCNR-SIM	1	93
	(with O.L. component)	2	98
CR-SIM	NCNR-SIM	1	93
	(feedback rule only)	2	100

Consider next the incentive for the blocs to renege on each other. Now we have to consider a possible switch from CR-SIM to NCR-SIM, NCR-OPT, NCNR-SIM or NCNR-OPT. Furthermore, the incentive to renege must be considered for either bloc.

Given the poor performance of NCR-OPT the possible switch to this regime is rather unlikely so we concentrate on the remaining three non-cooperative regimes. Of these only the possibility of reneging from CR-SIM to NCNR-OPT poses a problem. Within the constraint of the simple rules adopted, the probability of sustainability breaking down is small. If the complex rules implied by regime NCNR-OPT are feasible options, however, then the possibility of reneging becomes significant. In this case the rational expectations solutions of the system under control must take into account the significant probability of policy switches which requires a reworking of the analysis of sustainability.

VI Conclusions

This paper has developed and applied a general methodology for analysing the sustainability of international policy agreements in the form of simple rules. A number of objections to the use of feedback rules for the purposes of macroeconomic stabilization have been addressed.

Above all we have demonstrated empirically that policy coordination can be effective under the constraint that rules must be simple. Second, we have shown that there is considerable scope for using agreements in the form of simple rules as a surrogate for more far-reaching agreement on international policy coordination. Finally, we have shown that simple rules are sustainable; indeed, simplicity in policy design may actually improve the prospects of sustainability.

Future work will apply the methodology to an appraisal of other proposals for internationally coordinated policy rules, such as the target zone proposals of Williamson and Miller (1987), using a more developed multi-country model. The need for policy rules which are *robust* with respect to model misspecification will also be addressed.[4]

Appendix 1: Parameter values for Minilink

Table 11A.1   Parameter values for Minilink

	US		ROW
b_1	−0.0412		
b_2	0.1125		
b_3	−0.1863		
b_{11}	−1.577		
b_{12}	1.936		
b_{13}	0.856		
b_{14}	−0.215		
c_1	−0.573	c_1^*	−0.247
c_2	0.285	c_2^*	0.285
c_3	0.633	c_3^*	0.383
c_4	−0.127	c_4^*	0.124
c_5	0.158	c_5^*	0.140
c_{11}	0.754	c_{11}^*	0.721
c_{12}	0.246	c_{12}^*	0.279
c_{13}	0.952	c_{13}^*	0.952
c_{41}	1.413	c_{41}^*	1.194
c_{42}	−0.657	c_{42}^*	−0.447
c_{43}	0.245	c_{43}^*	0.253
d_1	0.5	d_1^*	0.5
d_2	0.0496	d_2^*	0.0496
d_3	0.945	d_3^*	0.907
a	0.01	a^*	0.01
b	0.01	b^*	0.01
c	0.005	d^*	0.005
d	0.005	e^*	0.005
λ	0.97	λ^*	0.97
μ_d	0.9	μ_d^*	0.9
μ_s	0.9	μ_s^*	0.9

Appendix 2: Details of regimes

1   The set up

The two-country model in the paper can be written in the following general form

$$\begin{bmatrix} z_{t+1} \\ x_{t+1,t}^e \end{bmatrix} = A \begin{bmatrix} z_t \\ x_t \end{bmatrix} + B \begin{bmatrix} w_t \\ w_t^* \end{bmatrix} + \begin{bmatrix} u_t \\ 0 \end{bmatrix} \tag{A1}$$

where z_t is an $(n - m) \times 1$ vector of predetermined variables, x_t is an $m \times 1$ vector of non-predetermined variables, $x_{t+1,t}^e$ denotes rational expectations of x_{t+1} formed at time t on the basis of the information set $I_t = \{z_s, x_s; s \leq t\}$ and knowledge of the model (A1), w_t and w_t^* are $r \times 1$ vectors of control instruments (* indicating the instruments for 'country' or 'bloc' 2), u_t is an $(n - m) \times 1$ vector of white noise disturbances independently distributed with $u_t \sim N(0, \Sigma)$, A, B (and C, D in (A2)) and Σ have time-invariant coefficients and Σ is symmetric and non-negative definite. The initial conditions at $t = 0$ are given by z_0. All variables are measured as deviations from some long-run trend. Further outputs of interest are given by

$$y_t = C\begin{bmatrix} z_t \\ x_t \end{bmatrix} + D\begin{bmatrix} w_t \\ w_t^* \end{bmatrix} \tag{A2}$$

Let $s_t = \begin{bmatrix} z_t \\ x_t \end{bmatrix}$ be the full state vector in (A1). Then the expected welfare loss for country 1 at $t = 0$ is given by $E_0(W_0)$ where

$$W_0 = \sum_{t=0}^{\infty} \lambda^t [y_t^T Q_1 y_t + w_t^T Q_2 w_t] \tag{A3}$$

which we rewrite as

$$W_0 = \sum_{t=0}^{\infty} \lambda^t [s_t^T Q s_t + 2 s_t^T U \begin{bmatrix} w_t \\ w_t^* \end{bmatrix} + [w_t^T w_t^{*T}] \begin{bmatrix} R_{11} & 0 \\ 0 & R_{22} \end{bmatrix} \begin{bmatrix} w_t \\ w_t^* \end{bmatrix}] \tag{A4}$$

where $Q = C^T Q_1 C$, $U = C^T Q_1 D$, $R_{11} = Q_2 + D_1^T Q_1 D$, $R_{22} = D_2^T Q_1 D_2$, $D = [D_1 D_2]$ partitioned conformably with w_t and w_t^*, Q_1 and Q_2 are symmetric and non-negative definite. R is required to be positive definite and $\lambda \in (0, 1)$ is a discount factor. A similar expression gives $E_0(W_0^*)$, the expected welfare loss for country 2 with Q_1^*, Q_2^*, Q^*, U^*, R^* and λ^* replacing their unstarred counterparts.

2   The cooperative optimal policy with reputation (CR-OPT)

We take as the joint welfare loss a linear combination of the individual countries' welfare losses, i.e. $E_0(W_0^c)$ where

$$W_0^c = \frac{1}{2} \sum_{i=0}^{\infty} \lambda^t [s_t^T s_t + 2 s_t^T U_c \begin{bmatrix} w_t \\ w_t^* \end{bmatrix} + [w_t^T w_t^{*T}] R_c \begin{bmatrix} w_t \\ w_t^* \end{bmatrix}] \tag{A5}$$

where $\lambda = \lambda^*$ is assumed and $Q_c = \alpha Q + (1 - \alpha) Q^*$, $U_c = \alpha U + (1 - \alpha) U^*$ and $R_c = \alpha R + (1 - \alpha) R^*$. The control problem is then to minimize $E_0(W_0^c)$ with respect to $\begin{bmatrix} w_t \\ w_t^* \end{bmatrix}$ subject to (A1). The details of the solution are given in Levine (1988) and for a slightly less general set-up in Currie, Levine and Vidalis (1987). The outline solution is

$$\begin{bmatrix} w_t \\ w_t^* \end{bmatrix} = -(R^c + B^T S B)^{-1}(B^T S A + U_c^T)s_t \qquad (A6)$$

$$= -F s_t$$

say, where S is a solution to the Riccati matrix equation:

$$S = Q_c - U_c F - F^T U_c^T + F^T R_c F + (A - BF)^T S(A - BF) \qquad (A7)$$

If we define N by

$$N = -\begin{bmatrix} S_{11} - S_{12} S_{22}^{-1} S_{21} & S_{12} S_{22}^{-1} \\ -S_{22}^{-1} S_{21} & S_{22}^{-1} \end{bmatrix} \qquad (A8)$$

where S has been partitioned so that S_{11} is $(n - m) \times (n - m)$ and S_{22} is $m \times m$, then we have that

$$\begin{bmatrix} w_t \\ w_t^* \end{bmatrix} = F \begin{bmatrix} -I & 0 \\ N_{21} & N_{22} \end{bmatrix} \begin{bmatrix} z_t \\ p_{2t} \end{bmatrix} = G \begin{bmatrix} z_t \\ p_{2t} \end{bmatrix} \qquad (A9)$$

say, where

$$\begin{bmatrix} z_{t+1} \\ p_{2t+1} \end{bmatrix} = T[A - BF]T^{-1} \begin{bmatrix} z_t \\ p_{2t} \end{bmatrix} + \begin{bmatrix} u_t \\ 0 \end{bmatrix} \qquad (A10)$$

is the saddlepath of the system under control.

$$T = \begin{bmatrix} I & 0 \\ S_{21} & S_{22} \end{bmatrix} \qquad (A11)$$

and the free variables x_t are given by

$$x_t = -[N_{21} N_{22}] \begin{bmatrix} z_t \\ p_{2t} \end{bmatrix} \qquad (A12)$$

The initial conditions in (A10) are z_0 as given and $p_{20} = 0$.

Equation (A9) expresses the cooperative, optimal policy in feedback form. Putting $H = T[A - BF]T^{-1}$ in (A10) and partitioning, we have

$$p_{2t+1} = H_{21} z_t + H_{22} p_{2t} \qquad (A13)$$

from which (A9) may be written as

$$\begin{bmatrix} w_t \\ w_t^* \end{bmatrix} = G_1 z_t + G_2 H_{21} \sum_{\tau=1}^{t} (H_{22})^{\tau-1} z_{t-\tau} \qquad (A14)$$

where $G = [G_1 \ G_2]$, partitioned conformably with z_t and p_{2t}. The rule then consists of a feedback on the lagged predetermined variables with geometrically declining weights with lags extending back to time $t = 0$, the time of the formulation and announcement of the policy. (It should be noted that $(z_{t-i}; \ i \geq 0)$ is part of the assumed information set I_t at time t.)

The expected welfare loss from time t onwards (the 'cost-to-go') is given by

$$E_t(W_t^C) = -\tfrac{1}{2} \operatorname{tr}(N_{11}(z_t z_t^T + \Sigma/(1-\lambda)) + N_{22} p_{2t} p_{2t}^T) \tag{A15}$$

3 Cooperative simple rules with reputation (CR-SIM)

In the paper simple rules are examined, which in their most general form are proportional-integral rules

$$\begin{bmatrix} \Delta w_t \\ \Delta w_t^* \end{bmatrix} = G \begin{bmatrix} \Delta y_t \\ y_t \end{bmatrix} = [G_1 G_2] \begin{bmatrix} \Delta y_t \\ y_t \end{bmatrix} \tag{A16}$$

where $\Delta w_t = w_t - w_{t-1}$ etc. and G is constrained to give the rule a particular assignment of instruments to targets. From (A2), (A16) may be rewritten as

$$\begin{bmatrix} w_t \\ w_t^* \end{bmatrix} = [I - (G_1 + G_2)D]^{-1} [(G_1 + G_2)C, -G_1 C, I - (G_1 + G_2)D] \begin{bmatrix} s_t \\ s_{t-1} \\ w_{t-1} \end{bmatrix} \tag{A17}$$

Augmenting the state vector in (A1) (adding s_{t-1} and w_{t-1}), (A17) may be written as a proportional rule on state variables. Without loss of generality, therefore, we may consider proportional rules of the form

$$\begin{bmatrix} w_t \\ w_t^* \end{bmatrix} = G \begin{bmatrix} z_t \\ x_t \end{bmatrix} = G s_t \tag{A18}$$

in conjunction with a model of the form (A1).

Substituting (A18) into (A1), (A5) becomes

$$W_0^c = \tfrac{1}{2} \sum_{t=0}^{\infty} \lambda^t s_t^T P s_t \tag{A19}$$

where $P = Q_c + U_c G + G^T U_c^T + G^T R_c G$. The system under control is

$$\begin{bmatrix} z_{t+1} \\ x_{t+1,t}^e \end{bmatrix} = [A + BG] \begin{bmatrix} z_t \\ x_t \end{bmatrix} + \begin{bmatrix} u_t \\ 0 \end{bmatrix} \tag{A20}$$

which has a rational expectations solution with saddlepath $x_t = -N z_t$ where $N = N(G)$ (Blanchard and Kahn, 1980). Hence

$$s_t^T P s_t = z_t^T (P_{11} - N^T P_{21} - P_{12} N + N^T P_{22} N) z_t \tag{A21}$$
$$= z_t^T T z_t$$

say, where P is partitioned conformably with $s_t = \begin{bmatrix} z_t \\ x_t \end{bmatrix}$. Write $J = A + BG$ and partition as for P. Then along the saddlepath we have

$$z_{t+1} = (J_{11} - J_{12}N)z_t + u_t \tag{A22}$$

It is now a standard result (see, for example, Levine, 1988) that the expected welfare loss from time t onwards is

$$E_t(W_t) = \tfrac{1}{2}\operatorname{tr}(V(z_t z_t^T + \Sigma/(1-\lambda))) \tag{A23}$$

where V satisfies the *Lyapunov Equation*

$$V = T + K^T V K \tag{A24}$$

where $K = \lambda^{\frac{1}{2}}(J_{11} - J_{12}N)$.

At time $t = 0$ the expected welfare loss may be decomposed into

$$E(W_0) = \bar{W}_0 + E_0(\tilde{W}_0) \tag{A25}$$

where $\bar{W}_0 = \tfrac{1}{2}\operatorname{tr}(V z_0 z_0^T)$ is the deterministic component of the welfare loss in the absence of any future shocks and $E_0(\tilde{W}_0) = \tfrac{1}{2}\operatorname{tr}(V\Sigma/(1-\lambda))$ is the stochastic component arising from future unanticipated shocks with known covariance $\operatorname{cov}(u_t) = \Sigma$. Corresponding to this decomposition we may write

$$\begin{bmatrix} w_t \\ w_t^* \end{bmatrix} = \begin{bmatrix} \bar{w}_t \\ \bar{w}_t^* \end{bmatrix} + \begin{bmatrix} \tilde{w}_t \\ \tilde{w}_t^* \end{bmatrix} \tag{A26}$$

for the policy design. The first term in (A26) is the open-loop component of policy formulated at $t = 0$ which we shall take as the optimal path given by (A9) and (A10) with $u_t = 0$. The second term is the stochastic component for which the simple feedback rule is appropriate. Thus the simple rule will stabilize the economy about its optimal open-loop trajectory in the face of unanticipated future shocks.

The optimal simple rule is found by minimizing $E_0(\tilde{W}_0)$ with respect to the non-zero elements of G given Σ. This is implemented by a standard numerical technique (see Gaines, al-Nowaihi and Levine, 1987). An important feature of the optimal simple rule is that unlike the optimal unconstrained rule it is dependent on Σ, i.e. *certainty equivalence* does not apply (see Levine and Currie, 1987b, for a detailed discussion of this point).

4   The non-cooperative equilibrium under optimal rules with reputation (NCR-OPT)

In Currie, Levine and Vidalis (1987) an NCR regime is used which is *open-loop* in character. Since this paper is concerned with comparing feedback rules, we now examine, as an alternative, a *closed-loop* form of NCR.

Suppose country 1 assumes $w_t^* = 0$ (no control) or some other initial rule and calculates an optimal rule with reputation. Following the analysis in the CR-OPT regime this will take the form

$$w_t = G\begin{bmatrix} z_t \\ p_{2t} \end{bmatrix} \tag{A27}$$

with

$$p_{2t+1} = H_{21}z_t + H_{22}p_{2t} \tag{A28}$$

and $p_{20} = 0$. Now consider the response of country 2 which faces a system under control of the form

$$\begin{bmatrix} z_{t+1} \\ p_{2t+1} \\ x^e_{t+1,t} \end{bmatrix} = \begin{bmatrix} A_{11} + E_{11} \\ H_{21} \\ A_{21} + E_{21} \end{bmatrix} \begin{bmatrix} E_{12} & A_{12} \\ H_{22} & 0 \\ E_{22} & A_{22} \end{bmatrix} \begin{bmatrix} z_t \\ p_{2t} \\ x_t \end{bmatrix} + B_2 w^*_t \tag{A29}$$

where $E = B_1 G$ is partitioned as for A. The optimal response will now be a rule of the form

$$w^*_t = G^* \begin{bmatrix} z_t \\ p_{2t} \\ p^*_{2t} \end{bmatrix} \tag{A30}$$

$$p^*_{2t+1} = H^*_{21} \begin{bmatrix} z_t \\ p_{2t} \end{bmatrix} + H_{22} p^*_{2t} \tag{A31}$$

and $p^*_{20} = 0$.

Now replace the initial rule of country 2 with (A30) and recalculate w_t for country 1. The new optimal response will be of the form

$$w_t = G \begin{bmatrix} z_t \\ p_{2t} \\ p^*_{2t} \\ \hat{p}_{2t} \end{bmatrix} \tag{A32}$$

p_{2t} is then up-dated with $\hat{p}_{2t}$ and country 2 responds in a similar way. Iterating in this fashion we arrive at stationary rules of the form

$$w_t = G \begin{bmatrix} z_t \\ p_{2t} \\ p^*_{2t} \end{bmatrix} : \quad w^*_t = G^* \begin{bmatrix} z_t \\ p_{2t} \\ p^*_{2t} \end{bmatrix} \tag{A33}$$

provided the algorithm converges. For Minilink and other models we have found no problem with convergence. The expected welfare losses in equilibrium are then given by an expression analogous to (A15) for both countries.

5 The non-cooperative equilibrium under simple rules with reputation (NCR-SIM)

As for (NCR-OPT) suppose country 1 assumes w^*_t and calculates a simple rule of the form (A18). Then country 2 faces a system under control

$$\begin{bmatrix} z_{t+1} \\ x^e_{t+1,t} \end{bmatrix} = [A + B_1 G]\begin{bmatrix} z_t \\ x_t \end{bmatrix} + B_2 w^*_t + u_t \tag{A34}$$

and responds with its optimal simple rule

$$w^*_t = G^* s_t \tag{A35}$$

Iterating in this fashion and assuming convergence we arrive at a Nash closed-loop equilibrium. As for CR-SIM we shall assume that the feedback component of policy applies to stochastic deviations about the open-loop component of NCR-OPT.

6   The cooperative optimal policy without reputation (CNR-OPT)

As for CR-OPT we only give the outline solution. This is given by the iterative scheme

$$J_t = -(A_{22} + N_{t+1}A_{21})^{-1}(N_{t+1}A_{11} + A_{21}) \tag{A36}$$

$$K_t = -(A_{22} + N_{t+1}A_{21})^{-1}(N_{t+1}B^1 + B^2) \tag{A37}$$

$$N_t = -J_t + K_t F_t \tag{A38}$$

$$F_t = (\bar{R}_t + \lambda \bar{B}^T_t S_{t+1}\bar{B}_t)(\bar{U}_t + \lambda \bar{B}^T_t S_{t+1}\bar{A}_t) \tag{A39}$$

$$\bar{Q}_t = Q_{11} + J^T_t Q_{21} + Q_{12}J_t + J^T_t Q_{22}J_t \tag{A40}$$

$$\bar{U}_t = U^1 + Q_{12}K_t + J^T_t U^2 + J^T_t Q_{22}J_t \tag{A41}$$

$$\bar{R}_t = R + K^T_t Q_{22}K_t + U^{2T}K_t + K^T_t U^2 \tag{A42}$$

$$S_t = \bar{Q}_t - \bar{U}_t F_t - F^T_t \bar{U}^T_t + F^T_t \bar{R}_t F_t + \lambda(\bar{A}_t - \bar{B}_t F)^T S_{t+1}(\bar{A}_t - \bar{B}_t F_t) \tag{A43}$$

where, to ease the notational burden, the subscript c has been dropped in C_c, U_c and R_c. If these converge to stationary values J, K, N, F, $\bar{Q}$, $\bar{U}$, $\bar{R}$ and S then the solution is given by

$$w_t = -F z_t \tag{A44}$$

$$x_t = -N z_t \tag{A45}$$

where

$$z_{t+1} = [A_{11} + A_{12}J - (B^1 + A_{12}K)F]z_t + u_t \tag{A46}$$

with z_0 given. The expected welfare loss from time t onwards is given by

$$E_t(W_t) = \tfrac{1}{2}\operatorname{tr}(S(z_t z^T_t + \Sigma/(1-\lambda)) \tag{A47}$$

7   Cooperative simple rules without reputation (CNR-SIM)

Consider a rule of the form (A18). In CR-SIM a saddlepath solution takes the form

$$x_t = -N(G)z_t \tag{A48}$$

policy makers with reputation can exploit this reaction function and so exercise *Stackelberg leadership*. For no reputation we propose a *Nash equilibrium* in which policy makers must take N as given.

In this Nash equilibrium we have $N = f(G)$, $G = g(\Sigma, N)$ with N given by the fixed point of f. g (given Σ). This can be arrived at iteratively as follows. The countries begin by assuming that $N = N_0$ is given. Then from the second stage of the CR-SIM solution an optimal simple rule can be found with $G_0 = g(\Sigma, N_0)$. Then the private sector response puts the system on the saddlepath $N_1 = f(G_0)$. The rule is then updated to $G_1 = g(\Sigma, N_1)$ and the iteration continues between the policy makers (together) and the private sector until convergence.

8 Non-cooperative equilibria without reputation (NCNR-OPT and NCNR-SIM)

Regimes NCNR-OPT and NCNR-SIM are Nash equilibria found by iterating between the two policy makers together and the private sector in a Cournot-like adjustment process.

For the case of two countries acting independently we now have three players. There are a number of ways in which the iteration may now proceed. The method we chose is to pass from country 1 to the private sector to country 2 to the private sector and so on. Then given initial values for D, D^* and N, provided the iteration converges, we arrive at the NCNR-OPT and NCNR-SIM equilibria. We have not investigated the convergence properties of the sequences in 7 and 8 but we have not experienced any problems even for quite arbitrary initial values.

9 The asymptotic covariance matrix for state variables

We require, for the sustainability analysis, the asymptotic variance of a system of predetermined variables under control satisyfing

$$z_{t+1} = Bz_t + u_t \tag{A49}$$

(see (A10) for example). From (A49) we have

$$z_{t+1}z_{t+1}^T = Bz_t z_t^T B^T + u_t z_t^T B^T + Bz_t u_t^T + u_t u_t^T$$

Taking expectations and using $E_t(u_t u_{t-s}) = 0$, $s > 0$, $E_t(z_t z_t^T) = V_t$ satisfies

$$V_{t+1} = BV_t B^T + \text{cov}(u_t) \tag{A50}$$

Thus in stochastic equilibrium $v = \text{asyvar}(z_t)$ satisfies

$$V = BVB^T + \Sigma \tag{A51}$$

where $\Sigma = \text{cov}(u_t)$. Equation (A51) is the Lyapunov equation.

Notes

1 This assumes that the private sector punishes reneging by the government by withdrawing belief in government announcements about future policy actions. This is the type of punishment mechanism assumed by Barro and Gordon (1983) except that in contrast to their one-period punishment we assume an infinite punishment period. Future work will investigate finite punishment periods.

2 See Currie and Levine (1987).

3 The 'bargaining' weight α is chosen to be $\frac{1}{2}$ throughout this paper.

4 See Christodoulakis, Kemball-Cook and Levine (1988) for a theoretical investigation of robust rules.

References

Barro, R. and D. Gordon (1983) 'Rules, Discretion and Reputation in a Model of Monetary Policy', *Journal of Monetary Economics*, 101–21.

Blanchard, O. and C. Kahn (1980) 'The solution of linear difference models under Rational Expectations', *Econometrica* **48**, 1305–09.

Bryant, R. and R. Portes (1987) *Global Macroeconomics: Policy Conflict and Cooperation*, Macmillan, London.

Buiter, W. and R. Marston (1985) *International Economic Policy Co-ordination*, Cambridge University Press, Cambridge.

Christodoulakis, N., D. Kemball-Cook and P. Levine (1988) 'Model Uncertainty and Policy Design', CEF Discussion Paper NO. 04–88, London Business School.

Cooper, R. (1985) 'Economic Interdependence and Co-ordination of Economic Policies', in R.W. Jones and P.B. Kenen, eds., *Handbook of International Economics*, Volume 2, North-Holland, Amsterdam.

Currie, D.A. and P. Levine (1985a) 'Macroeconomic Policy Design in an Interdependent World', in W. Buiter and R. Marston, eds., *International Economic Policy Coordination*, Cambridge University Press.

Currie, D.A. and P. Levine (1985b) 'Simple Macroeconomic Policy Rules in an Open Economy', *Economic Journal*, **85**, 60–70.

Currie, D.A. and P. Levine (1987) 'Credibility and Time Consistency in a Stochastic World', *Journal of Economics* **47**, 225–52.

Currie, D.A. and S. Wren-Lewis (1988) 'Evaluating the Extended Target Zone Proposal for the G3', Centre for Economic Policy Research Discussion Paper No. 221.

Currie, D.A., P. Levine and N. Vidalis (1987) 'International Cooperation and Reputation in an Empirical Two-Bloc Model', in R.C. Bryant and R. Portes (eds.), *Global Macroeconomics: Policy Conflict and Cooperation*, Macmillan.

Edison, H., M. Miller and J. Williamson (1987) 'On evaluating and extending the Target Zone Proposal', *The Journal of Policy Modeling* **9**, 199–224.

Gaines, J., A. al-Nowaihi and P. Levine (1987) 'An Optimal Control Package for Rational Expectations Models', CEF Discussion Paper no. 18–87, London Business School.

Hamada, K. (1979) 'Macroeconomic Strategy and Coordination under Alternative Exchange Rates', in R. Dornbusch and J.A. Frenkel (eds.) *International Economic Policy*, The Johns Hopkins Press, Baltimore.

Levine, P. (1988) 'Does Inconsistency Matter?', Centre for Economic Policy Research Discussion Paper No. 227.

Levine, P. and D.A. Currie (1987a) 'Does International Macroeconomic Policy Coordination Pay and is it Sustainable?: A Two Country Analysis', *Oxford Economic Papers* **39**, 38–74.

Levine, P. and D.A. Currie (1987b) 'The Design of Feedback Rules in Linear Stochastic Rational Expectations Models', *Journal of Economic Dynamics and Control* **11**, 1–28.

Masson, P., A. Blundell-Wignall and P. Richardson (1984) 'Domestic and International Effects of Government Spending under Rational Expectations', *OECD Economic Studies*, 177–90.

Pearlman, P., D.A. Currie and P. Levine (1986) 'Rational Expectations Models with Partial Information', *Economic Modelling* **3**, 90–105.

Taylor, J. (1985) 'International Co-ordination in the Design of Macroeconomic Policy Rules', *European Economic Review* **28**, 53–81

Vines, D., J.M. Maciejowski and J.E. Meade (1983) '*Stagflation*', Vol. 2, *Demand Management*, George Allen & Unwin.

Williamson, J. and M. Miller (1987) 'Targets and Indicators: A Blueprint for the International Co-ordination of Economic Policy', Institute for International Economics, Washington.

Discussion

Frederick van der Ploeg

The literature on the applications of dynamic game theory to problems of international policy coordination has taken off like a rocket in recent years and the present authors have provided most of the fuel. Most papers in this literature deal with linear (discrete-time or continuous-time) economic models, which incorporate rational expectations of future events, and quadratic welfare loss functions. The economic model is almost always a fleshed-out real-exchange-rate overshooting, symmetric two-country model with sluggish output and labour markets and efficient financial markets. This extended Mundell-Fleming framework typically means that monetary expansion is a beggar-thy-neighbour policy while fiscal expansion is a locomotive policy. The main feature of such economic models is that they are *ad-hoc* and without micro foundations. The welfare loss function almost always depends on output and inflation. I can therefore not see how within this framework economists can pretend to analyse properly the game between the goverment and private sector agents. Apart from the fact that the economic models are subject to the Lucas critique of econometric policy evaluation and that the welfare loss functions are *ad-hoc* as they are not consistent with the underlying behavioural relationships, I have never seen a textbook on game theory which does not specify the preferences for all players concerned. I therefore do not understand how this literature can begin to analyse games between governments and the private sector when the preferences of the private sector are never stated explicitly. It is important to remember that the seminal papers on time-inconsistency of monetary policy by Guillermo Calvo (1978) and on the time-inconsistency of optimal dynamic taxation by Stan Fischer (1980) used macroeconomic models with micro foundations. It is a pity that the recent literature is rocketing away with very advanced game-theoretic extensions when the foundations of the economic models and the associated preferences are so shaky. Recent work by Patrick Kehoe (1987) and myself (van der Ploeg, 1988) has shown, within the context of extremely simple perfect-foresight, two-country equilibrium models with micro foundations, the interactions between international policy coordination (the game between governments of sovereign states) and optimal taxation (the game between government and private sector agents). Future research should, in my view, be directed at applications of game theory to N-country models ($N \geqslant 2$) with micro foundations suitably modified to allow for realistic features such as unemployment. But I realize that this may be too much to ask in the short run and that this paper in the mean time provides worthwhile applications of game theory to a simple, empirical two-bloc model (MINILINK).

It is not clear at all that international policy coordination necessarily improves welfare for all countries concerned. So far, three reasons have been advanced to explain when and why coordination may be counter-productive. The most important one is probably when different countries base their choice of policy on different views on how the world economy reacts to changes in economic policy, because then coordination may well reduce welfare for some of the countries concerned. Given the different views prevailing in Germany today about the effectiveness of fiscal policy, this may be an important reason. The second reason is when countries coordinate their policies within a region, say Europe, but do not coordinate their policies with countries outside the region, say the US. Coordination within Europe may then be counter-productive, because it may provoke an adverse response from the US. The third reason is that coordination may aggravate the problems of credibility of each Central Bank versus its private sector agents.

The present authors focus entirely on this third reason. The point is that in the absence of coordination a surprise inflation induces a depreciation of the nominal exchange rate and this imposes inflation costs, while under coordination this does not happen. Hence, cooperation without reputation (CNR) may led to lower welfare than non-cooperation without reputation (NCNR). This led the present authors to conclude that cooperation without reputation as well as reputation without cooperation are counter-productive. Usually, one appeals to repeated games to show that reputational equilibria can sometimes be sustainable. In the Barro-Gordon game this arises when the discount rate is small, because then future punishments weigh heavily in the present and thus deter Central Banks from reneging. However, the present paper combines both structural dynamics from the economic model and behavioural dynamics arising from the game between the Central Bank and the private sector agents. Levine and Currie have extended the Barro-Gordon framework and allow for an infinite (rather than a unit) punishment interval and stochastic shocks. They also balance the temptation to renege against the enforcement or punishment of reneging. Of course, choosing an infinite punishment interval is more likely to give sustainability than in the Barro-Gordon game. This seems quite a sensible extension, but the arbitrariness of the length of the punishment interval bothers me and more intuition about why stochastic shocks can sustain reputation strategies would have been desirable. In any case, some have argued that if governments can maintain a reputation *vis-à-vis* their private sector then they can also maintain a reputation for international cooperation and vice versa. I am not convinced about the vice versa, but if this is so then the CNR regime does not make sense anyway. Before moving on, I would like to point out that the feedback Nash policy rules are not just correction mechanisms. In particular, subgame perfection implies time-consistency but time-consistency does not imply subgame perfection. This is the main reason why the feedback Nash equilibrium differs from the open-loop Nash equilibrium, but these two equilibria cannot be calculated by the present authors as they have a model without micro foundations.

The main objective of this interesting paper is, however, a methodology for analysing the sustainability of *simple* rules. I have not too many quibbles with the extension of their stochastic approach to the sustainability of simple rules, but I do have a few comments on the desirability of simple rules. The main reason why simple rules are desirable is that they are parsimonious, easy to understand and sell to the government, and robust when the operation of the economy is not well understood. A simple 'Deux Chevaux' is more likely to steer in an easy and robust way round a dark and narrow Welsh country lane than a complicated Ferrari racing machine that has to creep along the same lane. A simple rule may well be a car for most tracks. It is a pity that the paper offers little insight into the question whether simple rules are robust to parameter uncertainty and model mis-specification. The disadvantages of simple rules are that they no longer satisfy the certainty-equivalence principle (even though the authors seem to impose this principle) and that they are enormously complicated to calculate. If certainty-equivalence is not relevant, then proportional-integral policy rules of the form (33) with open-loop values as targets seem irrelevant as well. Another problem I have is that I do not know what simplicity means. A possibility is bounded rationality or lack of memory, but the present authors seem to imply that simplicity corresponds to diagonal policy rules as in the New-Keynesian policy packages advocated by James Meade and David Vines. This approach to simplicity bothers me, beause even though it is sensible to assign governmental institutions (such as the Central Bank, the Treasury, or the Wages Council) to their own targets it does not seem sensible to restrict their information sets to include only past realizations of their own target variable. This loss of efficiency seems, in my view, too large a price to pay for simplicity.

Finally, I shall comment on the particular economic model used by the present authors. This is a US–ROW stochastic version of MINILINK, the condensed version of the INTERLINK model of the OECD. This is a fleshed-out real-exchange-rate overshooting model with extensions to allow for lags of the effects of the terms of trade on net exports, current-account dynamics, a term structure of interest rates, and various AR(1) error structures. The main problem I have with this version of MINILINK is that there are no long-run trade-offs between inflation and output and thus no long-run international policy conflicts, that there are no intertemporal government budget constraints, that the specification of current-account dynamics and wealth effects is a bit too rudimentary for my liking (e.g. you would expect a fiscal expansion to lead to a short-run appreciation and a long-run depreciation of the exchange rate, but this is not the case), that there are no asymmetries (such as real and nominal wage rigidity) between the US and the ROW, and that the error structures do not seem to be estimated.

In summary, I think this paper makes considerable advances in the application of dynamic game theory to macroeconomic problems of international policy coordination, even though I am not quite convinced by the usefulness of simple rules and think that there are decreasing returns to scale in developing sophisticated technical tools and increasing returns to scale in developing small-scale empirical multi-country models.

References

Calvo, G.A. (1978) 'On the time consistency of optimal policy in a monetary economy', *Econometrica* **46**, 1411–28.

Fischer, S. (1980) 'Dynamic inconsistency, cooperation and the benevolent dissembling government', *Journal of Economic Dynamics and Control* **2**, 93–107.

Kehoe, P.J. (1987) 'Coordination of fiscal policies in a world economy', *Journal of Monetary Economics* **19**, 349–76.

Ploeg, F. van der (1988) 'International policy coordination in interdependent monetary economies', *Journal of International Economics* **25**, 1–23.

Index